Hidden Treasures

Hidden Treasures

Edited by ALAN CRITTENDEN

UNION SQUARE BOOKS
NOVATO, CALIFORNIA

Hidden
Treasures

Published by Union Square Books
P.O. Box 1150, Novato, California, 94948.

Copyright © 1985 by Alan Crittenden
ISBN 0-913153-04-4

Printed in the United States of America.

Library of Congress Catalog Card Number 85-50537.

This book was typeset by Unitype, Rohnert Park, California.

PHOTO CREDITS:

Page 85; SUPERMAN is a trademark of DC Comics
Inc. and is used with permission. Copyright © DC
Comics Inc. 1938, 1965.

Page 201; from *Jukebox: The Golden Age;* Lancaster
Miller & Schnobrich publishers, Berkeley, CA;
photograph by Kazuhiro Tsuruta.

Page 209; from *The Collector's Encyclopedia of Fiesta*,
Collector Books, P.O. Box 3009, Paducah, KY 42001,
copyright Sharon and Bob Huxford. Used with
permission.

Page 223; "Marchesa Brigida Spinola Doria;" Peter
Paul Rubens; National Gallery of Art, Washington;
Samuel H. Kress Collection.

Page 461; "Napoleon in His Study;" Jacques-Louis
David; National Gallery of Art, Washington; Samuel
H. Kress Collection.

Page 509; Helen L. Allen Textile Collection, School
of Family Resources and Consumer Sciences,
University of Wisconsin, Madison.

CONTENTS

D

E

F

G

P

Q

R

S

Hidden
Treasures

Introduction

How many of us know that our own homes—places so familiar to us—are filled with hidden treasures? How many of us know that they are hiding right now in the most obvious places, like a china cabinet, a grown child's room, the kitchen catchall drawer, even in a dusty bookshelf? Probably not many of us.

Why? Simply because we have not known where—and how—to look for them. Take, for example, that collection of baseball cards sitting in a shoebox in Bobby's room. It would seem to be worthless, at best a dust-catcher. But to someone who knows what to look for, it is quite possibly a fortune, and a major-league one at that. (Did you know that a mint-condition 1951 Bowman Company's Mickey Mantle card is worth $350 today?)

Or how about that everyday set of dishes you use year after year only because it is colorful and dishwasher-proof? Well, that "gaudy" old Fiesta ware is worth a great deal today. Its bright colors are prized by modern collectors and decorators, who are willing to pay handsomely for even a single piece of it. (Did you know that a sky-blue glazed Fiesta-ware marmalade bowl with cover is worth $40 to $55?)

Hidden Treasures will not only open your eyes to what is valuable, it will also become your treasure map, guiding you exactly to where values are found. In fact, I guarantee that after reading only the first few pages, you will *want* to clear out the attic or that Fibber-McGee-and-Molly hall closet just to see the treasures you have mistakenly called "junk" all these years. Not only will you be shocked at what you'll find, you'll also be thrilled to discover a source of wealth you never knew you had.

Once you have explored your home thoroughly, *Hidden Treasures* shows you how to find values in the marketplace. It will tell you how to identify other items of worth and where to find them in antiques shops and classified ads and at collectors' conventions and auctions.

All good treasure maps not only guide us to that precious spot marked "X," they also inform us of pitfalls along the way. This book not only tells you how to see and what to look for, it also alerts you to the hazardous side of assessing, negotiating, buying, and selling. It tells you how to distinguish a fake from the real thing. (When examining a chest of drawers, for example, that you think is homemade or have been told is so, look at the dovetailing of the boards. Is it so perfect that it could only have been done by a machine? If so, your "homemade" piece of country furniture most likely came from an assembly line.) It tells you when to hold on to an item and when—or if—you should sell. And, it tells you not only the dangers of entering the marketplace without enough information, it then instructs you on how to get the information—and the self-confidence—you need long before you approach dealers and other collectors.

In fact, the theme of knowledge is emphasized throughout this book. It is the one asset *no* hobbyist can do without if he or she wants to build a valuable collection of *anything*. And so each chapter ends with a well-rounded bibliography that lists other books on a subject, along with periodicals, catalogues, dealers, associations, clubs, and even some conventions. We encourage you to use the bibliographies long after your initial reading of *Hidden Treasures*. By staying well informed, you will gain the most pleasure and reward from your collections.

A FEW WORDS ABOUT THE AUTHORS...

I felt that doing a book of this size required the expertise of a group of authors, rather than just one, because a group would be more able to provide an overview of the collectors' marketplace. So I picked twenty-six top researcher/writers, each of whom I chose for his or her knowledge of specific items. Many of the writers are also recognized in their fields and are frequent contributors to other publications.

So, find a comfortable chair and settle down to begin an adventure that will not only be a great deal of fun but very profitable, too....

By the way, how long have you had that chair?...

—*Alan Crittenden*

Chapter 1

How to get the most from this book

My idea to create *Hidden Treasures* came from a nationwide tour I did last year to talk about a book I had just published on investments. Whenever I went on the air and discussed the most well-known, such as stocks, bonds, and mutual funds, studio phones remained silent. It seemed that listeners were not really interested. But the moment I mentioned comic books or porcelain, I couldn't answer the calls quickly enough.

It struck me that any information available to collectors on these items was exactly that: information that would only interest collectors. It did not mean much to those of us who had never gone into an antiques shop, or read a book on collectors' items, or gone to an auction.

I also realized that most of us hadn't the slightest idea that those "ordinary" things that make up our most familiar surroundings — and closet clutter—could be valuable in the marketplace.

So I put together *Hidden Treasures*. It is intended to give general but solid information about many everyday treasures found at home. It is also meant to spark your interest to find out more about them.

In order to make learning easier, each chapter has been broken down into sections. Not only does this format present the information more clearly, it makes the book ready to use as a reference in the future. Hence, all chapters are divided into the following sections:

- **History.** What makes an item valuable? Is it an intrinsic quality or is it public demand? The only way to answer these questions is to look back into the histories of each item or category to discover what forces and people created it. Knowing the history of a favorite item will also make you appreciate it more.

- **Values Outside the Home.** Once you realize what you like and what you would like to have more of, you must know what items to look for and what to stay away from. This section will point you in the right directions.
- **Where to Find Values.** This portion will be invaluable to anyone wanting to expand on items he or she already has at home. It will give information on how to buy from antiques dealers, other collectors, through the mail, and from auction houses. It discusses the positive and negative aspects of buying from each source, which is often different for different items.
- **Price Samplings.** Each chapter will present a brief list of *approximate* prices for a particular item. Because of the many influences on price, such as the passage of time and the area of the country in which you now live, these can only be general. However, they will give you some idea what you can *expect* to pay for an item and what to ask for it when selling.
- **How to Store/Display.** Most dealers grade items according to their condition. Comic books may be graded "pristine mint" (top of the line) or "poor" (showing many defects, such as tears, uneven printing, and missing pages). Since value is based directly upon condition of an item, it is of utmost importance to know how to display a piece without damaging it, and how to care for it to best preserve it.
- **How and When to Sell.** Collectors' items rise and fall with popular tastes, only to rise and fall again over time. With a little study and a developing awareness of the worth of your favorite items, you as a new collector will become a seasoned one, able to predict a trend, and with it the time to sell or the time to hold on to an item. "How and When to Sell" gives you tips on when to upgrade a collection and when it would be better to trade rather than buy or sell. And, best of all, it tells you what to look out for when selling. Is it best to offer an item directly to a dealer or to another collector? How should you price an item to sell it quickly? What are the dangers of dealing directly through the mail or at collectors' conventions? And when is it best not to sell at all?
- **Little-Known Facts.** Did you know that in 1906 a Tiffany Wisteria lamp ordinarily sold for $400, which was also the annual salary of a school teacher back then? Or that license plates with lower numbers are less common in the Southern states and therefore more valuable to collectors in the South than elsewhere? Valuable

information? Not at all. But it *is* a lot of fun to read, and it *does* give a bit more color and history to one's favorite treasures.

- **Bibliography.** As I stated earlier, this is one of the most important sections of each chapter because it expands your world as a beginning collector, pointing the way for you to learn as much as possible about the various items. All sources are listed in good faith, but your satisfaction can be guaranteed only by your own research.

Last of all I call attention to the many "success stories" that dot the pages of this volume. They were the result of my request to our writers to find people like most of us, who had either innocently stumbled across a valuable item or who had unwittingly purchased one, only to learn later that the article was somewhat—and in many cases, *extremely*—worthy. With this assignment our writers had no trouble, for it seems that dealers especially had endless tales to tell of just such cases of good fortune (names of individuals were frequently withheld due to their request for privacy).

So I pass them on to you, hoping they will not only entertain you, but will spark you to begin the hunt for treasures of your own.

A

CHAPTER 2

Advertising

Autographs

Automobiles

ADVERTISING

Attention, those of you who shriek at the sight of Mr. Whipple, Mrs. Olsen, and Morris the Cat. While mere glimpses of their folksy faces on advertising materials might drive you, whimpering, to the generic products section of your local supermarket, try to quell your distaste for, oh, about twenty-five years. It could well be that by that time "Where's the beef" will be passwords to wealth.

We all have them piled up around the house...those White Rock boxes and Campbell soup mugs and Budweiser wall clocks— possessions that can drive even the best marriages towards the rocks and cause Goodwill volunteers to weep. Some call these items "kitsch." But a good case can be made for the use of another description.

Try "gold mine."

Some examples:

- A Milwaukee housewife found a copy of Montgomery Ward's first catalogue in an attic trunk—and sold it for $1,000.
- The American Mail Auction group decided to sell an early Coca-Cola gum wrapper on the block—and was startled to see the bidding reach $90.
- A Hood's Sarsaparilla calendar that sold for six cents in 1896 went for $20 in 1977 and is worth $40 today.

Those willing to pay this sort of money for your dust collectors are everywhere—and delightfully eclectic. For instance, Ken D. Jones of Columbia, Missouri, will pay top dollar for your State Farm Insurance memorabilia, while Harvey Halpin of Albany, California, is a fanatic for Del Monte items.

Ours is not to reason why. Instead, let us swallow our natural hostility for such personalities as the Pillsbury Dough Boy, Clara Peller, and the obnoxious folks who grin from cornflakes boxes, and learn what we can about the dollar value of advertising collectors' items.

History. Although advertising is considered as American as...well... cornflakes, the ancient Egyptians get the credit for founding the first version of the grey flannel suit cult when they started posting runaway slave anouncements around 3200 B.C.

After the invention of moveable type, print advertising was launched with a 1477 German ad for a prayerbook sale.

While newspaper and catalogue advertising began in the United States as early as 1704, it was not until the late nineteenth century that J. Walter Thompson and several other advertising agencies pioneered the use of advertising giveaways.

Of course, these early efforts beat today's plastic key rings and pens by a mile. Many of them were carefully crafted from mother-of-pearl or celluloid. In fact, the period from the late 1890s through the Depression is considered the golden age for today's collector.

Although there is still an audience for post-1940s material, the items made before that time, such as signs designed by James Montgomery Flagg and Norman Rockwell and the trays decorated by old-fashioned lithography instead of the cheaper photolithographic process, bring top dollar in the marketplace.

However, there are exceptions. An Oklahoma man, who endured the mirth of his friends because he kept all of his old Cracker Jack toys (dated circa mid-1930s) found that his jumping frog, bulldog bookmark and Tooterville Trolley were worth, respectively, $10, $13, and...get this...$425.

★ **Los Angeles writer Lawrence Dietz bought two advertising trays from a junk dealer for 50 cents each and later found trays of the same vintage selling at one antique store for $17.50 and at another for almost $50.**

Values Outside the Home. Part of the joy of collecting advertising materials is the anticipation of generating wild excitement in future collector-buyers, who you hope will then be moved to pay handsomely for your favorite bit of kitsch however seemingly worthless, whether it be that advertising calendar for Bill's Hardware down the street or that pencil from your friendly neighborbood insurance company (down, Mr. Jones).

But there are certain items that you can count on to cause a stir, inciting even more excitement than, say, last year's State Farm key chain, and fetching considerably more. For instance:

Advertising Trays: These held tips or stood upright against the back of a bar or soda fountain and were adorned with pictures of beautiful women or stage stars. Recently appraised at $1,500 was a beer tray manufactured before Prohibition put a moratorium on breweriana production.

Calendars: No, not today's handouts from State Farm, (*down*, Mr. Jones), but those touting the wonders of its 1895–1930 counterparts, such as the 1904 calendar for Ohio Farmer's Insurance, which is now worth $300. The Winchester Rifle Company's 1920 offering, depicting a father and son toting guns and their collection of dead ducks, is worth almost $600.

Catalogues: Although early catalogues were not exactly parlor fixtures (they were, however, prominently displayed—and used—in an equally popular room), there is a huge market for those issued prior to 1925. The most sought after is the 1875 Montgomery Ward catalogue (worth over $1,000), but astonishing profits can also be made through ownership of Sears-Roebuck's editions from 1908, 1910, 1916 and 1918... and Montgomery Ward's 1925 edition.

Hand Fans: Before the days of air conditioning, hand fans were very popular, especially when adorned with pictures of celebrities, who usually had nothing whatsoever to do with the product (some things never change).

Pin-Backed Buttons: These brightly painted pieces of celluloid turned people into walking billboards, extolling the merits of everything from shoes to farm implements.

Celluloid Pocket Mirrors: These were meant to be carried in handbags and represented everything from tobacco to patent medicines to root beer. Although pocket mirrors were designed *for* women, many depicted hefty women in various stages of nudity. These are now understandably popular with male collectors.

And let us not forget other popular collectors' items, such as match holders, ashtrays, lunch boxes, signs and thermometers. They exist as proof that today's real estate man who deluges you with so-called worthless items is really a philanthropist and should be treated with respect.

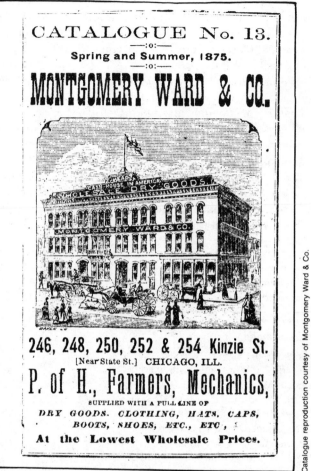

Although its interesting dimensions (shown here in actual size) make it a prize among collectors, this particular catalogue made for rather dull reading; it contained no illustrations, only listings of items and their prices.

Where to Find Values. Because advertising giveaways have been so widespread, you need not conduct a worldwide search for them. However, the good stuff is a little more difficult to find. Flea markets are excellent places to start looking. You should then try antiques dealers, auctions and ads.

However, before you buy, it is important to examine all items very carefully, no matter where you find them. Counterfeiting is not uncommon. Many old illustrations, for example, have been reproduced on new tin items, and some dealers follow the delightful practice of soaking new pieces in horses' urine to give them that lived-in look. Even *Fortune* magazine once fell prey to fakery when it innocently ran a full-size color picture of an extremely rare Coca-Cola cigar band. Old copies of the magazine have become gold mines for the unscruplous, who cut out the picture of the band and pass it off as the real thing.

★ Advertising collectors Howard and Flo Fertig bought a soda fountain despenser for Fowler's Cherry Smash for $35 in 1974 and recently found it to be worth $800.

A Price Sampling

Clock, "Sauer's Extracts," 1906	$1,150
Poster, "Cloth of Gold" cigarettes, 1895	295-350
Match holder, "Juicy Fruit" Gum, 1920	150-180
Mirror, "Pond's Extract for Inflammations and Hemorrhages," 1905	145-160
Tray, "Sanitary" ice cream, 1915	110-125
Thermometer, "Coca-Cola," 1941	65-80
Sign, "Baldwin's Wind Pills," 1904	40-75
Spoon and fork, Campbell kids, 1935	20-35
Calendar, Marilyn Monroe, 1952	15-50
Egg timer, "Mueller's Macaroni," 1895	22-40
Knife, "Planter's Peanuts," 1960	5-8

How to Store/Display. Because many marketable items are made of highly perishable celluloid, it is important to handle them with care. Keep them out of the sun, and keep them stored in cases where they can be kept dry. Some collectors even invest in humidifiers to control the storage environment as much as possible.

Keep your catalogues clean and wrinkle free, although unlike most specialties, it is often possible to unload even the most damaged of these. But since you can probably get twice as much for the well-preserved ones, it is wise to treat them kindly.

How and When to Sell. Because advertising collectors' items are so popular, and because the most desirable items are already considered antiques, it seems likely that they will continue to increase in value. Certainly it is possible to sell most items for a profit *now,* but why not wait? Time, for advertisers' pieces, seems to mean money. You might someday even be able to unload all those old real estate calendars you have been piling up.

After all, maybe Mr. Jones has a friend...

★ Aesthetic qualities aside, the most sought-after catalogue on the market is from Johnson-Smith, a Racine, Wisconsin, firm that sold exploding cigars, rubber rats and stink bombs. Although manufactured in the 1940s, the catalogue is already worth over $100.

Little-Known Facts. Coors Brewery, the pride and joy of Golden, Colorado, once produced pottery with the name of the company stamped on the back. It was manufactured from the turn of the century until the plant was destroyed by fire in the 1930s.

• Although advertisers pride themselves on their creativity, it should be noted that the slogan on one of Coca-Cola's calendars reads, "Good To The Last Drop." But breathe easy, Maxwell House. It was issued in 1908.

—*Sandra Hansen Konte*

Bibliography

Books

Dietz, Lawrence. *Soda Pop.* New York: Simon & Schuster, 1978.
Encyclopedia of Collectibles, Vol. 1. Alexandria, VA: Time-Life Books, 1977.
Mebane, John. *Treasures at Home.* New York: A. S. Barnes & Co., 1964.

Catalogues

Kovel, Ralph and Terry. *Kovels' Antiques & Collectibles Price List.* New York: Crown Publishers, 1984.

Associations

National Association of Breweriana, 475 Old Surry Rd., Hinsdale, IL 60521.

AUTOGRAPHS

Did you know that a letter written by George Washington during the American Revolution might sell for $2,500 today? Or that a signature from actress Greta Garbo could be worth over $500?

Collecting autographs has always been a popular hobby, but many who collect for fun are not aware that some of these autographs may be worth thousands of dollars.

History. Although autograph collecting has probably been around as long as celebrities have, this pastime was extremely popular during the 1920s, when the buying and selling of autographs became more than just a hobby. Composer Jerome Kern, for example, sold his collection of autographs and rare books for almost $1 million in 1929. A similar collection today might be worth several million dollars.

During the Great Depression, when money for everything was scarce, it was no surprise that the market for autographs declined. But in the 1950s, prices began rising again, and they have continued to do so ever since, generally increasing about 10% every year.

Values Outside the Home. Autographs are divided into several categories, which determine their value. *ALS* means "autograph letter signed," which refers to a letter written in longhand by the person who signed it. *LS* means "letter signed," which could be a letter or other document written by a secretary and signed by someone else. *DS* refers to a "document signed," which is a printed document bearing a person's signature. *S* means simply "signature."

When collecting autographs it is important to know that some individuals' names are worth far more than others. Presidential autographs are among the most valuable, particularly when the material upon which their names appear reveals something about the period in which they held office. An example would be a letter written by Abraham Lincoln during the Civil War.

Celebrities' signatures are also popular, but generally only if a celebrity's fame is secure, not fleeting. Signatures of value here would include those of Babe Ruth, Elvis Presley, and Albert Einstein.

Where to Find Values. Autographs can be purchased from several places. Some dealers specialize in autographs, and they can be found by looking through the phone book. Auction firms that sell rare books sometimes offer autographs as well. These are generally

Because of its scarcity and because of his place in world literature, a letter written and signed by William Shakespeare would be worth $2,000,000 today.

auctioned off in lots of two or more, so that one lot might yield signatures of several different individuals. Used and rare bookstores sometimes also carry signed letters and documents.

If one is interested in collecting autographs of famous individuals who are still alive today, it is best to write them directly with the request. Bernie Brown is a teacher in Philadelphia who began collecting autographs more than forty years ago. He has accumulated over one thousand, most of which he obtained by writing to celebrities and requesting them. Today his collection is worth thousands of dollars.

If one can get the signer to provide *more* than a signature, such as a brief description of what it is like to be a football player, or a statement of how old a star was when she started making movies, the autograph will be even more valuable.

A Price Sampling

	Classification	
Abraham Lincoln	ALS	$4,000-30,000
George Washington	DS	1,500-4,000
Thomas Jefferson	LS	1,200-3,000
Franklin D. Roosevelt	ALS	600-1,000
George Washington	S	450-600
Rudolf Valentino	Signed photo	225-300
John Belushi	Signed photo	75-100
Humphrey Bogart	Signed photo	50-110
Humphrey Bogart	S	6-9
Brooke Shields	S	5-8

How To Store/Display. The ideal way to preserve autographs is to place them in individual manila folders. It is also important to keep them away from heat and humidity, which cause paper to deteriorate, and to *never* glue them to another surface or leave them in direct sunlight (they will fade). Such precautions will help ensure their value. Collectors should also keep an inventory list of their autographs, so that all pertinent information will be readily accessible when the time comes to sell.

How and When to Sell. There are several ways of selling all or parts of a collection. One can consign his work to an auction firm, which will take care of the actual selling—but it will also take a percentage of any profits. Or one can offer them to a dealer. One advantage here is that if the price offered is not acceptable, one can refuse to sell and seek out another dealer.

Collectors can also print up catalogues of their offerings and send them to other collectors, who might be interested in buying. Or one can query institutions or individuals interested in any items belonging to a particular person. These would include libraries, archives, historians, and authors. Charles Hamilton began his career as an autograph dealer back in the 1950s, when he sold a letter written by abolitionist John Brown—a letter for which he had paid only $1—to a noted historian for $50. Today, Hamilton operates one of the largest autograph auction firms in the country.

Little-Known Facts. The world of autograph collecting is full of unusual facts and surprises. A letter handwritten and signed by President John F. Kennedy, for instance, may well be worth much more than one signed by George Washington, since Kennedy rarely wrote or signed his own letters. And the most valuable letter of all is probably that written by President Richard M. Nixon, resigning the office of president in August 1974. It is housed in the National Archives in Washington, D.C., and is estimated to be worth over $25,000.

—Andi Stein

Bibliography

Books

Hamilton, Charles and Diana. *Big Name Hunting.* New York: Simon & Schuster, 1973.

Rush, Richard. *Investments You Can Live With and Enjoy.* Washington, D.C.: U.S. News & World Report Books, 1974.

Sullivan, George. *Making Money in Autographs.* New York: Coward, McCann, and Geohegan, Inc., 1977.

Periodicals

Laird, Jean E. "Antiques Are Where You Find Them." *Saturday Evening Post,* August, 1984.

Catalogues

Walter A. Benjamin Autographs. P.O. Box 255, Scribner Hollow Rd., Hunter, NY 12442 (write for information).

Dealers

Federal Hill Autographs, P.O. Box 6405, Baltimore, MD 21230.

Mr. Autograph, P.O. Box 1075, Havertown, PA 19083.

Northern Co., 448 Henry St., Detroit, MI 48201.

Auctions

Charles Hamilton Autographs, 25 E. 77th St., New York, NY 10021.

Associations

Autograph Chapter of the American First Day Cover Society, c/o Jan Brennan, P.O. Box 433X, Elmwood Park, NY 07407.

Manuscript Society, 350 N. Niagra St., Burbank, CA 91505.

Universal Autograph Collectors Club, P.O. Box 467, Rockville Center, NY 11571.

AUTOMOBILES

On page 66 of the August 1954 issue of *Motor Trend* magazine, there is a section called "Sell 'N' Swap," which lists automobiles for sale. Among those offered are a "'33 V-16 Cadillac phaeton, $625"; a "'34 380-SK Mercedes-Benz supercharged sports roadster, $2,500 (includes delivery from Germany)"; and a "'37 Cord 812 convertible, excellent shape, $1,000."

It is interesting to consider that for a total initial purchase price of $4,125, one could have sold these three automobiles today for well over a quarter of a million dollars.

One could argue, with some justification, that there were even better things to invest in back in 1954 (how about IBM stock?), but detractors are really missing the point of the classic car hobby. What makes automobiles such attractive investments is not that they can make one rich overnight but that one can actually use, enjoy, display and be enormously proud of them. How could a handful of gold coins or some stock certificates stuffed in a drawer compare with driving a gorgeous old convertible on a bright and beautiful Sunday morning?

History. A strong interest in collecting cars for investment did not manifest itself in the United States until the late 1960s. There always was, of course, a small and devoted group of car collectors, but to most people old cars were heavy, outdated, old-fashioned machines that did not fit into space-age America. Most car buffs were content to customize their newer automobiles; quite a few even went so far as to take antique clunkers and skillfully weld, sand and paint until outrageous hot rods would spring forth from the bones of 1930s Fords and Chevys.

Old cars finally received notice after their competition—new cars—grew ordinary and dull. Around 1970, with certain rare exceptions, American cars were of two types: big and ugly, and small and ugly. It was no wonder that car lovers turned to the past. Anything was better than a Pinto, a Vega, or the countless other tedious variations, large and small, of those nondescript battleships offered by Detroit's Big Three.

The old-car hobby got a further boost from the oil crisis of 1973, which spawned the manufacture of domestic cars burdened with unworkable pollution devices. Ultimately, this affected the reliablilty of most American cars, and without reliability, there was no reason left to buy them.

By 1974, a 1964 Mustang convertible or a 1965 Pontiac GTO with full performance options looked great by comparison. So did American and foreign cars from the '40s and '50s. And it is no wonder. Good looks, reliability, power, a unique form of status, real chrome instead of plastic... all that *and* an appreciating investment besides! The car-collecting hobby started booming, and it has not peaked yet.

★ In 1977, a woman in Boulder, Colorado, was about to trade her somewhat tired and battered 1964 Mustang convertible to the local Toyota dealer for a $400 credit towards a new car; however, a friend advised her to restore her car instead, which she did for about $3,200. In the ensuing seven years, she has driven the car for over eighty-thousand trouble-free miles, and it is worth about $8,500. A 1977 Toyota would bring about $1,750.

Values Outside the Home. Buyers and sellers of collectors' cars have become very sophisticated in the last ten years. Gone are the days of the little old lady who does not know how much her clean, low-mileage Model A Ford is worth. She probably knows the market value within 10%! For this reason, one must approach an investment in automobiles with a realistic attitude and a fundamental knowledge of the market.

First of all, some clarification is in order, because terms such as *classic, vintage* and *collectors' car* have been terribly abused. Here is a partial list of definitions that many collectors, auctioneers and hobbyists go by:

- *Antique:* Cars made before 1935, although some auto clubs define an "antique" as any car that is at least thirty-five years old—that is, made in or before 1950.

Courtesy Daimler-Benz Press Department

Unique in its day for its unusual design, the 1954-1957 pristine Mercedes-Benz 300 SL Gullwing Coupe remains a prized collectors' item—an expensive one too, at $180,000.

- *Classic:* Any car appearing on a special list compiled by the Classic Car Club of America. At present, no car newer than 1948 is on the list.
- *Milestone:* Any post-World War II (1946 or newer) car appearing on a special list compiled by the Milestone Car Society. Milestone cars are recognized as such for their innovative characteristics. Many milestone cars will, no doubt, become recognized classics someday.
- *Special interest/collectors' car:* Certain cars built after 1935 that generate a particular interest, respect or admiration from collectors due to the car's special characteristics of styling, engineering and performance. Many, many cars can carry this label.
- *Vintage:* In the broadest definition, automobiles manufactured before World War I.

Second, one must realize that as with most hobbies, supply and demand determine value. Since there were usually far more 4-door sedans made in a particular model than convertibles and hardtops, the common sedan versions of most cars are less valuable than their sportier cousins. However, neither scarcity nor age are by themselves enough to insure a car's future value. This is where the phenonenon known as "demand" comes into play. For instance, the automotive neophyte might be surprised to learn that a fully restored 1964

Mustang convertible can command a higher price than a perfectly restored 1934 Ford sedan, or a 1924 sedan, or a 1914 sedan for that matter.

When one finally decides upon the type or types of cars to collect, he should keep in mind that his own affection for a particular model is just as important as its potential investment value. Collectors should seek out a car that will be an inspiration to drive, repair, polish and show off. Remember, part of any car's value lies in its ability to provide reliable transportation, to say nothing of an enthusiastic camaraderie with people who also have an abiding interest in similiar vehicles.

And what are some sound investments for car collectors in today's market? If one is rich, he has no problem. Just about any magnificent Rolls, Mercedes, Duesenberg, Bugatti, Packard, Pierce Arrow, Cord, Porsche or Ferrari will do. Expensive cars of magnificent design and craftsmanship will always appreciate in value.

But what if one is only a dabbler of sorts, or a person of some means, but cautious about investments? What cars will offer both enjoyment and a certain security for those hard-earned dollars? Are there still sleepers out there, delightful but not fully appreciated treasures that have somehow not fallen victims to the sky-high prices of speculation? Indeed there are, and here is a list of just a few up-and-coming models:

- *American convertibles:* The word might be out on Mustangs and Camaros, and, of course, it has always been out on Corvettes and '55-'57 T-Birds, but there are still plenty of lesser-known convertibles from the '50s and '60s that are available for reasonable prices. A good bet would be the 1973 Mustang convertible, which was the last of the full-size Mustang ragtops. The "compact" convertibles of the early 1960s, such as the Buick Special, Oldsmobile F-85, Plymouth Valiant/Dodge Dart, and Ford Falcon are sure to appreciate in value now that the more popular convertibles have been gobbled up by collectors.
- *Muscle cars:* The "muscle car" phenomenon began in 1963 with the introduction of the Pontiac GTO. Other manufacturers followed suit with the Chevy Chevelle SS 396, Mercury Cyclone GT, Olds 4-4-2, and Plymouth GTX, to name a few. These cars have been steadily increasing in value, and if one can handle the brute power, they are still good buys for the money.

- *English sports cars:* While the popular Jaguar XKE and Austin-Healey 3000 have always commanded high prices, the attractive MGB-GT (one of the world's first hatchbacks), the MGB & C roadster, the Triumph TR 250, and the TR6 roadster and hatchback are still undervalued. So, too, are the Sprite, Midget, and Spitfire models from Austin-Healey, MG and Triumph respectively, but these cars are less likely to appreciate quickly in the coming years. English sports cars are, however, great fun to drive, and repair costs are quite reasonable.

- *Other possibilities:* It may take a while, but someday the '65-'69 Corvair will be appreciated for the fine little car that it is. Another "orphan" that is slowly coming into its own is the very attractive '62-'64 Studebaker Gran Turismo Hawk. Buick Riviera "Boat Tails" ('71-'73) will have their day, and by all means keep an eye on the lowly VW Beetle.

- *Cars to avoid:* In general, any collectors' car that has been altered from the original is, by definition, devalued. Therefore, cars with incorrect engines, transmissions, or body parts must be assessed in terms of what it would cost to restore their originality. "Replica" and "kit" cars are generally also poor investments. These fiberglass and occasionally metal copies of classic or collectors' cars use modern drivelines and other up-to-date technology, their manufacturers claiming "an improvement" over the original car, which they have copied. This may in fact be true, but such cars have not shown themselves to be good investments. In fact, many old-car enthusiasts think quite poorly of the cars and the whole concept behind them.

Some Good Tips For First-Time Investors

1. If the three rules in real estate are location, location, and location, then in collectors' cars they are condition, condition, and condition. Low-mileage original owner cars are the most desirable. As the condition of the car worsens, the value drops dramatically.

2. Collectors should beware of cars that have been altered from their original state. It is wise to read up before buying, so that changes can be spotted.

3. Enthusiasts are advised to consult a reliable price guide before shopping. The prices listed in newspapers are rarely, if ever, representative of the true market value of the car advertised.

4. Collectors should request full documentation on any seller's claims made for a car's history or rarity.

5. Anyone interested should buy a collectors' car not only for its investment factor but for the amount of enjoyment it will give.

Where to Find Values. There is certainly no shortage of collectors' cars on today's market, but finding the right one at the right price can be a task requiring patience and persistence.

Most major metropolitan newspapers have a "collector car" section in their classifieds, and this is a good place to start. If nothing is available locally, both *Old Cars Weekly* and *Hemmings Motor News,* available at newstands or through the mail, offer an excellent variety of interesting cars at realistic prices.

A somewhat riskier source of old cars is the auction, which, contrary to popular belief, rarely offers the bidder a bargain. The main appeal of auctions is that unusual and often magnificent cars show up there. One may be fortunate enough to bid on a car that no one else is interested in, but that is unlikely. Besides, even if one is the only bidder, the car is likely to have a "reserve," or minimum bid, attached to it, so that a low bid would not be acceptable.

Likewise, there are reputable dealers who specialize in collectors' cars, but here, too, bargains are unlikely. What may be gained from buying from a good dealer is some sort of warranty as well as the legal recourse one usually has when buying from a licensed business.

★ **You never know where the car of your dreams may show up. One man found an antique International Harvester panel truck on the fifth floor of a toilet paper factory in New York City.**

A Price Sampling	Not restored, but very good	Restored
1968 Mercedes-Benz 280 SL Roadster	$7,500	$25,000
1964 Pontiac GTO Convertible	5,000	8,500
1969 American Motors AMX Fastback Coupe	4,000	8,500
1962 Studebaker Gran Turismo Hawk	3,000	6,000
1973 Mustang Convertible	2,800	6,250
1963 Falcon Sprint Convertible	2,500	6,000
1961 Buick Special Skylark Convertible	2,500	6,000
1963 Buick Riviera Sport Coupe	1,500	6,500
1967 MGB GT Coupe	1,800	4,500
1969 Corvair Monza Sport Coupe	1,500	4,200

How To Store/Display. Some people may disagree, but there seems to be no point in totally restoring an old car and then locking it up forever. A collectors' car can still retain its value without being placed in a museum. With proper washing and waxing and the use of a high-quality breathable car cover (in or out of the garage), a valuable automobile can be kept in top shape and still be driven as a transportation vehicle. Peace of mind can be carried further by properly insuring the vehicle or collection, either through a regular insurance company or through firms that specialize in old-car insurance. Either way, adequate coverage will, in part, consist of a proper written appraisal and some good photographs of the vehicle. These will help an insurance company to settle any claims in the owner's behalf.

Other than the proper weather protection, frequent oil changes and lubrication as well as that occasional tune-up and maintenance check are all recommended. A measure of care provides numerous benefits to both the beloved "classic" and the proud owner.

How and When to Sell. There is no great trick to selling a special automobile and getting the best price for it. It is mostly a matter of elbow grease and timing.

The hard work is necessary in order to make the car as attractive as possible. It may not be logical, but older cars, and perhaps all cars, sell on their looks more than on their mechanical condition. Potential buyers will often make up their minds about cars sometimes quite unconsciously, within the first minute or so after they see them. Torn upholstery, broken glass and unsightly dents will discourage buyers from paying top dollar. A few hundred dollars' investment in automobile cosmetics is always worth it.

Timing a sale is really just common sense. Convertibles sell better in spring than fall, and collector-car sales are slowest around Christmas and tax time.

One of the best methods of advertising an automobile is to put a sign in its window. Bulletin boards around universities and offices work well, too. Advertisements in local papers are effective, but sellers should make sure that the paper's readership is interested in the types of automobiles they want to list—Rolls Royces do not sell well in the local "pennysaver." National collector-car publications (see "Bibliography" at end of chapter) are very affordable and can sometimes bring in a buyer from out of state. Contacting a car club or clubs for a particular make of car will also bring benefits.

★ Neighbors laughed when a college student from New Jersey
dragged home a battered, torn, dented pile of junk that once was
a 1953 Mercedes 220 Cabriolet. It hardly looked like a car, much
less a classic. But after working for three years in his spare time,
scrounging parts all over the country and learning as he went, this
industrious hobbyist built himself a beautifully restored
automobile. He drove it for four years, finally sold it for $20,000,
and traveled around the world on his profits.

Little-Known Facts. The 1926 Ford Model T roadster sold brand-new
for only $260, which is about the price one would pay today for a
mediocre radio in a modern automobile.

• One of the world's largest, heaviest, and most expensive
automobiles ever built was the Bugatti Type 41 Royale. Six or seven
were made around 1930, one of which was a 2-seat roadster. It
weighed seven-thousand pounds, was 22 feet long, went 120 mph and
had no headlights because, as the owner explained, "I never drive at
night."

A Bugatti Royale today is worth over $2 million.

—Joseph L. Troise

Bibliography

Books

Brownell, Tom. *How to Restore Your Collector Car.* Osceola, WI: Motorbooks
International, 1984.

Georgano, G. N., ed. *The Complete Encyclopedia of Motorcars.* New York: E. P.
Dutton, 1973.

Langworth, Richard, and Graham Robson. *Complete Book of Collectible Cars,
1940-1980.* Skokie, IL: Publications International, Ltd., 1982.

Tax Guide for Auto Restorers and Collectors. Irvine, CA: Professional
Accounting Offices, 1984.

Periodicals

Automobile Quarterly. Kutztown, PA 19530.

Hemmings Motor News. Box 100, Bennington, VT 05201.

Old Cars Weekly. Iola, WI 54990.

Catalogues

Catalogues are best obtained by consulting the periodicals listed above,
especially *Hemmings Motor News* and *Old Cars Weekly.*

Gunnel, John, ed. *Standard Catalog of American Cars, 1946-1975.* Iola, WI:
Krause Publications, 1982.

Associations

The number of old-car clubs, associations and museums is too extensive to list. Here are four major organizations that can direct enthusiasts to others with the same interests. *The Encyclopedia of Associations,* available at local libraries, can also be very helpful:

Antique Automobile Club of America, 501 West Governor Rd., Hershey, PA 17033.

Classic Car Club of America, P.O. Box 443, Madison, NJ 07940.

Harrah's Automobile Collection, Reno, NV 89504.

Milestone Car Society, 22832 Buena Vista Rd., Rockbridge, OH 43149.

BASEBALL CARDS

In the timeless world of baseball cards, Willie Mays is still batting .320, or rather a *card* of Mays is. Today, the Willie Mays baseball card, issued and purchased for a penny, can bring its owner $275 if it has been kept in mint condition. The Mickey Mantle market is even better. Topps' 1952 Mantle card, for example, can fetch $1,000 mint. Duke Snider can go as high as $180, Satchell Paige $350, Ted Williams $625. Many rare turn-of-the-century cards are too expensive for the average person even to consider buying.

Since 1970 prices of most old ball cards have doubled three times. What was once the domain of little leaguers with big-league infatuations has also become a highly organized adult involvement fed by an enormous industry in which it is possible for hundreds, even thousands of dollars to be paid for a single item.

History. True to their source of inspiration, the origin of baseball cards is difficult to pinpoint. Who invented baseball? Well, who produced the first baseball card? No one can say for sure. The earliest known cards were versions of the product insert cards (of movie stars, cowboys and Indians, and the like), which took on a character of their own in the 1880s, when tobacco companies started including them in cigarette packs. Produced during two distinct periods (1886-1895 and 19091915), their first market was adult males, although many of the cards likely were passed along to sons.

By the time baseball entered the Babe Ruth era of the 1920s, candy companies had already discovered the youth market for baseball cards. Led by the American Caramel Company and Cracker Jack confectioners, they turned out sets that borrowed heavily from tobacco-card formats and illustrations. Their efforts were preludes to the boom period of the 1930s, when the Goudy Gum Company of Boston popularized what would become an American institution, the bubble gum card. The prototype for modern cards in size, packaging, and distribution, Goudy's six-year output equaled the premier tobacco issues for quality and ingenuity. Soon companies such as DeLong Gum, National Chicle, and Gum Incorporated joined the ranks, producing sets with such intriguing names as "Batter-Up," "Diamond Stars," and "Play Ball-America."

AP/Wide World Photos

Giant outfielder Willie Mays made this
spectacular catch, 460 feet from home plate,
during the 1954 World Series. His play saved the
game for the Giants.

The outbreak of World War II caused paper and rubber shortages, which plunged baseball cards into a Dark Age lasting until 1948, when the Leaf Gum and Bowman Gum companies resurrected them. Legal disputes over players' picture rights forced Leaf out of the market before the 1949 season, leaving Bowman unchallenged in the field until 1951. That year Topps Chewing Gum began the most comprehensive card-production campaign ever undertaken. For the next five years, the two companies competed hotly for the youngsters' nickels, until court battles over players' rights arose again and Topps bought out Bowman in 1956 to become lord of the baseball card empire. Its dominance prevailed until a 1980 court decision freed the market, and two other gum companies, Fleer and Donruss, began issuing annual sets as well.

For today's collectors, however, the history of baseball cards began the moment they opened their first pack of cards. They were the boys of the 1950s and 1960s, kids in every neighborhood to whom baseball was more than a summer pastime. Playing ball, watching it, listening to it on distant radio stations, emulating its heroes—to these kids the game became a culture unto itself, and baseball cards were its art form.

What made the cards so appealing? For one thing, Topps Chewing Gum, like the great card manufacturers before them, respected their customers' tastes and put out top-quality merchandise year after year. Improvising annually with the format, they consistently delivered excellent photographs of nearly every player, complete and accurate statistics, plenty of puzzles and other minutiae, and enough mystery and variety to bring kids back for another pack. Quite a lot for just a nickel.

And the cards had a million-and-one uses. They could be organized in countless ways, bound in rubber bands, and stored in shoe boxes. They could be used in fantasy ball games and trivia contests. They could be flipped, matched, and checklisted. But mainly they could be traded—for more cards or different cards or just for the thrill of it. An element of competitiveness figured into card-collecting even then, and smart traders took pride in the deals they engineered. A value system evolved from those boyhood transactions, the same system that governs card prices today. Now, as then, one Ted Williams equals fifty Wayne Terwilligers.

Unfortunately for many young collectors, baseball card history would come to an abrupt end. It usually happened on a grey October afternoon upon returning home from school and discovering that Mom had thrown that priceless card collection away. But some kids managed to keep their cards safely hidden and continued buying them throughout high school and beyond. By the late '60s, maturing collectors around the country started corresponding with one another. They conducted trades and held auctions by mail. They subscribed to mimeographed newsletters containing the latest hobby information. In 1969, a group of Southern California collectors held the first baseball card convention.

Gradually the meetings became more frequent and widespread. The newsletters became magazines. Hobby literature made its way to bookstore shelves. Non-collectors reading the price guides were amazed at what those old cards were worth. In the late '70s, hordes of enthusiasts took up the hobby, to the point where in today's collecting circles, baseball cards rank second only to coins in nationwide popularity.

★ **In 1954, seventeen-year-old Larry Fritsch of Spencer, Wisconsin, needed only a picture of Ted Williams to complete his annual set of Bowman baseball cards. When he purchased a five-cent package at Mabel's Pool Hall one day, he was amazed to find it contained not one but *eight* Williams cards. Easily the rarest card in the set, the '54 Williams lists at $625, or $5,000 for the eight. Fritsch, now the owner of the country's largest mail-order baseball card business, has never sold them.**

Values Outside the Home. Current card catalogues list tens of thousands of baseball cards. Besides the major tobacco, candy, and gum sets, ball cards have been used to sell everything from hot dogs to potato chips, newspapers to gasoline. Faced with so much from which to choose, newcomers to the hobby might feel overwhelmed.

Most potential collectors likely have a box of old cards stashed away in their attics gathering dust. If so, a quick evaluation using a current price guide will reveal some delightful surprises. Otherwise, the best way to start collecting is to pick up a few packs of current cards at the corner drugstore. Thirty cents will now buy fifteen cards, a slab of bubble gum, which itself tastes like cardboard, and a thrill of discovery that only a baseball nut can appreciate. Who knows, there might be a Steve Garvey or Reggie Jackson mixed in with the no-names. And save the wrappers. There are collectors for those, too.

Aside from the wealthiest and most advanced hobbyists, the majority of collectors concentrate on specific sets or players, allowing their collections to bespeak their love of the game and of those who play it. Most people sell or trade their duplicates or unwanted cards to finance their needs. Consequently, a steady stream of cards constantly filters into and out of the market.

Over the years, certain sets have become classics. Among the tobacco issues, those produced by the American Tobacco Company from 1909 to 1911 are considered the most distinctive. Goudy's first bubble gum set (1933) contains four different Babe Ruth cards and two Lou Gehrigs. Avid collectors consider Topps' 1952 set of 407 cards to be top of their line. The Mays and Mantle cards are particularly prized.

Not surprisingly, cards of any era featuring superstar-caliber players are the most expensive to buy. But they also should appreciate more as years pass. Pure investors would be wise to put their money in the Ruths and Cobbs, the Williamses and DiMaggios, the Mantles, Mayses, and Aarons—players with the broadest and deepest appeal.

In recent years there has been a growing interest in cards depicting star players in their first major league season, known as *rookie cards* in the trade. Many observers of this remain unconvinced of its logic since, with a few notable exceptions, these cards are no less plentiful than the average card.

Where to Find Values. There was a time when aggressive baseball card hunters could find abundant treasures at garage sales and antique shops. But as more and more people have discovered the value of old cards, these avenues have practically disappeared. Today's collectors are left with more conventional means to add to their collections.

The burgeoning baseball card industry has created hundreds of dealers around the country engaged in storefront and mail-order businesses. There are pros and cons to doing business with a dealer. On the one hand, since the major gum companies will not sell directly to individuals, dealers serve as go-betweens for acquiring the latest sets. Also, good dealers maintain extensive stocks of older cards and can often lay their hands on desired items not in stock. On the other hand, since dealers are in business for profit, customers should expect to pay book or near-book prices for cards purchased through them.

New collectors will get a good idea of what is available in the market by attending a baseball card show, usually held in a school gym or meeting hall. In highly populated areas, such shows or conventions occur as often as once a month. Most shows consist of booths full of sports memorabilia manned by dealers or serious collectors. They usually include auctions and drawings. Quite often, a major leaguer will be there to sign autographs. The greatest advantage to going to a show is the chance to make contacts. The major drawback is that card prices can be even higher there than at a dealer's shop.

Perhaps the best option for newcomers is to deal directly with other collectors. It is not uncommon for advanced collectors to sell part of their holdings to make way for new items. Unshackled by a dealer's overhead, collectors can offer price breaks, especially in selling large quantities.

No matter how a collector goes about buying cards, it should be understood that prices are never rigid. On the contrary, editors of authoritative guides stress that their listings simply reflect the going rates found at conventions, card stores, and in advertisements. In each card transaction, the buyer and seller alone determine what is a fair deal.

★ **Over a decade ago, Mike Aronstein of Peekskill, New York, embarked on a venture which any card fanatic would envy. He began issuing his own baseball cards. His first set, a series of drawings sketched by his uncle, proved successful enough to build upon. Today Aronstein has become the most prolific card producer in the history of the hobby, having put out close to eight-hundred different sets.**

A Price Sampling

Topps Series	Very Good	Mint
1952 Mickey Mantle #311	$650	$1,000
1952 Willie Mays #261	275	145
1951 New York Giants #5 (Team card)	47	74
1971 Pete Rose #15 (Greatest Moments)	42	70
1965 Hank Aaron #170	7	12
Bowman Series		
1954 Ted Williams #66	$500	$625
1949 Satchell Paige #224	170	320
1953 Casey Stengel #39	60	100
1949 Stan Musial #24	30	47
1954 Yogi Berra #161	15	20

How To Store/Display. The value of a baseball card is based on a variety of factors. Intrinsically it has no value at all; its worth is dictated purely by nostalgic attachment. But within that reality, the price of a card is influenced by its age, the player portrayed on it, the popularity of the set to which it belongs, its relative scarcity, and its physical condition.

Most experts agree that condition is the most important contributor to price. Therefore, it behooves anyone who plans to sell or trade cards to take proper steps to ensure their preservation.

The care and treatment of a baseball card are not the delicate matters they are with stamps and other fragile items. Most cards are sturdy. They will not wrinkle or fade unless abused. Naturally, they should be protected from dampness and extreme heat. Bulk cards can be adequately stored in thick cardboard boxes designed specifically for that purpose. Avoid binding cards in rubber bands, which can leave telltale marks.

Valuable cards are best kept in plastic sheets and fitted into albums. But *never* glue, pin, staple, clip or otherwise attach a card to a page if it is ever to be sold or traded. Damage done by such an action will drastically reduce its market value.

How and When to Sell. Every true collector would love to own one of every baseball card ever made, but no one ever has. It is likely no one ever will. Yet collectors continue buying, selling, and trading, sometimes on a grand scale.

By periodically adding to and selling from stock, the collector will remain active within the hobby and turn a small profit besides. It is important from the beginning, however, not to expect to make millions in the ball card market. Most card sales are in the $50 range. Except for those enthusiasts willing to give most of their spare time to the pursuit, earnings are calculated in hundreds rather than thousands of dollars.

An effective way to get into the action is to take out a series of "Cards Wanted" ads in the local classifieds, hoping to attract collectors who are selling all or part of a collection. Sales of this magnitude are usually made at around 50% of book price, leaving plenty of room for resale in smaller quantities.

At this stage, serious collectors usually pull out choice items to add to their own collections. With the remainder, they will then consider renting a booth at a card show and selling the remainder individually or in small lots. Most collectors come to a show looking for specific cards to complete personal checklists. Often the need for common cards is as great as for rarer items. Keep track of all transactions for tax purposes.

Remember, it is quite possible to be a baseball card investor without having the slightest romantic inclination towards the cards or, for that matter, for the game of baseball. In fact, such investors are likely more successful due to their detachment. But they can also be missing the joy of ball card collecting. Unless baseball cards conjure up visions of the ballpark, the smell of hot dogs and cigars, the sound of ball meeting bat, their meaning will be limited. In the end, the true collector focuses not on how much the collection is worth, but on how much enjoyment it brings.

★ **Thirty-one-year-old Gary Carter of Palm Beach Gardens, Florida, has been saving baseball cards for years. The walls of his office are lined with binders containing more than forty-thousand cards, some of them quite valuable. More important, however, Gary Carter has achieved the ball card collector's ultimate dream: As an All-Star catcher for the Montreal Expos, Carter has been pictured on a baseball card over a dozen times.**

Little-Known Facts. Estimated sales of baseball cards reached $45 million in 1984.

• Pittsburgh Pirates great Honus Wagner abstained from tobacco and was an outspoken critic of its use. When he discovered that the American Tobacco Company had issued a tobacco card of him in 1909, he ordered them to pull it off the market. Only forty to fifty of these cards are known to have survived. By far the most sought-after baseball card, it lists at $20,000 mint.

• The Metropolitan Art Museum in New York City owns the most comprehensive collection of baseball cards in the world. However, these cards once belonged to a single individual, the late Jefferson R. Burdick. The author of *The American Card Catalog*, Burdick amassed over three-hundred thousand cards of all types and donated them to the museum upon his death.

—Richard Keller

Bibliography

Books

Boyd, Brendan B., and Fred C. Harris. *The Great American Baseball Card Flipping, Trading, and Bubble Gum Book.* Boston, MA: Little, Brown, and Co., 1973.

Consumer Guide (eds.), *Baseball Cards: A Collector's Guide.* New York: Beekman House, 1982.

Periodicals

Baseball Card Magazine. 700 E. State Street, Iola, WI 54990.

Baseball Card News. 1049 Camino Del Mar, Del Mar, CA 92014.

Catalogues

Hudgeons, Thomas E. III, ed. *Official 1985 Price Guide to Baseball Cards.* Orlando, FL: House of Collectibles, Inc., 1985.

Dealers

Blazek, Ken. Pittsburgh Sports Collectibles, Inc., 3102 Banksville Road, Pittsburgh, PA 15216.

King, Dennis. King's Baseball Cards, 2132 Center Street, Berkeley, CA 94704.

Marchant, Paul. The Baseball Card Store, 4512 Hampton Street, St. Louis, MO 63109.

NOTE: Enclose a self-addressed stamped envelope with each letter to a dealer.

BEER CANS

Beer Can Collectors of America was formed in 1970, when a feature story on collector Denver M. Wright, Jr., of St. Louis prompted a group of five or six local beer-can fanatics to join together to discuss the wonders of brew and the cans it comes in.

A decade later, this same group has grown into an organization with thirteen-thousand worldwide members. The collecting of beer cans is "America's fastest growing hobby," according to *Newsweek* magazine, and recent estimates put the total number of beer can collectors as high as half a million. Some of these "canoholics" have paid over $2,000 for a single empty beer can!

History. Beer can collecting is a relatively new hobby, since beer cans have only been with us since 1934. At that time, the American Can Company had just developed a special can with an enameled lining and, along with the Gottfried Krueger Brewing Company of Newark, New Jersey, introduced canned beer to the people of Richmond, Virginia.

Within six months, Krueger's sales increased five times, and the big players—Pabst and Schlitz—came out with cans of their own the following year. These first cans are extremely valuable, and every change in can manufacturing technology since has produced prized collectibles.

Along with the scarcities caused by technological and marketing experimentation, such as the ill-fated cone tops,[1] came the forces of intense market competition and the resulting fatalities. Over 80% of the breweries operating at the time of the invention of the beer can are now defunct. Local and regional brand beer cans are, therefore, among the most sought after.

★ In 1979, when Bill Gaylord sold fellow collector Jon Bruscia a beer can for $5, he had no idea it would one day grace the cover of Josten Publication's *Beer Cans Unlimited* (by Art and Pete Ressel). The rare can, a demo put out by the American Can Company in the '30s before it went ahead with the famous Krueger can, brought $600 when sold later that year.

Values Outside the Home. Scarcity and condition determine a can's value. Approximately 5% of all beer cans are defective (such as missing a coat of paint), and these oddballs are the cream of the collectors' crop.

Some people just collect the cans of beer they consume. These people tend to laugh a lot and have big bellies. Others concentrate only on cans from another country, or on cans of unusual sizes, like the gallon-sized Koch's Deer Run Draft Ale. Other collectors' items include the so-called "flats," or unfinished cans in the form of unrolled, printed sheets.

Collectors have developed a grading system to determine the value of cans based on their physical condition. Graded On a scale of 1 to 5, 1 meaning mint condition and 5 meaning non-restorable, collectors judge a can's value by its dents, rust, faded paint, and scratches.

Where to Find Values. The best place to find beer cans is in the garbage. Neighborhood dumps, ditches and picnic sites are prime locations, as well as abandoned buildings (construction workers often deposited cans in the walls of buildings they were working on, so their bosses would not know how much brew they consumed).

People often trade and buy beer cans through the mail. When doing so, it is important to grade cans and inform prospective buyers

---

[1]The cone top was shaped like a bottle and introduced by Schlitz. It never really caught on because it was difficult to stack in the refrigerator.

of their condition and year of issue. Cans should be packaged carefully, wrapped separately in paper and packed into a strong box.

When traveling, collectors should concentrate on finding local brands. When overseas, they should search the beer-drinking countries of northern Europe—Britain, Germany and Denmark.

A Price Sampling

Haberle's Light Ale, cone top	$1,000
All-Grain Storz	750
IBC Crown Select, Indianapolis Brewery	400
Hop Gold, gold with white lettering, red star	325
Krueger's Cream Ale, first can	125
Altes Golden Lager, cone top	65
Burgermeister, San Francisco, man in eighteenth-century costume	41
Chief Oshkosh	23
Miller High Life, quarter-moon emblem above brand name	6
Blatz, pull tab	.60

How to Store/Display. One of the most important things to remember when collecting cans is how to drain the beer. The standard "church key" opener can be used with the old-fashioned seamed cans, but beer must always be drained from the bottom, so that punctures are concealed when the can is on display. It might be necessary to use the professional press-type opener on modern seamless cans, since seamless cans have no bottom rim to provide leverage for the standard opener.

Cans are often in need of restoration. Small dents can be popped out by hand. Larger dents can be removed by filling the can with water and putting it into the freezer. The water expands as it turns to ice, pushing out the dents. Rust can be rubbed out with emery paper. If the rust is bad, oxalic acid, available at most pharmacies, will most likely remove it.

How and When to Sell. With the large increase of collectors, the beer-can market is bottoming out. Price lists for 1982 were peppered with sales figures in the $2,000 to $2,600 range. Top prices for 1984 were about half that. High-quality cans still bring top dollar, but collectors who have antique cans that are not in the best shape are advised to hang on to them for a while. If one must sell, it is best to sell at an auction, where collectors are willing to pay full market prices. Since

Manning Bros. Collection

The nobleness of beer prevails in spite of today's emphasis on marketing gimmickry. The proud Stroh family of Detroit's Stroh Brewery traces its origins to sixteenth-century Germany and was one of several breweries that dominated early American beer production.

★ **Jon Bruscia, who owns a shop called "The Closet" in Old Sacramento, California, has made a habit of cashing in on beer cans. In 1981, someone walked into Jon's store and traded him a can of Pilsen Brau for a $25 glass. Jon sold the can for $1,000 to a collector who turned around and sold it for $1,500. It now appears on the cover of *The Class Book of U.S. Beer Cans* (Jefferey Cameron).**

---

there may be regional price differences, one may have to do some traveling to get the highest return.

Little-Known Facts. John Ahren is listed in the *Guinness Book of World Records* as having the biggest collection of beer cans in the world, with eleven-thousand specimens.

• Playmate Malt Liquor, marketed in the early '60s, was withdrawn from the market when Playboy Enterprises sued, claiming exclusive right to the trademark.

• Because of a false rumor that the brewery was destroyed during race riots in Los Angeles, cans of Soul beer, or Mellow Yellow, can fetch up to $225.

• The Rosalie beer can is the most famous among collectors, because only one can is known to exist.

—Peter Asmus

Bibliography

Books

Cady, Lew. *Beer Can Collecting.* New York: Charter Books, 1981.
Dabbs, Robert. *Worldwide Beer Can Collecting Guide.* Buckner, MO: Maverick Publishing, 1984.
Encyclopedia of Collectibles. Alexandria, VA: Time-Life Books, 1978.
Martells, Jack. *Beer Can Collector's Bible.* Palos Heights, IL: Greatlakes Living Press, 1976.
Ressel, Art and Pete. *Beer Cans Unlimited.* Buckner, MO: Maverick Publishing, 1979.

Periodicals

Beer Cans Monthly. P.O. Box 337, Buckner, MO 64016.

Dealers

Beer Foam Scrapers, P.O. Box 394, Vernon, NJ 07462.
J. Bruscia, 117 J St., Old Sacramento, CA.
J. Hosier, 301 N. Beauregard #704, Alexandria, VA.

Associations

Beer Can Collectors of America, 747 Merus Ct., Fenton, MO 63026.
World Wide Beer Can Collectors, P.O. Box 1852, Independence, MO 64055.

NOTE: Both associations also publish newsletters. Write to them for information.

BICYCLES

Bicycles have never gotten the credit they deserve. It was the bicycle lover, after all, who paved the way for good roads in America at the turn of this century, only to find himself almost driven off of

Smithsonian Institution

A bicycle built for two, the Sociable was only one of several variations of the somewhat dangerous but popular nineteenth-century high-wheeler, whose brakes were either nonexistant or very crude.

them by that noisy newcomer, the automobile. And it was bicycle technology, as much as horse-drawn buggy design, that give the first automobile builders some sound engineering principles.

Even the modern historian slights the bicycle, often insisting that the French invented it in 1791. In fact, the French contraption was a horse-drawn affair; the real father of the bicycle, a German named Baron Karl von Drais, receives little recognition for his achievement, a push-type scooter/bicycle made in 1818.

Today most of us can recall when bicyclists were usually depicted as a bit mentally unbalanced in movies and on television during the 1950s. It was not until the 1960s that the image of the bike—and of bicyclists—began to change. Americans are now enjoying a renewed love affair with the bicycle, after a seventy-year fling with the automobile. It is good to see this remarkable machine back in favor in this country.

History. Many first-time bicycle collectors are amazed when they see a bicycle that was made around 1900. It looks so modern! For this reason, many experienced collectors will only deal in cycles made during the nineteenth century, when they were called "high-wheelers" and were designed with huge pedal-driven front wheels, or they had more than two wheels (tricycles and quadricycles).

Since pre-1900 bikes are so hard to find today, most beginning collectors are content to gather up the more modern "safety" bicycles, which first appeared in small numbers around 1885. The safety bike employed a frame-mounted chain drive operated by pedals, which was a great improvement over the dangerous high-wheeler (whose brakes were either nonexistent or very primitive) and the complicated and expensive multi-wheelers. Later safety bikes, such as those made in large quantities after World War II, employed all kinds of fancy accessories; and with their white-walled balloon tires, two-tone paint, horn tanks, baskets, electric generators and white vinyl handgrips, they are still objects to marvel at.

Collecting antique bicycles is not yet a big hobby in the United States, but it will continue to proliferate as interest in modern bicycles grows, which it certainly seems to be doing in the 1980s.

★ Nothing rewards a collector like persistence. One collector of pre-1900 bicycles spotted a choice specimen from the late 1870s sitting in a modern bicycle shop in upstate New York. When he inquired about buying it, he was firmly turned down, the owner insisting that it would *never* be for sale. But the collector would not take no for an answer, and he returned to the shop every three months, asking politely if the old bike were for sale yet. He kept this up for over four years, and finally, when the owner needed room for other merchandise, he consented to sell this prize.

Values Outside the Home. The easiest collectors' bikes to find are those made after WW II with balloon tires, and the early ten-speed touring and racing bikes produced in Europe and the United States in the 1970s.

Learning which bikes are valuable requires a lot of research, since no reliable guide books on the subject exist. As a basic rule, however, any older bike in nice condition is certainly worth collecting. The issue here is supply and demand, and only a thorough reading of bicycle collectors periodicals and newsletters, as well as correspondence with dealers and collectors, can determine the true value of a particular bike. The value of the more "modern" ten-speeds depends greatly on their frames, which one can learn more about by talking to individuals who either custom build racing and touring bikes or who sell the better makes to serious enthusiasts.

Above all else, collectors should not pay too much for safety bikes that are incomplete or complete but with unoriginal parts. Finding authentic parts is difficult, and having them reproduced is not worth the trouble financially, considering the ultimate value of perhaps a few hundred dollars. For this reason, incomplete or non-original bikes are best left unrestored, and as such can still be very useful for riding, trading, and for learning about the hobby.

Where to Find Values. Safety bicycles still show up at flea markets, police and private auctions, and local antiques stores. Early ten-speeds will show up at police auctions but are more commonly advertised on bike shop bulletin boards and offered at private garage sales. The very old high-wheelers can sometimes be found at antiques dealers (be careful of modern reproductions), but a good deal of haggling is going to be necessary to get the price down to a reasonable level. The rarest "bicycles,"—the tricycles and quadricycles made before 1900—can only be found through experienced collectors and, on occasion, in museums that are disposing of duplicated or unwanted items.

Finally, collectors' periodicals are always a good source, and this includes publications devoted to old automobiles and motorcycles as well.

A Price Sampling. Current price lists for collectible bicycles are a bit sketchy, but as a general rule, an old safety bike in good, *original* condition can bring anywhere from $250 to $500. The really rare quadricycles of one hundred years ago can be worth as much as $4,000 fully and authentically restored. Some rather interesting old ten-speeds in decent condition can be had for $100 to $300.

How to Store/Display. Caring for an old bicycle is much like caring for a motorcycle (see "Motorcycles"). It should be kept high and dry, well-waxed and securely locked. The best preservative to use is a pure carbona wax without polishers or additives. Before applying, one should pre-clean the bike with a mild soap or a light automotive rubbing compound, such as Dupont White.

When storing a bike for a prolonged period, one should hang it by its frames. This will keep its tires from dampness and from going flat—it also keeps the bike out of harm's way.

How and When to Sell. Old bicycles sell well when they are displayed, at such places as flea markets and garage sales. The bulletin boards of local bike shops, as well as university boards, work well, too, especially when a Polaroid snapshot is attached. To sell really special items, collectors should advertise in the classified sections of collectors' periodicals.

Little-Known Facts. The world's largest high-wheeler bicycle has a front wheel that is sixty-four inches in diameter. The man who owns the bike spent $3,500 for its purchase and restoration.

• The Elliott Hickory Safety Bicycle of 1888 raised a few eyebrows back then as a possible misnomer: if its frame was made entirely of hickory wood, how could it be strong enough to be safe? But its creator thought hickory morally superior to metal and aimed to produce a bicycle that "a man or woman could ride, and still be Christian."

—Joseph L. Troise

Bibliography

Books

Alderson, Frederick. *Bicycling: A History.* New York: Praeger Publishers, 1972.
Ritchie, A. *King of the Road.* Berkeley, CA: Ten Speed Press, 1975.
Tax Guide for Auto Restorers and Collectors. Irvine, CA: Professional Accounting Offices, 1984.

Periodicals

Antique, Balloon and Classic Bicycles. c/o John Lannis, Jr., 5832 Lauder, Pittsburgh, PA 15207.
Hemmings Motor News. Box 100, Bennington, VT 05201.
Old Cars Weekly. Iola, WI 54990.

Catalogues

Catalogues for old bicycles are scarce, but occasionally they will be offered for sale in the periodicals listed above.

Dealers

Dixon, Box 765, Huntington Beach, CA 92648.

NOTE: Bicycle dealers occasionally advertise in the periodicals listed above.

Associations

Museum of Science and Industry, Attn: Curator, Chicago, IL 60637.
Smithsonian Institution, Attn: Curator, Washington, DC 20560.
Wheelmen, The, c/o Don Adams, Henry Ford Museum, Dearborn, MI 48121.

BOOKS

If you happen to find an anonymous little pamphlet with brown paper covers in your attic, do not throw it away without examining it closely. If the cover reads, *"Tamerlane and Other Poems / By a Bostonian,"* if it was printed in Boston in 1827, and if it is not a facsimile of the original, you may be holding one of the most valuable and sought-after books in the world. The author is Edgar Allan Poe, and *Tamerlane and Other Poems* was his first published work. The last time one was sold at auction (in 1974) it brought $123,000.

History. It is highly unlikely that another copy of *Tamerlane and Other Poems* will surface, but this classic example of a rare book provides an excellent illustration of what makes a book valuable in the quirky world of book collecting.

A book is not worth much if it is not in demand. Its rarity usually contributes to its desirability. Only a few copies of the Poe book are known to exist; that, coupled with the great number of collectors of the works of Poe, makes it extraordinarily desirable. If no one wanted the book, it would not matter how few copies there were; it would be worthless. Demand is usually the overriding consideration contributing to a book's value. All other factors are secondary, though they may affect the amount a book is worth.

Most old books stored in attics, even if they were published in the last century, are probably worthless, first, because they are unwanted, and second, because they are probably not in very good condition. There may be a few gems among the junk, but the important question is, how can they be recognized?

One alternative is to take them to a rare book dealer, who will most likely offer a disappointingly small sum, even for the more valuable items. A dealer cannot pay the full market value of a book because overhead and profit must be taken into consideration. He or she will usually offer half or less of what the book will sell for.

Such collections, however, should never be carelessly disposed of. A young man who now collects Tarzan novels, by Edgar Rice Burroughs, got his start because his father had had a few first editions of Burroughs's works that he hoped to someday pass on to a future son. Unfortunately, he unwisely stored them in the attic. Somone thoughtlessly labeled the box "Old Books" and then threw it away when the household was moved. A few Burroughs first editions are now worth hundreds, even thousands of dollars.

Not the least important factor affecting a book's price is its condition. Obviously, any copy of *Tamerlane and Other Poems,* considering its scarcity and desirability, will be valuable, but the worse its condition, the lower its price. The copy sold for $123,000 in 1974 was the best known to exist. Some books, however, become virtually worthless when they are in poor condition or, in the case of modern books, when they are missing their dust jackets.

During the '20s and '30s, it was fashionable to discard the dust jacket after a book was purchased. That practice made dust jackets from books of that period very scarce, hence highly valuable today. A first edition of *Soldier's Pay,* William Faulkner's hard-to-find first novel, published in 1926, is worth a few thousand dollars with the dust jacket and only a few hundred without it. Less-scarce and more recently published books will often have no value at all without the jacket.

Collectors, especially of modern books, also demand that books be in perfect or near-perfect condition. Each slight imperfection degrades the value of the book. Less-than-perfect books are usually termed, in descending order, "very fine," "fine," "good," "fair," and "poor."

With rare exceptions, a collector insists upon having the very first printing of a book. The identification of first editions is one of the most confusing aspects of book collecting. Not every book so marked on its copyright page is a true first—book club editions, for instance, are usually of inferior quality and without value. True first editions can be identified in several ways: some have "book club edition" printed on the inside flap of the dust jacket; they usually do not have a price printed on the inside front flap; and they almost always have a small indentation stamped into the back cover.

Some books are what is known as *first trade editions.* This usually means that the true first edition was a limited edition, often signed by the author and sold prior to the trade edition at a higher price. If this is the case, the collector will probably want to collect the limited edition, if it is affordable.

Many publishers do not print "first edition" on their copyright pages. To identify their first editions, the collector must be familiar with the various devices they use to indicate first printings. Books that list the methods of some publishers are *How to Identify and Collect*

American First Editions (Jack Tannen) and *Modern Book Collecting* (Robert A. Wilson).

★ **Scott Morgan of Woodstock, New York, was browsing through one of the many bookshops in Hay-on-Wye, Wales, when for no particular reason he put his finger on a book and pulled it out. It was a play called *Heliogabalus* by H. L. Mencken and George Jean Nathan. Because it was one of a limited first edition of sixty copies signed by the authors, he knew it had to be worth more than the tenpence on the price tag. It turned out to be worth over $300.**

Values Outside the Home. Book collecting entails endless possibilities. Before beginning a collection, the novice should narrow his or her focus to one subject area, time period, or perhaps to a single author. Some possible specialties: *incunabula* (books printed before 1501, when printing was in its infancy); *Americana* (a very broad subject area that could be further broken down by geographical area, author, time period, or in some other way); or *fine press editions* (expensive, high-quality books printed in limited editions that are collectors' items per se). Fine press books are good steady investments but rarely increase dramatically in value. Mysteries, science fiction, fantasy, and favorite living authors are fertile fields that might require a smaller initial investment. A collection might also be built around a rare book acquired serendipitously—received as a gift, found in the attic, or bought at a garage sale or thrift shop at a fraction of its worth.

The most important thing a new collector must remember is to be guided by his or her enthusiasms. Building a book collection can involve a huge investment of time spent learning about the chosen area and searching for the books needed to round out the collection. Obviously, no one wants to spend that much time on something that is not fun.

Once a field of interest has been chosen, the beginning collector should buy inexpensive reading copies of the books to become familiar with the material and to avoid handling and possibly damaging the pristine rare volumes themselves. Bibliographies of nearly every author and field are available and will help in the composition of a "want list" of desired books. Reputable dealers

Library of Congress

The demand for a book determines its value,
which is why a rare copy of Edgar Allan Poe's
Tamerlane and Other Poems sold for $123,000.

should be consulted for advice, information, and the names of
dealers who specialize in a chosen area.

The collector must learn to identify first editions of the books he
or she is seeking. There are telltale signs known as *points* that help to
identify the first printing of a particular book. A point might be a
typographical error that was corrected in subsequent editions. Once
they have been told of a collector's needs, friends and acquaintances
will often act as unofficial scouts.

Giving a collection a definite shape will make it more valuable.
Unless a collector is wealthy, a collection should be shaped slowly
and at prices he or she can afford. One particular collector's rule of
thumb is to never spend more on a book than the amount of pleasure
he can get out of it. Any increase in value is then just an added
pleasure.

Collecting Science Fiction. The same rules that apply to collecting rare books in general also apply to collecting science fiction, although there are some special considerations.

First, many science fiction titles were originally published in paperback; second, many of them were published by small presses in limited editions because most major publishers would not handle them.

The first factor contributes to the scarcity of titles, since paperbacks were meant to be disposable, and they deteriorate faster than hardcovers. Many prominent science fiction authors, including Ursula LeGuin and Larry Niven, had at least one paperback original.

Oddly, the second factor, the small printings (sometimes of five hundred or fewer copies) by small presses such as Arkham House, do not necessarily mean that a book so published is scarce. Because many of these titles were purchased by aficionados who treasured them, they are often easier to find than science fiction brought out in hardcover by a major publisher, such as Doubleday, the first big eastern publisher to make a commitment to science fiction.

Dust jackets are even more important to science fiction collectors than they are to book collectors in general, primarily because artwork is so important to science fiction fans. Often the dust jacket is worth more than the book it protects. The value of any book with artwork by a revered artist such as Frank Frazetta is automatically enhanced.

Where to Find Values. Rare books can be found anywhere that books are sold: garage sales, library sales, thrift stores, rummage sales, auctions, book fairs, used bookstores, new bookstores, and, of course, rare bookstores.

One source of potentially valuable books that most people overlook is the remainder table found in nearly every bookstore. Here, first editions of modern authors are often available for a few dollars. The trouble with this type of buying is that it is so speculative. The buyer has to be able to predict which authors will write books that will eventually become collectors' items, and then wait an unspecified length of time, probably many years, before the book becomes valuable.

The real challenge is to identify and collect an up-and-coming author, when first printings are small and before his or her books start to appreciate. This is where big profits can be made, but the only way a collector can begin to predict future collectors' items is to be constantly reading new writers.

Books can also be bought at book auction houses or at antiquarian book fairs, where dealers display and sell their wares. Few bargains will be had from these sources, however.

Surprisingly, valuable finds can often be made in used bookstores. A browser with a sharp eye recently bought a copy of *The October Country*, by Ray Bradbury, for a couple of dollars at a used bookstore in San Francisco. One of fifty copies signed by the author, it sold at auction for $1,300. That bookstore has since employed a more knowledgeable used-book buyer, and used bookstores in general are becoming more aware of the value of some books to collectors, to the point where they often overprice books that have little actual value. Even knowledgeable dealers cannot know everything, however, and used bookstores are still worth checking for bargains.

★ **A book scout picked up a book of photographs at a flea market for $1. He took it to a book auction house, where it was discovered to be the proof book of Eugene Atget, the French photographer whose work is now very much in vogue. The book sold at auction for $16,000.**

A Price Sampling

Dubliners by James Joyce, signed, with dust jacket	$11,000
English Bible, 1903, five volumes	6,500
Wise Blood by Flannery O'Conner, mint condition	950
Two Years Before the Mast by Richard Henry Dana, first edition, first issue	800
Lolita by Vladimir Nabokov, first edition, in fine condition	680
History of the Donner Party by C. F. McGlashan, first edition	300
The Shining by Stephen King, first edition, signed	160
Marginalia by H. P. Lovecraft, first edition, illustrated jacket	100
Stranger in a Strange Land by Robert Heinlein, first edition	60
The Black Mountain by Rex Stout, excellent condition, slight wear	45
You Only Live Twice by Ian Fleming, excellent condition, with dust jacket	40

How to Store/Display. Books are fragile, but in most cases excessive trouble need not be taken to preserve them. Storing them in glass-covered bookcases is an excellent way to prevent damage, but it is not absolutely necessary. Slipcases of paper or leather can also be used, but a less-expensive method is to wrap the cover of each book in transparent Mylar, available in art supply stores.

Books should be kept away from heat sources, direct sunlight, humidity, and dampness. Packing them too tightly or too loosely on a shelf is not good for them. Fluorescent lighting is much more harmful to them than incandescent lighting.

Extremely valuable books may be kept in a bank's safety deposit box or a fireproof safe or file cabinet at home, where one has easier access to them.

Obviously, valuable books should be handled with great care. Since condition is so crucial, it is advisable to read an inexpensive copy of a book to avoid handling a rare copy.

Common sense will protect books from most mishaps. Valuable books should not be kept on low shelves, where two-year-olds can reach them. Tape of any sort should never be used to repair tears, even (or especially) on dust jackets. Peanut-butter-and-jelly sand-wiches should not be eaten while examining a new find, and, of course, a book collector should never lend a treasured book to a friend.

How and When to Sell. There are several ways to sell a single book or a whole collection. The seller can offer it to a dealer, who will at best pay half of its estimated retail value. This may not be the best choice financially, but it is the most expedient. A dealer who specializes in the subject matter of the book will be more likely to have a true idea of its value.

Another option is to consign a collection or book to an auction house. The house will research the value of each item and reject bids that are below a threshold specified by the seller. The auction house will take 5% to 25% of the prices realized; the higher the value of the book, the lower the percentage.

A third choice is for the collector to find a buyer himself. This may be difficult and time-consuming. A dealer has the advantage of knowing many buyers and what they are looking for. An advertisement in *AB Bookman's Weekly* is the method used by many dealers, but the collector has to pay for the ad and take his chances on finding a buyer.

Obviously, the collector will want to sell at a time when the collection's value is highest. Anyone who has spent years painstakingly putting together a collection of the works of Longfellow and decides to sell it this year would probably be very distressed to find that Longfellow's popularity has waned to the point where there would be few interested buyers. Five years from now the tide may have turned.

Unfortunately, there is no way to predict the ebb and flow of an author's popularity in this sometimes-fickle field. Holding on to a collection or book until there is a strong demand for that author or field is the best hope for realizing a substantial return on the initial investment.

★ **In 1984, a Berkeley, California, woman brought eighteen original holograph sermons written by an anonymous preacher in California's Gold Country in the 1850s and 1860s to a book auction house. They later sold for $350. When asked where she had gotten them, she seemed embarrassed, but finally admitted that she had found them at the Berkeley dump.**

Little-Known Facts. A cautionary note: A love of books can be taken too far; it can lead to bibliomania and even death. Consider the sad case of Eleanor Barry of Long Island, New York. This elderly lady had collected so many newspapers, magazines, and books that the stacks reached to the ceiling. In 1977, she was trapped in her bed for days by a fallen pile of books. She died soon after being rescued.

• Collectors must also take care that their valuable books do not fall into the hands of the wrong people. Loved ones are sometimes the worst offenders: William Blades recounts in *The Enemies of Books* the case of a woman who used the pages of her deceased father's valuable black-letter books as toilet paper.

• There is also the story, perhaps apocryphal, of John Warburton's collection of seventeenth-century drama, including many works by Shakespeare. He claimed that he entrusted these rare works to his cook and that all but three were "unluckely burnd or put under Pye bottoms."

—Heidi Ellison

Bibliography

Books

Bradley, Van Allen. *The Book Collector's Handbook of Values,* 4th revised edition. New York: G. P. Putnam's Sons, 1982.

Carter, John. *ABC for Book Collectors*, 4th edition. New York: Knopf, 1966.

Currey, Lloyd W. *Science Fiction and Fantasy Authors*. Boston, MA: G. K. Hall, 1979.

Halpern, Frank M. *Directory of Dealers in Science Fiction and Fantasy*. Haddonfield, NJ: Haddonfield House, 1975.

Mandeville, Mildred S., ed. *The Used Book Price Guide*. Kenmore, WA: Price Guide, 1983.

Matthews, Jack. *Collecting Rare Books for Pleasure & Profit*. Athens, OH: Ohio University Press, 1981.

Peters, Jean, ed. *Book Collecting: A Modern Guide*. New York: R. R. Bowker, 1977.

Peters, Jean, ed. *Collectible Books: Some New Paths*. New York: R. R. Bowker, 1979.

Tannen, Jack,. *How to Identify and Collect American First Editions*. New York: Arco Publishing, 1976.

Wilson, Robert A. *Modern Book Collecting*. New York: Knopf, 1980.

Periodicals

AB Bookman's Weekly. Box AB, Clifton, NJ 07015.

Locus: The Newspaper of the Science Fiction Field. P.O. Box 13305, Oakland, CA 94661.

Catalogues

Leab, Katherine, ed. *American Book Prices Current*, Vol. 89. New York: Bancroft-Parkman, 1983.

Resnick, Michael. *The Official Price Guide to Comic and Science Fiction Books*. Orlando, FL: House of Collectibles, 1984.

Dealers and Auction Houses

William H. Allen, Bookseller, 2031 Walnut St., Philadelphia, PA 19103.

Best of Two Worlds (science fiction), 2411 Telegraph Ave., Berkeley, CA 94704.

Black Sun Books, 667 Madison Ave., New York, NY 10021.

California Book Auction Galleries, 358 Golden Gate Ave., San Francisco, CA 94102.

Caveat Emptor, 208 S. Dunn, Bloomington, IN 47401.

Christie, Manson & Woods International, 502 Park Ave., New York, NY 10022.

Colophon Bookshop, 700 S. Sixth Ave., La Grange, IL 60525.

Lloyd W. Currey (science fiction), Elizabethtown, NY 12932.

Fantasy, Etc. (science fiction and fantasy), 808 Larkin, San Francisco, CA 94109.

Goodspeed's Bookshop, 7 Beacon St., Boston, MA 02108.

Heritage Bookshop, 847 N. La Cienega Blvd., Los Angeles, CA 90028.

Other Change of Hobbit (science fiction), 2433 Channing Way, Berkeley, CA 94704.

The Phoenix Book Shop, 22 Jones St., New York, NY 10014.

Serendipity Books, 1790 Shattuck Ave., Berkeley, CA 94709.

Sotheby Parke Bernet & Co., 1334 York Ave., New York, NY 10021.

Transition Books and Prints, 445 Stockton St., San Francisco, CA 94108.

Associations

Antiquarian Booksellers' Association of America, 50 Rockefeller Plaza, New York, NY 10020.

International Society of Bible Collectors, P.O. Box 2485, El Cajon, CA 92021.

C

CHRISTMAS ORNAMENTS

During the 1983 Christmas season Washington D.C.'s Watergate Hotel exhibited Christmas ornaments collected by political celebrities. Called "Entertaining People," the exhibit included a life-size silver goose that sat on the Christmas table of Secretary of Defense and Mrs. Casper W. Weinberger. Also on display was a tree trimmed with a collection of ornaments inspired by the transportation industry collected by Secretary of Transportation Elizabeth Hanford Dole. Other displays included a holiday table from the British Embassy set by Lady Wright, the wife of the British ambassador.

Mrs. Clara Scroggins, author of *Silver Christmas Ornaments: A Collector's Guide,* is believed to have the most extensive collection of Christmas ornaments in the country. According to a *New York Times* account, Mrs. Scroggins is collecting ornaments at a rate of one-thousand a year. Each Christmas she decorates four Christmas trees in her Houston, Texas, home yet only uses a fraction of the over twenty-two thousand ornaments that make up her collection.

Just about everyone has a Christmas ornament collection, which they stash away in a hall closet or attic. Every year they make some additions to it and give a few older, hand-me-down ornaments a bit of extra attention and special positioning on the Christmas tree.

Collecting antique Christmas ornaments is rewarding not only because it satisfies a desire many of us have to prolong the magic and excitement of Christmases past, but also because it can bring profit along with the fun—resale prices for antique ornaments have been moving steadily up and promise to continue doing so.

History. The first Christmas ornaments appeared in both Christian and pagan legend simultaneously. According to one Christian myth mentioned by Maggie Rogers and Judith Hawkins in their book *The Glass Christmas Ornament,* St. Nicholas gave three bags of gold as dowries for three daughters of a poor man. The bags became stylized in paintings as three gold balls and later were symbolized by the hanging of gold balls on Christmas trees. (Some historians also have credited St. Nicholas' gold bags as being precursors to the traditional three-gold-ball sign of the modern pawnbroker.)

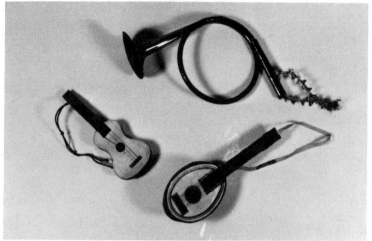

Courtesy Elizabeth M. Hartjens

The three-dimensional wooden Christmas tree ornaments made in Germany in the late 1800s were a departure from early designs, which were flat, geometric, and made of lead.

Store-bought ornaments made their appearance in America during the 1860s. An 1869 edition of *Harper's* magazine described some of the first ornaments imported from Germany as "grotesque figures suspended by a rubber string... exaggerated seraphim with flapping wings and strange-looking old women with heads larger than their bodies."

A few American manufacturers started producing ornaments when they became popular, but most were imported from Germany and sold on street corners. These early decorations often were flat geometric shapes, such as stars and crosses, and made of lead. Later versions were made of glass, cardboard, wax, or cotton and wool. Cotton-wool ornaments were children's favorites because they were unbreakable and therefore allowed by parents as playthings.

Blown-glass ornaments were first imported to the United States in fall 1880, when a German importer offered to sell $25 worth to a young dime store merchant in Pennsylvania named Frank Woolworth. Woolworth thought the ornaments were foolish but bought them when the importer agreed to refund his money if they did not sell. "In two days," said Woolworth, "they were gone, and I woke up." Within ten years Woolworth's annual order for blown-glass ornaments from Germany grew to more than two-hundred-thousand pieces, and Woolworth is credited with having discovered the German handcrafted ornament industry. He later made another contribution to its early success by getting the tariff status for ornaments changed from toys to glass articles. This greatly reduced rates for the German decorations and opened the way for the past fifty years for Japan, Austria, Poland, Mexico, and Italy to export large numbers of glass ornaments to the United States under the tariff protections of the Most Favored Nation trading policy.

Fortunately for blown-glass ornament collectors early German glass blowers shaped their ornaments with molds. The molds allowed for fairly high-volume production, which meant that a lot of turn-of-the-century glass ornaments have survived to the present. However, chemical imbalances in much of the glass that was used at the time have caused the ornaments to become more fragile as they get older. This increasing delicacy is good news for sellers because it is forcing the value for blown-glass ornaments to rise steadily.

★ Limited edition Christmas ornaments have been around long enough to command respectable resale prices. One mother has completed a set of "Twelve Drummers Drumming" limited edition silver ornaments by Towle for each of her four children at $28 each. If resale prices for silver ornaments continue to rise at their present rate, she hopes her investment will be worth roughly fifty times its current price when her children reach college age in the 1990s. She considers the ornaments an investment for their future and keeps impressing upon them the importance of keeping the original box, chamois bag and printed explanatory statement. "You are really collecting the whole thing," she said.

Values Outside the Home. A Christmas ornament's value is determined by its age and rarity. Collectors should pay attention to an ornament's construction, design, patina and material to ascertain its antiquity. Glass balls decorated with wire tinsel, cotton batting or silk tassels were most likely made between 1890 and 1910. Often the country of origin can be identified on pre-World War I ornaments by the design of the ornament's round metal cap.

No one knows for sure how many different types of antique glass ornaments have been made, but some collectors estimate it to be about five thousand. Of these, there are three general groupings: 1) points (treetop ornaments), 2) balls, and 3) figures. Antique ornaments made from other materials, such as cardboard, are also available in a variety of shapes, colors and degrees of quality. Embossed cardboard ornaments once fashioned in Dresden and covered with metallic paper are considered some of the rarest ornaments and the most valuable.

Light-bulb ornaments, which were used in the '20s and '30s, are also popular. The first bulbs were delicate pieces made by hand in Vienna when the electric light was relatively new. By 1919 General Electric was producing machine-made bulbs by the thousands. The most collectible light-bulb ornaments these days are the blown-glass designs made in Occupied Japan.

America's current nostalgia fad has given birth to limited edition and collectors' series Christmas ornaments, which join the company of collectors' series Christmas mugs, bells, plaques and plates. Limited editions of sterling silver ornaments made by American silver manufacturers are especially popular within this group.

Where to Find Values. No matter what a collector's price range, there are three basic rules to buying old ornaments: 1) buy what you like, 2) buy the best you can afford, and 3) never buy damaged or broken pieces for investment.

As the value of Christmas ornaments goes up, more and more ornaments are finding their way into antiques stores. Dealers buying estates are now discovering that it is more profitable to hold on to them, when once they considered decorations too fragile to bother keeping.

If one has the stamina to pick through dusty boxes, one can uncover interesting and lucrative items for himself and they will be less expensive than if bought through a dealer. Collectors should also read the classified sections of larger newspapers. In the late 1950s, a Washington, D.C. newspaper ran an ad for Jacqueline Kennedy, who was having a sale to dispose of some of her unwanted wedding gifts. Garage sales and flea markets are also good places to search for ornaments.

If beginning collectors are looking to buy or sell especially valuable ornaments, antiques and craft shows are excellent marketplaces. They are often held in fine hotels, where collectors and prospective buyers come prepared to deal. The best sources of

information about these shows are newsletters sent out by
sponsoring organizations and antiques associations (see bibliography). Many dealers are also aware of shows scheduled in their areas.

A Price Sampling

Ornament, bear with muff, blown glass	$45-55
Light, Humpty Dumpty, milk glass	18-32
Ornament, fence, wood	22-32
Light, zeppelin with flag	18-32
Ornament, umbrella, tinsel	22-28
Ornament, Santa Claus with plaster face	22-28
Ornament, ball, amber	22-28
Light, snowman, milk glass	12-22
Ornament, pinecone, blown glass	12-22
Light, elephant, milk glass	6-11

These are prices for pieces considered available enough for
acquisition and sale by collectors but not scarce enough to be *avidly*
sought after. The rarities fetch quite a bit more on the market: a 1934
Flash Gordon light bulb will bring $175; 1920 Charlie Chaplin glass
ornaments can be sold for as much as $220, and a boxed set of Snow
White and the Seven Dwarfs glass ornaments, produced by Disney
Enterprises in the 1930s, can be tagged as high as $500.

How to Store/Display. The most obvious place to display Christmas
ornaments is on a Christmas tree, but many collectors enjoy
exhibiting their pieces elsewhere all year long.

A few practical considerations for displaying Christmas ornaments include keeping the collection together. Seen as a group, even
the most ordinary objects take on interest. If one decides to hang his
ornaments on a wall, some interior decorators recommend grouping
them in a straight line to follow a distinctive architectural feature,
such as a window, door, or piece of furniture.

Most collectors feel their ornaments look best—and are safest—
stored away in cabinets, cupboards, and other types of enclosed
units. If using a cabinet, always check the shelves to be sure they will
support the weight of the collection. Also, place ornaments back
from the edge of a shelf. Repeated vibrations, common in every
home, can slowly nudge a prized piece to smash on a cabinet's floor.

If ornaments need cleaning, one should never use anything other
than a soft, dry cloth. Any sort of water or dampness will cause the
lacquer on an old ornament to peel right off.

Even the smallest collection should include a complete record of purchase dates, sources, prices and any additional information. In the event of a loss, such records will be the only resources one will have for obtaining insurance compensation or identifying stolen goods. Large collections, by the way, should be covered by a special home or renters insurance provision sometimes called a *floater policy*, which lets collectors distinguish certain items from their general household that are worth a good deal more than intrinsic value.

★ **Nineteenth-century German ornaments made in Dresden and Lauscha are popular among serious collectors, but as the number of these early pieces diminishes, collections from later years are climbing in value. One New York collector, Jerry Harmyk, co-owner of Johnny Jupiter antiques, collects ornaments made between 1920 and 1940. Common designs then were clear glass bells or globes often decorated with painted stripes. Today these are priced between $5 and $500.**

How and When to Sell. Ornament prices and availability vary widely in different geographical regions for different reasons. When Japan started making Christmas ornaments in large numbers for export, the Japanese people were unaware of Christmas. Now it is celebrated by many Japanese as a secular children's holiday which, of course, includes tree trimming. This means that fewer ornaments are exported here from Japan, making what does come here more valuable. In Germany Christmas ornaments are not nearly as popular as they are in the United States. According to one collector, "Emphasis (in Germany) has always been placed on having a beautiful Christmas tree, not on having a tree covered with unique figurals...." This makes decorations from Germany scarce also.

Collectors should be aware that the size of a collection can influence its worth. A large collection of almost anything will attract more buyers than a few items sold separately. Of course, if the few ornaments one does possess are in great demand, there is nothing to worry about. But if one has a few not-so-valuable ornaments, it would pay to build up a collection first before attempting to sell.

Among the more sought-after ornaments are nineteenth-century German glass balls called *Kugeln* (identified by thick glass and a dull sheen) and *free-blown* ornaments made by turn-of-the-century German artisans who did not use molds. Collectors' series favorites include "A Partridge in a Pear Tree," first in a "Twelve Days of Christmas" series of sterling medallions by Towle. The set sold for $10 when it was issued in 1971. It is valued today at around $500.

Little-Known Facts. Nineteenth-century Christmas tree stands are an uncommon variety of Christmas ornament but a collectors' item nonetheless.

• The idea of supporting Christmas trees with something other than a bucket of coal caught on in the United States about the same time tree ornaments became popular. The first American patents were issued in 1876 for a three-legged design that looked a lot like a flagpole stand.

• Mr. Martin Merk got a patent in 1891 for a two-pronged design that gripped the tree trunk. One of the more significant features of Mr. Merk's tree stand, as far as collectors are concerned, is that his name and the date of his patent are inscribed on the rim of the base, making the stand easy to identify.

• A famous center for ornamental glass blowing in the 1860s to the 1930s was the German village of Lauscha, sixty miles north of Nuremberg. Ornaments were made in family workshops, where a man and his sons usually labored at the kitchen table. Since similar molds were used to make most ornaments from Lauscha, families individualized their work by using distinctive colors and patterns. One family may have preferred a pastel combination while another might have chosen a configuration of gold, red, blue and white. Thousands of molds were produced by Lauscha glass blowers, and today Lauscha molds are worth as much as the ornaments that were made in them.

—*James W. White*

Bibliography

Books

Rogers, Maggie, and Judith Hawkins. *The Glass Christmas Ornament: Old and New.* Forest Grove, OR: Timber Press, 1977.

Scroggins, Clara Johnson. *Silver Christmas Ornaments.* San Diego, CA: A. S. Barnes and Co., Inc., 1980.

Snyder, Phillip. *The Christmas Tree Book.* New York: The Viking Press, 1976.

Periodicals

Antique Monthly. P.O. Drawer 2, Tuscaloosa, AL 35402.

Antique Trader, The. Box 1050-PG, Dubuque, IA 52001.

Spinning Wheel. Fame Avenue, Hanover, PA 17331.

Catalogues

Kovel, Ralph and Terry. *Kovels' Antiques Price Guide.* New York: Crown Publishers, Inc., 1981.

Scroggins, Wallace. *Hallmark Christmas Ornaments: A Collector's Guide.* Des Moines, IA: Homestead Book Co., 1983.

Periodicals

"The Golden Glow of Christmas Past" (bimonthly, $10 per year), Jerry Ehernberger, 9240 Irving St., Westminster, CO 80030.

Dealers

Gotham Book Mart, 41 West 47th St., New York, NY.

Jankauer, Paul, 9323 N. Kedvale, Skokie, IL 60076.

Jupiter, Johnny, 884 Madison Ave., New York, NY.

Associations

American Antiquarian Society, 185 Salisbury St., Worcester, MA 01609.

International Toy Buffs Association, 17 W. Main St., Alhambra, CA 91801.

National Ornaments and Electric Lights Christmas Association, 200 5th Ave., New York, NY 10010.

Annual Show

Gotham Book Mart Gallery (Dec. 16-Jan. 8) 41 West 47th St., New York, NY.

CIVIL WAR MEMORABILIA

The interest in anything related to United States history that began in earnest during the 1976 Bicentennial has driven up the prices of all objects related to the Civil War. Today, retail prices of those objects are so high that only the most affluent individual should consider collecting them. On the other hand, the situation makes it possible for someone to make a considerable amount of money from items that have been passed down through families or collected before prices rose.

History. The value of Civil War memorabilia comes from the fact that the objects were used by, or intended to be used by, anyone directly engaged in the hostilities, whether from the North or the South. Even the most everyday objects, such as pocket combs, prayer books, or bars of soap, are highly sought after because they are connected to a unique period in our nation's history. Items from the Confederacy tend to bring higher prices because many of them were destroyed once the Confederacy fell and because there was less uniformity in them to begin with.

★ **A Midwestern antiques dealer found a Civil War sword at a local auction for $150. When attending an antiques show a few months later, she saw the identical sword on display. The owner paid her $800 for the mate.**

Values Outside the Home. No matter how eager one is to begin collecting in this field, it is important to be highly knowledgeable about it, since it is so easy to throw money away on items of little value. Beginners can prepare by reading as much as possible about the Civil War and Civil War memorabilia. Libraries and bookstores have ample background material. It should be utilized to the fullest extent. It is important to understand first of all how both armies were outfitted, what individual items were issued, and where they originated. The Union, for instance, representing the established government, had official government issues of clothing, weapons, and equipment, while the fledgling Confederate Army had to rely on local communities and states to outfit their troops. As a result, there is a diversity of items that were carried by Confederate soldiers, depending on where they came from and when they mustered in. Many of the companies that produced uniforms, weapons, and camp gear for either army also supplied military academies before and after the war with similar, if not identical, items. While these objects may appear the same to the layman, they mean a world of difference to the collector interested only in the war.

To make the going more difficult, a large number of reproductions, some of them created as long ago as the early 1900s, have flooded the market. Collectors must be able to distinguish between a seventy-five-year-old copy and the real thing. They must also be able to authenticate any history offered with the item. Many dealers today fabricate the name of a soldier, complete with hometown and regiment, to add value to the objects. Unless the buyer can verify a history, he is taking a large gamble by purchasing the item connected with it.

Library of Congress

War memorabilia was prized from the moment Lee signed his surrender. Gen. Sheridan (standing between Lee and Grant) immediately bought the desk used for the signing for $20 and presented it to Maj. Gen. George A. Custer's wife for her husband's military efforts.

Once a collector knows what he is looking for and how to authenticate it, he has an entire world of items to choose from. Literally *anything* associated with the war is in great demand. To narrow one's focus, it is advisable to approach collecting in one of two ways: 1) collecting all versions of a single item, such as uniform buttons or belt plates, or 2) accumulating a complete uniform and gear that would have been used by a single soldier in a specific regiment. Either approach will provide a long-term search and challenge.

Where to Find Values. Collectors should buy only from dealers whose reputation for integrity can be verified by several other knowledgeable collectors. They should never buy anything that cannot be personally authenticated or that a reputable dealer is not willing to stand behind. Many of these dealers show at the annual Baltimore, Maryland, gun show and at the annual Gettysburg, Pennsylvania, relic show. Once a buyer has gotten acquainted with major collectors, he may be able to buy, sell or trade items without risk. Because large collections are often sold as a lot, collectors sometimes find themselves with duplicate items that they are willing to dispose of.

★ A woman with Southern ancestry discovered a Confederate soldier's shirt among her family's possessions and sold it to a dealer for $85.

A Price Sampling

The following are examples of recent purchases from dealers. Note the specific comments about each item, because they directly affect its value.

Presentation-grade Union officer's sword: name of famed
dealers Schuyler Hartley & Graham/New York etched
on blade, hand-engraved designs on solid brass guard,
solid German silver grip engraved with designs, solder
repair on rear of lower mount; "Presented to Lieut.
Geo. Krank by the members of Co. K, 7th N.Y. Artillery
as a token of their regard for him as an officer" engraved
on scabbard; excellent condition $2,495
Haiman-style Confederate "CS" two-piece belt plate:
prime quality; very rare   995
Sharps M1863 army rifle: original dark-blue barrel,
slightly thinned and aged, clear markings, excellent
rifling beginning to darken, fine pitting on breech
block, some surface wear, lacks rear sling swivel;
excellent condition   824
Union eagle drum: full color, hand painted, no flaking,
some wear, original heads, replaced rope, lacking
snares and label   750
Medical saddlebags: possible Confederate, flap on each
box embossed with large decorative diamond panel,
stamped inside "Manufactured only by Massengills/
Saddle Bags/The S. E. Massengill Co./Bristol
Tenn-Va.," tin-lined; rare, mint condition   424
Confederate frame belt buckle: unearthed at Sharpsburg,
MD; fine condition   139
Artillery water bucket: heavy black-painted sheet iron
with chain for suspension, surface rust patches in
original paint   97
Shaving mug and brush: said to have belonged to Capt.
Thomas McGuire, 2nd Reg., U.S. Light Art., but has
not been authenticated   65
Portable writing kit: buckram-covered heavy card exterior, opens like a book, somewhat faded exterior;
excellent interior condition   64
Curry comb: turned wood handle, sheet-iron head,
stamped by Brooklyn, NY, manufacturer; very good
condition   25

How to Store/Display. Because of the value of any authentic Civil War memorabilia, it is important that a collector properly store or display it. Photographs, which bring high prices, can deteriorate under certain climatic conditions. Wool uniforms that have survived a hundred twenty years can be destroyed by a single moth. Guns and metal field gear can rust. The best sources on proper care for these items are dealers who specialize in artifacts from the Civil War or in articles made of similar materials.

How and When to Sell. The best prices will always be paid by another collector, since dealers must add their markup before reselling. The collector who is searching for a specific item to complete a collection will pay more for that object than the collector who has more to accumulate. Sellers should obtain appraisals from two reputable sources. If one must pay for the appraisal, chances are likely it will be based on true knowledge and therefore reliable. Never indicate to the appraiser that there is an interest in selling, however, since he may want to buy the item himself and will therefore place a lower value on it.

★ **A Midwestern couple had the folding writing desk of a Union officer ancestor appraised at $1,000. They donated it to a museum and received a tax deduction at appraisal value.**

Little-Known Facts. *Cartes des vistas* were paper photos of individual soldiers. Today they are very valuable and more so if the soldier is portrayed holding a weapon.

—*Karl Nordling*

Bibliography

Books

Lord, Francis A. *Civil War Collector's Encyclopedia.* New York: Castle Books, 1965.

Sylvia, Stephen W., and Michael J. O'Donnell. *The Illustrated History of American Civil War Relics.* Orange, VA: Moss Publications, 1978.

Todd, Frederick P. *American Military Equipage, 1851-1872.* Providence, RI: Company of Military Historians, 1977.

Periodicals

Blue and Gray Magazine. Blue and Gray Enterprises, Columbus, OH 43228.

North-South Trader. 8020 New Hampshire Ave., Langley Park, MD 20783.

CLOCKS

Walk into the home of an antique clock lover and you enter a ticktock world where minutes are measured by the sway of a pendulum and hours are announced by a profusion of bongs, chimes, and cuckoos. These are the sounds of a vanishing era, which are being replaced by the occasional beeps of today's precision, digital timepieces.

If one is partial to modern efficiency, antique clocks may not be considered that interesting. Even the most inexpensive electric clocks are more accurate than antique clocks costing thousands of dollars. But if one enjoys the company of fine craftsmanship and can relax to the sound of gears, springs and pulleys in motion, this is a field worth exploring.

History. Timepieces of one sort or another have been around since the beginning of civilization. In the days of the Old Testament, sundials, water clocks and sand- or mercury-filled hourglasses marked the start of man's infatuation with timekeeping. Since then, a chief benchmark of technological growth has been the increasing sophistication applied to clockmaking and watchmaking.

Mechanical clocks first appeared in Europe during the thirteenth century. Although very few of these early clocks exist today, those that do show remarkable ingenuity and display the talents of many craftsmen, including jewelers, locksmiths, blacksmiths, carpenters and cabinetmakers. Handmade European clocks dating from the thirteenth to the sixteenth centuries are some of the finest and most desirable antiques.

America's clockmaking began in the early colonial settlements. Before 1700 there existed only a handful of clockmakers because anyone who could afford to buy a clock had it imported from Europe. By 1750, however, a number of skilled clockmakers were at work in Philadelphia, including David Rittenhouse. Clocks built by Rittenhouse and his colleagues, which sold for about $50 then, are often mentioned as examples of the finest in American clockmaking craftsmanship.

These beautiful Early American examples, primarily grandfather clocks that stood seven to nine feet tall, came out of the craftsman's shop at the rate of about four or five per year. Consequently there are not many around today, and the few genuine Peter Stretch, William

The Time Museum, Rockford, IL

Mechanical clocks originated in Europe in the thirteenth century. Depicted here is a reconstruction of an astronomical clock by Richard of Wallingford for the St. Albans Abbey of England, c. 1339.

Claggett or Simon and Aaron Willard-built clocks still on the market are worth many times their original price.

In the early 1800s, American clockmakers perfected methods of manufacturing interchangeable parts. This revolutionized the business not only in the United States but throughout the world. Clocks suddenly became affordable for most families, and the number of clocks manufactured skyrocketed.

Because of their size, even mass-produced grandfather clocks were too expensive for most people. But it was not long before one clockmaker, Eli Terry from Connecticut, began producing shelf clocks two feet tall that ran on wooden gears for $15. From that point on, clocks in America ceased to be rare. And venerable antique clock collectors have argued ever since about the validity of calling the thousands of nineteenth-century mass-produced clocks "antique."

Today, because there are so many types and sizes of antique clocks available, prices on the resale market are very unstable. Also, many Early American clockmakers are regional favorites. A grandfather clock made by Edward Howard will probably sell faster and at a higher price in Massachusetts, where he worked, than in New Mexico, for example.

★ **Antique pocket watches, a specialty among antique clock collectors, have their own history of technological achievements and spiraling prices. The record price for a pocket watch was set by Sotheby's in 1981. Manufactured by a Swiss clockmaker named Henry Capt in 1880, the pocket watch sold for $165,000. Along with being a split-second chronograph, the watch includes a perpetual calendar, notes the phases of the moon, and chimes.**

Values Outside the Home. Early European clocks are undoubtedly masterpieces and ultimate collectors' items, but they are so rare that most collectors can only see them in museums.

The majority of antique clocks bought and sold in America are the mass-produced clocks made in Connecticut and Massachusetts during the late eighteenth and nineteenth centuries.

Grandfather, or *tall-case,* clocks have always been popular. If one is looking for an authentic antique, it is important to check the dials on early grandfather clocks, which were made of brass with silver decorations. Usually the numbers were engraved on the brass dial and the name of the maker was added to the engraving. Interestingly, the roman numeral "VI" was placed upside down on all but the most recent grandfather-type clocks. Grandmother clocks, smaller-scale tall-case clocks that were less than six feet six inches high, were made in large numbers until around 1850.

Among the hundreds of styles made for hanging on a wall, banjo clocks are probably the best known. The name *banjo* comes from the shape of the clock, which was first created by Simon Willard in 1802. Because of their popularity, banjo clocks have been reproduced for years, and collectors should investigate any claim of authenticity before buying. Many collectors consider the girandole-style clock, an elaborate variation on the banjo, to be the most beautiful clock made in America.

Beginners investing in antique clocks should be sure they are buying authentic pieces. Quite often collectors and dealers are honestly mistaken about a clock's value. It should be in good working condition, with all original parts, including the glass panel, or faceplate. The case should also be complete, including the *finials* and *feet* (upper and lower ends of columns often added to the corners of decorative or mantel clocks). Collectors should also make sure that the key to wind the clock is included.

Mantel, or shelf, clocks are a very popular design that still command good resale prices if they are in good condition and can be authenticated. Early shelf clocks had elaborate cases with free-standing columns at the corners, scrolled tops and elaborately painted scenes below the clock face. Beehive shelf clocks are characterized by a rounded arch; steeple clocks have sharply pointed wooden steeples at the corners.

If one is looking for bargains, there are hundreds, if not thousands, of inexpensive old clocks around that are potential collectors' items in need only of some refurbishing. A common technique used by collectors is to buy any old clock, regardless of condition, for $25. People will often literally give away an old clock simply because the weight has been lost and the clock will not run without it.

Where to Find Values. There is such a large market for antique clocks that many dealers handle clocks exclusively. And because many collectors enjoy repairing old pieces, a lot of dealers will also buy and sell parts. (There are also those who will not do either, because old clocks can be temperamental. One dealer discovered that old mantle clocks cannot keep accurate time unless they sit perfectly level. Despite his telling customers this, some will continue pestering him with complaints that their mantle piece will not run.)

Collectors should also consider buying clocks at auctions, where prices are generally lower than those in a shop. Some estimate that auction prices are about 50% to 80% of an item's retail value. One reason for the lower prices is that auctions are usually attended by dealers. To be profitable, dealers must stop the bidding at a price that will allow them to add their own markup. Beginners need not be afraid of the high bids that are written up in the newspapers from time to time, either. At the well-known auction house, Sotheby Parke Bernet, two-thirds of the items auctioned off in 1982 went for less than $1,000 each. The only precaution that bidders should take before making offers on antique clocks is to inspect them thoroughly. The auctioneer rarely describes items accurately, and most auction catalogues are handed out more as conveniences than as sources of information.

More and more antique clocks are being bought and sold through the mail. There is probably a classified or display ad for nearly every antique clock in existence in some newspaper, antiques magazine or newsletter. But buying by mail can be risky; what is meant as "mint" or "very fine" to one collector may not mean the same to another.

Selling through classified ads has a chance of bringing more satisfaction than buying does because the element of ambiguity can be greatly eliminated. By describing an item in as much detail as possible, one decreases confusion and increases his chances of receiving nothing less than exactly what he advertised for.

A Price Sampling

	Prior year average price	Current price range
Ansonia Clock Co.		
Admiral 8-day strike, regulator, 1910	$1,100	$950-1,200
Queen Anne, Parlor wall, 8-day strike, 1898	570	540-600
Summit, cabinet, 8-day strike, 1883	175	165-185
Ingraham		
Betty Boop wristwatch, c. 1930	.98*	300
Buck Rogers pocket watch, c. 1935	1.89*	225
Official Boy Scout wristwatch, c. 1935	1.89*	200
Waterbury Clock Co.		
Glenwood Figure 8, simple calendar, c. 1900	500	450-550

Brittany, 8-day strike, regulator, c. 1910	355	335-375
Victorian kitchen shelf calendar w/thermometer, barometer, c. 1910	238	225-250
Ingersoll		
Mickey Mouse electric clock, c. 1933	3* (approx.)	500

*Original price

How to Store/Display. Aside from delicate novelty items, Early American clocks were usually sturdily built. If an antique clock is in good repair and serviced regularly, there is no reason why it should not run indefinitely.

Clocks mass produced from the late eighteenth century used machine-tooled brass movements, which wore well and today can still be replaced. Earlier clocks built with wooden gears are a different story, however. Wood gears did not last, and modern replacements for them are difficult to find. There are many books on clock repair (see "Bibliography"), and with a few tools, along with the patience to tinker, any collector can learn the riddle of an antique timepiece's movement.

Preventive care is the best policy for keeping antique clocks in good condition. Sensible precautions include keeping wooden case clocks away from sunny windows or any other source of heat. The wood will warp and dry out. It is tempting to display an antique shelf or kitchen clock on the mantle piece. One should keep in mind, however, that in doing so, one is exposing the antique not only to the drying heat of the fireplace but to soot and grime as well.

An antique clock's wooden case deserves the same attention given to antique furniture. First one must determine the kind of wood used and then find which product works best to preserve and protect it. Unsealed woods should be rubbed with an oil, such as lemon, to keep them from drying out. A paste wax, like Butcher's, works well for cleaning and protecting most other types of wood. To dust, one should use a clean, soft cloth free of loose threads that could catch and pull up a sliver of wood.

Antique clocks and especially watches with metal cases react to their environment in many ways: they can tarnish, rust, pit or scratch. If a clock is quite old, it may have developed a rich, deep glow called *patina,* which few collectors would willingly destroy. A patina is best preserved with a nonabrasive cleaner that will restore luster to the case but not destroy its rich color.

How and When to Sell. Most antique-clock enthusiasts dread the thought of giving up all or part of their collection, but there are plenty of good reasons for selling. As a collection grows, it may be useful to trade up or clean out some early mistakes. Collectors may also want to consider the amount of time they have owned certain pieces. Most antique clocks in good condition require about seven years for their wholesale prices (the price one can expect to get when selling) to reach the retail level (the price one probably paid for the clock). If one has the option of choosing among several clocks to sell, it would be best to sell those owned the longest.

Once a collector has decided to sell, he should gather all the information available on the clock—photographs, original bills, appraisals, and notes on repairs. Any background information that can substantiate an antique's authenticity will help get the best price possible.

Even if it is authentic, the age of an antique clock does not necessarily determine its selling price. If the clock's manufacturer is well known, it will very likely sell for more than a similar clock that was made by an unknown or unpopular maker. Also, the condition of the clock's case and works is important in determining its price. For example, an old clock's value is reduced if it has been electrified.

Collectors should keep in mind that antique parts of almost anything mechanical are hard to come by. One should always ask a dealer before throwing away any parts.

In general, any clock made during the 1800s and earlier, and in good condition, is salable as a collectors' item. Especially popular today are tall-case clocks that can be authenticated as having been made by David Rittenhouse, Eli Terry, Seth Thomas, Edward Duffield of Philadelphia, or Martin Shreiner of Lancaster. Other favorites are banjo clocks, Art Deco clocks, old schoolroom clocks, ships' clocks that combine a chronometer with the traditional ship's bell, and clocks from the 1930s, especially children's novelty clocks and watches.

To get the full resale value for a clock, one should select his selling strategy carefully. He should think creatively, considering as many markets as possible. Which of his clocks would attract a good price at an auction? Is there a neighborhood business he could approach? What about the local interior decorator? Perhaps he would be interested in a certain clock for one of his clients? Or might not a larger business be able to use a handsome clock to spruce up its reception room? Selling possibilities are limited only by one's imagination.

However or to whomever one sells his antique clocks, there are three general sales guidelines that are wise to follow: 1) collectors should know the value of their clocks *before* they buy or sell; 2) they should allow themselves plenty of time to sell a clock or collection; 3) they must adopt a *sales* frame of mind. This includes assuming that whomever one approaches in a sales transaction is interested in buying, and that if they do not buy, someone else will.

★ **Antique clock and watch dealers have a hard time keeping up with the changing values of their timepieces. Peter Fossner, a dealer in New York City, mentions how the price for one especially valuable watch went from $2,000 in 1973 to $25,000 in 1980. According to Fossner, the market has since bottomed out, and the same watch is now selling for $5,000.**

Little-Known Facts. Pocket sundials were popular in the seventeenth century. One type was made in the shape of a ring with a hook so that it could be held in the hand. Pocket sundials are now worth between $25 and $75, depending on the sundial's materials and condition.

• *Horology* is a little-used word that stems from the Greek word "hora" (hour) and means the science of measuring time and the art of constructing, regulating and testing sundials, clocks, watches and other timekeeping instruments. Clockmakers and salespeople were originally called *horologers,* and any sort of timepiece was called a *horologe.*

• Many Early American clockmakers also advertised as watchmakers. Ownership of a watch, or portable timepiece, was an important status symbol in revolutionary America. Watches were wound with keys and had inner protective and outer decorative cases. George Washington and Benjamin Franklin both owned watches, as did other more wealthy founding fathers.

—James L. White

Bibliography

Books

Baillie, G. H.; C. Clutton; and C. A. Ilbert. *Britain's Old Clocks and Watches and Their Makers.* New York: Bonanza, 1956.
De Carale, Donald. *Practical Clock Repairing.* New York: N.A.G. Press, 1968.
Drepperd, Carl W. *American Clocks and Clockmakers.* New York: Doubleday, 1947.
Palmer, Brooks. *The Book of American Clocks.* New York: The Macmillan Co., 1950.

Periodicals

Bulletin of the National Association of Watch and Clock Collectors. 401 Locust St., Columbia, PA 17512.
Hobbies. Lightner Publishing, 1006 South Michigan Ave., Chicago, IL 60605.
Spinning Wheel. Everybody's Press, Inc., Fame Ave., Hanover, PA 17331.

Catalogues

Babka, A. ed. *Antique Trader, Price Guide to Antiques and Collectors Items.* Dubuque, IA: Babka Publishing Co., 1971.
Ketchum, William C., Jr. *Catalogue of American Collectibles.* New York: Mayflower Books, Inc., 1979.
Massie, Henry, ed. *Clocks.* Hempstead, Herts, England: Model and Allied Publications, Ltd., 1978.

Dealers

Antique Gallery, 4303 S. Hanna, Fort Wayne, IN 46806.
The Clock Mill, 389 Belmont Ave., Springfield, MA 01108.
Corinthian Studios, 521 Sutter St., San Francisco, CA 94102.
Nelson R. Coleman III, Ltd., 2539 N. Charles St., Baltimore, MD 21218.

Associations

The Antiquarian Horological Society, New House High St., Ticehurst, Wadhurst, Sussex, England TN5 7AL.
National Association of Watch and Clock Collectors, Inc., P.O. Box 33, Columbia, PA 17512.

Museums

American Clock and Watch Museum, Inc., Bristol, CT 06010.
Museum of the National Association of Watch and Clock Collectors, Inc., Columbia, PA 17512.
Old Clock Museum, Pharr, TX 78577.

COINS

It is not hard to imagine the excitement of finding boxes of old Morgan dollars sealed in the wall of your house. It also does not seem likely, yet that is exactly what happened to a man in Portland, Oregon, when he remodeled his Victorian house. Although the coins' face value was in excess of $1,000, they were actually worth twenty times that amount, for many rare examples were included in the cache.

It is equally easy to understand why this man subsequently became a coin collector.

History. Few hobbies reflect the history of civilization more dramatically than *numismatics,* or coin collecting. Coins mirror the rise and fall of empires, the customs of many cultures, and the religion and symbolism of various countries—some of which no longer exist. Even in primitive times, man needed a tangible medium of exchange and used seashells, cattle, art objects, even slaves as money. Coins did not appear until 1091 B.C. in the Chou dynasty of China. These were not coins as we know them today. They were crudely made, bearing primitive artwork. But for some collectors, they represent items of great value.

Silver coins appear to date from 700 B.C. in Lydia, then a part of Greece. These early pieces were actually an alloy of gold and silver, since the two metals were frequently found together and were difficult to separate using that culture's technology. When the Lydians realized that gold's scarcity made it more valuable than silver, more effort was devoted to separating the two metals, and by 550 B.C., coins of pure gold and pure silver were being fashioned.

Coinage in the Americas can be traced to the lands south of the border, and even while the American government was issuing money, Spanish dollars were still considered legal tender. Prior to the opening of the United States Federal Mint in Philadelphia in 1792, only occasional coinage was used by the individual colonies. The primary American mint has always been in Philadelphia, and the coins made there are the only ones that do not carry the small initial letter, called the *mint mark.*

★ A *tickey* was a three-penny piece used in the Union of South Africa to make telephone calls. Mrs. L. Botha of that country used to save them to sell to collectors. One of those collectors told her to watch for one minted in 1931, because only 128 had been produced. He apparently did not tell her that 125 were already in the hands of collectors, or she would have been even more excited the day one turned up in her hand. It was worth the equivalent of $720.

Values Outside the Home. As a hobby, coin collecting is particularly adaptable to purposes of investment, because coins have value as metal. Needless to say, except for devaluation, coins are worth at least their face value. Thus, downside risk is scarely a factor.

For this reason, one criterion for selecting coins may include the collector's own special interest, but he must also specialize, for the history of coinage is too long and too broad to do otherwise.

Purchase is best limited to gold and silver coins of recent history. Ancient coins may have a certain mystique, but as collectors' items they are esoteric, and valuations are often subjective. Furthermore, the market for them is limited. Probably the best specialty for the beginning hobbyist in America is coins of the United States.

It must also be added that those coins which have consistently shown the greatest increase in value are those which have been obtained in *proof* (a coin struck from a highly polished die, not intended for circulation, and often of a different metallic content from those to be circulated) or in brand-new condition.

As with so many other collectors' items, it is rarity which constitutes value. The wise investor will seek those coins that were minted in smaller quantities. A 1938 *D* half-dollar, purchased brand-new, is worth almost $400 today.

Now, coin collecting does *not* provide instant gratification. Most enthusiasts will not make a profit overnight. But if enjoyment of the hobby is an objective, the fun along the way will at least make the time pass more quickly.

Even though gold and silver are more glamorous, there is still a lot of fun to be had by collecting the seemingly insignificant penny. If the collector is discerning and learns what to look for, he will find great value in those Indian heads or Lincoln cents that were minted in the smallest of quantities.

Generally speaking, whatever one sets aside each month to purchase coins will be better spent on one or two items with profit potential rather than on many coins that will ultimately provide minor returns.

★ **A nine-year-old boy in California decided to be a coin collector. An aunt, impressed by this, gave him a 1936 proof set that she had kept since that year in a box of memorabilia. Neither she nor her nephew realized that he was being initiated with a collection worth, at that time, over $500.**

Where to Find Values. The only legal ways to obtain coins are to find them, be given them, or buy them.

The most widely used method of finding coins is to search through one's own pocket change. It is a long shot, but once in a while it pays off. Boxes in the basement and trunks in the attic are always possible sources. Frequently, coins just get "put away" because they had modest value at the time, or because they were brought home from a foreign country as mementos.

Friends or relatives often give interesting or unusual coins to aspiring young collectors, many of whom got their start that way.

Buying coins, of course, is the most expensive way to acquire them. On the other hand, the odds of owning valuable coins are better. If one is willing to be separated from $25 to $50 a month, he is in a position to make careful purchases for his collection that will rapidly appreciate.

The most common source of coins will be a dealer. Finding a reliable numismatist who will suggest one or more reputable dealers is the best way to avoid painful experiences. The beginning collector should look for the logos of the American Numismatic Association or the Professional Numismatists Guild in a dealer's advertising. This usually insures a dealer's reputability.

Many coin dealers are seldom found in their shops, because they often go to auctions and shows. The collector can go, too, and these events are well worth considering both for fun and profit. The beginner should attend with a seasoned collector, though, until he has enough experience to "solo."

When the coin hobby was young, most collectors traded with each other. While this is practiced less today, it is still a good way to obtain coins. Numismatic clubs are excellent places to locate those who may want to trade.

A Price Sampling

The following representative sales of coins took place in 1984. All coins indicated are graded "very fine" or better:

1929	Liberty Standing, $20 gold piece	$2,140.00
1928	Liberty Standing, $20 gold piece	885.00
1870 *S*	Indian head gold dollar	535.00
1892 *CC*	Morgan dollar	55.00
1931 *S*	Lincoln cent	31.50
1980 *S*	Susan B. Anthony dollar (proof)	12.50
1931 *S*	Mercury dime	6.50
1966 *D*	Kennedy half-dollar	3.75
1928 *S*	Buffalo nickel	2.75
1906	Indian head cent	1.85

How to Store/Display. The care used in storing or displaying a collection is usually what distinguishes it from an accumulation. Because the value of coins depends so much, among other factors, upon their condition, even the fledgling collector must give immediate attention to storage. Coin folders and cardboard albums are popular with beginners. More experienced collectors use them, too, but not for long-term storage. Most cardboard contains acids that will spot or discolor coins over a period of time. Coin holders made of acetate and polyester are best for long-term storage.

No beginning collector should be without reference material. A general book on coin collecting, a catalogue of pricing information, and a grading guide are "musts."

How and When to Sell. Undoubtedly the simplest way to sell coins is through a dealer. Although this will not provide full retail value, it will give the owner a quick, uncomplicated sale.

Some dealers maintain a bid board, selling coins for collectors who patronize them. Fellow collectors register their bids, and sales are made on a regular, usually weekly, basis, with the dealer taking a modest commission. The dealer may also agree to take coins on consignment.

A coin show, at which many dealers are gathered under one roof, is one of the best sales alternatives. And coin shows are fun!

Coins may also be sold at auction; however, there is customarily a one- to two-month waiting period before final settlement is made.

It is usually necessary to hold on to a coin for a few years. This is not for purposes of letting it get older, for age has nothing to do with its value. It is primarily to absorb the disparity between wholesale and retail prices while the coin increases in value.

★ **The lucky fellow in Portland, Oregon, completed the renovation of his Victorian house with the proceeds from the sale of some of the rare Morgan dollars he found sealed in one of the walls. And he still possesses the rarest ones.**

Little-Known Facts. Coin counterfeiting has been discouraged by governments in a variety of ways, but the sternest warning seems to have been issued in seventeenth-century England. There, a counterfeiter was dragged to the gallows on a sledge and hanged. Public display of his body was meant to warn other would-be counterfeiters. Drastic punishment indeed, but most likely it was quite effective.

• In 1792, the United States Congress authorized the minting of a *disme*, or one tenth of a dollar, and the first disme bears that appellation. Soon the *s* was removed, making the word easier to pronounce. Today we simply say "dime."

—Robin C. Harris

Bibliography

Books

Andrews, Charles J. *Fell's United States Coin Book.* New York: Frederick Fell Publishers, 1981.

Bowers, Q. David. *Collecting Rare Coins For Profit.* New York: Harper and Row, 1975.

Bowers, Q. David. *Coins and Collectors.* Johnson City, NY: Windsor Publications, 1964.

Grierson, Philip. *Numismatics.* London: Oxford University Press, 1975.

Hoppe, Donald J. *How to Invest in Gold Coins.* New Rochelle, NY: Arlington House, 1973.

Kopkin, S., and Roberts, E. W. *Paths to Wealth Through Coin Investments.* Lynbrook, NY, 1965.

Lemke, Bob. *How to Get Started in Coin Collecting.* Blue Ridge Summit, PA: Tab Books, 1983.

Reinfeld, Fred. *Coin Collector's Handbook.* New York: Sterling Publishing Co., 1963.

82   *Coins*

Schmeider, Thomas K. *Collecting and Investing in United States Small Coins.*
Author, 1979.
Schwarz, Ted. *A History of United States Coinage.* San Diego, CA: A. S. Barnes
and Co., 1980.
Sutherland, C. H. V. *Art In Coinage.* New York: Philosophical Library, Inc.,
1956.
Wear, Ted G. *Ancient Coins.* Garden City, NY: Doubleday and Co., 1965.
Zimmerman, Walter J. *The Coin Collector's Fact Book.* New York: Arco
Publishing Co., 1974.

Periodicals
Canadian Coin News. P.O. Box 12000, Bracebridge, Ontario, Canada
POB 1CO (bi-weekly newspaper).
Canadian Numismatic Journal. Canadian Numismatic Association, Barrie,
Ontario, Canada L4M 4T2.
Coin World. P.O. Box 150, Sidney, OH 45365 (weekly newspaper).
COINage. 16250 Ventura Blvd., Encino, CA 91316 (monthly magazine).
Coins Magazine. Krause Publications, Iola, WI 54945 (monthly magazine).
Hobbies Magazine. 1006 S. Michigan Ave., Chicago, IL 60605 (monthly
magazine; contains large coin section).
Numismatic News. Krause Publications, Iola, WI 54945 (weekly newspaper).
The Numismatist. American Numismatic Association, P.O. Box 2366,
Colorado Springs, CO 80901 (monthly).
World Coin News. Krause Publications. Iola, WI 54945 (weekly newspaper).
World Coins. P.O. Box 150, Sidney, OH 45365 (monthly).
Young Numismatist. American Numismatic Association. P.O. Box 2366,
Colorado Springs, CO 80901.

Catalogues
Standard Catalog of World Coins. Iola, WI: Krause Publications.
Guide Book of United States Coins. Racine, WI: Western Publishing Co.
Handbook of United States Coins. Racine, WI: Western Publishing Co.

Dealers
Coin Gallery of San Francisco, Inc., 455 Powell St., San Francisco, CA.
Robert R. Johnson, Inc., 353 Geary St., San Francisco, CA.
Numismatics, Ltd., 9665 Wilshire Blvd., Beverly Hills, CA 90212.
Superior Stamp and Coin Co., 9301 Wilshire Blvd., Beverly Hills, CA 90212.
Century Stamp and Coin Co., 506 W. 7th St., Los Angeles, CA 90014.
Metro Coin, Ltd., 4455 E. Camelback Rd., Phoenix, AZ.
Rocky Mountain Coin and Stamp Co., 538 S. Broadway, Denver, CO 80209.
Florida Rare Coin and Stamp Gallery, 14231 S. Dixie Hwy., Miami, FL.
Coins and Stamps, Inc., 17658 Mack, Grosse Pointe, MI 48230.
Eastern Numismatics, Inc., 642 Franklin Ave., Garden City, NY.

Associations
American Numismatic Association, P.O. Box 2366, Colorado Springs, CO 80901.
American Numismatic Society, 617 W. 155th St., New York, NY 10032.
Canadian Numismatic Association, P.O. Box 226, Barrie, Ontario, Canada L4M 4T2.

COMIC BOOKS

Remember how your mother used to scold you for reading comic books, nagging you to stop wasting your time on junk? Read something good, she would say, so you could get smart, go to college and make a lot of money as a lawyer or a doctor. Well, if you were *really* smart, you paid no attention to your mother's advice and went out and bought the next issues of *Superman, Batman, Little Lulu* and *Donald Duck.* If you were really *really* smart, you bought so many comics they filled every corner of your room, barely leaving space for your bed. Like Uncle Scrooge diving into his swimming pool filled with money, you plunged into your private chamber filled with those wonderful stories of superheros, scheming villains, and one disaster after another. And like Uncle Scrooge, today you have little else to do but shovel your money from one pile to another after selling that treasured comic book collection.

But let's face it. You probably were not that smart or you would not be reading this chapter. You let your pile of comics dwindle to nothing, and now you hope to build it up again—first for nostalgia's sake, and second because nostalgia has become profitable.

History. Comic book collecting began only seriously in the early 1960s, and only since the early 1970s has there been real money in it. The original collectors gathered their favorite comics out of love; they bought them not to make money but to own books they remembered from childhood.

During the foment of the '60s, the notion of studying popular culture came into vogue. With it came a closer look at comic books and the realization that far from being junk, comic books were another kind of folk art. Certain illustrators were suddenly promoted to the status of artist-illustrators and ranked with such prestigious mainstream artists as N. C. Wyeth, Howard Pyle, and Maxfield Parrish.

At the same time, new blood entered the field, turning out a new breed of comic books that displayed an awareness of art and culture, which their predecessors did not do. Often highly educated, or at least highly intelligent, this new breed of artist was also critical but fun-loving and made comics—old as well as new—respectable.

Consequently, in only twenty years, the first issue of *Superman* has increased in value from next to nothing to an estimated $10,500. That first issue of *Captain Marvel* that you tossed into the garbage when you were sixteen is now worth $5,000. And your favorite *Green Lantern*—the one that got ripped to shreds in the fight with your kid sister—that is worth $1,150!

★ Stan Cornfield did not start collecting comics until late into the 1970s, well after the comic book craze had caught fire. He remembered the DC *Action Comics* from his childhood and wanted them both for their nostalgia and for use in a course he teaches in popular culture at a community college in California. Although he was not sure that paying $40, $50, $60 and even $100 a book made sense, he decided he wanted to acquire the entire opening series and was willing to spend the money for it. As it turned out, he chose wisely. Not a single one of his books has less than doubled in value since he bought it, and several of them—the ones he paid the most for—have as much as tripled.

Values Outside the Home. With prices that high, you may think you stand no chance of getting into the comic book market. Well, there are at least three ways available to the beginner in which he can become a serious collector. The first depends a lot on serendipity, the second on willingness and ability to invest a minimum of a few thousand dollars, and the third on wise advice.

The first approach involves a solid dose of good luck. Is there any chance that your attic or that of your parents might yield comic books you did not realize you had? It is worth checking. Even books from the past decade may sell for $50 or $60, and a few are worth a couple of hundred dollars.

Other recent books are now worth $5 to $10 apiece. Held on to for another ten years, a stack of these issues could fetch several thousand dollars.

The second approach to collecting involves the careful purchase of already valuable books. According to Robert M. Overstreet's *Comic*

The birth of Superman (June 1938) thrilled not only his millions of young readers but also those at DC Comics, who still watch comics featuring their man of steel appreciate by 15% per year.

Book Price Guide, Action Comics increase in value at a rate of approximately 11% per year. (In some years they have gone up by as much as 23%.) Overstreet estimates that *Superman* currently rises at about 15% per year, *Marvel Mystery* titles by 17%, and *Pep* comics by an astounding 29%. Thus, if you can afford to pay from a couple hundred to a few thousand dollars for a few of these or other comparably appreciating books, you can earn at least what you would have had you put your money into collecting more conventional items.

The third and most dependable way to begin stockpiling those comics on a limited budget requires selective purchase of more recent and even brand-new books. *Starslayer* went on the market in 1982 for $.45; its value in 1984 was $2.50—five and one-half times its purchase price. A reliable comic dealer can direct you to similar titles with potential for the same type of growth. For a relatively small outlay—even $100—you can reap a sizable return. Were *Starslayer* to go up at this same rate, by 1992, ten years after issue, it would sell for $90. A $100 purchase of issues of *Starslayer* in 1982 would yield $20,000 in 1992!

Where to Find Values. The best places to purchase new comics are local outlets that cater to collectors. The owners of these stores will be able to advise you on what is selling, what is going up in value, and what circumstances will affect future value, such as the death or retirement of a popular illustrator, the sale of a publisher, or the upcoming movie made from a comic book hero. Local stores are also good outlets for older comics, but unless you trust a dealer completely, be sure to compare his prices against others in the area.

Comic book periodicals (see "Bibliography") include advertisements from both dealers and individual collectors, but are usable only after you have gained some familiarity with the market. Although individual ads sometimes include amazing bargains, they also include ripoffs and occasional frauds. Use both caution and whatever legal protection you can when answering ads.

These periodicals also list comic book conventions and trade shows, several of which are held around the country each month. Look for those in your area and attend a few before you start collecting. They will give you a good idea of what is happening in the field and offer you an opportunity to learn comparison shopping. The large number of dealers at individual conventions also gives you the chance to pick up valuable insights into the market from experts in the field.

★ Ann Gregory of Portland, Oregon, inherited her grandmother's house, moving in shortly after the old woman's death. Stacks of old magazines littered every room of the house, reaching such heights in some rooms that she could move only along narrow paths between the piles. Her first thought was to clear the mess out, but after some coaxing by friends, she had several dealers come in to appraise the stacks. As it happened, among the piles were more than one-hundred fifty comic books from her father's childhood. Without bothering to sort through them herself, she let the lot go for just under $2,000. Not bad, but had she been willing to catalogue the books and sell them herself through comic periodicals, she probably would have made at least another $1,000.

A Price Sampling

Comic book prices vary greatly with the condition of the books, which are rated as "poor," "good," "fair," or "mint." Books in poor condition have value only when they are so rare that people have no choice but to settle for inferior quality. Usually it is best to select only copies that are in perfect condition—no folds, rips, or badly inked pages. Mint condition can mean as much as six to seven times more for a comic than it could fetch in only fair condition. The following are samples of 1984 selling prices:

	Good	Fine	Mint
Superman #1	$1,535	$4,600	$10,500
Whiz Comics #1	1,200	3,500	8,200
Captain America #1	800	2,400	5,200
Superboy #1	175	450	1,050
The Human Torch #3	150	450	1,000
Marvel Mystery Comics #2	82	245	535
Marge's Little Lulu	60	180	400
How Stalin Hopes We Will Destroy America	47	140	280
Casper the Friendly Ghost #1	13	40	80
Abbott & Costello #1	10	30	60

How to Store/Display. To preserve your purchases, seal them in airtight Mylar bags and store them in a cool, dry place away from light. Also, be sure to protect them from fire hazards! If you plan a quick turnover, you can use polyethylene bags rather than Mylar, but for long-term storage polyethylene is not adequate. If you plan to hold on to the books for a very long time (ten years or more), you might do well to have them chemically deacidified and then stored in a vault. This is a more expensive preserving process, but it can mean that twenty years from now you will have mint rather than good- or fair-condition books to sell, which will greatly increase their value.

How and When to Sell. Comic books are not diamonds. No matter how well you care for them, they will remain perishable, subject to rot, rips, and fire. Consequently, it is not necessarily wise to count on them as terribly long-term investments. You would do best to let them appreciate enough to have made a good return, then sell, putting back a portion of that return into a new collection.

Selling through dealers usually means a lower than market price, since the dealer will also have to earn a profit on a book he buys. More advisable is to sell to other collectors, particularly to those who want the books because they are true aficianados rather than for the money such books will bring them. Joining fan clubs, which advertise in periodicals and at conventions, is a good way to meet as many fellow collectors as possible.

Taste in popular culture can prove extremely erratic. On the positive side, this could mean that some comics of little importance now could suddenly become popular. The comic book market is not immune to social change—*Wonder Woman* gained prominence in response to women's liberation, as did *Little Lulu* and *Katy Keene*. On the negative side, the unpredictability of trends could mean that when today's children grow up, they will not care for the comic books they had when they were young (and certainly not for those that were popular during the childhoods of their parents and grandparents), and the market would slowly dry up. So pay close attention to trends. You do not want to hold on too long to books that may be going out of vogue.

In periods of minor recession, comic book values tend to go up slightly as people look for reminders of what were to them happier times. But when the economy goes seriously downhill, collectors are likely to turn to more durable goods. That marks a good time to buy but not to sell.

★ Mark Eastman, teacher of a course in popular culture, carefully chose $100 worth of new and recent comics in 1981 following the advice of the owner of a local comic book store respected for his fairness and knowledge of the field. Within three years, his collection had jumped to more than $400 in value. And it is still climbing!

Little-Known Facts. Like everything else in popular culture, comic books have attracted a diverse and, in some cases, peculiar set of fans. Japan's Emperor Hirohito was a great admirer of *Superman,* even during the war years, when *Superman* stories frequently featured the "Man of Steel" triumphing over various Japanese villains.

• Gloria Steinem claims that while reading *Wonder Woman* as an adolescent she first became aware that women need not be confined to their traditional roles. And, Steinem's recognition was exactly what *Wonder Woman*'s creator, a male psychologist, had intended by offering a female character to counter the usual stereotypes of women presented in the more male-oriented run of superhero stories.

• Stereotypes were just fine with author Mickey Spillane, however. Before he turned to writing pulp novels, he wrote for pulp comics; in fact, he originally intended detective Mike Hammer as a comic book hero.

—John McCloud

Bibliography

Books

Johnson, Brad L. *The Comic Collector's Handbook.* New York: Zanon, 1983.

Periodicals

Buyer's Guide for Comic Fandom. Dynamite Publications Enterprises, 15800 Route 84 North, East Moline, IL 61244.
The Comics Buyers Guide. 707 East State Street, Iola, WI 54990.
The Comics Journal. 707 Camino Manzanas, Thousand Oaks, CA 91360.

Catalogues

Overstreet, Robert M. *The Comic Book Price Guide,* 14th edition. Cleveland, TN: Overstreet Publications, 1984 (new edition published each year).

Capital City's Top 100 Titles, Capital City Distribution, 1774 Timothy Drive, #6, San Leandro, CA 94577.

Dealers

Comics and Comix, 2461 Telegraph Ave., Berkeley, CA 94704.
Joseph and Peter Koch, 1716 Central Ave., Yonkers, NY 10710.
James F. Payette, P.O. Box 750, Bethlehem, NH 03574.
Mickey Sullivan, 464 West Florida Ave., Sebring, OH 44672.

COMMEMORATIVES

To own a commemorative souvenir is to own a piece of today's history and yesterday's future. The modern commemorative is most likely an item from a world's fair or exposition. Some such souvenirs are very valuable because they were given away in honor of an outstanding achievement lauded at a particular fair or exposition, or because an event occurred at one of these celebrations that would mark a special point in history. So it is impossible to explore commemoratives without also reviewing the historical events they once stood for.

History. It is only in the last few centuries that man's preoccupation with his own history has grown. The earliest commemoratives were probably primitive pieces of art "commemorating" creators and gods. In the middle ages, history was recorded in art, music and eventually in books. But it was not until the nineteenth century that man began to celebrate his own achievements at exhibitions. As the exhibitions grew, commemorative items became more plentiful and varied. Everyone was given the chance to take home a piece of the times in which he lived.

The first of the world's fairs was the Great Exposition of London in 1851. Almost six million people made their way through the Crystal Palace to view the works of industry of many nations. There have been forty-five similar expositions since, the most recent held in New Orleans. Most have been held in the United States, but they have also been hosted by Britain, France, Spain, Belgium, Canada, Japan, and other nations. Each one put out a plethora of souvenirs.

Technology was central to expositions. The 1876 Centennial Fair introduced the sewing machine, the typewriter, the telegraph and the telephone. Electric lights made their exposition debut in 1893.

This amusement, created by George Ferris for the 1893 World's Columbia Exposition in Chicago, was an example of the extravagance that characterizes world's fairs.

The 1901 Buffalo Exposition made use of Niagara Falls for hydroelectric power. Atomic energy was the theme of the Brussels Exposition in 1958. The Seattle World's Fair of 1962 and the New York 1964 World's Fair commemorated the space age. The latest autos, homes of the future, and everyday miracle items, such as nylon stockings, delighted crowds at these gatherings. Fairgoers were given throwaways to sample the enormous array of new products.

Around the turn of the century, expositions were held to celebrate events, such as the Lousiana Purchase and the one-hundredth anniversary of the Lewis and Clark expeditions. Silver spoons honored the flight of Lindbergh, the Statue of Liberty, state anniversaries and monuments. Some fairs inadvertently held additional historic consequence, lending even more value to items commemorating them. (The course of America would have been quite different if President William McKinley had decided not to speak at the Pan American Fair in 1901; McKinley was assassinated at that fair on September 5, and Theodore Roosevelt assumed the office.)

Another celebration of human achievement has been the space program. Space may be the final frontier for collectors ... to seek out strange new souvenirs ... to boldly collect what no man has obtained before. Space items commemorate a record number of "firsts."

★ **Richard Reinhardt's parents returned home from the local 1939 San Francisco Exposition with a souvenir trivet. It was shaped like the Bay Area's Treasure Island and depicted various views of the exposition.**

The trivet was brought up to the family's mountain cabin and remains in use there today. Reinhardt was pleasantly surprised to see an identical item selling for $25 at a local flea market. This was not exactly a gold mine, but it was a fine example of appreciation from an initial investment of nothing.

Values Outside the Home. Collecting world's fair and exposition commemoratives is a relatively new and rapidly growing hobby. The inflation besetting more traditional collectors' items is only beginning in this field. Many relics can be found inexpensively, but there are exceptions. A Lenox vase from the 1939 World's Fair is worth more than $200, and a poster from the Columbian Exposition of 1893 is worth more than $300.

Age generally increases value. Memorabilia from the Centennial Exposition in 1876 has recently become quite expensive. But the most costly of these items is still way less than $1,000. And the least costly can still be had for what amounts to pocket change.

Souvenirs from the Centennial Exposition of Philadelphia (1876), the 1939 and 1964 New York World's Fair, the Chicago Fair of 1933 and 1893, the St. Louis Fair of 1904 and the Buffalo Fair of 1901 are still available and likely to appreciate.

Exposition commemoratives are created in most mediums, including paper, fabric, metal, glass, and ceramics, and are fashioned into clothing, paperweights, clocks, posters, glasses, trays, pins, tickets, silver spoons, booklets, postcards, ceramic plates, toys, flags, pencils, decals, matches, playing cards, and ticket books. Even full table settings exist from some fairs.

In general, most of the aforementioned may appreciate with age, but much of it can still be bought—and sold—rather inexpensively. It is only now that souvenirs predating the twentieth century are becoming valuable. Handmade items have good appreciation potential as do sophisticated pieces, such as clocks. Most mass-produced items will never gain much value.

Collectors should consider the historical importance of a piece as well as its construction and composition. For instance, ruby glass from the 1893 Chicago Exposition is rapidly gaining in value. And it may be an instinct to turn away from plastic, but collectors should keep in mind that synthetics change over the years, to be replaced by other synthetics; today's plastic could become tomorrow's valuable curiosity.

Authentic space souvenirs are rare and already valuable. By law, everything that has gone into space on an American mission is regulated by NASA. These never make it to the open market; almost every true space artifact now belongs to the Smithsonian Institute. In fact, the Smithsonian owns the Viking Landers now on Mars, as well as everything that Americans left on the moon. Moon rocks are carefully regulated, and any clothing worn by astronauts is NASA property. There is little chance to obtain an official space souvenir, but that only makes the rare find more of a treasure for collectors. For example, a very few remnants of space travel—commemorative flags—have been made into plaques and given to dignitaries. These could show up at an auction someday.

Official first-day postage covers are a little easier to find. In 1983, the United States Post Office sent two-hundred sixty-thousand first-day covers into space on the shuttle. Each numbered and stamped envelope was sold for $15.35. They now bring from $25 to $30.

And how about a piece of Skylab, which fell to earth and scattered future collectors' items over West Australia as well as two oceans? At least one woman is alleged to now own a Lucite-encased piece of the fallen craft.

A set of patches of manned space missions makes a beautiful display, but it will never become truly valuable because patches are still produced in unlimited quantities. In fact, a patch or tack (pin) worn by an astronaut in space is no different from those sold to the public, and there is no way to prove it was "official."

A number of space-influenced toys have also been produced, such as Gemini capsules and various scale models of spacecraft. Depictions of Neil Armstrong's famous steps and words are valuable and still available. These include magazines, posters, newspapers, and medals.

Where to Find Values. Garage sales and flea markets are the best places to find bargains and unrecognized treasures. They will also turn up at collectors' shows and at good prices.

The city in which an exposition was held is usually the best place to begin a search for specific items. But collectors should also keep in mind that people come from everywhere to attend these extravaganzas; the curios go back home with them and therefore may be found in the most remote places.

Space souvenirs are most easily found around the space centers, located in Texas, Florida and California.

★ **Karl Heuer of Northern California had been partial to world's fairs for some time when he decided to investigate an antiques fair held in 1965. He discovered a mint set of ten postcards from the San Francisco Exposition wrapped in the original plastic with the original picture stamps on them. He bought the pack (which fetched $.25 when new) for $15.**

Those world's fair commemoratives turned out to be the first United States prestamped postcards, and an unopened pack is very rare if not unique. Similar postcards now are valued at more than $10 each, and the packaging adds to its worth. Heuer's packet was worth over $100.

A Price Sampling

Drinking stein from 1904 St. Louis Louisiana Purchase Exposition	$125
Battery-operated space capsule toy with tethered astronaut	85
Ruby-glass pitcher from the 1893 Chicago Exposition	75
Official book of the 1893 Chicago Columbian Exposition	40
Sterling-silver spoon from Lousiana Purchase 1904 Exposition	37
New York 1939 Trylon & Perisphere pin	15
Official picture playing cards of the 1933 Chicago World's Fair	12
Official book of the 1939 New York Fair	10

July 20, 1969, newspaper depicting first astronauts
   to land on the moon   10
Spoon from 1933 Chicago and 1939 New York Fairs   8

How to Store/Display. Commemorative items can be attractively displayed, which experts recommend. Plates and containers should not be used, since beverages and dish detergent will affect the condition of the item by lodging in cracks and marring its appearance. Plates and spoons attain their highest values in mint condition; any wear will devalue them.

Collectors should buy or build an enclosed display case for plates, silver, and crystal. A glass case will allow a collection to be admired while protecting it from the elements and the temptation to use it.

Patches, banners and similar items fare well if mounted with pins on a felt or similar backing, and then framed and hung out of direct sunlight. Posters should be mounted on acid-free cardboard, covered with plastic or a glass frame, and hung.

Wood must also be kept out of the sun, and it will hold up best if polished with an oil-based wood polish or creme, which will prevent it from drying out. Water is one of wood's worst enemies and should be kept away from it.

Medals, coins and other metallic items should not be handled because the oils on a human hand will discolor their surfaces. Once an item is discolored, no polish will return it to its mint condition. Some polishes may even add to the discoloration, and some cloths may scratch a surface. It is best to enclose these pieces in airtight folders and admire them without touching them.

How and When to Sell. There are publications on world's fairs that are read by collectors. Placing a classified ad in those is a good way to find buyers who will appreciate an item's value. If one lives in or near a city that once hosted a fair, he should check with the historical department of the city's library. Oftentimes native alumni of a fair form clubs or give lectures. Libraries or museums may exhibit personal collections of fair memorabilia, where one can meet collectors. They will usually have knowledge of the value of a piece, which is important to know before selling. They may even want to buy it. Occasionally, alumni hold reunions or celebrations of the anniversary of a fair. These are excellent forums in which to meet potential buyers.

If one is fortunate enough to own a genuine item from a space flight, chances are he is going to want to hold on to it except to raise cash for an emergency. In that case, classified sections of science and space magazines are the best sources for leads to interested buyers who know the values of such rare articles.

Collectors interested in selling should stay away from the places in which they originally bought an item, such as flea markets and garage sales. While these events may net good finds, they will rarely net good prices. And if they do, they will only be at the expense of more ignorant buyers.

There are no particularly good or bad times to sell commemoratives. Most pieces are not affected by fluctuations in the costs of raw materials, except for those items made of silver and period pieces, such as rare glass.

★ **San Franciscan Raymond Clary has amassed one of the largest collections of memorabilia from the 1894 Mid-Winter Fair held in Golden Gate Park. One of his first finds was a hand-carved ivory letter opener. The handle of the opener unscrewed to expose a quill for writing. He examined it closely and discovered that when the handle was held up to a bright light, he could see a scene from the exposition through it.**

Clary bought the letter opener in 1966 for $9. Today the souvenir is so rare it is worth $150.

Little-Known Facts. Some fairs are best remembered for technology, but the 1933 Century of Progress Exposition hosted in Chicago is more fondly remembered for a burlesque act—Sally Rand's tantalizing and famous fan dance.

• The 1904 St. Louis Exposition held (a year late) to commemorate the one-hundredth anniversary of the Louisiana Purchase cost as much to hold as the actual Louisiana Purchase—about $15 million.

• Most fair buildings were razed eventually, but the Depression-era 1933 Century of Progress Exposition in Chicago is distinctive. Patrons spontaneously started tearing down buildings on closing night.

• In 1973, a West German stamp dealer admitted he had made $150,000 profit from the sale of twenty sheets of stamps autographed by astronauts. He obtained five-hundred autographs from eighteen of the space pioneers, and Neil Armstrong and John Glenn each contributed one-thousand autographs.

—Scott Calamar

Bibliography

Books

The Encyclopedia of Collectibles. Alexandria, VA: Time-Life Books, 1980.

Osman, Tony. *Space History.* New York: St. Martin's Press, 1983.

Stefano, Frank, Jr. *Pictorial Souvenirs & Commemoratives of North America.* New York: Sunrise/E. P. Dutton & Co., Inc., 1976.

Taxay, Don. *An Illustrated History of U.S. Commemorative Coinage.* New York: ARCO Publishing Co., Inc., 1967.

Periodicals

World's Fair. P.O. Box 339-A, Corte Madera, CA 94925.

Catalogues

Kovel, Ralph and Terry. *Kovels' Antiques & Collectibles Price List.* New York: Crown Publishers Inc., 1984.

The Antique Trader Price Guide. P.O. Box 1050 Dubuque, IA 52001.

Flea Market Trader, revised 3rd edition. Collector Books, P.O. Box 3009, Paducah, KY 42001.

Associations

Expo Collectors and Historians Organization, 1436 Killarney Ave., Los Angeles, CA 90065.

World's Fair Collector's Society, 148 Poplar St., Garden City, NY 11530.

Dealers

Spaceland, P.O. Box 775-D, Merritt Island, FL 32592.

Space Collectibles, Box 5108, Titusville, FL 32780.

CONFEDERATE MONEY

Those Confederate bills you used to play with as a child may be worth something today. But don't get too excited, because the smaller denominations in excellent condition may only bring 40% to 50% of their face value; only the larger denominations, in the best condition, are likely to bring anything near face value.

History. Confederate bank notes were issued from the beginning to the end of the Civil War (1861-1864), to finance the war effort of the South. Aware of the dangers of inflation, the rebel government originally intended to limit the amount of money it issued, all of it backed by a cotton standard. Planters were asked to contribute a portion of their crop to the government in exchange for interest-bearing bonds, or notes, to be redeemed at the end of a specified time. With the South producing most of the world's supply of cotton, Confederate leaders expected to raise $100 million dollars a year. What they did not foresee, however, was that England already had an abundant supply of cotton and that the North would impose a blockade on the Confederacy to halt cotton exports.

The oldest issue of notes, in denominations between $50 and $1,000, bears the origin of Montgomery, Alabama, the capital of the confederacy until it was moved to Richmond, Virginia, on May 24, 1861. These notes were engraved and printed by the National Bank Note Company of New York and smuggled across military lines into the South. When the Union confiscated the company's printing plates, the Confederacy turned to the New Orleans branch of the American Bank Note Company (which soon changed its name to the Southern Bank Note Company) to produce additional bills. Later issues were produced by several firms in the South, including Hoyer & Ludwig, J. T. Paterson, B. Duncan, Keatinge & Ball (which eventually became the leading engraver and printer), Archer & Daly and Archer & Halpin. All of these issues were produced by the simpler lithographic process.

One reason why so many of the notes remain in good condition today is that they were generally printed on paper made from rags, since at the time the South did not have the expertise to make its own paper from wood pulp, and it was also unable to obtain paper from England. Between 1861 and 1863 all notes were individually signed. By 1863, a mechanical device making it possible for one person to sign several notes at once was commonly used.

Values Outside the Home. Three factors determine the value of any note: 1) condition, 2) the issue and the engraver or printer who produced it, and 3) the signature, whether done by the hand of someone of historic reputation, or done mechanically.

To determine condition, one should examine the note for ragged edges, tears and holes. Most important, one should determine if it is

An example of the oldest issue of Confederate bank note, this bill, printed by the National Bank Note Company of New York, is worth four times more today, in mint condition, than its 1861 $1,000 face value.

still crisp. This can be done by folding the bill at one end. If it stands up straight, the crispness has been retained. A note considered to be in excellent condition will not have any of the printing worn off it, either.

Value as related to issue must be learned by studying the many books available on Confederate money. The fewer notes in an issue and the fewer notes within an issue printed by the same firm, the rarer the note.

Hand signatures by Confederacy President Jefferson Davis and leading members of his cabinet add to the value of the note. In some cases, these signatures may bring as much money from autograph collectors as from persons interested in Confederate money.

To many collectors, however, the most fascinating aspect of these notes is the wide variety of designs and design vignettes that were used (for more on vignettes, see "Stock Certificates"). As an expediency, many of the vignettes were borrowed from the North and from individual banks, who issued their own notes in those days. A $10 note dated 1862, for instance, bears a vignette of the mythological character Commerce reclining on a bale of cotton with ships in the background. This design had been used earlier on a $1 note issued by the Bank of Chicago. The engravers and printing companies apparently considered vignettes their property and used them for whatever client they desired. While most of the vignettes bear no direct association to the Confederacy, some feature everyday Southern scenes, such as slaves working in a cotton field or a wagonload of cotton bales being driven to market. Portraits of Confederate leaders, such as Jefferson Davis and Treasurer C. G.

Memminger, adorn some notes. But George Washington, who probably would not have approved of the South's secession, is featured on other notes. The most common vignettes are of mythological creatures, which were highly popular during the Victorian Era.

Where to Find Values. Beginning collectors should not buy any notes until extensive research has been done on the current value of specific issues. They should then buy only from coin dealers who specialize in paper money or from another collector. Counterfeiting was common in the late nineteenth century, creating potential disaster for anyone but an expert purchasing notes from any other sources.

For the potential collector seeking a field where he or she can make a profit, Confederate money is not the best choice. It is also a field that can be actively practiced only on the East Coast and particularly in the South. Individuals who already have Confederate notes may well be able to sell them for a decent price, however. But, unless one has a large collection of them, dreams of retiring on the profits are going to remain just that.

The beginning collector whose interest lies in the wide variety of vignettes used on the notes can have a great deal of fun accumulating a collection. Because these are items popular with a relatively small number of people, an impressive grouping can be put together at little cost.

A Price Sampling

Lucy Holcombe Pickens portrait on $100 note; 1864; excellent	$13.50
Jefferson Davis portrait on $50 note; 1864; excellent	10.00
Horses pulling cannon on $10 note; 1864; excellent	7.50
Capitol at Richmond, Virginia, on $5 note; 1884; excellent	7.50
Portrait of Clement C. Clay on $1 note; 1864; good	6.00
Capitol at Richmond, Virginia, on $5 note; 1884; very good	4.00
Portrait of Judah P. Benjamin on $2 note; 1864; average	3.50

How to Store/Display. All bills need to be kept in some type of enclosure that will protect them from air and moisture. Collectors who frequently show their bills keep them in albums that have plastic-encased pages. The more valuable bills, however, should be kept in metal security boxes or glass display cases that will give protection against fire and water. Bills should also be handled as little as possible, since their worth is based in part upon their condition.

How and When to Sell. Collectors will obtain the best prices by selling to other collectors, at shows, or through trade newspapers. Dealers will offer only about 50% of the value they think they can obtain in reselling. Follow the reports of auction prices to determine when specific notes are rising or falling in value. If one has collected strictly to have a complete selection of designs or design vignettes, the collection should be sold as a whole.

Little-Known Facts. The most commonly available Confederate note is the $10 bill bearing a vignette of field artillery soldiers and the bust of R. M. T. Hunter, a member of Jefferson Davis's cabinet. It was printed by Keatinge & Ball, who subcontracted some of the work to Evans & Cogswell in 1864.

• The bust of a woman appearing on a $100 note engraved in 1862 by Keatinge & Ball was thought for many years to be that of Mrs. Jefferson Davis. In 1917, however, numismatist H. D. Allen learned that the portrait was of Mrs. Lucy H. Pickens, who was apparently selected to represent Southern womanhood.

—Karl Nordling

Bibliography

Books

Criswell, Grover C. Jr. *Confederate and Southern States Currency.* St. Petersburg Beach, FL: Criswell's Publication, 1984.

Reinfeld, Fred. *The Story of Civil War Money.* New York: Sterling Publications, 1959.

Slabaugh, Arlie R. *Confederate States of America Paper Money.* Chicago, IL: Hewitt Brothers, 1971.

Periodicals

Bank Note Reporter. 700 E. State St., Iola, WI 54990.

D

CHAPTER 5

Decoys

Dollhouses

Dolls

DECOYS

As a decoy maker, Nathan Cobb was a perfectionist. He was a member of a sporting family from Massachusetts that had relocated on an island off Virginia's eastern coast in the 1830s, and his decoys bore the unmistakable qualities of his Yankee heritage. He carved bodies of white juniper and cedar, smooth enough to withstand the forces of a century without splitting. He sculpted each head with an individual character and pose. He calculated his paint strokes to render the most lifelike effects. The eyes he used were of the finest glass, imported from Germany. The weights he used he fastened to the bottoms with brass screws.

Cobb's decoys were beautiful, all right. But more important, they were effective. After the Civil War, scores of luminaries visited Cobb Island to hunt such forms of waterfowl as the Brant, an inedible bird popular only with sportsmen. Brants have the unusual habit of tilting forward as they rest in water, making them difficult subjects for the carver to imitate. Nathan Cobb perfected a way of making Brants' heads from the holly tree roots that would wash up on his shore during a storm. These heads gave his Brants just the right amount of lean, and many an unsuspecting bird fell victim to the wooden imposters.

In March 1983, the Bourne auction house of Hyannis, Massachusetts, put a Cobb Brant Goose on the block. It fetched $28,000, which at the time was the most ever paid for a decoy at a public sale and reflected the meteoric rise in value that decoys have enjoyed over the past several years. (Two years later, in February 1985, a William Bowman Golden Plover sold for $50,000.) Cobb's Brant, and the millions of decoys carved around it, are part of an American legacy. They speak of an earlier time in the nation's history, and no two tell the same tale. Because of all that they represent, they are relics highly sought by sportsmen and collectors of folk art.

History. Decoys have existed in some form since man first hunted the skies for food. Every civilization has had its own method of luring wild birds within capturing range. But it was not until the labors of

A fine example of Nathan Cobb's artistry, this Brant Goose displays the characteristic forward tilt and delicate sculpting of the head that distinguishes Cobb's decoys from all others.

the North American natives, as early as 1000 A.D., did decoys develop beyond the mud mounds and stacks of rocks employed by primitive man.

When the colonists arrived in America in the seventeenth century, they needed a readily available food supply before they could harness their own reliable sources through farming and animal husbandry. So they turned to food supplies that lay naturally at hand—waterfowl—and learned the art of decoy-making from the natives.

But the natives made canvasback decoys from dried skins and feathers, which were not durable. The settlers sought a more permanent lure that would stand up through years of heavy use. They chose white pine, and as years passed, the carvers strove for greater and greater detail in their work.

By the 1850s, hunting in America had outgrown its role as a means of personal survival. In Jefferson's time, duck hunting had been elevated to the level of an art, and the decoy was as important to one's arsenal as the gun itself. As the settler population increased and the breechloader rifle replaced its obsolete forebear, there grew an enormous culinary appetite for waterfowl and a means capable of satisfying it.

Thousands of market (commercial) hunters spread out along the eastern flyway, from Maine to the Carolinas. Some of them used rigs of as many as six-hundred decoys, mostly homemade. Gradually, decoy-making grew into a minor coastal trade. Old gunners whittled away the off season and were joined by others handy with tools, certainly oblivious they would one day be called the old masters of decoy-making. Nor would they likely have cared. They were simply producing what they considered the right equipment to get the job done.

As market hunting spread west, the demand for decoys intensified, and factories sprang up to fill it. The Jaspar Dodge Factory of Detroit was the pioneer manufacturer, soon joined and later superseded by the Herbert Mason Company, also of Detroit. A factory owned by the Stevens brothers of Weedsport, New York, turned out decoys with a distinctive brand. In 1926, the William Pratt Manufacturing Company bought Mason's equipment and moved it to the home base in Joliet, Illinois. From then until 1938, Pratt produced many fine decoys modeled after Mason classics.

But by then the age of the market hunter had vanished. By 1918, the systematic taking of birds had severely reduced their population and driven such species as the Labrador Duck and the Passenger driven Pigeon close to extinction. Finally, Congress enacted the Migratory Bird Treaty Act, prohibiting the commercial sale of waterfowl and shore birds. Thereafter, duck hunting became a sport full of heavily restricted seasons and limited bags, regulated by the federal government. Market hunters quietly took up new trades, and decoys—thousands of them—were abandoned to old boat houses in remote shanty villages.

But if the market-hunting era was a black mark in American conservationist history, it was the golden age of the duck decoy. This artful product of proud craftsmen's hands did not stay forgotten for long. In the summer of 1923, Abercrombie and Fitch sponsored a decoy show at Bellport, Long Island. In 1931, the Newark Museum included decoys (along with cigar-store Indians and figure heads of sailing ships) in an exhibition of American folk sculpture.

With the increase in appreciation, collectors emerged who identified specific examples and classified them. Noted collector Joel Barber wrote the earliest treatise, *Wild Fowl Decoys*, in 1937. Twenty-eight years later, William Mackey's *American Bird Decoys* became the bible for a burgeoning culture of serious collectors. Mackey was the first to bring objectivity to decoy evaluation. At last it was possible to compare an Oldsquaw decoy from New England with an Illinois River Mallard, or a gigantic Great Blue Heron with a tiny Least Sandpiper.

In the 1960s, folk art collectors joined sportsmen in the marketplace, driving prices out of sight. A George Boyd shore bird valued at $85 in 1965 was worth $3,600 by 1982. At today's auctions, the action does not really begin until they bring out the thousand-dollar-plus items.

★ **Of all the great men who ever took jackknife to wood block in quest of a decoy, Harry V. Shourdes of Tuckerton, New Jersey, was easily the most prolific. The tale is often told of Harry sitting down in a barber's chair with a knob of wood in his hand, and rising a half-hour later with a clean shave and a carved duck head. Endlessly whittling, Shourdes eventually went into the mail-order business, shipping his masterpieces by rail all the way to California and most points in between. No one knows how many decoys Harry Shourdes made in his lifetime. In his prime, he was said to have turned out as many as two thousand a year.**

Values Outside the Home. Most newcomers to the field of decoy collecting are struck by its enormous diversity. Throughout its history, decoys have been fashioned to suit a multitude of conditions and needs, each with its own peculiarity. Besides the normal ducks and geese, decoys have been carved in the likenesses of Godwits and Yellowlegs, Egrets and Terns, Sickle-billed Curlews and Black-bellied Plovers. There are stick-up decoys, full bodies or silhouettes mounted on a pole and stuck into the beach to attract shore birds. And there are the more traditional floating types used for waterfowl. There have even been decoys in the shapes of owls to lure crows, which despise them.

In fact, decoys have been made in so many shapes and sizes for so many different purposes that the consummate example would be difficult to conceive, although many a fine carver has given it his best shot. Decoys of prominent makers, preserved in original condition, accompanied by an interesting tale and proper documentation are the most highly prized specimens. Since most early carvers gave little thought to posterity, they neglected oftentimes to sign their work. Still, their style is signature enough. No trained eye could mistake the high, overriding breast of an Albert Laing model, the inimitable brushwork of Elmer Crowell, or Taylor Johnson's hump-backed tails. Top-grade decoys of this ilk naturally command the highest market value, sometimes $5,000 or more.

A more accessible level for most collectors are the thousands of factory-turned decoys from the market-gunning era. In this case, the term *factory made* is deceiving since most factories were teams of craftsmen who pooled their specific skills in an assembly-line operation. Some were adept at forming bodies with a lathe. Others would hand carve the heads and affix them to the block. Still others would paint the product to resemble the desired species of bird. Survivors of this mass-production effort have realized a healthy increase in value over time. There is great disparity in price among these decoys, however. A pair of Mason Challenge Mergansers may go as high as $5,000. Conversely, a standard-grade decoy by Pratt may be worth no more than $35.

Considering the magnitude of the decoy flock, most collectors tend to specialize. Hunters, drawn to decoys for their sporting significance and their rugged good looks, usually prefer decoys that have been shot over. Folk art collectors, appreciative of their artistic qualities and their deep connection with the American past, look for decoys of historical importance. Some people collect only certain types of birds. Others focus on specific carvers or different birds from the same locale. These broad personal tendencies mixed together create the rich fabric of contemporary decoy collecting and offer plenty of room for the fledgling hobbyist to explore.

Where to Find Values. The safest ways for beginning collectors to obtain valuable decoys is to buy them through a dealer, a recognized collector, or an auction house. Proper pedigree is the largest contributor to price, and considering the dollars involved, it is essential that a given piece be the real McCoy. *The National Directory of Decoy Collectors* lists hundreds of collectors and dealers from every state in the country. Major auction houses, such as Bourne in Massachusetts and the William Doyle Galleries in New York, hold as many as three auctions a year. They will often execute bids *in absentia* if so directed.

Those collecters who are short on funds but long on time and energy might consider going directly to the source. Like most forms of folk art, decoys occasionally can be found where they were left decades ago. Such decoy meccas as Stratford, Connecticut, and Barnegat, New Jersey, may have been picked clean, but the little objects continue to turn up in out-of-the-way villages, deserted barns, dusty attics, and other places inhabited by carvers or their descendants. Likewise, aggressive decoy hunters would be wise to investigate antiques shops and flea markets in search of their elusive prey. The yield from such adventures may not be plentiful, but the romance of it and the potential for a bargain can make the practice rewarding in many ways.

Of utmost importance is the ability to spot a genuine artifact from its more common kin. Identifying authentic decoys is a minute science. The greater the knowledge of decoy characteristics and those of their makers, the greater the potential for success.

Avoid replicas and beware of counterfeits. The production of old-decoy fakes is a red-hot cottage industry. It pays very well, so buyers should consider again if the deal seems too good to be true. Broken decoys can be reassembled in unusual postures to fool the unsuspecting buyer. The condition of the paint is often the best indicator of age and value—and of authenticity. Market hunters usually gave their decoys a fresh coat of paint every year, so cracked and chipped paint layers can reveal a desirable item. Watch out also for new heads married to old bodies. This is a common form of fakery. A simple X-ray may reveal a newly driven nail or a freshly laid spot of glue.

A Price Sampling

Brant Goose, Nathan Cobb	$28,000
Pintail Hen, Ward Brothers	9,700
Curlew, Elmer Crowell	8,000
Widgeon Drake, "Shang" Wheeler	6,750
Plover, George Boyd	3,000
Pintail Duck, Mason Factory	700
Canvasback Duck, Stevens Factory	295
Canada Goose, Madison Mitchell	275
Mallard, contemporary carved, paint, glass eyes	60
Stick-up Duck, tin	30
Mallard, Pratt Factory	25
Duck, cork	10
Carry-Lite Mallard, papier mache	6

How to Store/Display. Exposed as they have been to the ravages of time and wear, it is amazing how many old decoys retain their original luster. Seasons spent in salt water, violent storms, and misguided shots have conspired against them, and yet a good number remain intact. But then, they always have been a sturdy lot; that is how they were made.

Considering the craft that goes into making good decoys, it follows that they should be preserved with an equal amount of care. It also pays. Condition has a tremendous bearing on the value of a decoy.

Beyond the pecuniary reasons, collectors want decoys in top condition simply to enhance their enjoyment of owning them. But what if a prized find needs a bit of restoration? How should the new owner proceed? The best way to clean a decoy is gently, with soap and water. Then a universal sealer should be applied. Linseed oil is the cheapest and least objectionable way to preserve the wood, but one should not be too lavish with it, since it can yellow the paint a few decades down the line. If the decoy has suffered an abrasion or two, the marks should be considered for what they are—battle scars. To remove them from the decoy would be to wipe away its history. A restoration at this point must be approached with restraint. Too many fine decoys have been ruined in the process of being fixed. If professional help is necessary, the nearest decoy club should be able to recommend someone. Owners should try to find a restoration artist who is himself a carver or painter familiar with the old practices. Their services do not come cheap, but for a prized item, they can be well worth it. Having an old masterpiece restored by a modern master simply continues its legacy.

Short of restoration, one may do well to pick out a good spot in a favorite room and provide the decoy with a comfortable resting place. A room with neutral light and heat would be the most desirable. Avoid such places as the top of the TV. And stay away from the fireplace. That special decoy may look handsome sitting up there on the mantel, but it could fall into the fire, which would only serve to increase the value of all remaining decoys.

How and When to Sell. The only problem with decoy collecting as an active hobby is that once a prized specimen makes its way to a bookshelf, it tends to stay put. The huge prices paid for top decoys today are reflections of how scarce the truly valuable examples are on the market. There are far too few Elmer Crowell Mergansers or Ward Brothers Bluebills or even Mason Black Ducks to go around. Trends may come and go, but quality prevails.

Most collectors would agree that it should be enough to own the work of a master, whoever that master might be, without putting such an enormous price on it. But the prices exist, and more often than not they have been paid. Decoy collecting has become an intricate business, and it should not be pursued without sound preparation.

Before selling—or buying—enthusiasts should study decoys, their history, the tales of the carvers, and the relative scarcity of various examples. These are the elements that govern price. They should then study the market. What is out there? How much is it going for? The only way great numbers of decoys tend to make their way into the market today is when the owner of a large collection dies or decides to sell. This is usually done through an auction house, and prices will fluctuate depending upon the desire for that item or items. Sometimes the prices are beyond approach. Other times there are some real bargains.

Those wishing to sell should have no problem finding buyers. Serious collectors feel that it is always open season for new additions to their flocks. The best places to sell decoys are at local decoy collectors' conventions. If the items are truly valuable, their worth will be quickly recognized, with offers to follow. True collectors are an honest breed. They will not try to take advantage of each other, but they will bargain for the best price. This is why it is advised that sellers know their items and the market before putting valuable items up for sale.

Sellers should then develop a bit of patience to prevent them from closing a deal with the first interested party. Above all else, they must remember that top-grade decoys have created a seller's market; someone in possession of a genuinely valuable item need not jump at the first offer made for it.

★ The largest public repository of old decoys is held at the Shelburne Museum in Shelburne, Vermont. Spread throughout thirty-five buildings on forty-five acres of land, the Shelburne contains art and Americana ranging from carousel animals to quilts, turn-of-the-century carriages to Monet paintings. Its decoy collection numbers approximately fourteen hundred, including the entire Joel Barber collection. Although individual prices fluctuate, the collection would easily be worth $1 million on the open market.

Little-Known Facts. Throughout history, people have tried all kinds of methods to attract wildfowl other than using a simple decoy. King Tut purportedly used live birds. The Old World Europeans constructed elaborate net-covered channels with dogs placed at openings to funnel in hordes of fowl. Only in America, with its unrestricted hunting laws and widespread use of firearms, did the decoy gain enough popularity to survive.

• In 1924, archeologists excavating in Lovelock Cave, Nevada, came upon a round object made of reeds and feathers. Digging further, they found eleven more like it. They were decoys made by the ancestors of the Paiute Indians. Evidence shows them to date back to the tenth century, making them the earliest decoys known.

—*Richard Keller*

Bibliography

Books

Barber, Joel. *Wild Fowl Decoys.* New York: Dover Publications, 1954.

Kangas, Gene and Linda. *National Directory of Decoy Collectors.* Painesville, OH: 1981.

Mackey, William J., Jr. *American Bird Decoys.* New York: Bonanza Books, 1965.

Periodicals

Decoy Magazine. P.O. Box 1900, Montego Bay Station, Ocean City, MD 21842.

Ward Foundation News. 655 South Salisbury Blvd., Salisbury, MD 21801.

Catalogues

Kovel, Ralph and Terry. *Kovels' Antiques and Collectibles Price List.* New York: Crown Publishers, 1984.

Associations

Ducks Unlimited, One Waterfowl Way at Gilmer Rd., Long Grove, IL 60047.

Long Island Decoy Collectors Association, 92 Helme Ave., Miller Place, NY 11764.

Midwest Decoy Collectors Association, 1400 South 58th St., Lincoln, NB 68506.

Pacific Flyway Decoy Association, P.O. Box 536, Quincy, CA 95971.

West Coast Decoy Collectors Association, 6740 Boulder Rd., Loomis, CA 95650.

Auction Houses

Richard A. Bourne Company, Box 141, Hyannisport, MA 02647.

William Doyle Galleries, 175 East 87th St., New York, NY 10128.

DOLLHOUSES

Consider an eggbeater so tiny that if someone dropped it on the floor, he would have to hunt for it with a magnifying glass; or an edition of Robert Burns' poems printed on pages the size of postage stamps; or a pygmy piano with microscopic black-and-white keys that can tinkle a tune.

Anyone who finds himself entranced by these descriptions is ready to join the millions whose obsession is the miniature universe of dollhouses, a world in which planters are the size of toothpaste caps, Lilliputian fireplaces are formed from pea-sized bits of gravel, and chairs look just big enough to be the resting spots of baby mice. It is estimated that in the United States the collecting of dollhouses and other miniatures ranks among the top half-dozen most popular hobbies, somewhere behind stamps and coins, model railroads and antique dolls.

And it is more than child's play, which the prices of dollhouses reflect. At a recent Theriault's auction in New York City, the Bellamy House, a two-story wood Victorian built in the early 1890s by John Bellamy of West Newton, Massachusetts, as an exact replica of the 16-room home he once owned, was sold to an Arizona collector for $2,800. Even dollhouses built in the 1920s and 1930s have brought $500 to $600, while eighteenth-century European dollhouses have been known to sell for $20,000 to $30,000.

History. From their beginning, dollhouses have fascinated adults almost as much as they have children. The earliest-known recorded dollhouse was commissioned in 1558 by Albrecht V, Duke of Bavaria, as a present for his daughter. The duke was so entranced with the tiny house, which included a ballroom hung in tapestries of gold, a chapel complete with priest and musicians, and a stable, wine cellar and coach house, that he reportedly kept it for himself in his art chamber. Unfortunately for history, a fire in the Munich palace in 1674 reportedly destroyed the mini-marvel.

From the duke's time on dollhouses flourished, particularly in Germany and Holland, where girls often used them to practice their skills in managing households until their marriages. The Dutch were famed for their *poppenhuizen*, luxurious armoires and cabinets like those in which modern Americans house their VCRs and stereos. The cabinets could be opened to reveal several rooms of dolls and dollhouse furniture.

The eighteenth-century English called them *baby houses* and hired such famous architects and furniture-makers as Vanbrugh, Chippendale, and Adam to work on them.

American-made dollhouses began to gain popularity in the nineteenth century. One name that stands out from that time was the R. Bliss Manufacturing Company of Pawtucket, Rhode Island, founded in 1832. Bliss houses, made of lithographed paper on wood, were not as dramatic and ostentatious as those from Europe, but dollhouse collectors now compete avidly for them because of their colorful, rustic charm. All were richly decorated and usually featured porches and bobbin-turned pillars. Most seem to have had a lithographed stone or brick base. Small printed windows on doors and gables imitated stained glass. Some houses were only five by eleven inches.

During the nineteenth century throughout the world, children monopolized dollhouses. But in the twentieth century revival of adult interest began. Much of it grew from Queen Mary, grandmother of Queen Elizabeth II. She collected dollhouses throughout her life and often gave them as presents to others. In the 1920s she was given a spectacular dollhouse, designed by Sir Edwin Luytens, the architect who had laid out the city of New Delhi, India. The house took three years to complete. Its exterior was made of wood painted to resemble stone. The walls and roof could be removed electronically to reveal the interior. Famous artists and manufacturers made all of the objects in the house: Wedgwood and Doulton produced china, Singer supplied a working sewing machine, and Rudyard Kipling chose from among his verses and then handwrote them into a tiny book, which he also illustrated. Lapis lazuli and marble were used for the floors of the reception areas, and the roof was formed from thirty-eight-hundred slate tiles. The queen's bed was hung with blue and silver silk damask with seed pearls embroidered into the coverlet.

At the time, the house inspired thousands who viewed it at the British Empire exhibition, and a number of people went on to create dollhomes on a less ambitious scale. Even today, it is estimated that six-hundred-fifty-thousand people a year see the dollhouse at Windsor Castle, where it is now on display.

Unique among dollhouse rooms is the Queen Mary library, which includes not only drawerfuls of miniature prints and original watercolors by famous artists but also two-hundred tiny books written by renowned authors in their own handwriting.

Just ten years later another famous dollhouse was created on the other side of the Atlantic for child movie star Colleen Moore. Her twelve-foot-high $1 million dollhouse was furnished in fairy-tale whimsy and included a dining room set to serve King Arthur and his knights, a chapel with a fine gold miniature organ, and a weeping willow that dripped real water.

Dollhouses are not only entertaining; they have also served as important records of social change. Their exteriors chronicled architectural style, and their interiors told much about how their early creators lived. In real life, for example, stoves and utensils, lamps, furnishings and decorations change as the years do. But in dollhouses, these items are kept as they were, not modernized to catch up to a new era. In a dollhouse, time stands still.

★ **A great deal of money is also being made by craftsmen and artisans who produce dollhouses of stunning quality. Brooke Tucker, daughter of the actor Forrest Tucker, creates miniature rooms that sell from $500 for tiny rooms no larger than 6 by 9 inches to $3,500 for rooms 2½ by 18 inches.**

Values Outside the Home. Dollhouse collecting can be approached two ways: by buying antique houses or by purchasing new ones.

In general, fully furnished dollhouses are more valuable than unfurnished, and the earlier the dollhouse, the more likely it is to be interesting, original and steep in price. The eighteenth century was the dollhouse's prime, and the next one-hundred-twenty years to follow were its heyday.

Very old European dollhouses are usually found in museums. More accessible to American collectors are dollhouses made commercially from the turn of the century—R. Bliss dollhouses, for example, often identified by a trademark on their front doors.

The Morton E. Converse firm of Massachusetts made similar dollhouses, with lithographed designs placed directly on the wood. Although these are less appealing than the Bliss houses, they are also eagerly sought by collectors and command high prices. Another famous American manufacturer was Albert Schoenhut, and there was Tootsietoy, produced by the Dowst Brothers of Chicago.

Almost all dollhouses have some value. Highly prized are individual houses that were custom made for children by family members. For example, a house seen recently in a San Francisco antiques toy shop was sold to the storeowner by a woman who had played with it as a child. It was custom made, constructed during the 1930s, and now selling for $600.

For those interested in creating their own houses, kits are offered at prices from $150 to $800. Once assembled and furnished, the value of the dollhouse can soar to $10,000 depending on how well it is put together.

Where to Find Values. Old dollhouses are scarce and require real hunting. Auctions, estate sales and antiques shows sometimes offer them. Flea markets and yard sales are other sources. But here the risk is greater because the buyer may end up paying more than the item is worth.

Antiques dealers also carry old dollhouses, but most say they are snapped up almost as quickly as they arrive.

Almost every city in the country has shows featuring miniatures and their artists, many of whom specialize in dollhouses and dollhouse furniture and trappings. These are excellent resources for those who wish to make their own houses or to buy contemporary creations.

★ **Artist James Marcus of Bolinas, California, makes reproductions of Victorian homes that sell for $15,000 to $20,000.** The homes, decorated with brightly colored gingerbread, have coffered ceilings, stained glass windows, and are done entirely in natural woods so that their exteriors never have to be painted.

A Price Sampling

Two-story British-made dollhouse, one foot high, made from pottery, early nineteenth century	$3,900
Fully stocked pretend dollshop	800
R. Bliss dollhouse, two story, two rooms, 16¼″ × 11½″ × 7½″	650
Folding Victorian cardboard dollhouse, 15″ × 16″, marked "McLoughlin Brothers, New York"	650
R. Bliss dollhouse, two story, two rooms, 18″ × 12″ × 9″, c. 1900	575
Tootsietoy dollhouse, dated 1927, two story	475
French dollhouse, two story	310
Four-room wooden American-made house with gabled roof and door that opens, early twentieth century	200
Fisher-Price plastic dollhouse from 1960s	25

How to Store/Display. Buyers of antique dollhouses must approach restoration carefully. It is preferable to have a slightly shabby, chipped exterior than one coated with layers of modern paint. If restoration is needed, one should first carefully wash and clean the house and then repair any obvious structural damage. But be sure to consult an expert before attempting major changes, such as removing old paint.

Collectors should search for period furniture first, or well-made reproductions. Naturally, owners can build their own furniture, but they must be careful to avoid an artsy-craftsy hodgepodge.

When the work is done, many collectors, of course, want to share it with friends and relatives, but to avoid having enthusiastic spectators reach in to handle precious furnishings, open facades should be covered with glass or plastic.

How and When to Sell. The 1980s are an excellent time to sell dollhouses. The craving for miniatures is high throughout the country, with "miniature" clubs thriving in almost every major city and town.

Dollhouses can be sold to antiques dealers, but a collector can also sell them on his or her own via newspaper ads. Priceless items, on the other hand, are best handled by auction houses.

★ Although dollhouses frequently sell for steep prices, it is possible to find occasional bargains, as did Susan Hoy, owner of the antiques toy store Susan's Storeroom in San Anselmo, California. Ms. Hoy was attending a toy show when she happened to pick up a dollhouse stamped with the R. Bliss trademark and selling for $45.

She was sure it was a reproduction but, after buying it, discovered it was the real thing and valued at $300.

Little-Known Facts. Many famous people over the years have been dollhouse collectors, among them Vivien Greene, wife of British novelist Graham Greene.

• Her interest in dollhouses began in the 1940s, when the antiques shops of war-torn England had become collectors paradises, filled by the flotsam of disrupted families. A young woman then, she began by buying a few dollhouses. Very little had been written at the time about their preservation and restoration, so Mrs. Greene made it a personal crusade.

• She roamed the country to look at the houses that Britons had uncovered in their attics, stables and dairies and to assist people in deciding what to do with them. She is credited with having saved and restored some one thousand of the British miniatures, and she put fifty of her own into a museum near her home in Oxford, which is devoted solely to them.

—Rebecca Larsen

Bibliography

Books

Jacobs, Flora Gill. *A History of Dolls' Houses.* New York: Charles Scribner's Sons, 1965.

King, Constance Eileen. *Dolls and Dolls' Houses.* London: Hamlyn, 1977.

Latham, Jean. *Dolls' Houses: A Personal Choice.* New York: Charles Scribner's Sons, 1969.

Periodicals

Creative Crafts and Miniatures. Fredon Springdale Rd., Fredon Township, P.O. Box 700, Newton, NJ 07860.

Hobbies. Lightner Publishing Corp., 1006 S. Michigan Ave., Chicago, IL 60605.

Dealers

Theriault's (auction firm), P.O. Box 151, Department CC&M, Annapolis, MD 21404.

Associations

National Association of Miniature Enthusiasts, P.O. Box 2621, Brookhurst Center, Anaheim, CA 92804.

DOLLS

"If only the dolls themselves could speak!"—Wendy Lavitt, *American Folk Dolls*

During the 1920s, when stamps and coins were the undisputed kings of collectors' items, doll collecting was just becoming popular.

By 1980, dolls had become the third most widely collected item, replaced only by stamps and coins.

In 1984, doll collecting captured second place and threatened to overtake stamps as America's most popular hobby.

Current estimates place the number of United States adult doll collectors at over two-hundred-fifty thousand, 35% of which are men. (John Wayne, for example, collected Hopi Indian dolls, many of which are on display at the National Cowboy Hall of Fame in Oklahoma City.)

If only the dolls could speak... what exciting historical tales they could tell.

History. The word *doll* probably came from the word "idol," because the first known dolls were associated with ritual magic. Dolls have been used as talismans against evil, as representation of the dead, and as fertility symbols. (Dionne quintuplet dolls, made by the Alexander Doll Company between 1934 and 1939, were once sold as fertility dolls.)

Another fertility doll ranks as one of the finest examples of its kind from antiquity. The Willendorf Venus, discovered in Austria, dates from the forty-thousand-year-old Aurignacian culture. It was carved from limestone, with exaggerated hips and breasts, and still had traces of the original red paint when discovered.

The first Old World dolls were brought to America by English explorers. These wooden "Bartholomew babies," brought from London's Bartholomew Fair, were used for barter with the Indians.

In 1585, artist John White sketched the first known picture of a doll in America—a little Indian girl pictured with her mother, holding a properly dressed Elizabethan doll.

Ludwig Greiner, a German immigrant, patented the first doll in America in 1858—a papier-mache doll head. The work of Greiner marks the beginning of the commercial doll in America.

Until the mid-nineteenth century, most American dolls were homemade. These early folk creations were made of common materials and included rags and cloth, corn, wood, and apples, nuts, and beans.

Another German immigrant, Albert S. Schoenhut, son of a family of woodcarvers and toymakers, received a patent for his all-wood Schoenhut Doll in January 1911. The Schoenhut Company of Philadelphia is considered to be the forerunner of mass-market commercial dollmaking in the United States.

England's Queen Victoria began collecting dolls at age six. Her wooden dolls made up one of the first known collections. Another royal doll collector was Princess Grace of Monaco.

Doll collecting as a popular hobby dates to the 1920s. It has grown to such huge proportions that there is a collector for virtually every type of doll, from the highly prized German and French *bisques* (dolls made of matte-finish porcelain) made between 1875 and 1930 to the Cabbage Patch Kids of the 1980s.

★ **Butterfield & Butterfield doll expert Sheila Bradley recently examined the contents of an old wicker trunk in San Francisco, California, that had belonged to the elderly owner's mother. The trunk had been stored in a garage basement for many years. At the bottom of the trunk, Ms. Bradley found several broken doll parts and old doll clothes, including a rare Bru (named after Casimir Bru, a nineteenth-century French dollmaker) with a cracked head. Apart from the damage, when dressed the Bru sold for close to $2,000 at auction.**

Considered a national institution by many collectors and noncollectors alike, the Barbie doll has always displayed the latest fashions, from the sequined sheath of the early 1960s to the most current sports clothes.

Values Outside the Home. Faced with the enormous array of dolls and their various compositions, how does the novice collector begin to build a doll collection?

First, and most important, one should collect what he loves. Second, the beginner should learn as much as he can about his specialty, which includes the age, condition, originality and availability of the doll.

Values in doll collecting follow the laws of supply and demand. Value depends on how many originals were made and on how many are extant. Some antique dolls (seventy-five years old or older) are extremely rare because they were made from molds that were destroyed after only thirty or so samples were cast.

On the other hand, some modern mass-produced dolls are also quite valuable. A first-edition mint Barbie in its original box, which sold for $3 in 1959, can bring $900 to $1,200. Sans box, the doll alone might bring a mere $500!

Condition is an extremely important buying consideration. Most antique dolls have been restored to some extent; over-restoration can reduce value. Collectors should always examine the doll carefully before making a purchase. Does the doll bear a maker's mark? The more common the doll, the better its condition should be. Condition is also relative: a cracked head might reduce value by as much as 90%, while a cracked finger may be negligible.

Originality is related to condition. Are all of the parts original? Are the clothing and accessories original? The original fancy clothes on a mid-1880s Tete Jumeau in good condition could add 50% to the purchase price. Also, one should beware of fakes and reproductions sold as originals.

When buying, collectors should keep in mind the added cost of repairing and dressing the doll, if necessary. If a purchase requires restoration, the job should be placed in the hands of professionals. Doll "hospitals" are also excellent sources for estimates.

A doll's size is generally unrelated to price. A small pre-World War I Kewpie, which sold for less than $1 new, might bring $800 to $1,000, and some French miniatures bring $300 to $500. Some large dolls (over 36 inches tall) that sold new for $.95, are now valued at $1,500.

Where to Find Values. Doll-buying opportunities are everywhere, from flea markets and garage sales to specialty doll auctions. Other buying sources include dealers, private parties, collector shows and conventions, and mail order.

Dolls purchased from other collectors are usually less expensive than those bought from dealers, who may mark up prices 50% or more. However, dealers may offer the advantage of layaway buying, plus their valuable expertise.

Collector doll auctions are prime buying sources. Bids may be presented in person or by mail, either sealed or open. Remember that many doll auctions include a 10% "value added" premium to the bid.

Before bidding, buyers should study the "Conditions of Sale" listed in the auction catalogue. Is the merchandise guaranteed, or "as is"? They should also note that pre-sale estimates in the catalogue are only estimates and may bear little resemblance to actual selling price. Auction estimates tend to be conservative "fair market" prices. It is important to determine the seller's returns policy *before* buying.

About one-half of collectors buy limited-edition dolls. Limited editions may not always be profitable investments, however, because asking prices are top retail. And just because an edition is "limited" doesn't necessarily mean it will appreciate. Exactly how many editions were issued? Remember: rarity equals value. One advantage of buying limited editions is that they tend to be better constructed than store-bought dolls.

Some doll clubs offer the purchase of limited editions in lieu of membership fees. In 1975, when the Effanbee Doll Club was chartered, a new member had to buy one of 872 Precious Baby dolls at $40 each. These dolls brought $250 to $300 at auction in early 1984. Perhaps the queen of limited-edition dolls is the Marilyn Monroe, dressed in a genuine ermine coat and wearing real jewelry. A bargain at $7,400.

Brokerage services sell a wide variety of antique dolls by mail order. Advantages include credit-card buying, ten-day return privileges, layaways, and excellent selection. Disadvantage: a hefty 25% commission to locate some hard-to-find dolls.

One last piece of buying advice: *Caveat emptor!*

★ **A North Carolina woman heard doll auctioneers Florence and George Theriault describing an extremely rare doll on national television. The woman immediately recognized the description as matching that of a doll she had just thrown into the trash barrel. She rescued the doll at once. The same doll later tied the then-current world record auction price of $16,000.**

A Price Sampling

Jumeau "Long-faced" Bebe, with closed mouth, shaded lids, applied pierced ears, replaced blond wig, jointed body with straight wrists, wearing a garnet and cream satin dress, probably original; 25″ tall, minor body wear	$10,450
Bru Bisque-headed Bebe Teteur, with blue paperweight eyes, blond mohair wig, kid body with bisque arms, wooden legs; 18″ tall, eyelid flake, paint chipped on legs	3,300
Set of Alexander composition Dionne quintuplets, all with brunette hair wigs, wearing original organdy dresses and pins; 11″ tall, eyes cloudy, minor cracks; together with two Dionne books, a framed print, and a lamp picturing the quints on its shade and porcelain base	2,200
Kestner Bisque shoulder-headed Gibson Girl, with closed mouth, brown sleep eyes, brown mohair wig, kid body with bisque arms, dressed as a bride; 21″ tall, chipped finger, hairline on shoulder plate	1,045

S & Co. Bisque-headed Lori Baby, with fixed brown eyes,
open mouth, brush-stroked brown hair, bent-limb body,
wearing a white dress; 18″ tall, repaired finger   880
Schoenhut character boy doll "Tootsie Wootsie" with
molded blonde hair, painted blue eyes, open-close
laughing mouth, redressed in blue sailor suit; 14½″ tall,
paint wear   660
Small Bisque-headed Bye-Lo Baby, with blue sleep eyes,
cloth body with celluloid hands, wearing a white
lawn dress; 8″ tall   308
Black composition Kewpie doll, moveable arms, red heart
decal on chest; 10″ tall, minor cracks on arms; together
with earlier Kewpie composition statuette with move-
able arms; 12″ tall, paper label on chest   154
Ideal composition Deanna Durbin doll, with human hair
wig, wearing replaced organdy dress; 20″ tall,
cloudy eyes, minor face cracks   110
Ideal composition Shirley Temple doll, wearing tagged
white organdy dress printed with red flowers; 18″ tall,
face repainted; together with 1972 vinyl Shirley
Temple by Ideal   99

SOURCE: Christie's (East) Auction, May 1984.

How to Store/Display. A doll collection is an investment. Assuming
that one has bought only the best quality in terms of design and
craftsmanship, special steps must be taken to protect it.

The closer to mint condition, the greater a doll's value. First rule:
do not let children play with a doll collection. Instead, depending on
composition, dolls should be stored behind glass, where they can be
prominently displayed while being protected from dust, heat,
humidity, moths, and direct fluorescent light or sunlight.

Plastic dolls should be stored in a cool dark place to protect against
fading, soiling, and disintegration. Wax dolls are quite sensitive to
strong light and extremes of temperature. Collectors are advised to
leave cleaning and restoring to the experts. They should never comb
or wash a doll or its clothes. If clothing is changed, the discarded
clothing should be kept on file. Discarded clothing should also be
passed on with the doll whenever possible.

Personal property, such as a doll collection, is usually covered by
one's home-owner insurance, but it is still a good idea to insure a
collection separately if it is worth over $500. Certainly one should
make note of a collection on a home-owner policy and should

inform an insurance agent of the collection's existence. It is important to keep complete records of the collection as well, with photographs, count, and description of each doll (type, composition, year made, maker's marks and location, height, costume, repairs, purchase price, and estimated value). Collectors may want to purchase a special doll record book to note this information.

How and When to Sell. There is no firm consensus as to how long to hold on to a doll collection. Some experts recommend up to twenty years, while others prefer to sell when a doll has doubled in value—hopefully in about five years or sooner.

Doll collections should not be broken up for sale, if possible. It is better to sell the entire collection as a unit.

If one is unsure about the value of a doll, experts advise getting at least two estimates: one from a doll specialist, and another from a general antiques dealer.

Collectors should always check the copyright date in price guides. Are the prices listed current? They should also remember that doll prices can be regional.

★ Although rare dolls are becoming harder to find as the general public becomes more knowledgeable, dusty attics and garages still yield some excellent finds.

Early in their collecting careers, doll experts Pauline and Dick Madigan bought two small plastic Madame Alexander dolls at a garage sale. The Madigans were overjoyed to learn that they were rare Tommy and Katie dolls, issued to commemorate the 100th anniversary of F. A. O. Schwarz Company.

Little-Known Facts. As a little girl, Margaret Woodbury Strong wanted to acquire the world's largest doll collection. When she died, in 1969, at age seventy-two, her collection contained twenty-seven thousand dolls—and they only represented less than one-tenth of her entire collection of 300,000.

To say that Margaret Woodbury Strong was an avid collector would be an understatement. Her various collections consisted of some fifty separate catagories, including—in addition to dolls—dollhouses and furniture, carousel figures, silver thimbles, circus artifacts, books, ceramics, napkin rings, paperweights, and much more. The collections filled twenty-five rooms and spilled over into her five-room living quarters.

In 1970, Sotheby's estimated the value of the entire collection at $4 million. It took four major auctions between 1977 and 1981 to sell off the doll collection alone. Over $1 million was bid for the *discarded* dolls! Eighteen-thousand dolls were kept for display in the Margaret Woodbury Strong Museum, which opened in October 1982 in Rochester, New York.

—Gregory Frazier

Bibliography

Books

Coleman, Dorothy S., Elizabeth A., and Evelyn J. *Collector's Encyclopedia of Dolls.* New York: Crown Publishers, 1976.

Foulke, Jan. *6th Blue Book of Dolls & Values.* Cumberland, MD: Hobby House Press, 1983.

King, Constance E. *The Collector's History of Dolls.* New York: St. Martin's Press, 1977.

Periodicals

Doll Castle News. Box 247, Washington, NJ 07882.

Doll Reader. 900 Frederick St., Cumberland, MD 21502.

Doll Talk. Box 495, Independence, MO 64051.

Doll Times. 1675 Orchid, Aurora, IL 60505.

Doll Values Quarterly. 900 Frederick St., Cumberland, MD 21502.

Dolls. 170 Fifth Ave., New York, NY 10010.

The Doll Investment Newsletter. P.O. Box 1982, Centerville, MA 02632.

Dealers

James and Pauline Madigan, P.O. Box 1772, Canyon Country, CA 91351.

Auctions

Theriault's Auction. P.O. Box 151, Annapolis, MD 21404.

Brokerages

Magnificent Doll Brokerage Service. P.O. Box 1981, Centerville, MA 02632.

Associations

United Federation of Doll Clubs. P.O. Box 14146, Parkville, MD 64152.

E

CHAPTER 6
Erotica

EROTICA

Society has a particular fasination with erotic expression, whether some of us are willing to admit it or not. From the sacred, highly explicit Indian temple sculptures at Khajurako to the neon lights and buzz of San Francisco's Broadway Street, men and women through the ages have sought to explore ways of venting eroticism through a variety of artistic means.

The word "eroticism" is derived from the word *eros,* Greek for "love." Whereas Far Eastern religions often connected the erotic to the divine, we of the West have a more secular and reserved, though nonetheless earnest, appreciation for it.

Evidence of erotic art dates back to the Paleolithic era (30,000 to 10,000 B.C.), with cave paintings that associated sexual experiences with the hunt. Erotica can be found in all cultures, much of which has been the most sought-after—and controversial—art in the world. Some examples that created a stir were Michelangelo's statue "David," an idealized male nude that church officials eventually ordered "covered up" with the legendary fig leaf, and Constantin Brancusi's "Princess X," a bronze phallus that was banned from display after it was completed in 1916.

While most of us are not likely to find one of Picasso's famous steamy sketches in our attics or basements, there is a host of available contemporary erotica that can bring not only good money, but, well, a particular joy of ownership.

History. One of the oldest forms of this exciting art that one might find while digging through basements or attics is the French postcard. Produced during the first two decades of the twentieth century, French postcards did not hide much, and favorite collectors' items include the French maid and silk-stocking sequences.

While postcards were popular during World War I, the GIs of World War II preferred the airbrush fantasy girls of such artists as Rolph Armstrong, Alberto Varga, George Petty and Zoa Mozert—the latter being the only female cheesecake artist to achieve notoriety. GIs used to pin up the pictures of these luscious ladies on their lockers and trench walls; hence, the reference "pinup girl."

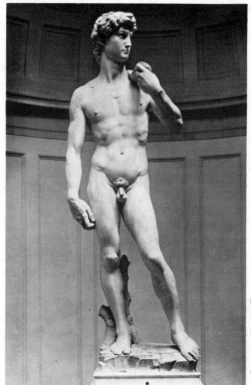

Art Resource, New York

The nudity displayed in Michelangelo's
masterpiece sculpture "David" caused outrage
among early European church officials, who
ordered that it be partially covered by the
strategic placement of the legendary fig leaf.

Esquire was the first magazine to publish centerfolds in 1933 as
well as reproduce the amorous Varga (also known as "Vargas") and
Petty girls in magazine format. Issues of *Esquire* from the early '40s
that feature both Varga and Petty girls can fetch up to $75 apiece. A
collection of all forty-seven issues that feature Varga girls would
bring in about $1,000, simply because it is very difficult to find these
magazines intact.

The '40s saw the introduction of the first exclusively men's
magazines, and they had titles such as *Titters, Wink, Giggle, Flirt,
Eyeful,* and *Beauty Parade.* Today they are currently worth around $15
each.

The '50s emphasized erotic photography. Irving Klaw's photos of Betty (also spelled "Bettie") Page made her extremely popular, "the most collectible cheesecake model ever," as one enthusiast put it. Klaw published several collections of Page photos in the '60s that stimulated interest in Page memorabilia.

Legs were also big in the '50s and the '60s and reflected in the names of the new breed of glossy magazines, which bore such titles as *Black Silk Stockings, Heels and Hose,* and *Garter Parade.* The magazines of Elmer Batters are the most desirable of this group and bring around $25 apiece.

Then along came *Playboy* and Marilyn Monroe. The popularity of *Playboy* and the developing art of cheesecake photography opened up the market to the masses, bringing credibility and prestige to packaged eroticism.

★ **When Joe (real name not available) of Los Angeles found a 1959 *Playboy* calendar in immaculate condition in an attic, he thought he was fortunate to get $50 for it. But the next day he found three more of the same calendar in the same attic, and one of them was printed with a double month—an oddity that collectors search for, in which two of one month may be printed while another month may be missing entirely. From the additional copies he received $250 more.**

Values Outside the Home. The most valuable collectors' items of this genre that are within reach of the modern collector are the first two issues of *Playboy* magazine. The first issues of all other major erotic magazines—*Penthouse, Oui, Playgirl*—are also valuable.

Although magazines are published in large quantities, the number of them in mint condition is extremely small. Mint copies of the earliest issues are diminishing, and as long as demand runs ahead of supply, their value will continue to increase.

The first issue of *Playboy* is not only valuable because it is a first issue, but because it features Marilyn Monroe, the top erotic draw of all time. Anything related to Monroe is worth hanging on to. She is to erotica what Elvis and the Beatles are to the world of music. With her death in 1962, people grabbed anything with her image on it, including the first *Playboy*.

That is why, at present, the *second* issue of *Playboy* is pulling a little more money than the first; because of the second issue's scarcity (people did not think about hanging on to the second issue), it is in greater demand and therefore worth more to hobbyists trying to complete their early-edition collections.

Whatever one decides to buy, it is important to buy only items in good condition. The collectors of the '80s are a fickle bunch, and only the best examples will draw top dollar. As for current issues of magazines, it is the unique and popular ones—such as the controversial *Penthouse* featuring then-Miss America Vanessa Williams—to pay attention to because they will be the most sought after ten to twenty years from now.

Other early erotic collectors' items include:

- The "eight-pagers." In their heyday, during the '20s and through the '40s (some are still made today), eight-pagers were takeoffs on popular cartoons or featured famous stars in humorous, erotic stories that lasted eight pages. If original, they can fetch $25.
- Pulp magazines, such as *Breezy* and *Snappy,* pulp paperbacks, and comic books. These are valuable mostly for their cover art. Enoch Bolles' covers from the '30s are becoming more popular all the time, and some paperbacks, such as the Diversey Romance title *Reform School Girl,* can bring in as much as $275.
- Erotic playing cards. Prices depend upon how old they are, whether the deck is complete, and whether the illustrations feature a popular personality. Some of the Marilyn Monroe playing cards can bring $50 a deck.
- Petty and Varga girls. Printed on everything from ties to movie posters to T-shirts, all samples of such are considered very valuable.

Where to Find Values. Erotica is not the kind of thing a local antiques shop or auction house is bound to carry. But neither does one have to sneak down dark alleys in his search either. Since most erotica is printed on paper, collectors should instead seek out those dealers and auctions that specialize in paper items, though chances are they will not be local, or prevalent.

A Price Sampling

Playboy, Vol. 2, Jan. 1954	$2,000
Playboy, Vol. 1, Marilyn Monroe cover, Dec. 1953	1,800
	($3,000 in Hollywood)
Esquire, all 47 issues, featuring Varga girls	1,000
Marilyn Monroe, "Golden Dreams" calendar, 1954	150

Penthouse, Vol. 1, No. 1, Sept. 1969	80
Esquire, Vol. 1, No. 1, Oct. 1933	50
"Petty Girl," 9″ × 12″ airbrush original, 1947	25
Varga Girls, any calendar page, '40s	20
Nude pinups, mid-'50s	15
Semi-clad pinups, '40s, early '50s	1

How to Store/Display. Collectors should pay attention to the overall condition of any valuable magazine or other paper item. A magazine cover is worth about 80% of the whole magazine. Tears, dog-eared pages, and spots are all detractors. Ideally, the item should be as close to new as possible.

Owners should store paper items in plastic, preferably Mylar, and should then place them in cool, dark, and dry places—never in cardboard containers, since cardboard can develop mold. Magazines should be stacked on end in an upright position, so that each magazine supports its own weight.

How and When to Sell. Prices for erotica may vary as much as 50% from those listed in price guides. Usually a dealer does not concern himself with the asking price of another dealer. He is only concerned with what supply and demand dictates among his clients.

Other traditional collectors' items seem to have firmly-established prices, but erotica does not. (Compare price of 1952 Marilyn Monroe calendar in "Advertising" to price of "Golden Dreams" Monroe calendar listed here.) Because it is so difficult to obtain (there are no erotica collectors' clubs or conventions), people who specialize may be willing to pay top dollar for a particular item. The best way to find such people is through major dealers.

★ When John Cairns of Tucson, Arizona, opened his shop in January 1983, he had no idea how he was going to get his hands on a first-issue *Playboy*—he only knew he wanted one. Then it happened. An elderly woman visited him one day in a wheelchair, having recently been in an accident. Under her arm was a first-issue *Playboy*, which she wanted to sell to finance her upcoming surgery. The other shop in town had offered her $150 for the magazine, but she felt it was not enough. So Mr. Cairns paid her $500 for it, and both dealer and customer parted happily—the dealer with his copy of a valuable, and coveted, magazine, and the disabled customer with the money necessary to pay for her operation.

Little-Known Facts. Famous sci-fi writer Ray Bradbury is collecting copies of all publications that printed the first edition of any of his stories. His search has led him to *Playboy* collectors. Copies of the 1957 hardback *Playboy Collection Special* contained a Bradbury story that was never published anywhere else and today is valuable not only as erotica but as sci-fi memorabilia.

• *Playboy* is also collected for its extensive interview with the Beatles in a 1965 issue. Copies in mint condition have fetched up to $100.

—Peter Asmus

Bibliography

Books

Bramble, Jack. *The Playboy Collector's Guide & Price List.* Montreal, Quebec: Budget Enterprises, 1982.

Connolly, Robert. *Paper Collectibles.* Florence, AL: Books Americana, Inc., 1981.

Webb, Peter. *The Erotic Arts.* Great Britain: Farrar, Strauss & Giroux, 1983.

Catalogues

Petty & Varga Pinup Price Guide. Denis Jackson, Box 1958, Sequim, WA 98382 ($2.75).

Dealers

Back Issues, John Cairns, Box 1257, Temple City, CA 91780.

The Magazine, 839 Larkin St., San Francisco, CA 94107.

Martignette, Charles, Box 9295, Boston, MA 02114.

F

FIGURINES

Figurines can be five-and-dime schlock or stunningly beautiful small sculptures, and learning the difference, and the gradations in between, will turn the attic or closet collector into a happy, if not a more wealthy, expert.

History. As long as potters have been working clay, they have been making human or animal figures, either for ceremonial or decorative purposes. The oldest and finest figures are museum pieces; the newest can be found in the local gift shop.

Most ceramic figurines are made of porcelain, bone china, stoneware, or earthenware. They are usually made in factories, from molds created by individual artists.

Some figurines are identified by their factory name. Most of the original ceramics factories declined by the late nineteenth century, although those that continued to produce fine tableware also continued to produce figurines. Familiar names of manufacturers were Royal Crown Derby, Royal Doulton, Royal Worcester, Royal Copenhagen, Haviland, Sevres, and Lladro.

Other figurines were known by their place of origin: Staffordshire, Dresden, Belleek, and Delft are examples. And some were known by the artist's name, such as Doughty, Boehm, or Hummel.

★ **A book about figurines, *The American Birds of Dorothy Doughty*, was published by Royal Worcester in 1962. It featured color plates and descriptions by Doughty, and was issued in a limited edition of fifteen hundred. The publisher's price was $65. Ten years later, the book was worth $1,000.**

Values Outside the Home. In judging the value of figurines, age can be less important than beauty, so a well-informed beginning collector can buy a newly produced object knowing it will increase in value.

Whatever its age, the bottom of a figurine will have marks indicating the maker and, after the McKinley Tariff Act of 1891, country of origin if imported. Antiques guides found on the shelves of every public library detail the marks.

CAMPBELL KIDS, Courtesy Campbell Soup Co., Camden, NJ

Reminding many of us of winter days, warm kitchens, and Mom serving up tasty hot bowls of chicken noodle soup, the Campbell Kids remain some of America's most popular collectors' items.

The collector should decide what to buy based on personal taste as well as investment acumen. Figurines are meant to be displayed and enjoyed, after all, not stashed in a vault.

Personal taste, of course, changes with the times. Today's fad figure can be tomorrow's treasure. But today's exquisite creation will not likely be a throwaway tomorrow. So the collector of figurines should look for quality of design and execution, no matter what the style. If in doubt, the buyer should stick with figures designed by established artists for established firms.

Figurines produced in limited editions or for a limited time will naturally grow in value. Reputable firms will produce a specified number of figures, and no more. As soon as an edition is sold out, its price usually rises by 35% to 50% or more, depending on demand. A bird figure created by Edward M. Boehm of Washington's Crossing, Pennsylvania, that cost $100 in 1950 was worth thousands by the mid-'60s.

It may help to choose a favorite artist and manufacturer and a favorite subject as a framework for new purchases. Perhaps a family treasure will provide the key to a long-term collecting career, or the investor will be enamored of horses or angels or little children wearing big hats.

Mass-produced figures may also be good investments if they at one time appealed to popular sentiments or have historical interest. Most of them will break or be lost through the years, so those remaining will be valuable. Kewpies, Campbell's Kids, Billiken figures, and Brownies are examples of popular figures that are now collectors' items.

Toby jugs are another. These often-ugly crosses between pitchers and figurines were originally made by Staffordshire potters in England, but are now made in Japan, France, and the United States as well. Tobies, like other Staffordshire figures, commemorated famous people good or bad, and were priced to appeal to the general public. In 1984, Royal Doulton character jug prices ranged from $27.95 for a small Mark Twain to $2,100 for a large Mephistopheles.

Where to Find Values. The novice collector should study a book like the Kovels' *Know Your Collectibles* before embarking on a buying spree or before selling any family heirlooms. A little general knowledge will help prevent the purchase of a well-executed copy or a sale at too low a price.

Major manufacturers choose distributors or dealers carefully, which is another reason for the cautious beginner to buy only brand names. The prices for new figurines are set by the manufacturer, but the price on resale is wide open.

Some manufacturers sell their limited editions only by mail, advertising in art or antiques magazines or mass-market publications aimed at upper-income readers, such as *The New Yorker* (see "Catalogues" at the end of this chapter). Duty on imported figurines is 4%.

The best source for a novice buyer of any collectors' item is a good antiques store. If the buyer has done some research and knows what to look for, the dealer will enjoy helping. Dealers often know the history of objects they sell, and they may be willing to hold expensive items with a deposit.

Prices should be marked, although they may be in code. If there is no price, the buyer can assume that bargaining is in order. Offering three-quarters of the asking price is acceptable.

The prices at antiques shows will be somewhat higher than those at a dealer's, to pay for expenses and dealer discounts. But browsing through the variety of figures at such a show can be a good education.

Major auction houses hold large auctions just for particular types of figures, such as Royal Doulton. Antiques auctions are fun, but they can be dangerous for the ill-informed novice. Sales are usually final, and no one guarantees authenticity. The descriptions in auction catalogues sometimes read like real-estate ads, so the buyer should not be surprised if a particular figurine in reality turns out to be smaller or more faded or coarser in design than what was written about it by auction-house copywriters.

Garage sales, flea markets and rummage sales are often good sources for older figurines if a wily dealer has not gotten there first. The collector who has found an interesting item at such a sale should never put it down, because the person walking several paces behind will most likely pick it up and become its new owner.

Antiques magazines and newsletters may run classified ads for specific figures. However, the wise collector will respond to ads only if the figure can be seen before purchase. It is also advised that once a purchase is made, buyers get a statement from the seller, unless it is a reputable dealer, warranting the sole ownership and "full and unconditional right of disposal" of the figure.

In general, the novice should avoid bargains, which are illusory, and buying on vacations from unknown sellers. With time, the collector will learn how to spot reproductions or fakes, how to judge the age of a piece, and how to feel and smell for signs of glue, which will indicate a repair job.

A Price Sampling

Royal Worcester: "Cardinals and Orange Blossom,"	
D. Doughty	$3,000
Hummel: "Good Hunting," No. 307	80-1,500
Royal Worcester: "Jumping Horses with Riders,"	
Doris Lindner	1,300

Royal Doulton: "Cleopatra," HN 2868	915
Belleek: "Meditation," marked	900
Staffordshire: "Prince and Princess of Wales on Horses"	550
Royal Copenhagen: "German Shepherd"	450
Hummel: "Little Fiddler," No. 4	60-300
Staffordshire: "Dog," Arthur Wood	50
Royal Copenhagen: "Frog on Rock"	25

How to Store/Display. The collector should store figurines away from little hands and frisky house pets. Keeping them behind glass will minimize dusting.

Ceramic objects should be washed in warm, soapy water in a plastic basin, or on a towel in a metal basin. A soft brush can be used on the piece. Salt or borax will remove stains, and a mild bleach solution will restore age-browned porcelain. Vinegar should never be used, because its acidity may affect the glaze.

Collectors should keep their figures catalogued, giving each item a number and including the following information: description, date and place of acquisition, price paid, present value, notes and comments, its present location if lent out, and a photo if possible.

Insurance, of course, is essential. Breakage insurance, however, is usually more than the average collector can afford.

How and When to Sell. To find a proper asking price for a figurine, the collector might offer it to several dealers for their estimates, or look for prices of similar figures listed in trade journals and price guides. *Antique Trader Weekly* lists current selling prices for selected items, as do the annual price guides available in library reference sections. Some antiques magazines answer questions from readers about value. One query should be sent at a time, accompanied by a self-addressed stamped envelope.

A dealer purchasing for resale cannot offer full value to the seller and still make a profit. By selling through classified ads collectors can avoid these dealer discounts. One dealer suggests selling two or three items together in order to get a better price.

A good auction house may bring a decent price, but the seller should set a reserve price high enough to justify the sale and low enough to attract bidders.

Anyone selling through auction should be aware that a transaction may be marred by the "dealer pool" technique, whereby a group of dealers holds back during bidding, allowing one of their number to acquire a figure at a low bid. That dealer will then resell immediately at a private auction, called a *knockout*. Dealer pools are illegal in most states, however, and most auctioneers can spot one before it has had time to hurt either the individual selling an item, or the house auctioning it off.

★ Just as a persistent Saturday-morning shopper can find great buys at garage or house sales, such sales also can bring small fortunes to the sellers. The contents of a middle-class house in Maryland, sold by an eighty-year-old man after his wife died, brought $33,000 in one weekend, only $1,500 of which was furniture. The sale was handled by a reputable dealer; thus the owner was assured that each humidor, each piece of jewelry, and each porcelain figurine brought full value.

Little-Known Facts. Porcelain-making was a Chinese secret until alchemist Johann Friedrich Boettger, failing at making gold for Augustus the Strong of Saxony, tried using kaolin, more readily known as wig powder, in a high-fired clay body. Augustus evidently forgave Boettger for his failure and rewarded his ceramic success with a factory at Meissen, now known as Dresden.

Early nineteenth-century Staffordshire figurines were made of separate pieces put together. After 1850, potters used single molds, so later Staffordshire pieces show less detail. The later pieces also have flat backs, because they were designed to be chimney ornaments. These figurines were sold to the general public to celebrate life events or relate amusing anecdotes. Later figurines commemorated historical events and even famous criminals. Prices for these figures range from $50 to $5,000 and more.

Some Staffordshire animal figures do not quite resemble the creatures they were supposed to because the potters who made them had never seen the real thing.

Berta Hummel was born in 1909, studied art in Munich, and became the Franciscan Sister Maria Innocentia in 1934. Her ceramic figures helped support the convent. She died in 1946, and the rights to her designs went to W. Goebel-Porzellanfabrik. The value of a Hummel figure depends on its mark, which indicates its period of manufacture. Hummel reproductions come from Japan.

Dorothy Doughty created ceramic birds for Royal Worcester between 1935 and 1960. Like Audubon, she sketched the birds in pairs in their native habitats. In 1972, an out-of-edition quail brought $36,000 at auction! Would-be collectors should look in their family trees for lovers of ceramic birds....

—*Elinor Lindheimer*

Bibliography

Books

Atterbury, Paul, ed. *English Pottery and Porcelain*. New York: Universe Books, 1979.

Cole, Ann Kilborn. *How to Collect the "New" Antiques*. New York: David McKay Co., 1966.

Cowie, Donald. *Antiques: How to Identify and Collect Them*. New York: Castle Books, 1970.

Davis, P. et al. *Wemyss Ware: A Decorative Scottish Pottery*. New York: Columbia University Press, 1984.

Degenhardt, Richard. *Belleek*. Huntington, NY: Portfolio Press, 1982.

Flayderman, Norman, and Edna Lagerwall. *Collecting Tomorrow's Antiques Today*. Garden City, NY: Doubleday & Co., 1972.

Fredgant, Don. *Hummel Figurines and Plates*. Florence, AL: Books Americana, 1984.

Hotchkiss, John F. *Handbook of Hummel Art*. Des Moines, IA: Wallace-Homestead, 1981.

Hotchkiss, John F. *Limited Edition Collectibles*. Available from Hotchkiss House, 18 Hearthstone Road, Pittsford, NY 14534.

Kovel, Ralph and Terry. *Know Your Collectibles*. New York: Crown Publishers, 1981.

Smaridge, Norah, and Hilda Hunter. *The Teen-ager's Guide to Collecting Practically Anything*. New York: Dodd, Mead & Company, 1972.

Periodicals

American Collector. P.O. Drawer C, Kermit TX 79745.

Antique Monthly. P.O. Drawer 2, Tuscaloosa, AL 35402 (sample copy, $1.50).

The Antiques Magazine. 551 Fifth Ave., New York, NY 10176.

Antique Trader Weekly. P.O. Box 1050, Dubuque, IA 52001.

Catalogues

Aynsley Bone China, 225 Fifth Ave., New York, NY 10010 (free brochures).

Carol's Gift Shop, 17601 S. Pioneer Blvd., Artesia, CA 90262 (free brochures).

Chinacraft Ltd., 130 Barlby Rd., London W10 6BW, England (biannual illustrated catalogue).

Hudgeons, Thomas E., III, ed. *Official Price Guide to Hummel Figurines and Plates*. Orlando, FL: House of Collectibles, 1984.

Kovel, Ralph and Terry. *Kovels' Antiques & Collectibles Price List.* New York: Crown Publishers, 1984.

———. *Kovels' Illustrated Price Guide to Royal Doulton.* New York: Crown Publishers, 1984.

Stephen Faller (Exports) Ltd., Mervue, Galway, Ireland (Fallers of Galway mail-order catalogue, $1).

Dave Grossman Designs, P.O. Box 8482, St. Louis, MO 63132 (Norman Rockwell figurines based on 300 *Saturday Evening Post* covers; free).

Hickory House Collector, 108 E. Main, Ottumwa, IA 52501 ($1).

Joy's Limited Editions, 851 Seton Ct., Wheeling, IL 60090 (free).

McDonald's Collectibles, 1229 17th St., Manhattan Beach, CA 90266 (free).

Pitt Petri, Inc., 378 Delaware Ave., Buffalo, NY 14202 (free newsletters: Boehm, Cybis).

Schmid Brothers, Inc., 55 Pacella Park Dr., Randolph, MA 02368 (free folder, "Limited Editions").

Dealers (see also "Catalogues")

Miriam and Aaron Levine's Antiques Market, 881 Whalley Ave., New Haven, CT 06515 (Belleek).

Staffordshire House, Inc., 450 East 78th St., New York, NY 10021 (Staffordshire).

Mrs. L. Vilas, 1804 Queensguard, Silver Spring, MD 20906 (Specializes in porcelain, including Royal Doulton).

Associations

Angels Collectors Club of America, Four Whitewood Dr., Trenton, NJ 08628.

Hummel Collectors Club, 12161 University Dr., Yardley, PA 19067.

FINE FURNITURE

Furniture collecting spans centuries and continents. It is probably one of the most revealing of all of our artifacts, telling future generations a lot about how we have lived.

Furniture is also the single largest investment in most households, although most of us would agree that we spend miniscule time thinking about it, do not consider ourselves experts on it, and simply buy it because we need it, the same way most of us buy an automobile.

To become knowledgeable about the subject is not an easy matter. But one who realizes that he has been bitten by the antiques bug can, with a bit of study and an armful of common sense, learn the basics about period pieces and be on the road to happy collecting.

And who knows? Some lucky person may well discover that he has been reading this very chapter while perched upon a small fortune.

History. Up until the seventeenth century, homes full of furniture remained the domain of the upper class. But with the mercantile expansion in England and France, a new industrial middle class emerged and established a need for well-constructed pieces. Local craftsmen quickly appeared to cater to this demand, and for the next two centuries their painstaking labor and ingenuity produced beautiful articles that remain so today.

Most collectors concern themselves with English, French and American pieces from the eighteenth and nineteenth centuries, since seventeenth-century pieces are rare. American antique furniture is usually categorized in one of a few specific periods: Pilgrim (1600-1700), William and Mary (1700-1725), Queen Anne (1725-1755), Chippendale (1755-1785), Hepplewhite (1780-1800), Federal, including Sheraton pieces (1790-1820), Empire (1810-1840), and Victorian (1837-1901). Other examples exist apart from these categories, such as Golden Oak furniture from the 1880s to the 1920s, which is now popular again.

England, the dominating influence in American furniture, followed a similar timeline for the same styles except that some were created a decade or so earlier than American equivalents, or were not produced at all in the New World. There are many beautiful French styles, two of which are Louis XV and its simpler counterpart, French Provincial. But most of the French pieces available today are reproductions of originals and may be valuable in their own right.

★ One famous dealer/collector tells the story of a lovely table he once found, bought in the early 1950s, sold and then watched surface in the market again and again. His initial expenditure for the piece was a mere $2 and after some delay he sold it for $125. Next time he saw it and bought it, its price tag was up to $400, but he was able to sell it the next day for more than twice that sum. Indeed, the latest valuation of the piece stands at $15,000, and its former owner is still smiling.

Values Outside the Home. Appraisers and collectors alike agree that there are three basic options available to the antique furniture

Art Resource, New York

Furniture remained lavish (as displayed by this Louis XV collection at the Palazzo Widmann, Venice) and an indulgence of the upper and ruling classes until the rise of a European middle class in the seventeenth and eighteenth centuries created a need for simple, attractive, yet affordable and functional pieces.

hunter. He can buy antiques at the lower end of the price scale and hold on to them tightly for a few years. Though not of prime quality, these pieces can increase in value up to 100% in a short time. He can also buy museum-quality expensive pieces, whose value will rise gradually through the years, or he may simply purchase a variety of antiques to use and enjoy, and consider them quality investments in the future.

As important as "what to buy" in the opinion of many collectors is "what to ignore." The legal definition of *antique* as an item that is "... at least one-hundred years old" allows for a lot of junk as well as treasure. But certain signs distinguish old gems from younger reproductions, and one can examine genuine pieces and pictorial guides to become familiar with such features. For example, one should feel for the rolling, irregular indentations of plane marks on a chest of drawers from 1820, not clean, circular saw marks. An item should also show signs of normal or even excessive wear and tear from constant friction and use, not sharp corners and curves.

In general, before a collector buys, he should read voraciously, search eagerly, and then approach prospective antiques suspiciously, as if they are on trial and must prove their innocence beyond a shadow of a doubt.

★ While at an estate sale at the Lubin Galleries in New York, a clever collector saw a brown commode with a marble top and decided he wanted it. He wrote "$30,000" next to the listing in his auction catalogue and proceeded to show off this high "bid" to other dealers and collectors so that he could scare them off before the auction got underway. In addition, once the bidding had started, he jumped substantially from $700 to $1,000, and then to $3,000 when countered. He frightened off the stragglers with this technique, and secured the piece for $3,000—a trifling sum, considering the piece was signed by a very famous designer and worth well into five figures.

Where to Find Values. Where are the *best* antiques and the *best* bargains? Everywhere, but be careful, say the experts. Consider the reputation of any dealer and check him out through an association, such as the Art and Antique Dealers League of America. In addition to antiques shops, auction houses such as Sotheby's in New York, antiques shows and estate sales provide a wealth of furniture, and a sly buyer will learn a few tricks of the trade to become a successful bidder. Other possible hiding places for antiques are thrift and commission shops. Antiques dealers haunt them and learn when deliveries are scheduled, and so can a clever collector. Garage sales can also be fruitful, as can newspaper and trade magazine advertisements and, believe it or not, house wrecking/salvage yards—these can be veritable treasure troves for collectors.

A Price Sampling

Pair of George III rosewood and satinwood parquetry cabinets (attributed to John Linnell's workshop), c. 1770	$125,000
Bachman and Sayre Federal style grandfather clock, Elizabethtown, NJ, c. 1805, mahogany, 8'4"	29,700
Chippendale mahogany display cabinet, c. 1840	4,575
Set of ten Thomas Moser ladderback chairs	2,500
English piecrust tilt-top table, c. 1750, with Queen Anne legs, mahogany	1,500
Acorn four-poster bed with rolltop on headboard, widened and restored	650
Very plain Hepplewhite chair of the period	450
Carriage lamps with beveled-glass lights, rewired and restored; the pair	250
Boston Rocker with heavy pine seat	175
Child's chair from New England, c. 1830-1850, in Boston Rocker family	100

How to Store/Display. Protecting one's antique treasures can be a simple matter, because they are sometimes covered by a standard homeowner's policy against fire, theft, and a long list of other perils and catastrophes. The security-conscious collector may opt either to install a burglar alarm or photograph his valuables and take out a special policy. Good locks on the home are a must, as is common sense in caring for pieces.

Antiques should be enjoyed and used, but one should save them from small children, pets and general mistreatment or excessive use. Insurance policies do not protect against wear and tear or deterioration caused by rot or mold, so treat antiques to a cozy home. Finally, check with an appraiser or museum before repainting or restoring a piece, even if it seems to cry out for repair.

How and When to Sell. The most important element in the demand for antiques is economic prosperity. Essentials first, extras later. Fortunately, what one author calls the "age of elegance" has now given rise to a demand for beautiful furnishings. In short, it is a seller's market. Though certain styles go in and out of vogue, and some years are better or worse than others economically, a top-quality antique always has a market, and the wealthy connoisseur always has his weakness.

Prospective antiques sellers can use private dealers, antiques shows, auction houses and flea markets to collect data and make transactions. Private dealers often buy at auction and from wholesalers, but they will certainly buy from a private seller if the deal is a good one.

Appraisals are important too, and each one should be updated periodically, because it represents the ever-changing market value of a piece.

Selling at auction can be quite rewarding for the *informed* antiques owner. He should begin by stating a "reserve," or bottom price, below which he will not go. He must then acquire patience, for auction houses will not guarantee anyone a selling price, and they will refuse to sell pieces not in their league. Finally, a seller may not receive his money for more than thirty days after the close of a sale. On the other hand, auctions offer both quality clientele and the advantage of head-to-head competition, which can drive a price sky high.

★ **On a collecting spree in New York in the early 1980s a couple spied a pair of dark wood knife boxes, each two feet high, with light wood inlaid bands. They inspected the pair and noticed a third, smaller box that went along with the set, and it sported a tag reading: "Art Treasures Exhibition of 1928, No. 129." What had they found? After deciding they had to have the boxes and agreeing with the dealer on a price of $170 for all three, the couple rushed home and started to research their treasures. After a lot of effort and some clever thinking, they found records of the 1928 exhibition and discovered their boxes were worth more than $2,000! Even the dealer had done well on that sale, as the couple found out some time later: The garbage man had come by with the boxes and sold them to him for only $40.**

Little-Known Facts. In 1937, the United States Treasury Department noted that $640,633,302 in "aged pieces" had entered this country since 1909. It also stated that 75% of the total import of so-called antiques in the last thirty years were fakes!

• The infamous Brewster chair was a carefully created fake made in 1969 to look like a typical Pilgrim piece. The Henry Ford Museum innocently proclaimed it a genuine Pilgrim era chair and paid $9,000 for it. Only after the transaction took place did an investigation reveal the deception and cause a huge stir in the world of furniture collecting.

—*Cynthia White Tolles*

Bibliography

Books

Aronson, Joseph. *The Encyclopedia of Furniture.* New York: Crown Publishers, 1938.

Colt, Charles C., Jr., ed. *The Official Sotheby Parke Bernet Price Guide to Antiques.* New York: Simon and Schuster, 1980.

Day, David, and Albert Jackson. *Antiques Care and Repair Handbook.* New York: Alfred A. Knopf, 1984.

Jenkins, Emyl. *Why You're Richer Than You Think.* New York: Rawson, Wade Publishers, 1982.

Kovel, Ralph M. and Terry. *The Kovels' Complete Antiques Price List.* New York: Crown Publishers, 1982.

Ramsey, L. G. G., ed. *The Complete Encyclopedia of Antiques.* New York: Hawthorn Books, Inc., 1962.

Rush, Richard H. *Antiques as an Investment.* New York: Bonanza Books, 1968.

Shea, John G. *Antique Country Furniture of North America.* New York: Van Nostrand Reinhold Co., 1980.

Periodicals

Antique Monthly. Boone, Inc., Drawer 2, Tuscaloosa, AL 35402.
American Collector. P.O. Drawer C, Kermit, TX 79745.
Art and Antiques. P.O. Box 20600, Bergenfield, NJ 07621.
The Magazine Antiques. 551 Fifth Ave., New York, NY 10017.
Antique Trader Weekly. Babka Publishing Co., Box 1050, 100 Bryant St., Dubuque, IA 52001.

Catalogues

Colt, Charles C., Jr., ed. *Official Sotheby Parke Bernet Price Guide to Antiques.* New York: Simon and Schuster, 1980.

Kovel, Ralph and Terry. *Kovels' Complete Antiques Price List.* New York: Crown Publishers, 1982.

Dealers

Butterfield's Auctioneers and Appraisers, 1244 Sutter St., San Francisco, CA 94109.
Sotheby's, 1334 York Ave., New York, NY 10021 (branches all over the U.S.).
Christie's, 502 Park Ave., New York, NY 10022.

J. Cohen, 1006 S. Michigan Ave., Chicago, IL 60605.

Washington D.C. Antiques Fair, P.O. Box 6147, Silver Spring, MD 20906.

Associations

American Society of Appraisers, 60 E. 42nd St., New York, NY 10016.

Art and Antique Dealers League of America, 353 E. 53rd St., #2G, New York, NY 10022.

Mid-American Antique Appraisers Association, P.O. Box 981 C.S.S., Springfield, MO 65803.

National Antique and Art Dealers Association of America, 59 E. 57th St., New York, NY 10022.

FINE GLASS

The sparkle of cut glass by candlelight, the fragile quality of a hand-blown piece of Art glass, delicately painted or richly tinted, the Early American salt cellar, small enough to fit into the palm of the hand, the shimmer of an Art Iridescent vase.... It is perhaps these ephemeral qualities—delicacy, fragility, and iridescence, like stars in a frozen sky—that make glass one of the most desirable of all collectors' items.

Glass has been a highly prized possession since the first sands were melted and blown into decorative or utilitarian pieces. Since the early 1800s, the United States has produced many unusual and beautiful types of glass, all of which are uniquely appealing.

History. For anyone intrigued by the charm and beauty of ornamental glass, Sandwich, Massachusetts, in the mid-1800s would have been a delightful place to visit. The Sandwich Glass Company, one of the best-known Early American glass manufacturers, was in full production, making what are now coveted collectors' items. Sandwich was not an industrial center but rather like the site of a giant cottage industry, employing the majority of the town's people. Men created the glass pieces, women and girls decorated them, and boys carried wood to the furnaces. The factory in Sandwich, like those of other glass companies in the Northeastern United States, was producing pressed glass, which was a form of glassware that was available and affordable to the majority of Americans.

Initially molded, or pressed, glass was made into door knobs and drawer pulls. These items were so well received that manufacturers

The New England Glass Company produced both cut and hand-blown pieces, which were highly valued by wealthy Victorians.

began making curtain tie-backs, salt cellars (small salt dishes), and cup plates, which were designed to hold a tea cup while the tea first cooled, and then enabled the user to sip the tea directly from the saucer. The Sandwich Glass Company was well known for its decorative salt cellars. They came in many shapes and designs, were sometimes on pedestals, had scalloped bases, scrolled or claw feet, and were shaped like boats, sleighs, and sofas. Some had covers, others did not.

The earliest pressed glass was known as *Lacy glass*. It was made from about 1825 until the late 1850s, and was stippled, or covered with small raised dots, except where the design was molded. It was made and sold in individual pieces, not sets. The lace pattern and stippled effect were designed to conceal imperfections, but in the 1850s, a new process, called fire polishing, corrected the bubbling and other imperfections, and *Pattern glass* was introduced.

Pattern glass was produced from the 1850s until around the turn of the century. It was usually unstippled and made to be sold in matched sets. Pattern glass was enormously successful, and during the time it was produced, more than three-thousand different designs were created.

One way to determine the date of a piece of Pattern glass is by its design. The early pieces were simple and geometric; after the 1860s they became elaborate. Soda-lime-based glassware replaced lead, or flint, glass. Because very few manufacturers marked their work, and because the glass styles can be very similar, even pressed glass experts can mistake the identity of a particular piece.

At the Centennial Exhibition in Philadelphia in 1876, an enormous fountain of cut glass introduced this exciting new product. Only ten of the forty-three glass companies exhibited cut glass, but it was such a hit that within decades hundreds of glassmakers produced the showy pieces that were considered stylish wedding and anniversary gifts at the turn of the century. During the height of its popularity, almost anything normally made of glass was also made of cut glass. *Brilliant glass,* the most desirable form of this type, had red lead added to it to make it soft enough for cutting. Design motifs were achieved by making deep cuts into a glass blank with an abrasive wheel and then polishing the finished piece. Initially Brilliant glass was polished with pumice or jeweler's rouge on a wooden wheel, but after 1900 an acid dip was used that did not reproduce the same level of brilliance. The finest pieces of Brilliant glass were made between 1876 and World War I.

Good cut glass is a choice collectors' item. Household wares usually have less value than unusual pieces; colored pieces and custom-made pieces are more valuable. Special pieces were usually inscribed, especially if they were for exhibition or special occasions.

To assess the value of cut glass, one should make certain that no parts of the piece are ground down. Flowers and other designs should be whole, and nothing should run into the edges. There should be no flakes or chips on either the rim or the base. To check for invisible cracks, one should listen to the sound made by the glass when tapped. Genuine cut glass rings when tapped with a finger; the sound will be deadened if the piece has cracks. One should also check for mismated pieces; for instance, bottle stoppers were often replaced because they were easily dropped and broken.

Some cut glass was marked by some of the more popular manufacturers, such as Libby Glass Company and T. G. Hawkes and Company, but not all important glass companies used marks. Marks were applied with small rubber stamps that had been dipped into acid. Marks were stamped inside the centers of shallow bowls and plates and on the edges and bases of bottles and decanters. It may be necessary to use a magnifying glass to find them.

There are, of course, many inexpensive imitations of cut glass. Real cut glass is *always* sharply cut, usually with a characteristic V-shape that defines the major divisions of the pattern. Imitations are usually made of pressed glass or else cut on a pressed blank rather than being blown by hand. Pressed glass will have cuts with rounded edges. Imitation cut glass will also look somewhat worn.

During the latter years of the nineteenth century, hand-blown and painted pieces were made for wealthy Victorians, who had an almost unbelievable passion for collecting fancy bric-a-brac. *Art glass,* as it was known, was colorful and unusual, and is now considered one of the most sought-after and coveted collectors' items. It was initially made by commercial glass companies.

The special techniques necessary to produce the beautiful colors and shapes of Art glass were brought to America by Bohemian immigrants in the 1850s. There are a large number of colors and styles and several famous names in the field of Art glass. One very popular style was created in 1883, when Joseph Locke of the New England Glass Company invented and patented a technique of shading colored glass by reheating it. Called *Amberina,* it was made by adding gold powder to the glass, which created a shading from amber to ruby red. This lead to the production of many colors of heat-sensitive glass. Glassmakers would add glass beads, colored glass threads, and metallic flakes to the molten glass and to the surface of already-formed pieces. They also painted, engraved, and layered glass, and created frosted and crackled pieces as well as those that imitated mother-of-pearl and tortoise shell.

Some of the many popular types of Art Glass were *Quezal glass, Burmese, Bohemian* (colored glass that was etched or cut to the clear layer, its colors usually ruby, amber, or green), *Rainbow Mother-of-Pearl, Cranberry glass* (one of the best known), and *Peach Blow.* Among the best-known Art glass producers were Tiffany, Durand, and Thomas. *Tiffany glass* was produced from the late 1800s until just after

World War I by the flamingly redhaired Louis Comfort Tiffany. Made for the cultured and wealthy, his exquisite windows, dishes, desk pieces, vases, and lampshades were suddenly passe by the 1930s and were tossed in junk heaps, attics and basements. The prices they now collect are astonishing. A medium-size Tiffany window (admittedly a rare find) goes for over $50,000! But collectors should beware of both old and contemporary look-alikes, many of which are very convincing.

Steuben glass, made during the time of Tiffany, was equally as elegant and expensive. Decorative Steuben pieces, often in the shapes of animals, are quite precious and fetch large sums.

Emile Galle was the biggest name in *Cameo glass,* which was made of several layers of glass molded together and then cut through to show the different colors and to make details stand out in relief. *Wave Crest,* produced by C. F. Monroe Company, was also very well received. Known for its hand-painted, projected shapes, it is considered an important collectors' item. Art glass was produced from the 1880s until just before World War II.

Another glass that was popular during this period, though not really Art glass, was *Custard glass.* Custard glass—either milk white or yellow—was quite prevalent during the 1880s and was revived as a collectors' item some time ago.

★ **Roberta Hise has a shop in a collectors' cooperative in San Carlos, California. She recommends that people use their intuition as well as good taste in choosing collectors' items. She did just that at a garage sale a few years ago when she spotted a pretty vase for sale at $10. She bought it because she liked it and because something about its style suggested that it could be valuable. Indeed, Roberta later discovered she had purchased a piece of Quezal Art glass appraised at $750.**

Values Outside the Home. Those interested in accumulating valuable glass should begin by evaluating any pieces already collected. If they are unusual or special, it will be worthwhile to find out more about them either from an appraiser or through books, and then create a collection around them.

Those collecting for the first time should consider any of the types of glass mentioned in this chapter, for all of them have value. There are also contemporary companies making exquisite pieces that are already valuable and that will continue to appreciate over the next twenty years.

Since it is increasingly hard to differentiate between original and contemporary pieces and the variety of Art glass, one should consult an appraiser or a specialist if there is any doubt about authenticity.

Where to Find Values. A lot depends on the type of glass one is collecting as to where to find the best prices and selections. Checking through the ads of weekly newspapers is often fruitful, and some cities have special collectors' tabloids that specialize in a certain item. Collectors' associations that publish their own newsletters will also be represented in tabloids. It is helpful to subscribe to any newsletter that covers one's field of interest. They are excellent places to get names of other collectors and often to find items for sale or for trade.

One should also get to know local dealers, who can be valuable stepping stones towards knowing other dealers or collectors specializing in particular items.

A Price Sampling

Cut-glass pitcher, signed	$300
Crystal goblet, decorated with gold leaf, c. 1930s	75
Lacy glass salt cellar	75
Cambridge glass crystal bowl	70
Cameo glass from Phoenix Glass Co., c. 1920s	55
Art glass, a small piece (most Art glass is very valuable and can be priced into the thousands)	35

How to Store/Display. Because it is so easily broken, glass needs special attention. The ideal way in which to display it, and also to protect it, is to place pieces in a glassed-in cabinet. Clear glass sides will allow in light to show off items to their best advantage, but they will keep dust out and eliminate the chance for breakage. One might also place pieces on a glass window shelf, but it is important that the shelf never be exposed to direct sunlight, which could fade colorants used in the pieces. When displaying glass, it is important that individual pieces are well supported.

Glass can be washed in warm water and a *mild* soap. If possible, one should use a plastic container as a basin rather than one made of metal or enamel, to avoid chipping the item. Pieces should be washed individually, rinsed thoroughly, and then dried with a lint-free cloth.

How and When to Sell. Most collectors' items will continue to become more valuable over time, so that selling has less to do with items hitting a peak than with upgrading or disbanding a collection.

Before selling, the items should be appraised, so that one becomes aware of current market values. The same tabloids and newsletters used to obtain new pieces also can be used to sell pieces. Swap markets and gun (surprisingly) or special collectors' shows are always good places to sell.

★ In 1906, a Tiffany Wisteria lamp cost $400—the annual salary of a school teacher then. In 1984, a small Tiffany piece bought fifteen years ago at a San Francisco Bay Area yard sale for $5 and used as a jelly bean holder sold for $500!

Little-Known Facts. Prior to the late nineteenth century, all factory-produced glass, whether free blown, mold "blown" or pressed, remained unmarked. Most glass companies, instead, stuck a paper label to the bottom of a piece. This makes identification difficult today. Additionally, many pieces that were not made by a famous manufacturer may later have been marked by someone trying to create a more "valuable" item.

• Louis Tiffany chose not to go into the family jewelry business, but instead took off for New York and Paris to paint. In 1892 he formed the Tiffany Glass and Decoration Company. Although all pieces bear his name, many of his most famous works were created by other designers under his supervision, who remained anonymous. They *were* well paid, however.

• True Cranberry glass was made with gold powder. In the late 1800s, copper powder was substituted because it was less expensive. However, it also created objects with an orange tinge to them. Later still, color was *applied* to a piece by a process called "flash firing." Items made this way can be discovered by holding a piece to the light.

—*Patricia Rain*

Bibliography

Books
Boggess, Bill and Louise. *American Brilliant Cut Glass.* New York: Crown Publishers, Inc., 1977.

Koch, Robert. *Louis C. Tiffany: Rebel in Glass.* New York: Crown Publishers, Inc., 1964.

Periodicals

Kovels on Antiques and Collectibles. P.O. Box 22200, Dept. BPL, Beachwood, OH 44122.

Catalogues

Schroeder, Bill. *Collectors Illustrated Price Guide, Cut Glass.* Paducah, KY: Collector Books, 1977.

FIREARMS

Firearms have been with civilized man since the fourteenth century in every shape, size and caliber, but few have survived to the present. Whether lost, broken, discarded or just stuck away and forgotten, it is these long-buried relics that raise the adrenalin level of collectors, who all seem to be looking for that 1735 .50-caliber Flintlock pistol worth $6,000.

History. No one knows where, when or by whom the first firearm was discharged, except that the event took place sometime in the 1300s. It is also recorded history that a monk of the Franciscan order, Roger Bacon (1214-1296), did in fact experiment with gunpowder, often disturbing his fellow monks and more than once blowing holes in the walls of his laboratory.

At least a century passed from those first days of experimentation before survival overcame gallantry and firearms replaced swords and lances. Previously, firearms were considered cowards' weapons, and generals and knights alike demanded and enforced a death penalty for anyone using them on the battlefield. Yet, firearms survived and became popular, achieving an efficiency and a powerfulness that early proponents could not have foreseen.

Today, beginning collectors hear such terms as *matchlock, wheel lock, percussion, breechloader* and *repeated.* All of these refer to some stage of firearm development, and each stage either directly or indirectly touches on the sciences of mechanical engineering, mathematics, chemistry, physics, thermodynamics, pneumatics, metallurgy, kinetics and metrology.

★ Shortly after their grandmother died, a family was sorting through her personal effects. Hidden in the back of a closet was a canvas bag. Remaining unopened, it was given to the youngest heir. Later he found out that the bag contained a Civil War sniper rifle complete with scope. No dealer would put a price on it, and it was later sold at auction by sealed bid for a large, undisclosed amount. But there was speculation that the winning bid exceeded $50,000.

Values Outside the Home. The beginning collector should buy what interests him, although he should also be aware of several things before he makes his first purchase. First he should understand that there are three main categories of firearms. They are:

Handguns	*Rifles*	*Shotguns*
Antique	Antique	Antique
Revolvers	Single shot	Single shot
Automatics	Lever action	Over/under
Small caliber	Bolt action	Double-barrel
Larger caliber	Automatic	Pump
Limited edition	Commemorative	Automatic
Manufacturer	Manufacturer	Manufacturer

Each category has been further broken down into seven different configurations, which again could be further classified by time period, origin, specific caliber, and design. With over eighty-four total classifications from which to choose, it does not take a whiz kid to know that a little research is in order before one can even begin to think about buying.

What gives value to a collectors' firearm is a combination of desirability and scarcity. The Colt pistols are more in demand than Colt rifles. Why? Because they take up less space. Rifles are preferred for other reasons, perhaps because there have been more commemorative rifles offered than handguns.

There are only three simple rules for collectors to live by: 1) collect what you feel comfortable with, 2) learn everything possible about your area of collecting, and 3) deal with someone you trust.

Rules 1 and 2 are simple enough, but what about No. 3? Finding a dealer with whom one feels comfortable may require visiting a number of shops in the beginning, but it will be a wise investment of

Library of Congress

Firearms, which were once integral to everyday life among American colonists and settlers, are today purchased primarily for their exquisite workmanship and their value to other collectors.

time, since the new collector can be assured of getting a genuine article at a fair price.

What to buy first is another problem. There are 84 manufacturers of handguns, 109 for rifles and 64 for shotguns listed in the *Gun Trader's Guide,* which gives you 5,397 guns of all kinds to choose from. Refer to rule No. 1.

Where to Find Values. Attending a gun and collectors' show will be an experience one does not soon forget. All of that fire power under one roof! There are enough guns, knives, ammo, books and clothing to more than outfit a small army. The uninitiated can be intimidated, unless they understand that most dealer–sellers are very helpful and more than willing to answer questions.

Certain firearms are always in demand and hard to find. The Walter PPK was made famous by James Bond; John Wayne increased the demand for the Colt .45 and Winchester rifles; and Tom Selleck helped make the Army Colt .45 automatic scarce. So beginners should be realistic in their search; it lessens the chances of being disappointed.

Magazines such as *Soldier of Fortune, Eagle* and *Survival* give the impression that anyone can order a handgun through the mail. This is not true. Only licensed federal firearm dealers can *legally* sell any handgun, no matter when it was made, where or by whom. Anything that deviates from this can land one in a federal prison. (Refer here to rule No. 3.) Before buying any handgun, it is best to check with local law enforcement agencies.

Rifles and shotguns are other matters. Anyone can walk in off the street, put down his money and walk out carrying either one. But, as with handguns, only a licensed firearm dealer can sell either through the mail.

★ A gun dealer in San Jose, California, invested in a Colt Saur-drilling rifle in 1979 for $1,690. It had two barrels on top for shotgun shells and a single-shot rifle barrel below. Made in West Germany for Colt, it now sells for $3,382 — a profit of over 200%, if the dealer were to sell, which he won't.

A Price Sampling

The following are prices for firearms in excellent condition:

Luger Parabellum (all models), 1900-1945	$ 700-$45,000
Holland & Holland (any shotgun, any year)	2,300-17,500
L. C. Smith Hammerless double-barrel shotgun	1,050-15,000
H & H Limited Edition Springfield carbine, 1873	3,500
Weatherby Deluxe Magnum rifle (discontinued 1958)	900
Weatherby Deluxe rifle (discontinued 1958)	800
Colt Peacemaker Centennial .45 (1,501 produced), 1975	635
Smith & Wesson Texas Ranger Commemorative (8,000), 1973	625
Remington Wingmaster field gun	225
Harrington & Richardson model 155 single-shot rifle	80

How to Store/Display. Any collectors' item requires a certain amount of tender loving care. Firearms need just a little more. Susceptible to rust, firearms should be stored in an area where the temperature and humidity are consistent. Just stacking guns in the corner of a closet is a sure way to downgrade a collection. The serious collector also might think about buying a gun vault, available from most dealers. They not only protect firearms from moisture but from thieves as well. One collector converted a spare closet into a vault ten feet by ten feet. His collection, valued at over $150,000, is wiped clean at least once a month and is cleaned internally twice a year.

If one prefers not to use a gun vault, then make certain each firearm has its own case. It will at least keep the gun from being scratched and the finish from fading.

Another item that is cheap compared to replacement price and frustration is insurance. The National Rifle Association offers a replacement policy with membership, and some home-owner insurance policies cover such items.

Finally, remember, firearms sell best in mint condition. If one has bought a gun as an investment, do not take it out on the firing range with any intention of shooting off a few rounds. To do so will reduce the gun's worth by approximately $100 per shot.

★ Recently, an article ran in the *San Francisco Chronicle* about cowboy legend Doc Holliday's great-granddaughter, who found his Colt .45. It is alleged to be the same gun he used in the shootout at the O.K. Corral. No one will attempt to put a price on such a relic until it is authenticated, which began late in 1984. If it is indeed the same gun used by Holliday, it could bring at least $25,000.

How and When to Sell. If one has been doing his homework, he will know what each of his prized firearms is worth and what it is currently selling for. To know less is like swimming in a small pond with sharks, where one will lose more than his shirt.

Gun, antiques, and collectors shows are the best places to sell guns (as well as buy them). But one should check local laws carefully if selling handguns. It is easy to get into a lot of trouble by offering one for sale without a federal firearms license.

Nor should one overlook advertising in reputable gun publications, such as *Shotgun News* and *Guns and Ammo*. The drawback here is that it may be months between the time the ad runs and one begins to receive responses to it. Then weeks or months may pass before the transaction is completed. The advantage to advertising, however, is that one reaches more potential buyers at one time.

It is important that collectors keep track of what their investments are doing. If prices go up, it is a sign to hang on to those guns. If they begin to drop and show a steady decline, it is time to sell. Or one might be lucky and foresee a trend before the rest of the market does.

Above all else, a wise collector should never be in a rush to sell, for no matter how good he may think he is at bargaining, there is always someone out there who is better. Instead, the smart collector will know what he has, what it is worth, and exactly what he will sell it for.

Little-Known Facts. The most valuable gun in the world is a 1610 Flintlock pistol made for Louis XIII by Pierre le Bourgeoys. It is one of the three oldest flintlocks known to exist. The Metropolitan Museum of Art in New York City paid $305,000 for it at a sale in London.

• During the 1870s, an occasional Winchester rifle barrel was especially engraved with "One in a Thousand" because of unusual performance tests. These are now prized collectors' pieces.

—John Shriver

Bibliography

Books

Allen, W. G. B. *Pistols, Rifles and Machine Guns.* London: English Universities Press, 1953.

Bearse, Ray. *Sporting Arms of the World.* New York: Harper & Row, 1976.

Ezell, Edward Clinton. *Small Arms of the World.* Harrisburg, PA: Stackpole Books, 1977.

Hatch, Alden. *Remington Arms in American History.* New York: Rinehart & Co., 1956.

Madis, George. *Winchester Book, The.* Dallas, TX: George Madis, 1961.

Wahl, Paul. *Gun Trader's Guide.* South Hackensack, NJ: Stoeger Publishing, eleventh edition.

Periodicals

American Handgunner. 591 Camino De La Reina, San Diego, CA 92108.

Guns & Ammo. 8490 Sunset Blvd., Los Angeles, CA 90069.

Guns. 591 Camino De La Reina. San Diego, CA 92108.

Shotgun Sports. P.O. Box 5400, Reno, NV 89513.

G

CHAPTER 8

Gemstones

Greeting Cards, Postcards, Labels

GEMSTONES

Shimmering rich green emeralds, beaujolais rubies, moss green peridots, soft pink kunzites, cloudy violet amethysts, dreamy Brazilian tourmalines, champagne imperial topazes—a riot of exploding colors. Symbols of kings, of power, of love. And money. Your pulse increases, your head spins. You are Ali Baba, and Sesame just opened. Or you are merely browsing through Tiffany's.

History. It all began with a legend. Prometheus became the first collector of jewelry when he made a gem-set ring out of the rock to which he was bound and the chain that bound him. Renaissance princes passed their time breeding horses and hawks and collecting jewels and jeweled works of art. Jewels were early considered a resource for rainy days—there were pawnbrokers even in the time of the Ptolemys. Marcus Aurelius sold his own jewel collection at public auction to defray the cost of war. A king would carry gems on a journey or into a battle to buy off possible captors.

Since ancient times, gemstones have been thought to possess magical powers. Drinking water mixed with crushed aquamarines cured laziness. Emeralds were good for the eyes, yellow stones cured jaundice, red stones would still blood and soften anger. No wonder they were so sought after.

★ **In the spring of 1984 a poorly dressed woman came into Butterfield & Butterfield, San Francisco, asking for the jewelry department. She began pulling Tiffany bracelets, pins and sapphires out of her bulging pockets. The jewelry staff gasped. She had inherited the "stuff" from her mother, she said, but was afraid to wear it. Was it perhaps worth something? Butterfield & Butterfield sent her a check for close to $50,000.**

Values Outside the Home. There are four "Cs" which the beginning gem collector must consider before buying or selling. The first is *color.* In a gemstone it should be vivid, pure and intense. As for

Smithsonian Institution

Although the market for gemstones is fickle, fascination with certain baubles will never diminish. The Hope diamond is still revered in spite of diamonds' dwindling value.

diamonds, the most valuable are completely colorless (there are some fancy pink and blue ones that bring equally fancy prices: in 1983 at Sotheby's, New York, a 9.58-carat pink diamond worth about half a million dollars was stolen while on display—the clever thief dabbed pink nail polish on a stone of much lesser value and exchanged the two).

The other three Cs are *cut, clarity* and *carat.* Cut determines brilliance. Clarity is the absence of internal and external flaws. Carat is the international standard for weight. Weight should not necessarily influence a purchase: a large but flawed stone is less valuable than a smaller gem of finer quality.

The market is fickle. Since its dazzling performance in 1980 the diamond has deflated like a pricked balloon. Even top-quality rubies and blue sapphires are below their all-time highs. However, many semi-precious stones have held their own. Some, like tourmalines and aquamarines, have even risen in value. When any of these stones are set by the likes of Tiffany, Van Cleef & Arpels, Harry Winston, or Cartier, they cease being just gems and become works of art. And, it follows, pricey.

Where to Find Values. There is no bargain basement for gemstones. It is imperative to buy only from reputable jewelers, dealers or auction houses and to stay clear of high-pressure sales tactics. Sales people can be very persuasive indeed, as a woman learned a few years ago, just before the diamond market collapsed. While she was out shopping, her husband committed $145,000—their entire retirement nest egg—to a smooth-talking saleswoman who told him there was no time to lose; the price of diamonds was going up over the weekend....

Retail jewelers mark up their merchandise 100% or more. But, as Mark Twain pointed out, "Let's not be too particular. It's better to have old second-hand diamonds than none at all." Experts from top auctions tend to agree. At auction one pays only one-quarter or one-third of retail. New collectors are encouraged to go to auctions and watch the dealers, who are easy to pick out because they are bidding on fifteen or twenty pieces rather than one or two. Novices should watch what they bid on and how they bid.

★ One day in 1974 a young man from a small southern town walked into the Smithsonian in Washington, D.C. with a ruby his father had brought back from World War II. As he recalled, his father had said something about the stone being worth some money. He was right. It turned out to be the finest 10-carat Burma ruby the Smithsonian curator had ever seen. He told the young southerner not to take a penny less than a quarter of a million dollars for his ruby—if he ever decided to sell it.

A Price Sampling

The following jewelry and gems were sold at top auction houses around the country. Prices are current as of 1984.

Ring, 27.52-carat Kashmir sapphire set by Tiffany & Co. (Sotheby's)	$220,000
Ring, 46-carat blue star sapphire set in platinum (Butterfield's)	25,000
Bracelet, Art Deco, diamond, emerald, platinum by Yard, approx. diamond weight 14.7 carats (Butterfield's)	9,000
Ring, Lapis Lazuli set in gold with ten small diamonds, approx. diamond weight 1.0 carat (Butterfield's)	1,800
Ring, turquoise, diamond and black onyx by David Webb (Christie's East)	1,600
Pin, amethyst pearl heart (Butterfield's)	400
Ring, oval tourmaline set in gold with one star sapphire, four Biwa pearls, one red tourmaline (Butterfield's)	400
Aquamarine, unmounted 2.24 carats (Christie's East)	110
Sapphires, three unmounted totaling 3.88 carats (Christie's East)	60

How to Store/Display. It seems a shame to hide gems in safe deposit boxes (although many collectors do). Gems were not meant to shine in bank vaults, nor can they. They were meant to be worn and enjoyed. And while they are being worn, their value will probably increase.

Opals should be stored in moist cotton to maintain their beauty. Turquoise rings should be removed before washing hands, or they will turn a nasty shade of green (turquoise is called the "stone of love" because it supposedly changes color when a lover is being unfaithful).

How and When to Sell. All gem investing is done with the distant future in mind. Appreciation takes time, so patience is a must if an investment is to pay off.

In 1981 a woman decided to sell her rare 5-carat blue diamond. She took it to a dealer. Not knowing the full market value, the dealer showed it to another dealer and asked $100,000 for it. The second dealer promptly wrote up a check. He knew what he had. He then turned around and sold the diamond for half a million dollars to a third dealer, laughing all the way to the bank. The moral? One should sell only through a dealer who knows the market of a particular stone. And he should always ask for a second opinion, either from another dealer or a reputable auction house. At auction houses stones may not always be recognized for their full worth, but at least they will have the chance to be seen by knowledgeable persons. And chances are they will bid it up to a fair price.

★ **Before going off to World War II, a young man gave his girlfriend a necklace. He never came back. The young girl eventually forgot the young man—and the necklace. Thirty years later she found it in a drawer. She took it to Butterfield's, wanting to know if it was gold. It was. And not only that, it was also a superb example of French Art Nouveau jewelry—a *plique a jour* with golden sapphires and diamonds, signed by the great French designer Gautrait and first sold by the famous Baily, Banks and Biddle in Philadelphia at the turn of the century. It sold at auction to a New York collector for $14,000.**

Little-Known Facts. Jewel thieves seem more romantic and resourceful than ordinary crooks, to judge by the following:

The comtesse de Lamotte-Valois convinced Louis XVI's grand almoner, the Cardinal-Prince de Rohan, to buy, in greatest secrecy, a necklace of 647 diamonds weighing 2,800 carats for Marie Antoinette (the queen's appetite for jewels was well known). A meeting was arranged between the cardinal and the queen in the moonlit garden. The necklace was exchanged, and the "queen," who was really the comtesse, disappeared without a word. So did the necklace.

• Ali Pasha, who ruled Albania for the sultan of Turkey, had two most valuable possessions: a magnificent diamond, and a young and beautiful wife whose name was Vasiliki. The sultan wanted both and planned to chop off Ali's head. Ali got wind of the plot, and to foil the sultan he ordered one of his men, d'Anglas, to destroy the diamond and kill Vasiliki. As Ali watched, d'Anglas smashed the diamond. The sight so shocked Ali that he fell down dead. Happy ending? Yes! D'Anglas scooped up the now-multiple gems, fled, and lived happily—with Vasiliki—ever after.

• Dario Sambucco, alias Dante Spada, was a legendary thief with great style. His heists on the French Riviera in the 1950s made headlines. His only weapon was a penknife to pry open difficult jewel boxes. He left no signs of entry, no fingerprints. When he was finally caught, he sued film director Alfred Hitchcock, from his jail cell in

Milan, for using his life as the basis for the film "To Catch a Thief" (starring Cary Grant). He lost.

—*Birgitta Hjalmarson*

Bibliography

Books

Goldemberg, Rose L. *All About Jewelry.* New York: Arbor House, 1983.

Kovel, Ralph and Terry. *Kovels' Collectors' Source Book.* New York: Crown Publishers, Inc., 1983.

Matlins, Antoinette L., and Antonio C. Bonanno. *The Complete Guide To Buying Gems.* New York: Crown Publishers, Inc., 1984.

Schumann, Walter. *Gemstones of the World.* New York: Sterling Publishing Co. Inc., 1984 (reprint).

Snell, Doris J. *Antique Jewelry with Prices.* Lombard, IL: Wallace-Homestead, 1984.

Zucker, Benjamin. *Gems and Jewels: A Connoisseur's Guide.* New York: Thames and Hudson, 1984.

Periodicals

Art & Auction. 250 West 57th St., New York, NY 10019.

Connoisseur. P.O. Box 10174, Des Moines, IA 50374.

Gems and Minerals. Box 687, Mentone, CA 92359.

In Focus. GIA Alumni Association, 1660 Stewart St., Santa Monica, CA 90404.

The Jade Collector. 33112 Lake Rd., Avon Lake, OH 44012 (newsletter).

The Lapidary Journal. P.O. Box 80937, San Diego, CA 92138.

Ornament, A Quarterly of Jewelry & Personal Adornment. P.O. Box 35029, Los Angeles, CA 90035-0029.

Precious Stones Newsletter. 7315 Wisconsin Ave., Suite 1200N, Bethesda, MD 20814.

Catalogues

Hudgeons, Thomas E., III, ed. *The Official 1985 Price Guide to Antique Jewelry.* Orlando, FL: House of Collectibles, Inc., 1984.

Auction Catalogues

Butterfield & Butterfield. 1244 Sutter St., San Francisco, CA 94109.

Christie's. 502 Park Ave., New York, NY 10022.

Christie's East. 219 East 67th St., New York, NY 10021.

Dealers and Specialists

Carl D. Lindstrom & Sons, Inc., 624 South Grand Ave., Los Angeles, CA 90017.

Don Gruenberg, Inc., 9431 Brighton Way, Beverly Hills, CA 90210.

Hansen Minerals, 1223 Port Royal, St. Louis, MO 63146.

James Robinson, 15 East 57th St., New York, NY 10022.

Klaus Murer, 370 Sutter St., San Francisco, CA 94108.

Murray & Appel, 210 Post St., Suite 306, San Francisco, CA 94108.

Paul Fisher, 608 5th Ave., New York, NY 10020.

Shirley Molbert Leass, 14 Pound Hollow Rd., Old Brookville, NY 11545.

S. J. Shrubsole, 104 East 57th St., New York, NY 10022.

Associations

The Bead Society, P.O. Box 605, Venice, CA 90291.

GIA (Gemological Institute of America) Alumni Association, 1660 Stewart St., P.O. Box 2110, Santa Monica, CA 90404.

International Club for Collectors of Hatpins and Hatpin Holders, 15237 Chanera Ave., Gardena, CA 90249.

Sotheby's, 1334 York Ave., New York, NY 10021.

William Doyle Galleries, 175 East 87th St., New York, NY 10028.

GREETING CARDS, POSTCARDS, LABELS

If colorful, artfully designed graphics and remembrances of things past tend to warm the cockles of your heart, maybe it is time to look into collecting postcards, greeting cards and fruit crate labels.

These paper products, among others, fall into a category of perishable collectors' item defined by the Ephemera Society of America as "the minor transient documents of everyday life."

History. *Philocarty* or *cartephilia,* words from the Greek meaning "a hopeless lover of cards," is what the early collectors called their hobby. Present-day collectors call it *deltiology,* combining two Greek words meaning "small picture" and "knowledge."

People began collecting picture postcards in Europe in the late 1800s, and by the turn of the century, the craze had reached the New World. In 1913 alone, Americans bought 968 million postcards, with subjects in more than fifteen-hundred categories, including modes of transportation, expositions, street scenes, politicians and political events, national monuments, novelties, advertising, natural wonders, and oddball restaurants and diners.

Most of the cards collected today date from 1910, although collectors are now beginning to turn their attention to the "view" cards of the 1940s and 1950s, which captured such scenes as the Golden Gate Bridge, Niagara Falls, and Mt. Rushmore.

Actually, 1912 proved to be the high point of the postcard craze in America. A few years after World War II, the postcard collecting frenzy died out completely, not to be revived until the 1960s. What started the craze all over again was perhaps an awareness on the part of a new generation of collectors that the old picture postcards had exquisitely captured, in miniature, a part of the past gone forever.

World War II was not the only cause for the decline of interest in collecting postcards. About the same time, the greeting card was introduced in America. With its beautifully drawn designs, colorful artwork and larger message space, it soon took over in popularity with collectors. Developed and first published in England, c. 1850, the greeting card actually evolved from the formal "visiting" cards, used for calling on friends at Christmas, and the decorated writing paper of earlier times.

Fruit crate labels have a much shorter history as a collectors' item. Originally, they were colorful lithographs that displayed a company's name and a romantic scene oftentimes showing an Indian chief or maiden, early California, or plump, appetizing pieces of fruit. Growers in California, Florida and other fruit-growing regions of the country affixed these to the ends of crates used to ship oranges, lemons, grapes and other fruit during the late 1800s. In the 1940s and 1950s, when growers switched to cardboard boxes, the bold, brightly colored lithos became collectors' items.

★ **One California dealer recently reported two occasions on which his clients found old albums containing postcards in their attics, brought them in to be appraised, and were pleasantly surprised to find that the cards were worth $1,000 — apiece.**

Values Outside the Home. As with any collectors' item, whether acquired for pleasure, profit or both, the first rule applies: Buy what you like.

The best investment buy in cards and labels, however, is the rare and unusual item, preferably in excellent condition and signed by the artist.

For postcard collectors, the signed-artist cards of the Art Nouveau and Art Deco movements in Europe and the early twentieth-century schools in America are highly recommended. These high-quality postcards should be collected with long-term goals in mind. Names of key artists to remember in this category are Mucha, Kirchner,

Q. David Bowers/*The Postcards of Alphonse Mucha*

The works of Art Nouveau artist Alphonse Mucha are prized today. Postcards printed with artwork bearing his signature can fetch up to $700.

Humphrey and Greenaway. Five years ago, postcards by the famous Art Nouveau artist Alphonse Mucha sold for $50 to $75 each; today, the same cards are priced at $200 to $700.

Somewhat less expensive but also popular with collectors are the postcards designed by Ellen Clapsaddle (children and suffrage motifs); Grace Gebbie Wiederseim-Drayton (Campbell soup kids); and Rose O'Neill (Kewpies), with works by the latter two artists being somewhat rare and therefore fetching higher prices. Other popular American artists include Charles Dana Gibson, Harrison Fischer, James Montgomery Flagg and Phillip Broileau. A signed Gibson now sells for $15 to $20.

Many of these artists, including Howard Chandler Christy, and William and Rebecca Coleman, also created designs for the then fast-emerging greeting card business. The most popular of this group was

Kate Greenaway, who later became famous as an illustrator of children's books.

The most sought-after greeting cards were published in England by Charles Goodall & Sons, Marcus Ward & Company, De La Rue & Company, and Raphael Tuck & Company; and in America by L. Prange & Company between 1860 and 1890. Also collected are the early cards by modern American publishers, such as Rust Craft Greeting Cards, the Gibson Art Company, and Hallmark Cards.

While the serious collector sticks to Christmas and New Year cards, many collections also include Valentine, Easter, Thanksgiving, birthday and novelty cards. Some cards are prized for their design, others for their signatures and still others for their messages, but only the rarest of antique greeting cards are worth very much money.

Rarity among fruit crate labels is not the only guiding factor in making a purchase: design is also important. Labels were printed in great quantities in the late 1800s, and more imagination went into some than others, especially the orange crate labels. Fruit labels from 1880 to 1920, showing highly detailed three-dimensional scenes, for example, are scarce and bring high prices, often as much as $500.

Labels from California growers are generally worth more than those from Florida and other fruit-growing states, and citrus labels are more desirable than those showing apricots, pears, apples and other fruit.

Some valuable brand names include Angora, Tiger, Strength, Fearless, Red Riding Hood and John Alden. Others are Wildflower, Orange Blossom, La Loma Queen, Diving Girl and Southern Plantation. The Strength label, depicting an elephant, now sells for $25 to $30.

Where to Find Values. Good buys in postcards can be found at general and special auctions and shows throughout the United States, through sales lists published by dealers, and in the bulletins published by the numerous clubs that formed after the revival of collecting in the early 1960s. Postcards, greeting cards and other paper products often turn up at garage sales, flea markets, estate auctions and rummage sales. Fruit labels may be purchased at the large paper shows, from dealers, and through advertisements in collector periodicals. Many dealers will upon request send out photocopied lists of their card and/or label inventories free to the buyer who includes a self-addressed stamped envelope.

A Price Sampling

"Eugene V. Debs" postcard (Socialist Labor Party candidate for president in 1908)	$100-110
"Kewpies" postcard signed "Rose O'Neill," with signature painted over on original	60-75
"Tiger" label (oranges)	45-50
"Endurance" label (camel)	35-50
"Animals" postcard, Wain & Theill, signed	30-50
"Interior of St. John's Church" postcard (Richmond, VA)	30-35
"Athlete" label (three runners)	7-10
"Diving Girl" label	5-10
"Sunflower" label (citrus)	3-5
"World's Fair" postcard (New York, 1939, linen)	1-2

How to Store/Display. Since cards are usually collected according to rarity, publication date, artist and subject matter—and fruit labels by plant location, subject matter and fruit type—it is essential for the new collector to learn to identify the various artists, paper stock, publishers and growers to insure that he/she is buying items of value.

A word of caution: the quality of a purchase should be in excellent-to-mint condition. The cards and labels should have clear, sharp images, no writing or other markings on the surface of an illustration, and no tears, creases, worn edges or bent corners. Cancellation marks on the *back* of postcards neither add to nor detract from the value of the item.

One should remember, too, that he will be dealing in items that are transitory. Therefore, care should be exercised in the handling and storage of them. Some collectors prefer to protect items in loose-leaf binders with clear plastic pages; others practice more elaborate methods. For long-term storage of a valuable collection, the serious collector might even take into account the acid content of the storage container and the moisture level of the room.

When starting out, one should bear in mind that most collectors specialize—some of the more popular categories are history, Thanksgiving greetings, art, transportation, California oranges, politics, Christmas greetings, geography, airships, and photography. Due to the enormous number of cards published, the possibilities here are unlimited, which is why many collectors select a category in which there is cross-over; that is, a collector of railroad memorabilia collects train postcards, or a collector of erotica crosses over to greeting cards featuring female nudes.

How and When to Sell. Collectors generally rely on two channels for buying and selling their wares: the network of clubs related to each specific collectible, and the United States mail. Card and label dealers will often mail out bundles of their inventory to a prospective buyer. The buyer picks out the items he/she wants and returns the rest along with payment for the items selected. Cards and labels are also bought and sold at flea markets, secondhand stores, antiques shops, and real estate auctions and sales.

Like the seasons, the public's interest in collecting paper products runs in cycles. As with other collectors' items, the best time to sell is when interest is running high. There are no fixed rules, no guidelines.

★ **A San Francisco, California, man presented a dealer with what he termed an "ugly" card, gray in tone with no picture, just little colored specs in the card stock, apparently worthless. Upon closer inspection, the dealer realized that his client had a mascerated money card, printed on stock made from currency destroyed by the government. Value: $150.**

Little-Known Facts. Almost every city in America has had its main street immortalized on a picture postcard, which usually can be found for sale near the checkout counter of the local drugstore.

• Postcards were originally published for collectors.

• Since postcards provide a vivid, graphic representation of the change and growth of a city or town, many institutions, museums and historical societies have become avid collectors.

—*Gregory Frazier*

Bibliography

Books

Buday, George. *The History of the Christmas Card.* New York: Spring, 1954.

Carline, Richard. *Pictures in the Post.* Deltiologists of America: 1971 (see "Associations" for address).

Chase, Ernest Dudley. *The Romance of Greeting Cards*. New York: Tower Books, 1971.

DiNoto, Andrea, ed. *The Encyclopedia of Collectibles*. Time-Life Books. Alexandria, VA, 1979.

Klamkin, Marian. *Picture Post Cards*. New York: Dodd, Mead & Company, 1974.

Miller, George and Dorothy. *Picture Postcards in the United States — 1893-1918*. New York: Clarkson N. Potter, 1976.

Range, Thomas E. *The Book of Postcard Collecting*. New York: Dutton, 1980.

Salkin, John, and Laurie Gordon. *Orange Crate Art*. New York: Warner Books, 1976.

Periodicals

Better Postcard Collector. 10 Felton Ave., Ridley Park, PA 19078.

Hobbies. Lightner Publishing Corp., 1006 S. Michigan Ave., Chicago, IL 60605.

Postcard Dealer. P.O. Box 27, Somerdale, NY 08083.

The Postcard Collector. Padre Productions, P.O. Box 1275, San Luis Obispo, CA 93406.

Associations

Citrus Label Society. 16633 Ventura Blvd., Suite 1011, Encino, CA 91436.

Deltiologists of America. 10 Felton Ave., Ridley Park, PA 19078.

Ephemera Society of America. 124 Elm St., Bennington, VT 05201.

International Postcard Collectors Club. Charles von der Ahe Library, Loyola-Marymount University, 7101 W. 80th St., Los Angeles, CA 90045.

International Seal, Label and Cigarband Society. 9815 E. Bellevue St., Tucson, AZ 85715.

National Valentine Collectors Association. Box 1404, Santa Ana, CA 92702.

Prang-Mark Society. Old Irelandville, Watkins Glen, NY 14891.

CHAPTER 9

Homemade American Furniture

HOMEMADE AMERICAN FURNITURE

That old chest or chair on Grandmother's back porch you've thought about stripping and refinishing may be worth twice as much with the paint left on it. That table in the garage made by your great grandfather that appears best suited for kindling may bring several hundred dollars and end up in the living room of a sophisticated home.

History. The recent surge of patriotism in the United States has brought with it a demand for anything made by hand during the nation's earlier days. While furniture and artifacts made by the more sophisticated craftsmen have been valuable for many years, the current tendency to cling to any aspect of the American past has increased the value of a wide range of items that were previously considered crude and ordinary.

The most sought-after pieces among antiques collectors and discriminating homeowners today are examples of homemade American country furniture that were originally painted and still retain some evidence of those colors. Usually made by the man of the house or a local craftsman before the Industrial Revolution, this furniture has long been labeled "primitive." Now it is viewed as an important part of the American heritage, valued for the very imperfections that caused recent generations to look down on it. In fact, many dealers today will agree that there was nothing primitive about these handcrafted pieces, that far from being crude, they were designed and assembled by sophisticated craftsmen with sophisticated tastes.

★ **A Midwestern family had always cherished a small bedside table with a single drawer because it had been handmade by an ancestor in the mid-nineteenth century. A recent appraisal established a value of $450 for the primitive item.**

Values Outside the Home. To determine the value of family heirlooms or that ugly duckling discovered at a flea market or a garage sale, it is necessary to pursue a four-point examination: (1) Was it made by

Philadelphia Museum of Art

Excellent examples of Shaker furniture show the beauty of uncluttered lines and straightforward functionality. The hand-rubbed finish gave pieces an elegance that concealed their true physical strength.

hand? (2) How old is it? (3) Was it originally painted? (4) Has it been drastically altered or repaired?

To learn whether a piece was made by hand or by machine, one must search for imperfections in the craftsmanship. Are the legs identical, or is there some deviation? One should not be misled by recent repairs; there must be enough similarity in workmanship to prove that all parts were made by the same person. When examining chests, it is important to go over all the drawers. Is the dovetailing of the boards so perfect that it could have been done only by a machine? Are there marks from a carpenter's plane on unfinished wood? If so, there is evidence that no machine was used. Factory-produced pieces are always smooth. Marks from a circular saw usually indicate that a piece was made by hand after 1830, when that tool came into common use.

In the investigative process, one should be aware that there are many excellent reproductions on the market today. Even the experts can be fooled by some of them. Unless one is willing to take a chance on a purchase, he is safest buying only from an antiques dealer who will stand behind the authenticity of the furniture. If one is determining value of something he already possesses, he should seek the opinion of two or three knowledgeable dealers. He should offer to pay for the appraisal without indicating an interest in selling, since the dealer may be interested in acquiring the item himself at a bargain. Collectors should also consult the many books on homemade American country furniture as aids in identifying period and style.

Now to determine whether any paint is original. A visual inspection should suffice in detecting recent paint, as both latex and enamel are modern finishes. Any drips will also provide evidence of twentieth-century finishes. To learn what lays beneath recent coats, the surface should be gently scratched with a coin. In coats beneath the topmost, one should look for signs of aging. Separation of paint, known as "crazing" or "alligatoring," comes only with age. Muted color is another indicator. As one begins stripping away top coats — and this should be done only after consulting experts on how to do it — cracks and joints should be examined to see if they are free of the initial color, since they would have separated with the aging of the wood. Nicks and scratches free of paint indicate they were made after the paint was applied.

Earlier furniture paints were actually stains. Buttermilk was used frequently as a base because of its binding quality. The colors were produced from whatever was available, including berries, tobacco leaves and animal blood. Red, black and yellow were used from the seventeenth century onward. Blue, which brings the highest price today — as much as two-thirds more than other colors — was popular in the nineteenth century. Red, white and gray came into use after the 1830s. An undercoating of red was used frequently during the eighteenth and nineteenth centuries and is highly desirable to collectors.

Other evidence of original paint includes kitchen tabletops free of paint, resulting from daily scrubbing after use. Even on the most worn furniture, however, there should be evidence of paint on legs and supporting members. In today's market, it does not matter how little paint remains; it is the verification that the paint is original that counts. Decorators and collectors love the appearance of the worn, faded colors. Many people prize furniture that has more than one early color showing, no matter how strange it may appear. Such a condition gives evidence of the furniture's "paint history." The earlier painted furniture is worth as much as twice the price of a similar piece from the same era without paint.

Even more valuable is furniture with fake wood graining. A common technique in earlier centuries, it is in demand today because of the rare art form it represents. A wide variety of techniques was used, including application by combs, crumpled newspaper, feathers, candle smoke and sponges. The elaborate multicolored decorations usually associated with the Pennsylvania Dutch are sometimes found on furniture from other parts of the country. These pieces bring top dollar from collectors.

Shaker furniture, made by members of religious colonies on the East Coast, has been prized for many years and continues to increase in value. It includes both painted and unpainted versions, all recognizable by their simple, functional forms. The most common examples are slat-backed chairs, which were sold commercially throughout the nineteenth century.

The final step in the evaluation process should be to check for major repairs. The replacement of one leg of a table or the feet of a corner cabinet will not diminish value to any great extent, but the fewer repairs, the higher the price. The demand for homemade country furniture is so high, however, that well-made attractive pieces bring top dollar even with major alterations—someone seeking a special accent piece for a home is less concerned with perfection than the serious collector.

★ A large corner cupboard with original green paint was purchased from an out-of-the-way secondhand shop in Tucson, Arizona, for $1,500. A Scottsdale, Arizona, antiques dealer, who estimated the origin at early-to-mid-nineteenth century and verified the paint as original, paid the purchaser $2,000 for it a few weeks later.

Where to Find Values. If one's interest is authenticity, it is best to buy only from a reputable dealer who will guarantee the history of a piece. Collectors may expect the highest prices from the better antiques shops and at large, well-established antiques shows. They should not expect any bargains in today's market unless they have the knowledge to spot a valuable piece in an unsophisticated shop out in the country or on the edge of town. Collectors may want to investigate flea markets and garage sales, but unless they get there before the doors open, they can count on the dealers having beat any competition to any diamonds in the rough.

A Price Sampling

Triple-back Windsor, New England (1740-1780), with comb-back above bow-back (rare), once a rocker, stripped, refinished	$2,500
Continuous-arm Windsor chair, Rhode Island (1780-1790), some repairs; stripped and refinished	1,750
Stepback hutch, New York (1815-1825), weathered gray second coat; some evidence of red undercoat	1,650
Extra-long settee, New England (1820-1830), evidence of original paint	1,500
Ladderback commode chair (early nineteenth century), original finish	1,250
Fireplace mantel, wood with original paint (c. 1800)	1,200
Corner cupboard, New England (mid-nineteenth century), some original paint on exterior, newly painted interior, upper doors removed	1,100
Four-slat Ladderback chair (mid-nineteenth century), original rush seat	750
Bedside table, Pennsylvania (1820-1830), no drawer, stripped but with slight evidence of original paint	675
Three-slat Ladderback chair (mid-nineteenth century), original finish, rush seat	375

How to Store/Display. Unlike many other collected items, the average individual can appreciate owning homemade American furniture only if it is functional within the home. The most valuable examples belong in museums. Because of their primitive character, however, maintenance is no problem. The arid Southwest is a poor environment for any wood furniture; unless it is thoroughly oiled on a regular basis, it will dry, crack and separate from joints.

How and When to Sell. The only practical way to sell individual pieces is to offer them to dealers, who can be expected to pay about 50% of retail value. If an item is known to be of special worth, one may want to advertise it in one of the many antiques magazines or in local and regional antiques newspapers. A periodic check of dealers' prices on similar furniture will help determine fluctuations in the market.

Homemade American has been very popular for several years, but most experts believe prices have not yet peaked. Now is a good time to obtain top dollar for any furniture from the period.

★ **A family decided to get rid of an old Windsor chair that had been gathering dust in the attic for many years. Although one foot was badly damaged, a dealer, estimating it as an early-twentieth-century version, purchased it for $75 and resold it, without repair, for $145.**

Little-Known Facts. Furniture from the earlier days of this nation was painted to hide the fact that several types of wood were used in the construction. Local craftsmen used whatever wood was available, since they were interested only in the function of the finished piece. Pine and other soft woods were often painted because they tend to darken with age.

—Karl Nordling

Bibliography

Books

Fales, Dean A., Jr. *American Painted Furniture 1660-1880.* New York: E. P. Dutton, 1979.

Marsh, Moreton. *The Easy Expert in American Antiques.* New York: J. B. Lippincott Co., 1978.

Raycraft, Don and Carol. *Collector's Guide to Country Furniture.* Paducah, KY: Collector Books, 1984.

Voss, Thomas M. *Antique American Country Furniture.* Philadelphia, PA: J. B. Lippincott Co., 1978.

Periodicals

The Antiques Magazine. 551 Fifth Ave., New York, NY 10176.

Art & Antiques. 1515 Broadway, New York, NY 10036.

The Auctioneer. 867 Madison Ave., New York, NY 10021.

CHAPTER 10

Inventions

INVENTIONS

"How can *women* learn to type?" was the male outcry when, around the turn of the century, New York City's YMCA instituted its first women's typing course. Today one wonders how *anyone* could have learned to type on those early, clumsy "writing machines," whose keys often jammed and whose peculiar construction prevented the operator from seeing what he—or she—was actually putting down on paper.

Those clattering machines are collectors' items now. But in their time they provided women (who *did* learn to type) with the opportunity for "respectable" work outside the home, and in so doing, struck the first important blow for women's liberation.

History. Typewriters, sewing machines, telephones, cameras...history buffs and people fascinated by technological advances have always considered inventions to be milestones in the progress of civilization, but it was only in the 1960s that inventions started to gain popularity as collectors' items. Today, collectors throughout the world share the historian's fascination with these objects that changed—and made—history and which, through their evolution, show us not only where we have been, but where we are going.

★ When a broken hot-water tank flooded their basement, Harry and Eleanor Smythe were forced to clear out huge piles of old things they had not used in years. Among them were, a forty-year-old Royal portable and two ancient Singer sewing machines. Eleanor decided to have the items appraised, and to her delight, the money she was paid for the old machines was enough to buy a new hot-water tank and a bottle of champagne to celebrate.

Values Outside the Home. With so many different kinds of inventions, the beginning collector may have some difficulty deciding which one to choose. Even once he decides, there are additional choices to be made. Should he collect by period? By style? By manufacturer? How

Library of·Congress

Inventions attract collectors who not only appreciate the item for its function but also for what it signifies historically. The typewriter was a passkey for women who wanted to work outside their homes, the significance of which now is unquestionably historic.

about by specific features, or even by certain colors? One person will collect only Singer sewing machines; another, cameras with leather bellows, and a third will search for Eliot Ness-type telephones of the 1920s. On the other hand, one might want to follow the example of a Mr. Joseph M. Updegraff, whose typewriter collection was eventually donated to Oregon State University; at one time he had attempted to locate a model of every typewriter ever invented.

To those would-be collectors who find the elimination process overwhelming, do not despair. It is usually at the point of desperation that an unexpected "find" will appear.

Where to Find Values. The seasoned collector searching for specific items will make his interest known to specialty dealers and will pore over their catalogues. But for the beginner, flea markets, garage sales, estate sales and church bazaars are unique treasure houses where prices may be low and where the excitement of the hunt is surpassed only by the thrill of discovery.

★ **Looking at fancy new cameras she could not possibly afford, aspiring photographer Ella Brooks spotted an illustration of an antique camera in an advertising poster. "I have one that looks just like it," she remarked to the store owner. He looked interested. "I know a collector who would want it. If it's really that antique model, we might make a deal."**

The next day, Ella walked in with her ancient, obsolete camera—and walked out half an hour later the proud owner of the expensive, late-model camera she had been dreaming about!

A Price Sampling. Though a certain amount of wear is to be expected, general condition of an item reflects on its price. Pieces in reasonable working order are the most highly valued. Any item that also comes with a case that is still in good condition is worth even more. The following are recently listed dealer prices—thrift bazaar or garage sale prices can be quite different.

Telephones

Western Electric wall model, oak	$190
AT&T candlestick, patented 1892	100
Desk model with dial, 1939	7

In general, early models with carved oak boxes and the "candlestick" type from the early part of the century are the most sought after.

Cameras

Bell & Howell Foton, 50mm	$300
Agfa 5×7 field view, 250mm	80
Keystone, model C, handcrank, 16mm	10

Special note: Detective cameras disguised as books, handbags, candy boxes, and other everyday items are popular for their clever concealments.

Sewing Machines

Singer, ornate iron, carved, 1900	$225
New Wanzer, with instructions and parts list, patented 1882	100

Typewriters

Hammond, 1904	95
Underwood portable, 1922	50

Next to enthusiasm, what the collector of inventions needs most is *space* — a collection of typewriters or sewing machines can hardly be stored in a box or pasted into an album. But if space is no problem, such a collection can turn a home into a museum. In fact, many collectors have become respected authorities on their subjects, and their collections are often exhibited in museums and other public viewing places.

Apart from being careful not to trip over them, inventions require little care. Items with cases or covers should be kept in their protective housings, dusted or oiled as needed, and generally looked after as any other comparable item in one's home. Be cautious, however, when testing electrical appliances, because old, frayed wiring could be dangerous.

★ **Fourth-grader Joanie Wilcox was thrilled when she got an *A+* for her project on the history of inventions, which involved an old Brownie camera, an ancient adding machine and a candlestick telephone from her grandmother's attic. Grandma Wilcox was even more pleased when, the day after, the father of one of Joanie's classmates, an antiques collector who had seen the exhibit, offered her $200 for the three old machines.**

How and When to Sell. Because inventions require the specialist collector to appreciate their rarity or historical value, an advertisement run in the daily classifieds or in one of the collectors' periodicals will often draw good response from other enthusiasts. Sellers can also profit by doing business directly with a specialty dealer, who will either buy outright or handle the sale on commission.

With the modern acceleration of technology, interest in inventions as collectors' items has grown steadily. There can be no doubt that by basing his collection on relics of the past, the farsighted collector can reap a worthy profit in the future.

Little-Known Facts. "My God, it talks!" exclaimed the King of Brazil upon being shown the remarkable telephone of Mr. Alexander Graham Bell. A colorful story, though not very likely? Actually, a Brooklyn teacher eventually confessed to having invented the tale in order to inspire his pupils with a love for science.

• When William Seaward Burroughs produced his first fifty adding machines, no one but he and one of his salesmen were able to operate them. It is recorded he later went to the storeroom and threw the fifty machines, one by one, out of the window.

—*Vera Abriel*

Bibliography

Books
Hudgeon, Thomas E. III, ed. *Guide to Antiques & Collectibles.* Orlando, FL: House of Collectibles, 1984.

Periodicals
Photographic News. P.O. Box F, Titusville, FL 32781.

Dealers and Collectors
Bays, C., 3214 Foxhall St., Columbia, SC 29204 (sewing machines).
Lippman, Paul, 1216 Garden St., Hoboken, NJ 07030 (typewriters).
Weiner, Allen and Hilary, 80 Central Park West, New York, NY 10023 (cameras).

Clubs
Antique Telephone Collectors Association, P.O. Box 94, Abilene, KS 67410.

J

CHAPTER 11

Jewelry

Jukeboxes

JEWELRY

The word *jewelry* connotes a certain mystique, with images of exotic places, precious metals, sparkling gems, carved ivory, and luxuries known only to royalty and the aristocracy.

Body adornments seemed to have been a part of man's apparel since he began walking upright and wearing skins. Beads fifty-thousand-years old have been found by archeologists. But jewelry has always been more than just a way of enhancing one's appearance. It also has been a symbol of status and prestige, used to advertise a family's wealth, and equated with—and often used as—money.

Jewelry is also something that will never lose its appeal and desirability, or its value. So it is well worth the time it might take now to rummage through one's attic and closets, for it is quite possible that wearable—and valuable—treasures are stashed there simply collecting dust.

History. In order to provide an overview of current valuable jewelry, it is necessary to go back to the 1830s. At this time jewelry was crafted by hand, from the preparation of metals to the faceting and polishing of stones, the carving of ivory, bone, seeds or coral, to fashioning a finished piece. Jewelry was expensive not only because of the materials and labor involved in making it, but because only a limited number of pieces could be produced by one craftsman.

It was during the reign of Queen Victoria, with the advent of the Industrial Age, that machines were created which could mold and stamp jewelry as well as produce quality synthetics to substitute for the real thing. By the third quarter of the nineteenth century, the middle class was wealthy enough to purchase jewelry, and by the end of the Victorian era, mass-produced jewelry was affordable to the working class.

During her long reign as Queen of England, Victoria dictated fashion throughout Europe and North America—and Victoria *loved* jewelry. In the early years of her sovereignty her taste in jewelry was

Library of Congress

Queen Victoria's fondness for jewelry influenced both Europeans and Americans, who learned to love silver, jet, opals, and sentimentality.

ornate and fanciful. Through her, silver gained status and to a certain extent replaced gold. Coral, ivory, jet, and bog oak, all of which could be carved and hand turned, were used. Semi-precious stones were quite popular, though diamonds were the favored gem during the 1890s, and a piece displaying one large stone was preferred to one holding several smaller stones. The Australian opal mines were discovered during this period. Amber and *gutta percha,* a natural plastic from the resin of Malaysian trees, were also very popular. Snakes were common motifs in Victorian jewelry because

Victoria was so fond of them that she even had her wedding ring styled to look like one.

It was during this time that ancient artifacts were being excavated in Italy and Egypt. Designers incorporated motifs and even duplicated pieces. This gave rise to the Classic Revival, the Renaissance, and the Gothic Revival styles of jewelry.

The prevailing attitudes during the Victorian era were sentimental love, family solidarity, and obsessive mourning for those who had "passed on." The jewelry clearly mirrored these.

Although mourning jewelry was at a peak after the death of the Prince Consort, it was popular as early as the seventeenth century. But in 1861, when Albert died, Victoria imposed upon herself a strict discipline of mourning for the rest of her life, a style adopted by many of her subjects.

Jet became the most popular jewelry to be worn while in mourning. Found along the Yorkshire coast, the jet industry, centered in Whitby, employed over fifteen-hundred workers to produce elaborate beads, pins, brooches, medallions, bracelets and rings, often carved and polished. The jet industry was short lived, however, due to the introduction of cheaper substitutes.

Bog oak was also popular for mourning jewelry as was ivory and tortoise shell. However, the most curious jewelry was fashioned from the hair of the deceased. Watch chains and bracelets were the most common, but very few pieces of hair jewelry have survived. On the other hand, brooches and lockets with a sealed central frame and containing plaited hair are not uncommon finds in homes where family jewelry has been inherited. Mourning lockets usually have the initials of the deceased inscribed on them.

In the 1880s, photographs began to replace hair in mourning lockets, which were not exclusively for mourning but were meant also to carry the picture of a sweetheart or family member.

By the late 1880s, mourning was replaced by love-oriented and sentimental jewelry. Silver love brooches became the rage. They were fancy pieces, sometimes depicting the name or initials of the wearer, or they were covered with hearts, flowers, birds and butterflies. Meaning was attached to each symbol on a piece of this type of jewelry. Flowers, hands, anchors, knots, and hearts were symbolic of emotions, attitudes and aspirations. A heart meant love and affection; a crown meant "queen of my heart." A heart, anchor, and cross together symbolized faith, hope and charity. Coral intimated love and warmth. Pearls on mourning jewelry symbolized tears. These sentimental pieces continued to be popular into the Edwardian period and even after, and can be found in family collections and antiques stores.

In the middle of the 1880s, the school of design known as *Art Nouveau* began in England with the Arts and Crafts movement, which preached a return to the old ways of handcrafting jewelry, furnishings, and books.

The Art Nouveau school flourished in France, where jewelry became lavish and extravagant. The work was sensuous, incorporating maidens, nymphs, bats, dragonflies, and fish. Enamel was used more than gems, and silver was often the metal. American jewelry during this period copied French styles. Companies such as Unger Brothers, William Kerr and Company, and Marcus and Company were the leading names. Because Art Nouveau jewelry emphasized hand work, good jewelry was not made in quantity. However, machine-made Art Nouveau jewelry is available and quite desirable.

During the first decade of the twentieth century a number of designers began to adapt ideas from Cubist art, Aztec temples, abstract African art, and Egyptian motifs, as well as the streamlined, sharply defined lines of the new machinery being used in industry, creating a style that later became known as *Art Deco.*

The fluid, languid lines of Art Nouveau gave way to startling contrasts and geometric forms. Brilliant colors replaced muted tones, and manmade materials replaced gems and precious metals. Although synthetics were used, they were of good quality. The finest Art Deco jewelers were, again, French, but Americans produced unusual and innovative jewelry of their own. A lot of the Art Deco jewelry was mass produced and is still widely available. The most attractive pieces to collectors are massive plastic bracelets set with rhinestones, and earrings made with enamel, rhinestones and chrome. Synthetic amber was quite popular also, and was made from Bakelite, a synthetic resin invented in 1909 by Leo Bakeland. Bakelite was used extensively in the 1920s and 1930s for jewelry and later by industry for its adaptability. Celluloid too was popular and often known as French ivory. Art Deco jewelry was produced up to the 1940s.

In the late 1940s and the 1950s, the emphasis was on costume jewelry. Anything that glittered was in, and rhinestones in multitudes of colors became popular. Many of these items were very inexpensive, but if brand names such as Trifari, Patti Carnegie, Lisner, and Weiss (specializing in rhinestones) were stamped on a piece, it became valuable.

During the early 1970s the work of Native Americans became prized among collectors. All American Indian tribes made some jewelry, but the fairly recent jewelry of the Navajo, Hopi, and Zuni Indians has become the most commonly collected.

Navajo jewelry is massive, simple, and mainly of cast silver, which is heavy, thick, and has a roughened finish. The Zuni used semi-precious stones and unusual settings. The Hopi initially copied other Indians' techniques but developed their own style in the 1930s, placing polished silver ornaments on backgrounds of oxidized silver. The oldest Southwestern Indian jewelry is known as *old pawn* and is now hard to find.

Age, value of the materials, and craftsmanship are the factors that determine the quality of Native American pieces. The finest jewelry was that made for personal use or to be traded within a tribal community. Heavy coin silver that was evenly polished, and clear-blue, hard turquoise are the key materials to seek.

★ **As Michelle Tomlinson was picking through a box of jewelry "dress-ups" the children frequently played with, she found an old glass necklace given to them by an older relative. Curious, she took it to a bead store, where she discovered the "glass" necklace was actually faceted rock crystal, worth $100. The store owner gave her a clue to determine whether an item is made of crystal or glass: Rock crystal is cold to the touch and will remain cold when held in the hand; glass will quickly absorb the heat and become warm.**

Values Outside the Home. The value of jewelry depends on materials, craftsmanship, condition, and the availability of a piece or style. Gold is more valuable than silver; sterling silver is more valuable than alloys or coin silver; and pieces that are marked are generally more valuable than ones that are not.

Knowing some of the terms used in the art and craft of jewelry and ways of determining what a piece is made of is essential in deciding what to buy and whether an item already in one's possession is worth having appraised.

Appraisal is the best way of determining authenticity, and this should be done by a specialist, not well-meaning family members, one of whom might overrate a piece, while another declare it to be nothing more than junk.

Naturally, older jewelry, such as true Victorian or Art Nouveau pieces, will be valuable, especially if they are gold or sterling silver and in good condition. However, pieces only twenty years old, and fortunate enough to be of rhinestones or unusual, can also be in demand.

Where to Find Values. Buying and selling jewelry can be a challenge because the styles and values are so variant. Most Victorian, Art Nouveau, and Art Deco jewelry is sold in antiques stores or jewelry stores that feature antique or estate items. Although older valuable jewelry occasionally shows up in estate sales, collectors' markets, or even at garage sales, it is possible to be "taken," sometimes as much by one's own ignorance as by the person doing the selling, *unless* one is familiar with hallmarks (stamps certifying purity of the precious metal, often identifying maker, date and place of manufacture), testing for authenticity, and how to refer to the various types of jewelry.

Quality costume jewelry may show up anywhere. There are a number of new small shops and boutiques in most big cities that carry vintage and unusual pieces. Remember, marked jewelry is more valuable than unidentified pieces in most cases, and gold or sterling is more valuable than coin silver or metal. However, collectors should not overlook jewelry being made by local crafts people or quality "primitive" or "ethnic" jewelry. Handmade jewelry, if unusual or of any quality, always has value as a collectors' item.

A Price Sampling. Jewelry prices vary enormously. Geography, awareness of value, age of the piece, condition, quality, desirability and availability are all factors in determining worth.

Baltic amber necklace	$200-$500
North American Indian pieces, top quality	200 plus
Art Nouveau pendant	125 plus
Peking Glass necklace	75 plus
Ivory bracelet	75
Bakelite necklace	12-60
Art Nouveau piece, machine made	45 plus

Cut-steel pieces	30 plus
Celluloid bracelet	18 plus
Weiss rhinestone earrings	16-18

How to Store/Display. Jewelry should be kept in boxes or containers that minimize contact with dust, airborne minerals, or chemicals that may cause tarnish or discoloration. Also, earrings have a way of disappearing or losing mates, so it is wise to be consistent and keep them in one spot.

Gold, silver, and jewelry set with real stones should be cleaned periodically with commercial cleaning solution or by boiling for about five minutes in water to which a few drops of liquid soap and ammonia have been added. *Never* use this solution, however, to clean pearls, opals or amber. These should be cleaned with warm, soapy water only, then dried with linen or terrycloth. Rub a little oil on opals and jade to discourage drying and to add luster. Never expose opals, pearls or amber to hair sprays, perfumes or harsh chemicals. Rhinestone and other synthetic jewelry should be washed in warm, soapy water occasionally, and perhaps even scrubbed with a fingernail brush to remove oil buildup. Do not use a commercial solution on synthetic jewelry, because it might dissolve glues or even the piece itself. Jeweler's cloth, also known as *rouge cloth,* can be purchased in jewelry stores and is an easy, effective way to polish gold, silver, and other metals quickly.

If a jewelry collection includes some valuable pieces, it is wise to keep the pieces in a safe or safety-deposit box. Travel with inexpensive jewelry if possible, or leave valuable pieces in a hotel safety-deposit box.

How and When to Sell. Jewelry can be easily sold through ads or in collectors' trade newsletters. Many boutiques or collectors' cooperatives will take jewelry on consignment. However, one should remember that when selling this way, the profit is apt to be minus 30% to 60% of the going price. So it is worthwhile to hold on to a piece a little longer, since it will likely appreciate anyway.

Sometimes a trade can be arranged, and that may be more profitable to the seller. This is also a good way to upgrade a collection. While jewelry may have a high appraised value, it can be difficult to get full value for most pieces unless there is a current trend for a particular type of item and a scarcity in the marketplace (this is what is currently happening with rhinestones—now is an excellent time to sell). Any good gold, platinum or sterling silver jewelry is bound to become more valuable over time and should be kept in a safe place to sell in the future or to pass on to a relative or loved one.

★ **Joe McPherson discovered a tarnished silver and turquoise Indian belt buckle in a drawer. When he had the buckle appraised, he discovered that it had been made for the tourist market around the turn of the century and has a current value of $200.**

Little-Known Facts. Up through the time of Queen Victoria's reign, opals had been considered bad luck, partly because they chip and shatter easily. Sir Walter Scott fed this superstition by maligning the opal in one of his novels. However, Victoria put an end to the belief by buying and wearing huge quantities of the stones.

• Celluloid was the first synthetic plastic to be produced. Invented in 1869, it was first made from the pulp cotton plant, solvents, and camphor. It became the generic name for plastic.

• A lot of jade available today has been dyed to give it a richer appearance.

• The finest ivory comes from the tusks of African elephants. It has a fine white appearance, as opposed to Asian ivory, which is more yellow. Teeth and bones of animals are sometimes used and referred to as ivory. Vegetable ivory is carved from a type of palm nut. It has lines and dots running through it and is far softer than true ivory.

• West Bengal has 22-karat gold, and West Bengali goldsmiths are considered the best in the world.

—Patricia Rain

Bibliography

Books

Armstrong, Nancy. *Victorian Jewelry.* New York: MacMillan Publishing Co. Inc., 1976.

Fregnac, Claude. *Jewelry.* New York: G. P. Putnam Sons, 1965.

Goldenberg, Rose Leiman. *Antique Jewelry: A Practical and Passionate Guide.* New York: Crown Publishers, 1976.

Hothem, Lar. *Collectors Identification and Value Guide: North American Artifacts.* Florence, AL: Books Americana, Inc., 1978.

Mourey, Gabriel, and Aymer Vallarice. *Art Nouveau Jewelry and Fans.* Mineola, NY: Dover Publishers, Inc., 1973.

JUKEBOXES

There's a famous photograph from *Life* magazine's "Miscellany" section depicting a normally dignified feline sprawled happily next to a Wurlitzer jukebox—the very picture of a hep cat.

An evening spent bopping around the jukebox was the joy of many two-legged cats and kitties in the '40s and '50s. "Jukebox Saturday Night" is a phrase that symbolizes an era of zoot suits, saddle shoes and uncomplicated fun. It's no wonder that a shot of a jukebox was used at the start of the TV show *Happy Days.*

Although half a billion dollars is still spent annually on five-hundred thousand jukeboxes, the truly valuable are what remain from those innocent times.

★ **Rick Botts, of** *Jukebox Collector* **newsletter, tells of a Little Rock, Arkansas, businessman who bought a 1940s Wurlitzer Model 1015 for a nominal amount and spent about $100 fixing it up. Now at least two experts have told him that the restored box is worth up to $5,000.**

History. The nickelodeon, with its tinkling sentimentality, is considered, believe it or not, the prototype of the modern jukebox, that flashy showcase that first turned heads with the hot sounds of Benny Goodman and other Big Band maestros.

The Regina Music Box Company (a nickelodeon manufacturer) was using an automatic arm mechanism and mass-producing metal discs as early as the 1890s, even though the phonograph was in its infancy, and the first cylindrical coin-operated jukeboxes weren't perfected for two more decades!

However, one-selection machine manufacturers finally recognized the practicalities of the flat phonograph disc and began producing fairly contemporary-looking jukeboxes by the late 1920s. Only then did they "introduce" the new automatic arm mechanism—thirty years after its invention.

The late '30s to the early '50s—the days of elaborate case variations and garish colors—are considered the classic period in

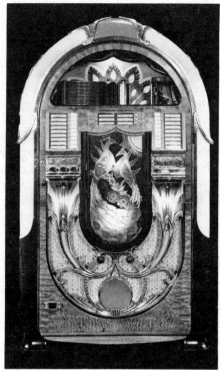

Jukebox: The Golden Age; photograph by Kazuhiro Tsuruta

The Wurlitzer 850 was created during the classic period in jukeboxdom, which was characterized by the use of bright, rich colors, a single well-executed theme (peacocks here), and the capacity to play twenty-four tunes.

jukeboxdom. In fact, during World War II and the immediate postwar period so many Americans became dependent on jukeboxes for entertainment that more than fifty-six thousand Wurlitzer models were produced in 1946 alone.

It was the advent of disc jockeys and video music that brought most Jukebox Saturday Nights to an end. In 1974, Wurlitzer, which over a period of forty years manufactured over a million jukeboxes, announced it was discontinuing production, convinced that these wonderful machines were finally obsolete.

Values Outside the Home. Jukeboxes are divided into three periods: 1934-1949, which played 78s; 1950s-1960s, which played 45s; and 1961 to the present, which are still in service but not considered truly valuable, yet.

Wurlitzers from the '40s are the most sought after. But Seeburgs from the '50s as well as other jukeboxes from the post-classic era are easiest to find and in some ways are more practical investments.

To identify your jukebox, look on the upper backside for a metal ID plate that gives the name of the manufacturer and model number. If it's a rare one, cross your fingers that it is operational or that the parts are available somewhere to restore it. You could end up with either a multi-thousand dollar profit—or a nice planter. (In this specialty, "rare" does not necessarily mean "valuable." Parts may not be available for many rare machines, and an unplayable jukebox is just not cool... or profitable.)

Where to Find Values. In the annals of jukeboxdom, they talk in hushed tones about the San Francisco bar owner who inherited a Wurlitzer 950 Classic model (c. 1941) along with his rundown establishment and found it to be worth more than the establishment... like $9,000.

Now, don't run out and buy a bar, ferheavensake! It's a nice story, but it does not offer the best way to purchase a jukebox. Most experts recommend participating in estate and house sales as the only foolproof ways to buy operational models, followed by attending auctions and, finally, by making the rounds of dealers. Antiques shops, they believe, run a poor third as sources, but since dealers seem to have most jukeboxes these days, let's take a look at this area. Yes, you *can* expect to pay a 50% markup. Yes, you can *also* sometimes expect to be had... unless you know what to look for. So... Rule No. 1: Educate yourself as much as possible about the machine before you purchase it. What should it sound like? What should it look like?

If you are planning to buy one that is *not* operational, find out what missing components could lower the value of the machine, and how difficult it would be to find the parts to restore it.

Rule No. 2: Do *not* play the machine! "You Break It, You Buy It" should be emblazoned above every machine on the floor. A demonstration is critical, but by the dealer only. Yet, obviously, this is a real neat trick when purchasing by mail, so make some arrangement with the seller whereby a refund will be made if the item does not prove operational.

And if you *still* prefer to buy from your friendly neighborhood antiques dealer, listen up! Most *honest* jukebox dealers will provide a written guarantee, but this is seldom obtainable from a general antiques dealer, who only sells the things every once in awhile.

A Price Sampling

1941 Wurlitzer 850 Peacock (stylized peacock design)	$5,000-$7,000
1946-1947 Wurlitzer 1015c (revolving lights in plastic bubble tube)	3,500- 5,000
1941 AMI Singing Tower (resembles Art Deco skyscraper)	2,500- 3,000
1939 Mills Empress Model 910 (large metal decorated front section)	1,250- 1,750
1953 Rock-ola Comet (modern case, curved glass top)	1,000- 1,500
1935 Packard Pla-mor (Capehart), 24 selections	750- 1,250
1941 Seeburg Commander (space-age look)	750- 1,250
1930s Carryola Cabaret (top lifts to reveal turntable)	700- 900
1941 Wurlitzer 780 (front panels, grill and viewing window)	400- 600
1936 Galel's Charme (wood rectangular case)	275- 375

How to Store/Display. Since jukeboxes are only valuable when in mint condition, it's important to know how to tune, refine and perform minor and major surgery. Jukebox repair is costly and, like auto repair, fraught with people who hope to talk you into shelling out $200 to replace some obscure, defective thingamibob.

Once in good working order, make sure to keep records dusted, the body polished, nuts and bolts oiled, and your machine away from dampness (bad for nuts and bolts) and excessive heat (bad for records).

And although it's tempting, try not to play it too much. Every *A-Wop-Bop-Alu-Bop-A-Wop-Bam-Boom* will depreciate the item.

How and When to Sell. There is a veritable army of jukebox junkies out there, so selling your treasure isn't a real problem. Even if you've been taken to the cleaners by a hipster huckster, be cool, mama . . . many collectors will be happy to take salvageable parts off your hands.

But if you have a classic model in prime condition, why not enjoy it a little longer? As more and more bars, honky tonks, ice cream parlors, restaurants, taverns and social halls trade their jukeboxes for video screens, prices should go sky high, and you just might have the opportunity to buy that little bar and the Wurlitzer bubble top that goes with it.

Crazy, man, crazy. . . .

★ **David Rubinson, a San Francisco, California, recording studio owner, became interested in jukeboxes and decided to repair, restore, and sell some of them in a small specialty shop. His greatest finds were what he called a "bunch" of Wurlitzer 1015s that had been left in a San Jose field for years. He bought the lot for a song, so to speak, and resurrected them all. Today they are each worth approximately $6,500.**

Little-Known Facts. The jukebox got its name because it was first used extensively in jukehouses, the Southern designation for brothels and roadhouses.

• The jukebox was primarily responsible for the success of the classic tunes "The Music Goes Round and Round," "A Tisket A Tasket," and "Three Little Fishes." In fact, in its heyday, the jukebox was responsible for the sale of thirteen-million records per year.

• Gustave Brachhausen of the Regina Music Company was the first to attempt assembly-line music machine discs—and almost the last. On the company's first day of work, he erected partitions so his laborers would not talk to each other. They staged a mass walkout. He hastily removed the barriers and music-machine mass production was born!

—*Sandra Hansen Konte*

Bibliography

Books

Kirvine, J. *Jukebox Saturday Night.* Secaucus, NJ: Chartwell Books, 1977.

Lynch, Vince and Bill Henkin. *Jukeboxes—The Golden Age.* Berkeley, CA: Lancaster Miller, 1981.

Rinker, Harry, ed. *Warman's Americana & Collectibles*. Elkins Park, PA: Warman Publishing Co., 1977.

Catalogues

Gould, Susan. *The Official Price Guide to Music Machines and Instruments*. Orlando, FL: House of Collectibles, 1984.

Dealers

The Antique Jukebox Co., 2363 E. Olympic Blvd., Los Angeles, CA.

Jukebox Saturday Night, 1552 N. Wells, Chicago, IL 60610.

Organizations

Automatic Musical Instruments Collectors Association, 824 Grove St., San Francisco, CA 94117.

CHAPTER 12

Kitchen China

Knives

KITCHEN CHINA

"Oysters and teacups have the same growth curve."—Anonymous

Anyone who has tried to preserve a collection of "the family's best china" will agree to the truth of this saying and recall how the ravages of time, trips to the kitchen sink, and things that go bump in the night have taken their toll on the most coveted saucers and serving dishes. China and ceramics have traditionally been considered collectors' items because of their eventual rarity, and also because they are decorative and often unusual in some way.

There has since been a shift in the china collectors' market during the past few years. Although rare and unusual items are still sought, there is now an emphasis on functional pieces that can be used daily as well as be admired—and that are not prohibitively expensive. Many pieces made in this country, therefore, are considered valuable, and there are few families today that do not have at least something of this ilk stashed away in a cupboard or attic.

So, pour yourself a cup of coffee in a possible collectors' cup and read on. The dining room hutch or kitchen cupboard may just be housing a collectors' treasure trove.

History. The earliest commercial earthenware made in the United States was hazardous to the health of its users. Produced in Massachusetts in 1635, *Redware* was made from clay with a high iron content that made it turn red when fired (bricks and flowerpots are classic examples of redware). Since Redware was extremely porous, it had to be glazed to hold liquids, and the early glazes were generally made with lead. In 1785, the *Pennsylvania Mercury* warned its readers that lead glaze was a slow but sure poison. But the warnings went unheeded and Redware remained popular until 1850, when *Stoneware* replaced Redware storage containers, and inexpensive *Whiteware* replaced the Redware table service. Economics, however, not health, was the reason for the replacement.

The earliest pieces of Redware are the most valuable, especially if they have clear interior glazes. The more elaborate or intricate the design, the more valuable the piece.

Handmade *Stoneware* became the major source of utilitarian containers until 1890, when machine-made wares replaced it. Salt

Color largely determines the value of Fiestaware, which was not produced after 1973. This extremely popular disk water pitcher is most scarce in medium green and chartreuse. Tumblers were not made after 1946 and are most difficult to find in turquoise.

glaze, which was clear, thin, and pitted, with a texture similar to orange peel, was the most popular. It was made from salt heated and thrown into the kiln at maximum firing temperature. Other glazes, such as Albany, Michigan, and Texas slips, were used, especially in the interiors of containers, where salt could not provide an adequate seal. In the South, where salt was more difficult to come by, an alkaline glaze with a dribbled effect, called "Tobacco Spit," was used. Cobalt often colored Stoneware. Simple blue designs and dabs of blue at the handles usually indicate pieces made before 1850. After the 1850s, stencils were used.

In the middle to late 1870s, Stoneware was replaced with glass and tin storage containers. Some Stoneware is made today but is seldom marked. The most important factors in determining the value of Stoneware are shape, decoration, and glaze, though origin and age are also important.

Concurrent with the popularity of Stoneware was *Staffordshire china,* which was produced in England to compete in quality and price with Chinese export porcelain (see "Porcelain"). It was soon in such demand that in 1822, a Boston china merchant wrote to his

Staffordshire supplier, "You have created a monster! My gates were stormed today by wives wanting dark blue Staffordshire china."

Indeed, by the late eighteenth century, tens of thousands of barrels of Staffordshire china were shipped to the United States. The most popular version of this tableware was *Historical Blue*. It was produced especially for the United States and depicted primarily American scenes, although some foreign scenes, such as the Willow pattern, were very popular.

Bone china and *Feldspar*, made by Josiah Spode, a famous Staffordshire potter, were enjoyed by the gentry, the professional classes and prosperous merchants. *Stone china* was created for the expanding lower and middle classes. It was also known as *Ironstone* because it had a dense body and was hard and durable.

Wedgwood, another Staffordshire china, was exported extensively, making it relatively easy to locate today. *Jasparware*, a china with a colored background and white-relief Greek motifs, was invented by Josiah Wedgwood in the 1770s. It was most popular in blue, familiar now as Wedgwood Blue. All Wedgwood is marked with different styles denoting the period in which it was produced. This makes it fairly easy to pinpoint its age and value.

Lustreware, a beautifully decorated china, found a ready market in the nineteenth century. It was based on the Hispano-Moresque wares of the early Renaissance. The lustre decoration was achieved by applying metallic film to earthenware or china. The piece was then painted with enamels. It was especially effective at night by candlelight or gaslight, the metals catching the light and sparkling.

Nipponware and *Noritake*, two Japanese chinas, were made from the late 1800s to the 1930s. They were elaborate, gold painted, and based on Bavarian designs. Although many people preferred German or English china, assuming that it was of superior quality, in fact both Nippon and Noritake were of the same high quality as European wares. All Nipponware and Noritake pieces are marked.

Majolica, a brightly colored earthenware, became popular after being exhibited in 1851 in London. Several English and American potters noted the public's enthusiasm and began producing the gaudy but functional ware. Majolica was considered by its critics to be vulgar, but Americans bought it because it was inexpensive. During the 1880s it was given away at the A&P grocery chain with the purchase of baking soda. Most American Majolica is found in the Eastern and Midwestern United States, though it, like other collectors' items, has become more available nationwide as families become more mobile. Its value is determined by workmanship, design, and condition. It is difficult to find Majolica ware in mint condition because the lead glaze was brittle and became chipped and crazed with use.

In the 1870s, rebellion against mass production encouraged the creation of beautiful ceramic pieces. Called *Art pottery,* they were designed for their aesthetics and fine workmanship, although they could also be functional. A number of wealthy women became involved with Art pottery, either as a creative outlet for their talents or to help other women establish themselves in the arts. Through the course of its evolution Art pottery was produced in thirteen states by 118 potteries. Today it is highly valued as a collectors' item.

The Homer Laughlin China Company in West Virginia, one of the top manufacturers of inexpensive American pottery, produced the most popular pieces of the twentieth century. Known as *Fiestaware,* it was turned out from the 1930s to the early 1970s. Less than five years after it went out of production, over twenty-five thousand people were actively collecting it, causing its value to jump dramatically. It is an easily obtainable collectors' item, since thirty million pieces a year were produced during the 1940s.

Prices for Fiestaware are higher on both coasts than in the Midwest. Those items made in limited quantities, such as vases, compotes, nesting bowls, and carafes, are the most desirable. Color is another important factor: chartreuse, grey, and rose are especially valued. However, the most popular is Fiesta Red, introduced in 1936 and used until 1973, except for the years 1943 to 1959.

Fiestaware is easy to identify: it has a band of six concentric rings close to the rim of each piece. Also, anything larger than salt shakers or cups is marked.

Other wares made by the Homer Laughlin Company are often confused with Fiestaware. *Harlequin* and *Riviera* are very similar but neither is marked. Riviera ware was inexpensive, lightweight, and made to be sold in dime stores. *Kitchen Kraft,* made only from 1937 through the 1940s, is the most valuable of all Homer Laughlin wares because not much was produced.

In the 1930s through the 1950s a variety of companies around the country produced china that now is considered valuable. Two California companies, Bauer and Pacific, produced china from the 1930s through the 1950s. In the 1950s, Jewell Tea, Westinghouse, and a few other companies gave out inexpensive china as promotional items when their products were purchased.

One other product requiring mention is *Occupied Japanware*. Produced during the two years after the war in which the United States occupied Japan, the Japanese ceramic dinnerware, figurines and animals made then helped rebuild that country's economy. The materials were inexpensive, and the items were intended only for tourists. Occupied Japanware is, for the most part, quite unremarkable, but it is valuable because it was only made between 1946 and 1948. All Occupied Japanware is marked.

★ **In 1965 author Patricia Rain of California had picked up a piece of Stoneware in a junk shop in Georgia for $2. She knew nothing about her purchase other than that it was attractive and would function as an umbrella holder, which is what she had originally been looking for. In the late 1960s, a friend informed her that she had purchased a butter churn, and that a similar churn with a wooden clabber was for sale in a decorator's shop for $70. At that point she turned the churn into a lamp. Later, she discovered that her "lamp" had been made in the early 1800s and today is worth at least $150.**

Values Outside the Home. Choosing to build a kitchen china collection is partly contingent on what one may already possess. Unusual teacups, a special pitcher, or a partial set might be good items to expand upon.

Another factor to consider when collecting is geography. The major national pottery companies were originally located near sources of good clay. Virginia, Ohio and Pennsylvania still have a reasonably large proportion of locally produced pieces.

Where to Find Values. A number of tabloids are published nationally in which one can advertise free or inexpensively. These are good sources for collectors' items. Hobbyists should also consult newsletters and periodicals that specialize in a certain item, such as Fiestaware. These are excellent places not only to find items but to get a good sampling of current prices.

Garage sales and flea markets are often excellent places to buy china. When buying, one should not pass up the "specials" tables. A collector of Staffordshire pottery found a fine early Wedgwood creamer on a table marked "Every item 50¢." The piece was in reasonably good condition, but the seller did not know how to read the marks that indicated its early—and aristocratic—origin. Needless to say, the piece was quite valuable.

A Price Sampling

Prices of china will vary tremendously from area to area. The most inexpensive pieces can often still be found in the Midwest.

Nipponware and Noritake, tea set from turn of the century	$500
Art pottery, large piece	300
Occupied Japanware, highest-priced pieces	85
Fiestaware vase or pitcher	65
Art pottery, beginning prices	50
Spongeware, Yellowware, Brownware	45 plus
Nipponware and Noritake, single piece	25
Occupied Japanware, small figurine	4

How to Store/Display. Because china is reasonably fragile, a certain amount of care is necessary in washing, displaying, and storing it. Pieces are best displayed in cabinets or mounted on sturdy stands or wall racks. Rather than store a valuable set of china loosely in a cupboard, where it can easily be chipped, one should put the pieces in china bags (zipper-closed storage bags). One collector, who lives in earthquake country, keeps her china in drawers, believing it minimizes the likelihood of damage more than if it were stored in cupboards.

China should be washed in warm water using a *mild* soap. Harsh detergents or dishwashers should never be used to clean handpainted pieces or Lustreware, because the paint or metal will rapidly deteriorate.

★ **Jan Lindstrom began collecting Spongeware bowls twenty years ago, when she was newly married and living in Pennsylvania. She picked up bowls of all sizes, choosing them for the quality of color and design. She recalls never spending more than $3 per item. Her collection of twenty-five bowls was recently appraised at $900—not a bad price considering her initial investment.**

How and When to Sell. Upgrading or disbanding a collection are the only major reasons one would want to sell, since a collectors' item tends to increase in value over the years, not decrease.

Before selling, one should have items appraised to find out their current values. It is also advised to study the tabloids on the subject to get an idea of the going advertised prices. Sellers should also consider trading as an excellent way to get the best value for a piece and to upgrade a collection.

Little-Known Facts. During the 1870s, noted potter F. B. Norton created delightful imitation tree stumps to be used as outdoor chairs. He is reputed to have sat in each one before the wet clay hardened in order to create the special contours of each seat.

• The popularity of Chinese porcelains diminished because of political upheavals in China and competition from European manufacturers. A set of special-order Chinese porcelain could take up to three years to reach a customer, and occasionally disastrous mistake˜ ˜vere made. One particular American family had ordered its motto "ɪ think, I thank" to be inscribed on each piece. The order arrived with the words "I stink, I stank" printed instead.

• As Staffordshire potters grew, it was often difficult for them to stock enough clay. In order to obtain the fine white clay quickly and easily, workers sometimes dug it up from roadbeds and then filled the holes with shards of old pottery. From this practice grew the term *pothole.*

• In 1943, United States government officials arrived at the Homer Laughlin China Company and demanded to know why the factory was using up most of the country's uranium oxide supply and requested that they please stop doing so. Factory managers pointed to the red Fiestaware they had been producing and explained that they had been using the compound for years as the coloring agent. But they agreed to halt production even though the government's urgency remained a mystery. It was not until the bombing of Hiroshima, in 1945, that the reason became clear: uranium oxide had provided the atoms necessary for the manufacture of the atom bomb. The Homer Laughlin China Company did not resume production of its red Fiestaware until 1959, this time using "depleted" uranium.

—Patricia Rain

Bibliography

Books

Evans, Paul. *Art Pottery of the United States.* New York: Charles Scribner's Sons, 1974.

Huxfort, Bob and Sharon. *The Collectors Encyclopedia of Fiesta, with Harlequin and Riviera.* Paducah, KY: Collector Books, 1976.

Ketchum, Wm. C., Jr. *The Pottery and Porcelain Collectors Handbook: A Guide to Early American Ceramics from Maine to California.* New York: Funk & Wagnalls, 1977.

Kovel, Ralph and Terry. *Kovels' Collector's Guide to American Art Pottery.* New York: Crown Publishers, Inc., 1974.

KNIVES

The folding pocket knife is part of that particularly American ritual that begins a boy's journey to manhood. What modern American son has not been given his first—and very own—pocket knife by a father who also carefully instructed him on how, and on how not, to use it? Some estimate that at least 90% of the adult male population carries a knife of some kind, an activity that most likely resulted from that little ceremony that took place years earlier between a father and his son.

History. Man most likely began to make stone knives about fifty-thousand years ago. These were tools used for cutting and shaping wood implements, and for preparing food and hides. They were small, and their primary functions were to cut and scrape, not pierce. By 6500 B.C. copper replaced stone as the preferred metal for knives, daggers and swords. Copper was easy to work with, but it soon proved to be too soft to be functional. Knife blades fashioned from it were short and thick and often would bend under pressure.

Then came bronze, made by adding tin to raw copper during forging. Bronze blades could be made larger and thinner without bending and were chosen by champion warriors instead of iron, which would not hold an edge.

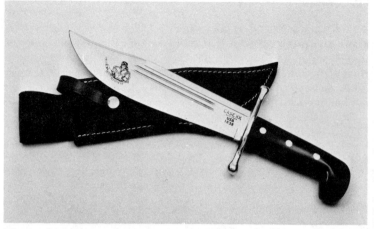

W. R. Case & Sons Cutlery Co.

The bowie knife was an all-American design, perfectly suited to life on the frontier. It was big (10-inch blade), well aligned for powerful thrusting, could be hand-honed to shaving sharpness, and provided exceptional hand protection.

Around 2000 B.C. an obscure blacksmith discovered that when iron was heated in a charcoal fire, it became harder because iron picked up carbon from the charcoal and became steel.

The earliest examples of folding knives have been salvaged from the ancient ruins of Rome and Pompeii. From these examples one can see that there has been little change in knife design since 1600 A.D., except in degree of bulkiness. Today's knives have lighter, thinner blades and compact handles made by true craftsmen.

★ **Richard Young traveled across the United States at the beck and call of the Navy many times. Wherever he stopped, he always spotted a knife that caught his interest. Whether it was simply an unusual knife or a numbered, limited-edition folding pocket knife, he would eventually add it to his collection. Today, if asked to put a price tag on his collection, including those knives that are irreplaceable, he replies they are worth a minimum of $5,000. He also adds that he is not ready to sell.**

Values Outside the Home. Whether one invests in a $10 utility knife or a $500 commemorative Bowie, the choice is personal. Whichever it is, there are a few things the beginning collector should look for.

First, he should check for quality and craftsmanship, but he should also understand that this is not going to be a speedy process, since so many knives today are so well made.

Next, he should look for fine steel in the blades, at least 440 (the gauge of steel's hardness) or better. Brass hinges, brass or nickel bolsters, and ornaments on the handles are necessary embellishments.

After quality, one must look for rarity. This can be determined by low serial numbers—1 to 100 or 1 to 500—which are stamped right into the blades. Knives with low numbers are sold at premium prices, and their resale value goes up rapidly.

The final consideration should be source. Knives offered by the better-known collector groups and clubs can be counted on to become collectors' items.

One should also consider knife reproductions. A five-inch copy of an early Winchester Trapper was crafted in Germany with top-quality steel and beautiful workmanship. It was not offered as anything but a copy. However, it was part of a limited edition of slightly over twelve-hundred pieces and originally sold for $45. Today it sells for $75 to $90.

Where to Find Values. The beginner should go to gun, antiques and collectors shows, and to flea markets and state auctions. The object is to personally inspect the knives, looking at each of their features and getting the feel of the blades. He should also talk to sellers and get prices and histories. Once he has decided on a purchase, he should ask for a detailed bill of sale, describing the item fully. This will protect both himself and the seller.

★ **Sgt. Michael Shriver, stationed at Andrews Air Force Base, Maryland, took advantage of his three tours of duty in England by adding to his collection of stag-handled knives of every size, shape and purpose. Presently his collection numbers over fifty, which is quite a undertaking to pack and unpack every four years. However, with an overall value of $7,000, his troubles are certainly worth it.**

A Price Sampling

NRA Special Edition with presentation case
(limited to 100 made) $400

Buster Warenski Pahvant	141
Buster Warenski Tushar	139
Winchester 1920 single-blade w/bone handles	100
Remington #R4353, two-blade w/stag handles	100
Winchester	70-85
Browning #3018	20-25
Case three-blade whittler	9-12

How to Store/Display. One should ask himself, if he owned a 1928 Cadillac convertible, would he let his teenager drive it? Most likely not. The same precaution can apply to owning a valuable knife: One does not peel potatoes with a Jimmy Lyle acid-etched presentation blade. In fact, owners should handle their collections as little as possible, since even the small amount of moisture on one's hands can tarnish a new blade and start the rust process on an older one.

How and When to Sell. Knives can be sold or traded in the same places from which they were purchased: collectors shows, gun and knife shows and flea markets. Only the roles are reversed: the buyer becomes the seller.

It is most important for anyone who wants to sell to do his homework. It is also important to know that the person selling in the next booth has most likely been doing his also. Homework will keep one from pricing too high or too low.

Sellers should also consider trading, which can be as much fun as receiving cash. The trick here is to always trade up.

★ A collectors' knife can turn up in the most unlikely places. A woman from San Carlos, California, was going through an old cigar box that had belonged to her father. Still bound with a well-worn rubber band, the box contained miscellaneous items, such as screws, nuts and bolts, and pencil stubs. It also contained one small pocket knife. Slightly rusted, the name on the knife was still legible. The knife turned out to be a three-blade Remington worth $70 to $85.

Little-Known Facts. Jim Bowie's famous knife was not made from a piece of meteorite, as shown in the movie starring Alan Ladd. In real life, James Black, a cutlery craftsman from Washington, Arkansas, fashioned the famous blade using a twelve-step tempering process known only to himself. His process produced a steel harder than any known at the time.

• Black is also credited with creating the clipped point, which is a cutting edge formed from the top two inches of a blade. Bowie was thankful for this feature when he was jumped by thugs—he quickly dispatched all three.

—John Shriver

Bibliography

Books

Lewis, Jack, and B. R. Hughes. *Gun Digest Book of Folding Knives*. Northfield, IL: DBI Books, Inc., 1977.

Periodicals

Antique Trader Weekly. Box 1050, Dubuque, IA 52001.
The Blade. P.O. Box 22007, Chattanooga, TN 37422.

Organizations

Knife Collectors' Club, 1701 Highway 17 North, Springdale, AR 72764.

LACE

In centuries past, nobles, affluent gentlefolk, and even prelates of the church flaunted ruffles and flourishes of lace at their throats, sleeve ends, petticoat hems, and even shoe tops.

The works of the old masters attest to the fascination of lace. Rembrandt's subjects wore *millstone* ruffs around their necks that required as many as sixteen yards of lace. The English government took steps to curb these excesses in 1711 by laying an embargo on the importation of gold and silver lace. A similar maneuver was tried in Puritan Massachusetts when an edict against lace was issued. It appears that even the devoutly sober liked a little lace edge on their collars and hankies.

Though lace fanciers are prone to show more restraint in dress today, becoming "hooked" on lace is a pleasant addiction, easily acquired. It has abundant eye appeal, and many a fantasy has been woven around lace both black and white. Those who love textiles usually have a piece or two packed away somewhere, and valuable pieces still turn up in old trunks and boxes. Antiques dealers have until recently ignored lace, but things are changing. Lace may be the collectors' item for those who love it and are willing to wait awhile.

History. Perhaps lace was born when someone attempted to twist the frayed threads at the end of a worn sleeve into a pleasing pattern. Examples of mesh and network were found in ancient Egyptian tombs, and there is evidence that the craft traveled throughout the Middle East to Europe via Italy.

The familiar form known as *needle lace* probably originated in Italy in the fifteenth century as *Reticella,* or "little net." Based on embroidery, threads were pulled from a foundation fabric, leaving a grid into which designs could be embroidered. Lacemakers then abandoned the grid and began taking "stitches in the air," or *punto in aria.* In this style, free-shaped designs or ornaments were joined only where necessary by *bars,* or as they were sometimes called, *brides.* Knitted and crocheted lace are variations of needle lace.

Bobbin lace, the other major classification, was made by twisting or plaiting many threads from a group of bobbins according to a

National Gallery of Art, Washington; Samuel H. Kress Collection

It is obvious why seventeenth-century lace collars such as this were called *millstones;* a single "ruff" could contain up to sixteen yards of material.

pattern. Simple designs used at least twenty separate threads, and the finer ones called for hundreds or even thousands. The edges and other important points were often held in place by pins stuck into a pillow or other form. *Macrame lace* belongs to this category.

Examples of bobbin lace existed before the sixteenth century in Italy and in the Low Countries. Both Italy and Belgium claim that bobbin lace originated within their borders.

Both types of lace were extremely popular, especially with royalty. During her reign, Queen Elizabeth I undoubtedly believed that the high lace ruffs she wore were becoming to her, while her courtiers and subjects whispered behind her back that they hid the "yellowest neck in England." Though inordinately fond of the stuff herself, this royal lady issued edicts forbidding her subjects to use excessive amounts of lace.

Ruffs and high Medici collars went out of fashion in the seventeenth century, giving way to softly falling collars, such as those worn by Charles I and his family in Van Dyke's portrait. At the same time, lace became heavier, richer and more beautiful. Status was measured in yards of lace finery. Some laces were worth their weight in gold, and more. The skill of Italian lacemakers was so desired that governments tried to lure them away from their homeland, and smugglers got rich carrying contraband lace across borders.

Louis XIV founded a lace-making school near Alençon in 1665. He was so pleased with the lace produced there, he made it compulsory for his courtiers to wear it, and he forbade the importation of foreign lace. Fashion changed rapidly, however, following the revolution. Egalitarians disdained the exquisite lace associated with the nobility. They even killed some of the lacemakers.

Lace made a comeback under Napoleon, however, because he had an eye for elegant attire. He ordered his wife, Josephine, to dress up a bit, and she gladly spent over one million francs a year on her wardrobe, most of which was embellished with fine lace.

In the nineteenth century, efforts were made to revive the craft of making lace by hand. Another revolution, the Industrial, had changed the craft forever because it was possible to produce the foundation net for lace-making by machine. Nevertheless, some exquisite pieces of handmade lace have been produced commercially in Belgium, France, Ireland, and Italy during the nineteenth and twentieth centuries. English queens, including Mary II, wife of William of Orange, Victoria, Alexandra, and Mary, have done their best to encourage hand lace-making in England and Ireland. But even though beautiful examples of the lovely *Honiton* (a bobbin lace) were produced, nothing could compete successfully with the machine.

★ **Lace dealer Kaethe Kliot of Berkeley, California, once had a woman walk into her shop with four yards of the rarest needle lace from France, which she had inherited from her great-grandmother and now suspected might be worth something. She was right—the pieces were valued between $500 and $3,000 per yard.**

Values Outside the Home. Learning how to identify, date and care for old lace requires many hours spent looking at examples in dealers' shops and museums, poring over books on the subject, and talking to experts. Associating with others interested in lace and comparing notes adds to the fun and helps the learning process. At first, lace lovers tend to accrue everything that pleases their eye. With experience, they grow selective.

A magnifying glass can help to distinguish between types of lace, whether handmade bobbin or needle laces, or machine-made imitations. Under magnification, telltale loose ends and irregular filling stitches of machine-made lace are obvious. Handmade needle lace has finely finished buttonhole stitching and clipped outline stitches at the end of each motif; bobbin lace will have evenly worked filling stitches.

Sixteenth- and seventeenth-century Venetian needle laces are probably the most valuable. *Gros point* and *rose point,* or *point de neige,* are well-known types of raised-design laces. Some flat laces were also produced. If you are lucky enough to find entire articles of clothing or collars made of lace, they may be even more valuable. *Point Plat de Venise a Reseau* is an eighteenth-century Italian needlepoint lace most prized by collectors.

Point de France is similar to *Point de Venise* with its large ornamental designs, but the French developed a method of making mesh-like bars, or joinings. *Point d'Alençon* and *Point d'Argentan,* both needlepoint laces, were also made in France after 1650. A French bobbin lace called *Blonde de Caen* was made of delicate silk net with large flowers. Spanish ladies loved *mantillas* made from this. It is not rare, but an entire article made of it is a find. Another famous French bobbin lace is black *Chantilly,* with motifs set off from the ground by *gimps,* or outlining threads.

Examples of valuable Flemish laces are *Point d'Aiguille* and *Point d'Angleterre,* both bobbin, or pillow, laces. The latter was made in Brussels, though some experts argue that it originated in England and was copied by the Flemish. Others suggest that it was so named to facilitate smuggling past English customs. Extremely popular both in England and other places during the seventeenth and eighteenth centuries, it was produced from extremely fine hand-spun thread of twenty-inch lengths knotted together. The knots, angular outlines, and the loose threads carried across the back of the designs help to identify this lace.

Dainty *Mechlin* is another Flemish bobbin lace often found on borders of nineteenth-century Indian muslins. In learning to identify it, one should look for a flat silky thread that outlines the design.

The English got into lace-making a little late, but *Honiton,* a bobbin lace, is one of the most costly and beautiful. During the eighteenth century, lace became a patriotic issue in Ireland. Both the making and wearing of the flat needle version made at Youghal was encouraged. Another Irish lace, *Irish Point,* was mostly made at the Convent of the Poor Clares in Kenmare County. Made of flax thread, it is light and delicate, and many believe it to be superior to what was made at Youghal.

Lace produced in the Victorian era is more available. It was used in parasol covers, fans and dresses and for trimming. *Point de Graze,* a Brussels lace, is one of the better known types. Recognize it by the gauzy sheerness of the net ground, each loop made from a single buttonhole stitch.

A hint to collectors: In your search you may run across some lace-making tools. Antique bobbins and patterns may be very valuable.

Where to Find Values. Rare items can turn up in places such as thrift shops, flea markets, and yard sales. The informed collector has a great advantage in being able to spot valuable pieces mixed in with a tableful of junk. Nor does he overlook Salvation Army depots and estate sales.

When poking around in antiques shops, collectors should not be put off by a dealer's reply that there is no old lace in his shop. Examining the contents of old sewing baskets and scrapbags and going through the old clothing racks will often yield valuable finds.

A Price Sampling. Prices quoted below are derived from *The Official Price Guide to Antiques and Other Collectibles* (The House of Collectibles, Inc., 1984). They reflect nationwide values derived from collectibles experts, auction houses, and specialized dealers.

Collar of Gros Point de Venise, mid-1960s	$260-$360
Rectangle, Point Plat de Venise a Reseau, c. 1720	210- 285
Mantilla, cream-colored, Blonde de Caen lace, c. 1820	110- 150
Handkerchief, linen with Point de Gaze lace, c. 1829	85- 125
Gloves, cotton crochet, c. 1890s	14- 20
Doily, tatted, intricate design, oval, 10 inches long	9- 13

How to Store/Display. Laces such as Chantilly and Alençon should be dry cleaned. Cotton and linen items can be washed with mild, pure soap. Very dirty pieces should be soaked in cold water for an hour, then gently simmered in a saucepan for about ten minutes, stirring with a wooden spoon. They should then be lifted out gently, rinsed with clear water, squeezed, not wrung, in a towel, and then laid flat to dry.

Venise and other raised laces can be ironed face down on a well-padded ironing board. The iron should be set at the lowest temperature.

Brownish stains on old cotton or flax (not silk) lace can often be removed by dabbing for a half hour or so with a very weak solution of household bleach. Rinse carefully when the stain is almost invisible. Hydrogen peroxide can be used for black or greenish mold stains.

Lace is best stored in a cool place with good circulation. If it is to be stored for long periods, it should be refolded occasionally to prevent creases from wearing out its delicate threads.

Lace should never be wrapped in colored paper because dampness can make material absorb the color. Acid-free paper and boxes are ideal for storing it, but larger pieces such as tablecloths can be wrapped in old sheets and stored on shelves. This will prevent the yellow edges caused by pollution that are often seen on articles kept in storage. Smoke from tobacco is the worst offender here.

Cedar chests are also best avoided for lace storage. Sap from the wood may leach out onto lace articles, making them look as if they have contracted a case of measles.

Displaying lace treasures between two pieces of glass is a fine way to show them off, but they should never be wrapped or stored under plastic, which will make them turn yellow.

★ Years ago collector-expert Michael Auclair of New York City was poking around in a thrift shop looking at odds and ends when he found a treasure—a complete piece of sixteenth-century Italian lace done in one of the earliest forms, *reticella* with a border of *punto in aria*. He walked out with it after paying less than $50. Clearly, no one at the thrift shop had any idea of its true value.

How and When to Sell. Lace is currently an undervalued collectors' item. That means there is good hunting, but the seller's market is a few years down the road. Still, through networking, one may be able to find a collector who is interested in buying. Sellers can also seek out organizations of lace collectors and magazines that carry "wanted" and "for sale" listings.

Taking lace to a dealer should be a last resort. Many antiques dealers do not yet know the value of old lace, and specialists who do know the value will buy an article for quite a bit less than they hope to sell it for.

Little-Known Facts. Until the middle of the nineteenth century, laceworkers' eyes often failed by the age of thirty. They had to work in damp cellars to keep the extremely fine and delicate linen thread from becoming brittle and breaking. Four at a table they sat, each with a globe of water placed to concentrate the light from a single candle into a beam that lit up a portion of the pillow they were working on.

• Henry III of France was quite a dresser, who even delighted in "doing up" his elaborate lace ruffs himself. He took endless pains clear-starching them and ruffling them with poking sticks until they crackled like paper. His ruffs finally disappeared after growing so enormous that even Henry could not tolerate them.

—Joyce Hecht

Bibliography

Books

Bath, Virginia Churchill. *Lace.* Chicago, IL: Henry Regnery Company, 1974.

DiNoto, Andrea. *The Encyclopedia of Collectibles: Inkwells to Lace.* Alexandria, VA: Time-Life Books, 1979.

Eveleth, E. Lolita. *Chart for Lace Identification and the Meshes of Handmade Lace.* Lithographed in the United States by Britta Dorothy Jeppson, 1974.

Huetson, T. L. *Lace and Bobbins: A History and Collectors' Guide.* New York: A. S. Barnes & Co., 1973.

Moore, N. Hudson. *The Lace Book.* New York: Frederick A. Stokes Company, 1904.

Pond, Gabrielle. *An Introduction to Lace.* New York: Charles Scribner's Sons, 1973.

Periodicals

Real Lace: The Journal of the Bobbins and Shuttles Lace Guild. (A valuable resource for patterns, instructions, and historical information.) 305 Hoodridge Ave., Pittsburgh, PA 15234.

Dealers

Andrews, Eva Marie, Antique Lace and Linens, 330 Utah St., San Francisco, CA 94103.

Dempsey, Sherri and Jack, 4142 Pine Ave., Erie, PA 16504 (will buy old lace; collectors should send photo and description of article).

Lacis Antique and Textile Center, 2982 Adeline St., Berkeley, CA 94703 (an extensive collection of antique lace, appraisals, lectures, classes and workshops).

Associations

International Old Lacers, Martha Fry, 4212 Bel Pre Rd., Rockville, MD 20883 (membership open to any interested lace collector or maker).

LATIN AMERICAN ART

Albrecht Durer, the German engraver and painter whose works were pinnacles of sixteenth-century European art, was stunned by the beauty and creativity of the objects that Spanish conquistadores brought back from the New World. Today, the works of modern Latin American artists stand alongside those of Picasso and the European modernists in both aesthetic and monetary value.

History. During the sixteenth and seventeenth centuries, Spanish and Portuguese explorers came to what was then called the New World to find gold. They found a lot of it, which they took back with them to their mother countries. They also found sophisticated cultures that were skilled in social and political organization, craftsmanship, and in scientific and civil technologies. Unfortunately, those of the New World lacked horses, gunpowder, wheels, and a few other innovations that were already basic to European development. The clash of cultures resulted in a quick and easy conquest of Central and South Americans by the Spaniards and Portuguese, who then established colonial empires that melded native cultures with those of Western Europe.

Today the art from Latin America can be divided into three eras: Pre-Columbian, Colonial, and Modern, all of which differ from each other in form and character. In the Pre-Columbian civilizations of central Mexico and the western coast of South America, artisans made brightly colored and patterned cloth, pottery, and figurines, and ceremonial objects of gold and silver. Not only the culture but most of the traditional craft techniques were destroyed along with much of the art during the European conquests. Surviving examples of the arts are rare and very valuable.

In some areas of Latin America, however, certain craft traditions are still alive, and artisans continue to make such items as bowls and fabrics of the same materials and in the same ways as their Pre-Columbian ancestors. The beautiful lacquered wooden ware made in the Mexican village of Olinala is such an example. Known as *folk art,* it is bought both by tourists and serious collectors.

European aesthetics dominated the Colonial period. Great cathedrals in the Spanish Baroque tradition were being built and artisans were enlisted to make ornamentation for them.

European influence continued into the Modern era as young painters went from the emerging republics to Paris to study under the Impressionists. They returned to their native countries and began developing styles that combined European sophistication with expressions and themes from their national backgrounds. Some, like Diego Rivera and the artists of the Mexican Renaissance, and Brazilian Candido Portinari of Brazil, became commentators through their art on social and economic conditions. Mexican Rufino Tamayo and Chilean Roberto Matta combine Pre-Columbian colors and shapes in contemporary abstract paintings.

★ *Americas* **magazine describes how recently retired freelance writer Alvadee Adams read of the rising values of Modern Latin American art. She wondered if she could sell a Candido Portinari painting entitled "Family" (1939) she had acquired for $100 while living in Brazil in the 1940s. The painter, now deceased, had become Brazil's most famous artist. Adams had no art or sales background, but she contacted a major New York auction house. The painting sold for $26,000!**

Values Outside the Home. Collecting Latin American art can lead one in very different directions depending on the tastes and pocketbook of the collector. Pre-Columbian antiquities and modern painting and sculpture are very pricey, while folk art can be just as pleasing aesthetically and is reasonably priced. Its one drawback is that it is not likely to appreciate in value unless the art form itself dies out.

Brazilian artist Candido Portinari combined the influences of early twentieth-century Parisian painters with his native landscapes and social conditions. "Family" (above, 18″×15″, 1939) reflects all three.

Most of the Pre-Columbian treasures that survived the conquistadores have found their way into museums, and modern Latin governments have strict laws about the exportation of antiquities. Some countries have even pressed, through diplomatic channels, for the return of national heirlooms taken to Europe during the Colonial period.

One Pre-Columbian item, the Peruvian textiles of the Chavin and Incan periods, are available and currently in demand by collectors. Vast quantities of textiles for clothing, ritual gifts and ceremonies were produced by the Incas. Largely ignored by the conquistadores and post-Colonial art collectors, they survived intact in Peru's very dry climate. Today, their beauty and craftsmenship are recognized by the art world.

Paintings and sculpture of established contemporary artists who are still living also are considered good buys.

Where to Find Values. Both Pre-Columbian antiquities and modern Latin American painting and sculpture are generally acquired through dealers and auctions. Sotheby's now has two Latin American auctions a year in New York City, where total sales are approaching $3 million per showing.

Folk art can be purchased at reasonable prices from dealers and importers throughout the United States. A more satisfying way to collect folk art is to travel to the countries and locales where it is produced. In the larger Latin American cities there are publicly or privately operated centers where authenticated folk art is on display and for sale. These are not museum stores selling reproductions, but genuine craft centers that sell authentic articles that continue to be made by thousand-year-old methods. Collectors may even want to travel to the villages where the objects are being made. Buyers can bargain with artists in native surroundings for pieces being crafted in exactly the same ways as they were before the arrival of Columbus.

Enthusiasts must beware of expecting to find bargains in Latin American *city* marketplaces, however, for few if any will be found.

A Price Sampling

Portrait, Diego Rivera artist, Mexico	$210,000
Painting, Fernando Botero artist, Colombia	176,000
Painting, Roberto Matta artist, Chile	160,000
Chavin fabric, c. 1000 B.C., Peru	65,000
Painting, Candido Portinari artist, Brazil	26,000
Incan textile, c. 1500 A.D., Peru	3,000
Woven panel, traditional design, Bolivia	100
Lacquered bowl, fold design, Mexico	10

How to Store/Display. Textiles, especially antique pieces, must be kept dry and dust free. They can be washed, but this can also remove dyes. A safe way to clean them is to use the flat plastic attachment that goes on the end of the vacuum-cleaner hose. But this should be done carefully and avoided altogether if a fabric is delicate, worn out in places, or torn.

Paintings should be kept at a constant degree of humidity and away from drafts and heat. The treatment of paintings by museums should be studied and followed as closely as possible.

How and When to Sell. Latin American paintings of the Modern period are currently hot in the art world. One of the reasons for this is that well-to-do Latin Americans have been bidding extensively for them. Any radical political or economic changes affecting this aristocracy may cause owners to sell the canvases, thus lowering prices.

Values of Pre-Columbian items will continue to grow, while those of folk art probably will not unless the traditional methods of producing it disappear.

Little-Known Facts. The ancient Peruvians, before burying their dead wrapped in the remarkable textiles of that era, took these garments on a "tour" of the places in which the deceased had lived and worked. Relatives then washed the garments in a local river. This custom is still carried on in many Andean villages.

• Some Pre-Columbian thread used to make textiles was so fine that it was actually several times thinner than thread produced by modern industrial techniques using the same materials.

—*Donald Mayall*

Bibliography

Books

Bardi, Peter M. *New Brazilian Art.* New York: Praeger, 1970.

Graburn, Nelson, ed. *Ethnic and Tourist Art: Cultural Expression from the Fourth World.* Berkeley, CA: University of California Press, 1976.

Keleman, Paul. *Art of the Americas: Ancient and Hispanic.* New York: Crowell, 1969.

Lothrop, S. K. *Treasures of Ancient America: The Arts of the Pre-Columbian Civilization from Mexico to Peru.* Geneva: SKIRA, 1946.

Panyella, August, ed. *Folk Art of the Americas.* New York: Abrams, 1981.

Parsons, Lee A. *Pre-Columbian Art.* New York: Harper and Row, 1980.

Periodicals

Americas, Administration Building, 19th St. and Constitution Ave., Washington, D.C. 20006. ($21).

Dealers

Treasure House of Worldly Wares, Dept. CC, 1414 Lincoln Ave., Calistoga, CA 94515.

LICENSE PLATES

Jim Fox of California, a former drummer for the rock band The James Gang, has been a license plate collector since he was seven years old. His collection of twenty-thousand is only eighteen short of his lifetime goal of owning one of every plate ever made in the United States. He feels that the value of a plate is based 100% upon how much someone wants it, and tells the story of a collector in Alaska who owns one of only two 1921 Alaska plates. The Alaska collector is certain that eventually he will get $100,000 for it.

One-hundred-thousand dollars for a license plate? Well, the collector has yet to make that particular sale, but the other 1921 Alaska plate already holds the unofficial record for commanding a five-figure sum.

History. Auto licensing was introduced around the turn of the century in New York City to help injured pedestrians identify dangerous drivers. The car owner's initials, according to the new law, would be displayed on the back of the vehicle in letters three to four inches high.

By 1909, license plates were standard throughout the states, and a year later, annual plates were introduced (the first plates were issued only once and meant to be permanent).

The Automobile License Plate Collectors Association was formed in 1954 and has a current membership of three thousand. License plate collecting increased dramatically after 1976, when special bicentennial issues were available. They provided beginning collectors with ample opportunities to pick up novel plates at little expense.

★ In the early part of 1984, Ted Cline was rummaging through some debris at a flea market in North Carolina. At the bottom of a box he found a 1933 District of Columbia inauguration plate, the first inauguration plate ever produced. Cline purchased it for pennies and later collected $250 for it.

Values Outside the Home. A common starting goal for beginners is to own a tag from all fifty states. Some have the lofty goal of possessing the first plates ever issued by each state.

A pair of plates is always worth at least double the value for a single plate, and the lower the number on the plate, the higher its price.

Library of Congress

It is still possible for plate collectors to find treasures nailed to old barn doors, walls, and interiors.

(Traditionally, No. 1 from any state is reserved for the governor and therefore the most valuable plate of any state, any year.) Many of the early plates were made of porcelain steel and so are quite durable. Porcelain plates are worth at least twice that of standard enameled issues.

Multi-colored bicentennial plates are recent popular collectors' items. In some states, such as Georgia, special-issue plates—which cost patriotic drivers an extra $10—are valuable. There were twelve-thousand five-hundred special-issues produced in Georgia, and each one is worth about one-hundred dollars.

Vanity plates are the newest fad. A plate printed with a common name, such as "Tom," is worth about $20, depending on who wants it and how rare it is. A 1920 plate bearing the letters TOM, and in good condition, would be worth a lot more.

In Britain, where vanity plates are known as CNPs (Cherished Numbered Plates), and the quirks of the law often require individuals to purchase an entire automobile to get a desired plate (CNPs belong to the cars, not to the people), prices have skyrocketed 3,000% in the last ten years. In fact, so much money is being made on CNPs that the British government now wants a part of the action and has begun to sell unregistered issues on the open market.

Where to Find Values. The best places to find valuable plates are, of course, auto junkyards and auto-wrecking sites. A determined collector will be eager to tramp through the rust and dust in order to get that special item. Flea markets, yard sales and antiques shops are also good sources for old plates.

Collectors can obtain information about specific plates by contacting certain organizations, such as the Automobile License Plate Collectors Association. Many associations also publish their own newsletters.

★ Four years ago, when Eugene Gardner, a resident of Georgia, went searching through his neighborhood junkyard, he was not expecting much. Within two hours, however, he had found two special-issue Georgia bicentennial plates in prime condition and walked away from a local dealer with $200.

A Price Sampling

Vermont, 1905 $700*

New York, 1903	100
Montana, copper, 1967	50
Montana, U.S. senator	40
Texas, pair, 1932	25
Alabama, pair, 1940	20
California World's Fair, 1939	19
Ohio, 1931	10
New Hampshire, 1925	4
Quebec, 1960	.75

*Current known record, available to the public. Sale of Alaska plate was a private transaction and therefore not considered a record-breaker in this listing.

How to Store/Display. Many of the plates picked up in flea markets, yard sales, and out of their hiding places in garages and basements will be covered with dirt and rust. Soap and warm water can clean soiled plates, and even paint thinner can be used, provided one does not scrub the plate too hard. Although paint on most plates is oil-based enamel and there to stay, it can also be removed if not treated gently.

Most collectors use car polish as a final cleaner, shiner and preservative. Once plates are spruced up, they are usually mounted as a display and often organized around a theme, or "run," such as a plate from every state or a plate from every year in a particular state.

How and When to Sell. Because the license plate market is young, prices are bound to keep rising for a while. The best way to make the most profit is to know more about a favorite hobby than one's fellow collectors. Armed with the right information, collectors can make their plates produce lucrative results. Recessions are the recommended times to buy, because prices are their lowest, as well as the best times to sell, before prices sink too low.

★ When Dr. Edward Miles paid $2,600 for an estate museum collection, he knew he had struck a license-plate gold mine. Antique plates from New Jersey, Pennsylvania, and elsewhere have already brought him over $7,500, and he still owns the most valuable plates of the lot—ten New York 1912 porcelain plates worth $75 to $100 each.

Little-Known Facts. New popular collectors' items are the B. F. Goodrich key chain license plate tags made between 1939 and 1944. They used to cost ten cents, then a quarter, but now they command $25 to $35, and their prices should soon reach $50.

• Lower number plates are more rare in the Southern states and therefore more valuable than low-number plates in Northeastern states, where they can often be traced through generations of a single family.

• One license plate collector from South Carolina built an entire clubhouse from plates in 1975. One of the walls appears as a replica of the United States flag (stars were painted on the backs of blue plates for the appropriate effect).

—*Peter Asmus*

Bibliography

Books

Land-Weber, Ellen. *The Passionate Collector.* New York: Simon & Schuster, 1980.

Encyclopedia of Collectibles. Alexandria, VA: Time-Life Books, 1978.

World Almanac of Buffs, Masters, Mavens and Uncommon Experts. New York: World Almanac Publications, 1980.

Periodicals

ALPCA Newsletter. (See "Associations" for address.)

Catalogues

Kovel, Ralph and Terry. *Antiques and Collectibles Price List.* New York: Crown Publishers, Inc., 1983.

Dealers

Fox, Jim, 10176 Page Dr., Mentor, OH 44060.

Gardner, Eugene, Route 1, P.O. Box 166, Palmetto, GA 30268.

Miles, Dr. Edward (considered an authority on plate pricing), 888 8th Ave., New York, NY 10019.

Associations

Antique Automobile Club of America, 501 W. Governor Rd., Hershey, PA 17033.

Automobile License Plate Collectors Association (ALPCA), P.O. Box 712, Weston, WV.

Michigan License Plate Collectors Association, 601 Duchess Rd., Milford, MI.

LIMITED EDITIONS

Among serious antiques collectors limited editions are considered to be nothing more than "instant antiques." Although purists often look down their noses at ceramic and other ornamental-type limited edition items, they have become popular collectors' pieces. With well over four-million active collectors in the United States alone, the limited edition industry is a lively business.

History. Compared to antiques, ornamental and commemorative limited editions are a recent phenomenon. Some plates, spoons, figurines and books have always been produced in limited quantities, but the idea of selling an advertised number of pieces as a business enterprise did not catch on in America until the 1950s.

Limited editions as collectors' items were first recognized outside of this country about fifty years earlier, with production of the Bing and Grondahl blue and white Christmas plate, made in Denmark in 1895. The plate bore the word "Christmas" in Danish and the date, which was incorporated into the design. The following year, Bing and Grondahl created a new design using the current date and, at the same time, halted production on the previous plate. There is no record of how many plates were made in 1895, but some collectors have estimated the run at four hundred. The plates sold for $.50, which was considered high in 1895. Current resale value is estimated to be more than $3,000.

The limited edition business remained a Danish idea until the 1940s. It was then that antiques dealers began to offer Christmas plates dated from past years, and collectors began to buy limited editions in order to own every piece in a series.

Serious collecting began when limited edition price lists became available in 1951. Before then, the prices quoted by manufacturers did not change significantly (aside from inflation), whether pieces were made that year or ten years earlier. After the appearance of lists, prices for a previous year's limited editions climbed or fell according to supply and demand.

During the early 1970s, the limited edition business reached an all-time peak and a large number of manufacturers entered the market. They offered plates and other items made of porcelain, pottery, wood, silver, gold, glass, copper, pewter and countless combinations of these materials.

Courtesy Bing & Grondahl, Copenhagen Porcelain Inc.

The world's first Christmas plate, created in 1895 by Bing and Grondahl and titled "Behind the Frozen Window," sold then for 50¢. Today it is valued at $4,000.

Eventually many collectors realized that not all limited editions were of equal value, and they developed a shaking-out process that remains today. Over the past few years dozens of companies discontinued their products for lack of buyers. More established companies have continued producing and promoting their limited editions, and prices have begun to rise for many items. Some of the more popular limited edition manufacturers today are Edward Boehm and Burgues (porcelain sculpture); Royal Doulton, Bareuther, and the Gorham Collection (cups and plate); Baccarat and Whittemore (paperweights); and Lalique (crystal plates).

Especially handsome limited edition books, sometimes called *press books,* date back to the nineteenth century. The pioneer publisher in the press book field was the Kelmscott Press, founded by English poet William Morris in 1891. Only a few Kelmscott editions are available today for less than $200. One of Kelmscott's first books, a 46-copy limited edition of Chaucer, bound in white pigskin, sold in 1975 for $10,630.

Limited edition publications are usually not original works, but reprinted standard works, such as the Greek and Roman classics and the works of Shakespeare and Dante. Classic American authors, such as Mark Twain, Edgar Lee Masters, Jack London and Sinclair Lewis, are also popular. In many instances these books are illustrated by distinguished artists, who frequently sign all of their copies—so do many modern authors (see "Books"). One limited edition of James Joyce's *Ulysses* included illustrations by the French painter Henri Matisse. The publisher, Limited Edition Club, ran fifteen-hundred copies. Matisse signed all fifteen hundred; James Joyce signed two-hundred fifty.

The limited edition market as a whole began to specialize in the 1970s. Clubs formed, conventions gathered, and trade magazines appeared. Today, many collectors consider limited edition collecting and selling to be like investing in the stock market, and everyone has his own system or theory on how to make money at it. Amid all the hype and dubious promises, many buyers have forgotten that the primary reason to buy a limited edition is for its beauty; manufacturers, on the other hand, are still very much aware that the main reason to produce a limited edition is for its profit.

★ **Prices for china of all sorts are increasing rapidly, and a major cause for this is our present energy crisis. The ovens in which china is glazed must be kept at constant temperatures twenty-four hours a day. Skyrocketing increases in overhead costs have also dramatically affected antique china prices.**

Values Outside the Home. The best advice for anyone interested in collecting limited editions is to buy only those items that one admires, since many limited editions are works of art.

If one is more interested in investment possibilities, it is important to know that items with the potential to rise significantly are the first pieces issued in any new production run. First issues, called *first editions* in the book trade, have increased in value simply because they are the first and therefore considered unique. The first glass plate, the first copper plate, the first Rockwell figurine, and the first Baccarat sulphide paperweights, for example, have all increased in value. Many who begin their collection after a first issue is released spend much of their time acquiring back issues.

It is important before buying limited editions as investments to find out the number of pieces that make up an issue. If that information is not available, it is reasonable to assume that the limited edition is not limited at all. *Limited* can sometimes misleadingly refer to a limited production time rather than to the number of pieces produced. In such cases usually there are quite enough of a particular piece to satisfy market demand.

Limited edition books are most often published by private or university presses. Sales are generally not made through regular bookstores but to subscribers by mail or through selected book dealers. Press runs are generally small, with a maximum printing of around twenty-five hundred. To be of appreciable value a press book must be in excellent condition—as untouched as possible. In 1979 the University of California Press offered twenty-five-hundred limited edition copies of the *Plan of St. Gaul,* a three-volume illustrated study of a ninth-century Carolingian monastery. Considered a masterpiece of scholarship as well as a major publishing undertaking, it sold for a subscription rate of $185. All of the copies have been published and the book is now selling on the secondary market for approximately $500.

Where to Find Values. Plates seem to be the most favored limited edition item for collectors buying investments. Advertisements for limited edition plates often claim that a $2.50 piece could be worth thousands of dollars in the future. But keep in mind when looking at an advertisement that if it puts more emphasis on display cases, souvenir folders and the like, the piece itself is not very valuable.

Plates and other limited editions can also be purchased through dealerships that specialize in particular styles, prices and combinations of items. The best place to find dealerships is in the Yellow Pages under *antiques.*

Official price guides are published by the manufacturers of famous limited editions, such as Hummel and Royal Doulton, and many more manufacturers' prices can be found in general price guides published by such trade groups as Kovels and the House of Collectibles. If price guides are not available at the bookstore, try the library. Most libraries carry at least a few antiques and limited edition guides under catalogue number 738.

When using manufacturers' price lists, heed the figures quoted as general prices only. Sometimes an increase in cost can be attributed to efforts by the manufacturer and not to conditions in the marketplace. Many plate manufacturers, for example, willingly buy back editions of their wares and resell them at new—and higher— prices. Although it's rare, occasionally collectors themselves will organize and agree to bid more than market rate on certain figurine pieces so that resale prices will increase. The wise collector will, therefore, always get at least two opinions before settling on a price.

A Price Sampling

Manufacturer/piece	Issue number	Issue price	Current price
Paperweights			
Baccarat/			
Winston Churchill, 1954	81	$75	$1,500-$2,000
Robert Bryden/			
Blue & White Ribbons, 1978	150	60	60
Gentile Glass/			
God Bless America, 1973	1,800	7	7
Plates			
Hamilton Mint/			
Picasso, Tragedy, 1972	5,000	$25	50-125
Bing & Grondahl/			
Navigators, 1977	Year	30	30
Bareuther/			
Toys for Sale, 1971	10,000	14	8-25
Figurines			
Boehm/			
American Eagle, 1957	31	$225	$250-$8,500
Cybis/			
Apple Blossoms, 1977	400	350	350
Colonial Mint/			
Eastern Cougar, 1976	9,500	65	65
Miscellaneous			
Borsato/			
Mustangs plaque, 1974	250	$1,650	$1,650
Calhoun/			
Queen Mary bell, 1977	3,000	39	39
Blue Delft/			
Christmas spoon, 1970	Year	7	7

How to Store/Display. There are a lot of official and unofficial rules about caring for and displaying limited editions. According to the National Association of Limited Edition Dealers, it is not enough to just buy a limited edition plate, for example, and plan to resell it for a profit. Resale buyers expect the plate to be in mint condition and preferably accompanied by the original box and papers. One ad in an antiques newsletter offered $50 for the empty box that had held a much sought-after 1971 plate.

Collectors should keep complete records of limited edition purchases, including source, date of purchase, and price. Taking a photograph of the piece is also advisable.

Any large collection should also be covered by a special insurance policy. (Regular homeowners or renters insurance will not adequately cover a loss in case of fire, theft or breakage.) To further insure against damage, breakable collections should be kept behind glass, where they can be displayed yet kept out of the reach of admirers and over-enthusiastic housecleaners.

The same collectors' guidelines hold true for limited edition books. Many publishers include a variety of deluxe features with limited edition press runs, such as boxes, broadsheets or prints, special bindings and museum-quality production embellishments. These are considered integral parts of the product, and any damage to or omission of them will affect a book's resale value.

How and When to Sell. Commemorative limited edition pieces, such as Christmas and Mother's Day plates, bells and spoons, usually go through a price cycle. When they are first announced, most dealers ask for retail prices. A good shopper can sometimes find an isolated dealer who will offer a few items at discount to lure in new customers. Every January, when the next year's editions are available, prices for last year's pieces often go down. Of course, last year's prices may go up later in the year if demand for certain pieces increases.

Investors should never buy part of a set if a full set is offered at issue time. A popular limited edition manufacturer, the Franklin Mint, for example, makes a variety of limited editions that are offered for sale over a period of years. Most of them have no resale value until the final piece is issued.

Despite the pitfalls, limited edition collecting can be financially rewarding. Porcelain figures by Edward Boehm and Royal Worcester have been bought and sold at auctions, shops and sales for years, and prices for some pieces are up far more than expected if compared with the present rate of inflation.

Among the most desirable pieces are Hummel annual plates from 1971 through 1973, Royal Copenhagen Christmas plates from 1911 through 1973, and Edward Boehm porcelains, such as the 1957 "California Quail" edition of five hundred that sold for $300 and now sells from $1,600 to $2,600. Paperweights also have enjoyed a rising secondary market. Baccarat was the first to make limited edition paperweights, which are now very popular. The 1954 edition of 81 pieces entitled "Churchill" sold for $75 then and now goes for $1,500 to $2,000.

Remember that no limited edition, or any other piece of art, can be *quickly* converted into its best cash value. To take advantage of a rising market price an investor must wait for the right auction, sale or classified ad by an interested buyer.

★ **In 1977, a well-known independent antiques appraiser, Emyl Jenkins, was asked by a bank to appraise a large collection of pre-World War II Meissen china. When Jenkins asked for a pre-auction estimate from Christie's auction house, he was told not to expect more than $675 for the lot. Three years later a similar set of 226 pieces sold for $10,000.**

Little-Known Facts. These days in any shopping mall or along many neighborhood shopping streets there will be at least one poster shop or framing business that offers posters as a sideline. As the poster market has grown, limited edition posters, called broadsheets, have become popular among press book publishers and collectors.

• Broadsheets are usually printed in small quantities (one thousand or less), and are of the finest quality. Paper is either 100% rag or especially commissioned to come as close to museum quality as possible. Pieces are usually numbered and/or signed, sometimes by the printer as well as the artist.

• Often, small independent printers who specialize in high-quality, low-volume publications will join with a related business to produce limited edition broadsheets. Peter Koch, a well-known press book printer in Oakland, California, for example, recently worked with a Berkeley bookstore to produce a limited edition sheet promoting

Pasta, Pizza and Calzone, a popular cookbook created by Berkeley's famous Chez Panisse restaurant. The three-color poster was distributed with the book and signed by author Alice Waters. Two other artists whose works are famous among press book and broadsheet collectors are Barry Moser, who runs Penny Royal Press in West Hatfield, Massachusetts, and Andrew Heuem, a San Francisco, California, artist and printer who owns Arion Press.

• In 1984, limited edition plate enthusiasts probably attended the auction in Norfolk, Virginia, held aboard the luxury liner *United States.* Easily one of the most expensive antiques events of the year, the auction grossed over four-million dollars. Over a million available items were taken from what was once the pride of the American maritime fleet.

The ship's eagle-embellished dinner plates were good examples of what was offered. When bidding opened, the first set of twelve plates quickly topped the $700 estimate and were sold for $1,000 to a buyer who flew in from Denver just to buy them.

• Malcolm Forbes, publisher of *Forbes* magazine, sent an employee to bid on the dinnerware and bought the last offering of plates for $2,200. They are intended to be used on Forbes' new yacht.

—*James W. White*

Bibliography

Books

Donovan, Hedley, ed. *The Encyclopedia of Collectibles.* New York: Time-Life Books, 1975.

DeForrest, Michael. *Antiquing From A to Z.* New York: Simon & Schuster, 1975.

Kovel, Ralph and Terry. *The Kovels' Guide for Collector Plates, Figurines, Paperweights and Other Limited Editions.* New York: Crown Publishers, Inc., 1978.

Krause, Chester. *Guidebook of Franklin Mint Issues.* Wisconsin: Krause Publications, Inc., 1977.

Periodicals

Annual Bulletin of the Paperweight Collectors Association. P.O. Box 128, Scarsdale, NY 10583.

Antique Trader. P.O. Box 1050, Dubuque, IA 52001.

A. B. Bookman's Weekly. Box AB, Clifton, NJ 07015.

Catalogues

Hudgeons, Thomas E., ed. *Official Price Guide to Antiques and Other Collectibles.* Orlando, FL: House of Collectibles, Inc., 1984.

Kovel, Ralph and Terry. *Kovels' Antique and Collectibles Price List, The.* New York: Crown Publishers, 1980.

Dealers

Flynn, E. (collectors' plates), Box 4111, Thousand Oaks, CA 91359.

Henry A. Clausen Bookshop (press books), 224 N. Tejon St., Colorado Springs, CO 80902.

Macklowe Gallery (general), 1088 Madison Ave., New York, NY 10028.

Associations

American Limited Edition Association, Box 1034, Kermit, TX 79745.

Hummel Collectors Club, P.O. Box 257, Yardley, PA 19067.

Rockwell Society of America, P.O. Box 176, Slatersville, RI 02876.

M

MAGAZINES

Few of life's pleasures are so appealing as curling up with a cup of coffee and a favorite magazine. We all wait for the mail or newsstands to bring the latest issues of *Life, Esquire, Playboy,* and *Ladies Home Journal,* and this is an eagerness that our parents and grandparents also enjoyed. For our magazines *are* us, in their slick, sleek design, their period graphics or photographs, their fine and often disturbing articles and fiction. What happens to us, decade by decade—the people, places and events we adore and despise—are distilled into words, photos and illustrations in pamphlets and inside the glorious covers of magazines, which have brightened over a century of American coffee tables.

History. Magazines and pamphlets were the logical vehicles to convey information and style to masses of readers. *Harper's Weekly* dated back to the 1770s, as did some other early favorites, and *Ladies Home Journal, Vogue,* and *Vanity Fair* had their heyday during the 1850s. Magazines as we think of them today however—glossy, colorful, packed with interesting tidbits and articles—did not really catch on until the 1920s.

From their beginnings, magazines immediately held the public's attention. They were portable, slim, less bulky and perishable than newspapers, and printed on high-gloss paper. And they were easy to collect; one issue neatly followed upon the other. Today there is scarcely an American household that at one time has not enjoyed at least one national glossy.

★ **One lucky collector found an Art Nouveau illustration by the renowned artist Mucha, signed by him and printed as a magazine cover. The collector sold it for $400.**

Values Outside the Home. Magazines are most desirable because of their graphics. Prior to 1930, illustrations were used for articles, advertisements and covers, and many are exquisite works of art.

Magazines were an immediate hit with an increasingly literate public. They were easy to carry and read and were packed with articles, fiction, and remedies for everything from chilblains to infidelity.

Special finds include any magazine with graphics by J. C. Leyendecker, Norman Rockwell, Coles Phillips (especially his "Fadeaway Girl" covers), Maxfield Parrish, Varga, Petty, and Elfgrin.

Beginning in 1930, photographs replaced illustrations in most national magazines. Noted photographers were Edward Steichen, Margaret Bourke-White, Cecil Beaton, and H. P. Horst.

The following magazines, containing the work of many of the above artists, are the best known and most profitable: *Life, Saturday Evening Post, Collier's, McClure's, Ladies Home Journal, Vogue, Vanity Fair, Esquire, Playboy,* and *Sports Illustrated.* Any issue with a foldout of any kind is automatically worth more.

In a class of its own is *National Geographic* and its maps, supplements, and books. The earliest issues, going back to the 1880s, are very rare and worth a great deal.

Equally interesting are magazines with literary works by famous, or infamous, people. Any issue with an early article or story by Faulkner or Hemingway, when they were not popular with critics, is worth a good deal. James Joyce's *Ulysses*, for example, was serialized in twenty-three issues of *The Little Review* in the late teens and early 1920s. Four of those issues were burned *en masse* by the post office for obscenity. Today those missing issues, or the entire series, are worth a gold mine.

And there is, of course, *New Yorker* magazine, full of valuable literary pieces and cartoons, including work by E. B. White, S. J. Perelman, James Thurber, and Peter Arno. The *Literary Digest* is another collectors' item, known for publishing the early works of well-known writers.

Collectors should be on the lookout, too, for *Camera Work*, published between 1903 and 1917. Although short lived, it contained the photographs of the famous Alfred Stieglitz. A complete run of the magazine sold for $33,000 in 1975. Old *Harper's Weekly* magazines from 1857 include Civil War illustrations by Winslow Homer, and issues from 1887 to 1906 contain Frederick Remington articles and illustrations and are rare and precious.

Condition of a magazine is critical if it is going to be worth anything. Even a Norman Rockwell cover, if moldy or tattered, is worthless except for its nostalgic value.

Pamphlets, an often over-looked collectors' item, can be separated into areas of interest. Some of the more popular are travel and historic booklets, army information, railroad paraphernalia, theater playbills, and political tracts.

Where to Find Values. The best source of old magazines and pamphlets is the neighborhood pack rat. Many who do not consider themselves collectors have heaps of old *Ladies Home Journal*s or *National Geographic*s, dry and in excellent condition, in their attics.

Thrift shops often have unsorted stacks of magazines in a corner, and libraries only keep periodicals for five to ten years before calling a dealer or charity organization to pick them up.

Many collectors' shops and secondhand bookstores have a magazine/pamphlet display, as do flea markets. Garage sales are an excellent source of old material, but the most precious pieces are often available only at auction.

A Price Sampling

Playboy issues, 1950s (except the first issue) with centerfold	$200
Life, first issue, November 23, 1936	75
Book of Art Printing (Bound collection of Deco prints from various magazines, 1928. Could be dismantled and each print sold for $20)	75
Sports Illustrated, first issue, August 16, 1954, with baseball card foldout	65
Tourist pamphlet on Alameda, California, 1930, pen and ink illus.	30
First issue of the short-lived *Ken* (full of collectors' Deco ads), April 7, 1938	20
Life, April 7, 1952, with Marilyn Monroe cover	20
Harper's Weekly, 1863	5
Theater playbill featuring Paul Robeson in "Othello"	5

How to Store/Display. Condition is critical to value and, unfortunately, twentieth-century paper ages poorly and will disintegrate because of its high acid content. Pages will yellow and crumble, and colors will fade. Keeping magazines and pamphlets in plastic sleeves can help preserve paper, as does keeping them out of direct sunlight. Most important is making certain that paper remains dry. Many a precious stack of old *Life* magazines has turned to mold in someone's damp basement.

★ **Early material from the Old West is always popular and often lucrative. An 1800s broadside pamphlet, depicting and describing Calevaras trees, ended up in the collection of a Prussian king. When he died, the broadside made its way back to America and sold for $1,000. Originally the pamphlet, of course, had been *given* away.**

How and When to Sell. Age will not necessarily affect the price of an old magazine or pamphlet. Price often depends on the ebb and flow of cultural interest in a subject. For instance, recent curiosity about Marilyn Monroe has made any magazine with photos of her worth many times more than an issue of the same magazine produced just a week earlier or later. Collectors should try to capitalize on the waves of nostalgia that sweep over us and sell when a personality, graphic artist, or particular magazine is in vogue.

Little-Known Facts. So fabulous were the graphics in magazines that in one month during the early 1920s a man depicted in a Leyendecker illustration advertising Arrow shirts received over seventeen-thousand fan letters, including suicide threats.

• Although twentieth-century paper disintegrates easily, nineteenth-century paper remains intact. Many a paper publication from the early 1800s is in pristine condition.

—*Robin Solit*

Bibliography

Books
Clear, Richard. *Old Magazines.* Gas City, IN: LW Promotions, 1974.
Hinds, Marjorie and Donald. *Magazine Magic.* Laceyville, PA: Messinger Book Press, 1972.

Periodicals
The Girl Whirl. Box 7244, Washington, D.C. 20044.
National Geographic Collectors. Edwin C. Buxburn, Box 465, Wilmington, DE 19899.
Paper American Auction. 736 N. Frazier St., Baldwin Pk., CA 91706.

MECHANICAL BANKS

The little man sits at a desk. His expression has not changed in a hundred years. His only purpose is to sweep coins across the desktop with his arm and push them into a slot. Then he wiggles his fingers, his arm goes back, and he sits still again.

These simple actions are part of the charm of the legendary antique cast-iron Freedman mechanical bank, of which only five or six are known to exist. The price? You better sit down for this. Around $100,000.

History. Some historians insist that the existence of mechanical banks can be traced back to Roman days (when even a version of the yo-yo existed). But today's collectors hover over the small mechanical

Courtesy Stephen A. Steckbeck

One of the most valuable mechanical banks of all is the rare Freedman. A fortunate collector found one in Mexico several years ago and paid only $4.50 for it. Today it is worth $100,000.

banks that were manufactured between the late 1860s and the early 1930s.

It is estimated that over two-thousand varieties of banks were manufactured and patented during this heyday, when silver coins were a much more trusted and hoarded medium of exchange than paper money.

Many banks, including those made of tin, came from England and Germany and are collected today. The leading producer of mechanical banks in America was the J. E. Stevens Company of Cromwell, Connecticut. Other American producers, such as the Kilgore Manufacturing Company of Westville, Ohio, and Kyser and Rex of Philadelphia, competed with Stevens and tried for elaborate machanisms that placed a premium on animation.

By using wheels, springs, levers, and delicate balancing mechanisms, designers of cast-iron banks created such mechanical activities as dogs flipping coins through hoops, Uncle Sam dropping coins into bags, cannons firing coins, girls skipping rope, three baseball players pitching and catching coins, football players kicking coins, clowns and monkeys swallowing coins, and music playing at the drop of a coin.

Irresistible, inexpensive and colorful, the banks were popular in the days when being frugal was a necessity—children needed to learn the virtue of saving pennies. The banks were also used for promotional advertising by car companies such as Buick and Chevrolet, food and drink companies such as Gerber's and Bosco, Red Goose shoes and, of course, by many banks.

Mechanical banks bought in stores could cost anywhere from a dime to as much as $2. For instance, in 1932, Montgomery Ward sold a monkey and parrot bank for $.21. Today the bank is worth $250.

Banks made with no mechanical parts are called *still banks*. Their use preceded the popularity of mechanical banks. Still banks were made as early as the 1800s from glass, ceramic, brass, tin and iron.

The star of all banks, still or mechanical, was the piggy bank, symbol of the household word for savings. A still piggy bank on today's market is worth from $25 to $125.

Many comic strip characters of the day were served up to the public in bank form. So were Charlie McCarthy, Santa Claus, General Sherman, Teddy Roosevelt, Professor Pug Frog and other historical or humorous characters.

The need for steel and iron during World War II brought an end to iron bank manufacturing. Along with the shrinking value of the dollar and the growing irrelevance of loose change after the war, small banks became an obsolete novelty—obsolete, that is, until people rediscovered them.

During 1983 an important event in the world of mechanical banks occurred. The amazing bank collection of Edwin Mosler, Jr., was sold following his death. Mosler, the grandson of the founder of the Mosler Safe Company, had the world's most comprehensive and complete collection of banks. He had not just one of almost every bank made since 1876, but sometimes two and three, his collection numbering in the thousands.

Mosler was a generous, gregarious man who loved toys and anything mechanical. When his banks were sold by lottery, collectors

and dealers worried that prices would nosedive because such a large number of banks would suddenly be on the market. But that did not happen. Instead, several million dollars worth of banks served to feed a hungry market and prices went up. Mosler's lottery also enabled new collectors to buy in.

★ **Collector Bill Norman bought a bank from a shopkeeper for $200 and then had second thoughts. The paint on the bank was faded, and overall it was not impressive. But he took it home anyway thinking he might return it. At home he discovered that nearly fifty years of soot had accumulated on the bank and it had actually protected the paint. He washed the soot off and realized the bank was really worth $1,500.**

Values Outside the Home. Although a beginning collector can buy mechanical banks for as little as $50 to $70, the truly rare banks, in fine condition, begin in the $500 to $800 range. Generally less expensive, and not as unique, are the still and advertising banks beginning for as little as $25.

The beginning collector should be aware that reproductions as well as forged banks exist in the market. Forgeries were discovered as far back as the late 1930s, and some price guides today indicate which banks are known to have been forged and in circulation. Reproductions are usually identified and sold as such. But because some of them were made over forty years ago it takes an experienced eye to tell the difference between them and copies.

The first steps to collecting, according to veterans, are to research and read about mechanical banks and then to select a *type* of bank to collect. Penny banks for instance. Or animal banks. One beginner focused on banks in the form of buildings because he liked architecture.

Collectors and dealers like to talk about banks and share their knowledge with beginners. One can also check in his area for museums with toy or bank exhibits. More and more books about collecting are being published, and getting information about specific items within a field of collecting is not as hard as it used to be.

The same thorough, patient approach should be used when collecting still banks, whether one is interested in glass, steel or ceramics.

Register banks (similar to real cash registers) are also on the market. There is a Popeye bank made in 1929 that takes only dimes. Another register bank from the Bennett Brothers of New York takes nickels, dimes, quarters, half-dollars and even bills. Each time the total amount hits $10, the bank opens.

A mechanical bank, to be in good condition, must have a high percentage of original paint. All the original parts must be present and in working order. Certainly rarity is a factor in value, but other factors that make a bank valuable are its animation and its history. A particularly popular design can bring a higher price than a rare bank.

Where to Find Values. The weekend antiques show is not the best place to buy old banks, although a few may be discovered there. But they will probably be in poor condition and overpriced. The antiques toy and advertising shows, on the other hand, present the best opportunities for the beginner. These are often advertised in newspapers.

The Mechanical Bank Collectors Association has regional conventions each year. A rare-bank show is usually part of the festivities. Here, collectors are able to see banks (usually not for sale) that cost thousands of dollars and will also learn to judge condition and appeal. They may also want to make their first knowledgeable buy at this kind of a convention, perhaps with a little bargaining to test buying skills.

Local newspapers sometimes carry classified headings for memorabilia or Americana that include mechanical banks. The Yellow Pages of the phone book will also have a section on antiques.

Auctions usually attract professional dealers who will sometimes allow themselves to be caught up in the emotion of the bidding. This can drive up the price of a bank beyond that of what it might bring at a show. The beginner should stay clear of bidding at an auction until he is no longer a beginner.

A Price Sampling

Baby elephant (mech.)	$10,000
Acrobat (mech.)	2,000
Darktown battery (better condition)	1,150
Darktown battery (mech.)	650
Artillery (mech.)	600

Chocolate Menier (mech. tin)	80
Turkey (still, cast iron)	80
Lion (still, cast iron)	50
Popeye (register, metal)	40

How to Store/Display. Mechanical banks are durable, but collectors have differing opinions about suitable care. The bottom line seems to be, when in doubt, do nothing. Some collectors will spray clear acrylic paint on the bank in order to enhance the brightness of the original color. But other collectors contend they would never buy a bank with acrylic on it.

Banks can be gently and lightly waxed, but waxes should be free of cleaners—old paint is sometimes too fragile for cleaners. Banks should also be kept out of direct sunlight and away from moist environments.

How and When to Sell. Even though some of the prices paid for mechanical banks cause the uninformed to blink and swallow, the market continues to be strong.

If one is collecting out of a sense of hobby, he need sell only when he wants to. One can sell directly to dealers, at an antiques advertising show, through ads in collectors' publications, or through an auction if a collection is noteworthy.

Little-Known Facts. Edwin Mosler, Jr., once had a man come to him and offer to sell him a bank for $50. Mosler wrote out a check for $50 and asked the man if he was satisfied. The man said yes. "You cheated yourself," said Mosler and wrote out another check for $500. The bank was rare and Mosler wanted the man to get the proper value for it.

• Some banks have delightful names, such as "Always Did 'Spise a Mule," "Thrifty Tom's Jigger," "When My Fortune Ship Comes In," "Poor Weary Willie," or "Smiling Jim & Peaceful Bill."

—David Holmstrom

Bibliography

Books

Hughes, Stephen. *Pop Culture Mania.* New York: McGraw Hill, 1984.

Meyer, J. *Penny Banks: Mechanicals and Stills.* Watkins Glen, NY: Century House, 1960.

Moon, Susan and Andy. *Penny Bank Book.* Exton, PA: Schiffer Publishing, 1984.

Norman, Bill. *The Bank Book: Encyclopedia of Mechanical Banks.* Burbank, CA: Collectors Showcase, 1985.

Periodicals

Periodic Reports: Mechanical Bank Collectors of America. P.O. Box 128, Allegan, MI 49010.

Schroeder's Insider & Price Update. P.O. Box 3009, Paducah, KY 42001 (occasional bank coverage).

Catalogues

Cranmer, A. *Encyclopedia of Toys and Banks with Price Guide and Identification.* Gas City, IN: L. W. Productions, 1984.

Huxford, Sharon and Bob, editors. *Schroeder's Antiques Price Guide.* Paducah, KY: Collector Books, 1985.

Dealers

Griffith, F. H., P.O. Box 323, Sea Girt, NJ 08750.

Norman, Bill, 2601 Empire Ave., Burbank, CA 91504.

Suozzi, Marx, Box 102, Ashfield, MA 01330.

Associations

Mechanical Bank Collectors Association of America, P.O. Box 128, Allegan, MI 49010.

MILITARIA

Adventurous-minded collectors may be drawn by the noble sweep of the guardsman's cape, or the gleam of the horse soldier's spurs. As well, those of us whose sentiments reside in family memories may embrace military objects such as these with a fondness that respects the nobility they represent. Many of us have a parent or grandparent who fought in a war, and we attach a lot of emotion to those old buttons, jackets and stripes. Military memorabilia—"militaria"—is part of our past, and interest in it has been increasing with each passing year.

History. Swords, a primary example of militaria, have been collected since ancient times. Over the centuries, an evolution of the weapons, clothes and accoutrements of soldiering has occurred. These objects have been assembled and displayed by museums and academies

Library of Congress

One of the most memorable profiles in modern
American military history was that of General Douglas
MacArthur. Rarely did the public see photos of him
without his aviator's glasses or his corncob pipe.

throughout the world. Today militaria is increasingly collected by
individuals who have a general interest in the history of war or who
appreciate the well-made artifacts of this ageless activity. Perhaps due
to the growing interest in war gaming and model soldiering (creating
accurately detailed regimental miniatures), many younger people
are collecting militaria. There are also those collectors whose
interests have come from their personal war experiences.

★ **Rudy Garcia of San Diego, California, built a collection of naval
hats and caps by buying them from American and foreign sailors
whose ships had docked in San Diego Bay. His collection was
recently appraised for insurance purposes at seven times what he
had paid for it.**

Values Outside the Home. Because militaria includes items from the armies and navies of all the countries of the world, a beginner must exercise a measure of discrimination if he is to build a collection that is manageable. Some broad categories to base a collection on are military weapons; helmets and headdresses; uniforms; medals, badges and buttons; and military prints, books and ephemera. Within these categories numerous specialties are possible.

Military weapons is a term that collectors apply to the weapons used by regular armed forces. Most sought after here are pikes, muskets, rifles, bayonets, swords, and pistols. Armor is also considered a weapon; armor skirts, breast plates, and helmets were integral parts of the early soldier's wardrobe.

Helmets have been worn since ancient times. Sumerians and Egyptians wore leather caps to protect themselves in battle. Before long, helmets were adorned with horns, feathers and furs. The local knight in shining armor wore a *close helm*—a classy-looking piece of headgear descended from the huge, cylindrically shaped *great helm*. Collectors can sometimes find close helms dating back to the seventeenth century in antiques shops or at auctions.

Eighteenth-century soldiers looked rather smart under their *jockey caps* and *tricorns,* dressed with plumes and tufts of lace. Units of several European armies wore bearskin hats fitted in front with a nobleman's arms or the regimental badge, plaited cords draped gracefully around the top. Simpler headdress included the *kepi* and *shako* (similar in shape to the familiar *bandsman*'s cap worn by Robert Preston in *The Music Man*).

Uniforms kept pace with the changes in headdress. From complete informality evolved a standardization of the soldier's livery, probably the result of a ruling power's desire for greater authority. By the middle of the nineteenth century, many European armies were standardizing everything from belt buckles to cartridge boxes. Uniforms are interesting pieces for individual display, but storage problems dampen their popularity as collectors' items.

More popular are the medals, buttons and badges that were fastened to uniforms, distinguishing one regiment and one soldier from another. The value of a medal depends on its rarity and condition. Also important is its association with a person, event, unit, or with other medals that together comprise a particular group. Medals may be naval or military, commemorative or campaign, observing an order or award. General issues of medals were not commonly made before the middle of the nineteenth century, and awards for acts of bravery or long service are more rare than campaign medals. Some approaches to medal collecting include: concentrating on one regiment; obtaining a complete sample of the issue from a particular campaign; completing a sequence of medals covering a particular period; or developing a historically representative selection. Manageable size and expense make medals popular collectors' items, the abundance of ribbons adding color to the pursuit.

Badges and buttons are interesting and inexpensive. Badges that fasten to breast, cap, collar and sleeve often carry a symbol in their design, such as a cannon for artillery, or wings for parachutes or airplanes. Nineteenth-century badges of rank were of metal and worn on the epaulettes of an officer's tunic. More recent badges were made of cloth and worn on the shoulder, bearing a variety of designs and insignia. Buttons evolved from flat to convex shapes, and those from this century are still plentiful. Gilt buttons, made from a brass alloy, have been employed on uniforms since the 1750s, but military buttons can be of tin, pewter, brass, silver, ivory or gold. Not many gold ones will be found in a dealer's button bins, however.

All this regalia can be appreciated through military prints, many of which portray the dress of the period in splendid (if not always accurate) detail. Hand-colored book plates were produced in the late eighteenth century, followed by plates with printed color in the 1840s. These colored plates sold well, and print shops realized they could make a larger profit from the sale of individual plates than from a complete book; many dealers proceeded to remove the plates and throw away the text.

Military prints are popular because of their artistic qualities and because they provide information about the dress, tactics, and strategy of armies during a particular historical period. Reprints are often so good that they are hard to distinguish from the real thing. Care must be taken to avoid purchasing a copy for the price of an original.

Printed works also of interest to collectors include accounts of campaigns, regimental histories, general histories, instruction books, and official publications. Fly leaves containing signatures, names or notes add value in excess of an unsigned copy.

Within the broad range of military ephemera may be found wartime money, propaganda leaflets, military magazines, postcards, curios, and the work of prisoners of war. The latter objects commonly include dominoes, small toys, and crucifixes made from scraps of leather, odd pieces of wood, straw, and bones. Sometimes a ship was fashioned from these materials, often rigged with the maker's hair.

Where to Find Values. Dealers and auctioneers provide a ready source of militaria in all categories. Membership in clubs and associations can provide access to many objects, with possibilities for trading. More recent military memorabilia can often be acquired through friends and relatives who served in a war or who know someone who has. Inquiries placed in the classified section of newspapers also help locate particular objects.

A Price Sampling

British "Brown Bess" musket, c. 1760	$900
American Navy pistol by Colt, 1851	575
American cavalry saber, 1818	300
Japanese samurai sword, World War II	175
British officer's saber, single-edge blade and black leather scabbard with brass mounts	125
Luftwaffe raincape	90
Nazi M42 helmet, steel, with liner and chin strap	45
Nazi iron cross, 2nd class, with ribbon	22
Nazi swastika armband, red on white	8
Nazi shoehorn, Bakelite	3

How to Store/Display. Displaying a collection of militaria provides an opportunity to share the experience with friends, perhaps to relay the story behind this item or that. Weapons always make conversation pieces. Helmets and headdresses are similarly striking, and can be displayed on a simple wire or, for realism, on a model head. Uniforms may be shown the same way; one may use a well-shaped clothes hanger, even a lifelike mannequin. Military prints of course take on an added elegance when framed.

Preserving objects will require a variety of techniques. Leather may be treated with neat's-foot oil or a similar dressing. Brass or silver fittings will gradually be worn by polishing, and an alternative is to lacquer metal parts. Clothing should be cleaned by experts; storing it in plastic bags will preserve fabrics from moths, dust and air pollution. Some collectors think medals should be kept in their original condition. Others believe in cleaning dulled surfaces and replacing tattered ribbons. Medals are best preserved in cases sealed from impurities in the air.

Military prints will often be dirty, and a very soft eraser or even semi-stale bread applied to superficial marks will remove most of them. Larger jobs should be approached on an individual basis, since some papers will dissolve by exposure to moisture after a long period of dryness, or by exposure to the wrong cleaning agent.

★ **Mary Roberts was cleaning her grandfather's attic in preparation for an estate sale when she discovered a beautiful sword wrapped in cloth and lying in a dusty wood box. A note wrapped over the blade translated from French read, *"Thank you, Edward, for saving me. Forever yours, Jean Roland. 1917."* The sword was appraised by a Chicago dealer at over $1,000.**

How and When to Sell. When to sell is a personal choice, though the current popularity of an item is worth taking into account (objects from Imperial Germany and the Nazi regime are glamor pieces today). Consignment shops, dealers, auctioneers, and newspaper ads are good places to pass along military collectors' items.

—Terry Parker

Bibliography

Books
Gaylor, John. *Military Badge Collecting.* London: Secker and Warburg, 1983.
Wilkinson, Frederick. *Militaria.* New York: Hawthorn Books, Inc., 1969.

Periodicals
Military Collector News, Box 7582, Tulsa, OK 74105.
Military Images, 706 Mickley Rd., Whitehall, PA 18052.

Catalogues
Rankin, Robert. *Official Price Guide to Military Collectibles.* Orlando, FL: House of Collectibles, 1981.

Dealers
Military Research International, Box 264, Merrifield, VA 22116.
U.S. Surplus Center, 715 Camden, San Antonio, TX 78215.

Associations

American Military Society, Frank G. Frisella, 1528 El Camino Real, San Carlos, CA 94070.

Imperial German Military Collector's Association, Dr. Eric Johanson, Box 651, Shawnee Mission, KS 66201.

Japanese Sword Society of the U.S., Ron Hartmann, 5907 Deerwood Dr., St. Louis, MO 63123.

MINIATURES

Chances are there has never been a single object made by man for his day-to-day use that someone did not also make in miniature. And in the Victorian era, someone put almost everything ever made in miniature into a dollhouse.

Since the early 1970s, a renewed interest in dollhouses has led to a renewed interest in miniatures. Not many Victorian dollhouses have survived, but their tiny yet valuable contents may turn up anywhere, from an attic trunk to a flea-market bargain table.

History. It is likely that miniatures were originally created by craftsmen who were already successful toymakers. As miniatures became popular, factories specialized in them. As interest waned, the factories closed, creating valuable collectors' items out of the tiny toys that were once produced with such skill. Today, even the market for newly made miniatures is growing.

The Victorian passion for dollhouses provided a market for miniatures that appealed to another Victorian fancy: fine furnishings. Expert cabinetmakers crafted tiny versions of Queen Anne, Chippendale, Hepplewhite, and Sheraton designs. In Rhode Island, Tynietoy factory workers made authentic period pieces with a child-size circular saw until the 1930s.

Painted tin was another favorite, which appeared in nineteenth-century kitchens, creating a taste for painted tin miniatures. A nineteenth-century tin stove from Germany came complete with alcohol trough and wicks. A tin lavabo (a washbasin with a water tank and spigot) from England had a reservoir for water. Tiny tin pots and pans, utensils, and canisters were hung on tin walls of complete miniature kitchen sets. Automobiles, trucks, and airplanes were produced in miniature, as were pressed glass and china, tapestries, and guns.

Photograph by Roger Bartelt

The Tootsietoy Overland Bus, Mack Truck, and Ford Model A Coupe are some of the metal miniatures made by the Dowst Brothers of Chicago in the early 1930s. The scarcity of Tootsietoy items today has made them valuable.

★ **Missionary Ralph Partelow of Denver was having trouble supporting his wife and daughter, going to school, and making unpaid missionary trips to Africa. Ten years ago he began making miniature grand pianos. His pianos are so well known and in such demand that they have supported his family and his work ever since.**

Occasionally, miniatures were used for advertising. Murad cigarettes gave away doll-size rugs. A tin cradle advertised Victory lozenges. And English biscuits came in tins shaped like miniature castles.

Miniature bookmaking began with stone tablets several thousand years ago, and as soon as Gutenberg's printing press was in operation, it, too, was producing miniatures. A miniature book was defined as any volume made three inches or less in any direction. Dollhouse books, known today as microminiatures, are one inch or less. The Japanese are currently printing ultramicrominiatures, measuring under a quarter of an inch. The number of miniature-book presses and collectors is growing, attested to by the vigor of the Miniature Book Society, created in 1983.

Miniature painting is more art than artifact, and so better studied along with full-size paintings.

Values Outside the Home. The new collector might consider specializing in a certain material, such as wood, tin or glass; or in a room type, such as kitchen, living room or bathroom; or in a type of object, such as trucks, tea kettles or books. The wise buyer studies the market, goes to museums, talks to other collectors, and spends cautiously while learning.

Most miniatures are not considered good investments—buyers are usually looking for pleasure rather than capital gain. Within these limits, however, good buys can be found. Painted tin furniture is very rare, for instance, and valuable even if broken. Miniature china from an established factory, such as Royal Beyrouth or Wedgwood, will always be valuable. A pressed-glass butter dish or creamer that used to sell for $2 is now worth up to $50. "Ecology furniture" was made recently from tin cans. It will be valuable in the future. Tootsietoy metal furniture, trucks, and trains were produced by the Dowst Brothers in Chicago between 1925 and 1935. It is hard to find and thus valuable. A year and a half ago, Mattel began a line of metal furniture. The wise collector will grab up a good selection before the line is unavailable.

Quality furniture reproductions are still being made, signed and dated by the cabinetmaker. Melville G. Davey, one of the original Tynietoy craftsmen, is still making furniture reproductions, which his wife, Elizabeth, hand paints. John and Ellen Blauer create miniatures at their shop in San Francisco. Brass chandeliers and lamps, wood furniture, and ceramic Christmas plates with their mark also will be good buys.

Miniature books are valued according to quality or rarity. Like figurines, they are produced in limited editions. A book purchased for $20 three years ago may still be worth $20, or it may have gone up to $60. Most books retail for $18 to $80, but the most unique will cost as much as $300. An ultramicrominiature Ten Commandments, for instance, costs $150. Hard-to-find issues by Achille St. Onge, who died about four years ago, are already worth up to $1,500.

Where to Find Values. An excellent mail-order source for would-be collectors is *Nutshell News,* which has classified ads and a "Private Eye" column, in which buyers are given help in locating specific items. *Nutshell News* also lists dealers by state and had two-hundred-sixty display advertisers in one recent issue. No source, however, is better than a well-informed local dealer. And some dealers, such as those of San Francisco's Miniature Mart, specialize in mail order.

Finally, the collector should join the association dealing with his or her particular interest. The list of associations at the end of this chapter attests to the variety of miniatures both old and new available to the collector.

★ **Edgar L. Roy, a machinist in West Roxbury, Massachusetts, started making miniature automobiles in 1955, when he was afflicted with a nerve disorder. He now works thirty-five to fifty hours a week in his basement, making most of the parts himself, including tires with miniature valves. His perfectly detailed cars are said to be worth $35,000 to $40,000.**

A Price Sampling

Sewing machine, Singer; iron, tin cabinet, 5¼"	$600
Living room set, German; 8 pieces, marble top, c. 1880	260
Washer, Federal Tin, lithographed, w/wringer, 4¼"	130
Dining room set, Tootsietoy, 12 pieces	100
Cook stove, Venus, cast iron, 7½" × 5"	65
Volume of *Pinocchio,* pub. by Barbara Raheb, w/hand-painted porcelain Pinocchio doll 1¼" tall	39
Windsor chair, hand painted	35
Washtub and washboard, tin, 6½"	30
Casserole dish and cover, Ellen Krucker Blauer	14
Kerosene lamp, glass	7

How to Store/Display. Although once used as children's toys, miniatures should be kept far from their reach if they are to remain in good condition. Keeping them behind glass will not only show them off well, but will eliminate dusting.

Cleaning methods depend on the composition of the piece. The local library will have books detailing such methods.

Miniatures need to be shielded from direct sunlight and kept from extremes of heat or cold, dry or damp. A dish of calcium chloride concealed in a miniatures display will help absorb potentially damaging dampness. The dish should be refreshed often.

Miniatures look best displayed against a pastel background. Collectors specializing in furnishings and fixtures often create room settings or furnish dollhouses, including wallpaper and floor-tile reproductions.

Books can be kept in miniature bookshelves, tiny glass cases, or Oriental lacquer cabinets. For $65, Miriam Irwin (Mosaic Press, 358 Oliver Rd., Cincinnati, OH 45215) sells a regular-size book that is actually a storage box for miniatures.

How and When to Sell. Most miniatures are not considered investments to be bought and sold as the market changes. Rather, they are hobby items bought and kept for pleasure.

If a collector wishes to sell an entire collection, or if a death in the family forces such a sale, appraisals should be sought from several dealers. The seller might also compare prices for similar items in local stores or in catalogues available from miniatures dealers.

Membership in a miniatures society will open up new markets, as members buy, sell, and trade among themselves. Some associations hold swap meets and annual shows, at which buyers and sellers can mingle.

★ **A half-inch book published in the Netherlands in the 1720s was the smallest volume in the world for over one-hundred years. Then all of the copies mysteriously disappeared. One day in the 1950s a browser in a New York antiques store noticed five copies of the book inside a bowl priced at around $200. He bought the bowl, of course. At a British auction, the books sold for a total of 9,000 pounds (or $25,110).**

Little-Known Facts. Toys made of celluloid are very valuable, very breakable, and very dangerous. The material was outlawed in 1970 because of its high flammability. Collector Edith Morris tells of the time a big doll exploded in her hands. She was not deterred, however, and the visitor to her Hansel and Gretel Doll House Museum on Martha's Vineyard can see fine examples of celluloid miniatures.

Jack Norworth, the songwriter who wrote "Take Me Out to the Ball Game" and "Shine On Harvest Moon," was an avid collector of miniatures. W. C. Fields once gave him a set of miniature drinking glasses. His collection was bought by John Blauer and can be seen at the Miniature Mart (see "Bibliography").

Mrs. James Ward Thorne, heiress to the Montgomery Ward fortune, commissioned various artists to construct over eighty miniature American and European rooms. Most of these are on display at the Chicago Art Institute.

Barbara Raheb is the most prolific publisher of miniature books today. Two of her books were ordered by West Point for shipment to Houston and a trip on the Discovery space shuttle flight in August 1984. One was Shakespeare's *Sonnets,* the other, Chaucer's *Canterbury Tales.* The books are now the property of the Department of Literature at West Point.

Stanley Marcus of the Neiman-Marcus family is a miniature-book enthusiast. His Somesuch Press has produced a dozen three-inch books in the last few years.

—*Elinor Lindheimer*

Bibliography

Books

Bondy, Louis. *Miniature Books.* Available from Bromer Booksellers, 607 Boylston St., Boston, MA 02116.

Cook, Catherine and Edith Morris. *Fascinating Tin Toys for Girls, 1820-1920.* Available from Edith Morris, Hansel and Gretel Museum, Box 1454, Oak Bluffs, MA 02557.

Cowie, Donald. *Antiques: How to Identify and Collect Them.* New York: Castle Books, 1970.

Flayderman, Norman and Edna Lagerwall. *Collecting Tomorrow's Antiques Today.* Garden City, NY: Doubleday & Co., 1972.

Greenhowe, Jean. *Jean Greenhowe's Miniature Toys.* New York: Van Nostrand Reinhold, 1980.

Jacobs, Flora Gill. *A History of Doll's Houses.* New York: Scribner's, 1965.

Jacobs, Flora Gill. *Doll's Houses in America: Historic Preservation in Miniature.* New York: Scribner's, 1978.

Jensen, Gerald. *Early American Dollhouse Miniatures.* Radnor, PA: Chilton Books, 1981.

McClinton, Katherine M. *Antiques of American Childhood.* New York: Clarkson N. Potter, 1970.

McClinton, Katherine M. *Antiques in Miniature.* New York: Scribner's, 1970.

O'Brian, Marian M. *The Collector's Guide to Dollhouses & Dollhouse Miniatures.* New York: E. P. Dutton, 1974.

Smaridge, Norah and Hilda Hunter. *The Teen-ager's Guide to Collecting Practically Anything.* New York: Dodd, Mead & Company, 1972.

Periodicals

Miniature Collector. Collector Communications Corp., 170 Fifth Ave., New York, NY 10010 (bimonthly, $12/year).

Nutshell News. Clifton House, Clifton, VA 22024. Monthly ($29/year; sample copy, $3.25).

Catalogues

Bromer Booksellers, 607 Boylston St., Boston, MA 02116.

Craft Products, 2200 Dean St., St. Charles, IL 60174. *Doll Houses and Furnishings.*

Dawson's Book Shop, 535 North Larchmont Blvd., Los Angeles, CA 90004.

The Enchanted Doll House, Route 7, Manchester Center, VT 05255.

F.A.O. Schwartz, 745 Fifth Ave., New York, NY 10022.

Federal Smallwares Corporation, 85 Fifth Ave., New York, NY 10003. *Collector Miniatures.*

Happy Things, 73 Spring St., Eureka Springs, AR 72632.

Manhattan Doll Hospital, 176 Ninth Ave., New York, NY 10011 (send stamped self-addressed envelope for list of catalogues and prices).

Miniature Mart, 1807 Octavia, San Francisco, CA 94109.

Miniature Silver, 317 South Prospect Ave., Park Ridge, IL 60068.

Pizazz Ltd., 1510 W. 15th St., Amarillo, TX 79102.

Rombin's Nest Farm, 117 W. Main St., Fairfield, PA 17320.

Dealers (See also "Catalogues")

Bromer Booksellers, 607 Boylston St., Boston, MA 02116.

Dawson's Book Shop, 535 North Larchmont Blvd., Los Angeles, CA 90004.

House of Miniatures, Box 1156, Terre Haute, IN 47811.

Miniature Mart, 1807 Octavia, San Francisco, CA 94109 (by appointment only).

Mountain Valley Miniature Shop, 201 Union St., Occoquan, VA 22125.

Pizazz Ltd., 1510 W. 15th St., Amarillo, TX 79102.

Washington Doll's House and Toy Museum, 5236 44th St. N.W., Washington, DC 20015.

Associations

Liliputian Bottle Club, 5626 Corning Ave., Los Angeles, CA 90056 (wine, beer, and spirit bottles).

Miniature Arms Collectors/Makers Society, c/o Joseph Macewicz, 104 White Sand Ln., Racine, WI 53402.

Miniature Book Society, c/o Kalman L. Levitan, 6586 Eastpointe Pines St., Palm Beach Gardens, FL 33410.

Miniature Figure Collectors of America, 102 St. Paul's Rd., Ardmore, PA 19003.

Miniatures Industry Association of America, 1130 15th St. N.W., Washington, DC 20005.

Miniature Truck Association, c/o Ferdinand Zegel, 3449 North Randolph St., Arlington, VA 22207.

Motoring in Miniature Association, 147 Pin Oak Dr., Williamsville, NY 14221.

National Association of Miniature Enthusiasts, P.O. Box 2621, Anaheim, CA 92804.

MODEL TRAINS

Political columnist George F. Will wrote that the world of the 1940s was divided into two warring camps: on the one side were the Lionel train fans, who were loutish children with dark pasts clouded by dangerous futures; on the other side were the precocious, more discerning children who preferred and rejoiced in the American Flyer. Today, instead of being split between American-made models, the camps are divided between factions who prefer collecting and investing in either the American tinplate type or the highly detailed brass trains made overseas in such limited editions that a king's ransom may be enough to buy only one complete set.

History. Railroading in the nineteenth century was so popular that it inspired the manufacture of model trains in large numbers. From the late 1800s to the 1950s, when Lionel Corporation made 622,209 locomotives and 2.4 million cars, two track-gauge sizes became standard among American manufacturers: 2⅛″ and 1¼″, with the 2⅛″ width corresponding to the larger model trains made up to World War II. Trains on these tracks were popular during the '20s and '30s and had cars measuring nearly two feet long. The Lionel State set, made mostly by hand between 1929 and 1935, had hinged roofs to expose plush car interiors. They would also bring high resale values to collectors.

The Standard-gauge railroad sets gave way in the 1930s to the smaller 1¼″-width track. The reduction in track size replaced the Standard-gauge with O-gauge trains, which were fashioned from blueprints of actual operating trains and labeled with their names.

Though the pre-World War II Standard-gauge trains are more popular as collectors' items, O-gauge models have increased in value more rapidly due to the greater details of such operating accessories as automatic cars that deliver milk, load coal and logs and perform a host of movements by remote control. Joshua Lionel Cowen, who founded Lionel Corporation, created a long line of these movement-oriented cars for kids who quickly grew tired of seeing their trains only travel in circles. His insight produced some of the most exciting model railroading available to children. Unfortunately, his trains are ignored as collectors' items because most hardcore investors and collectors do not actually run their trains but keep them in mint condition for maximum resale value.

★ **A collector-surgeon acquired a boxful of miscellaneous items that he bid on at auction. Before he placed the winning bid, he had quickly examined the objects and discovered several German-made trains dating to the early 1900s. Once the box was his, he realized that for $300 he was now the owner of trains worth as much as $1,500, not to mention the worth of other cast-iron toys in the crate that were also of collector quality.**

Values Outside the Home. The major American toy train-makers were Lionel Corporation, American Flyer Manufacturing Company, Ives Corporation, and Louis Marx and Company. The large volume of trains manufactured by Lionel has made them easier to collect than the rarer American Flyers. Marx engines and cars were brightly painted, low in detail, relatively inexpensive, and sold in dime stores. Ives trains, originally manufactured in 1868, were meant to appeal to an elite market, but because of their earlier reputation as inexpensive wind-up models, the company went bankrupt in 1928.

Collectors often suggest that beginners put their love for trains ahead of their desire to make a profit, since one may have to hold on to a collection for years before making a substantial gain.

Brass model trains exist in a world apart from the tinplate American trains and might be thought of as model railroading's high-tech foreign counterparts. Unlike the lesser-detailed American models, brass trains are intricately detailed to duplicate to scale former engines, cars and entire lines.

So many model trains were produced by Lionel Corporation up to 1950 that today they are relatively easy for collectors to find. This car is part of Lionel's State Set, which featured hinged roofs that exposed the cars' interiors.

Compared to the mass-produced plastic models and die-cast trains of today, the foreign-made brass locomotives are produced in limited editions and require a high standard of craftsmanship. Their value lies in their reputation as historically correct replicas. Their production rate is often so low that a collector-investor who wants to purchase them must contact a dealer that receives brass trains from a particular manufacturer and place an order long before the unit arrives.

Brass-train collectors look for exact duplications of the most intricate details—anything less will often lower a selling price. An astute collector will make use of good photos taken of the actual life-size locomotive to check for alterations or imitations.

Where to Find Values. An obvious starting place is one's neighborhood hobby store if it features the sale and purchase of model trains. Many local dealers have private collections and are eager to share their knowledge. However, these same collectors and dealers are reluctant to discuss prices and values of their own pieces. Instead, they will usually suggest that a beginner look at one of the recent issues of

R. A. Brown's *The Brown Book* for prices on foreign-made brass sets, and Bruce C. Greenberg's *Greenberg's Price Guide to Lionel Trains* for the values of Lionel locomotives.

Associations, clubs and conventions are all excellent places to make contact with collectors and buyers. The Train Collectors Association in York, Pennsylvania, is one of the country's largest enthusiast groups and meets every April and October.

Occasionally complete train collections and serious collectors can be discovered by reading newspaper ads or through word-of-mouth. For example, a writer went to interview ex-Brooklyn Dodger Roy Campanella for a book and discovered he had a large collection of post-World War II model trains and two rare Lionel steam locomotives. The writer left with a 773 Hudson, a 746 Norfolk, Western pieces by Lionel and a deal to buy the entire set.

Buyers should beware of purchase through newspaper ads. A rule here is to know one's hobby. Only knowledge will protect buyers from dishonest craftsmen, who produce bogus pieces that only experts can quickly recognize.

Operators are a different breed of collectors and are usually excellent sources of information on specific lines.

A Price Sampling. The following prices reflect values in the West. Model prices are often regional, often gauged by the demand for a particular train line. Southern Pacific Cab-forward locomotives, for example, are higher in the West, while replicas of eastern railways are a better buy in the East.

American-made Trains (mint conditon)	
Ives O-gauge set No. 576, the Commodore	$2,400
American Flyer set No. 1387	1,700
Lionel locomotive No. 2345, Western Pacific	650
American Flyer No. 1093 locomotive	100
Lionel locomotive No. 201	35

Brass Trains (mint condition)	
Union Pacific 4000 Big Boy locomotive	$1,500
Canadian Pacific G-2 locomotive	350
Union Pacific 9000 Union Pac locomotive	250
Southern Pacific #966 Switcher	225
Logging locomotive #5 Georgia Pacific	200

How to Store/Display. To maintain the best condition possible, cars should be individually protected in styrofoam or bubble-wrap while in storage. This is especially true for brass trains. Locomotives should rest in an upward position, so that oil from their engines will not drip down on brass surfaces and spoil the finish. To display trains, many collectors arrange them on short sections of track and place them under dustcovers.

How and When to Sell. The *Wall Street Journal* reported that the investment potential of brass locomotives has raised their value beyond that of a number of listed stocks. Even the so-called *orphans*—locomotives made by companies that have gone out of business—have continued to increase in worth even though they might not be part of complete sets.

Collectors should check their phone books for retailers who buy new and used model trains. They should also look for model train magazines, where they can place ads that will be read by train buyers all over the country.

Although there are no steadfast rules for buying and selling, the beginner who understands the growing demand for models, who develops a sense of supply and demand, and who stays alert to trends practically guarantees himself that his investment will bring a good return and a lot of fun.

★ A collector-dealer intent on assembling a complete collection of mint sets of trains and individual cars received a call from a man anxious to sell a Lionel 400E, which is in great demand and sells readily for $1,000 to $1,500. When asking the price, the collector stated, "Not a penny less than $500." The dealer proceeded to buy the set for at least half of what he would have had to pay from someone more knowledgeable.

Little-Known Facts. The "Girl's Set" was made by Lionel in 1957 to 1958 aimed at, obviously, young female train enthusiasts. The special trains came in a variety of pastels. Unfortunately, only a handful were sold. Originally priced at $25, today a mint set (still retained in its original package) can fetch $500 to $750.

• Many pre-World War II standard-gauge models ended up in metal scrap piles to support the war effort. To make certain that the public did not forget the idea of owning a model train, however, Lionel produced lithographed cardboard punch-out train sets, in 1943, with wood axles and paper wheels. They sold for $2. Today the rare sets sell for about $300.

• In 1948, Lionel needed money for the manufacture of its popular F-3 diesel models and decided to approach General Motors. GM responded with an advance of $50,000 under the stipulation that its logo be seen on each set of the new diesels.

—Billy Cache Lewis

Bibliography

Books

Brown, R. A. *The Brown Book*. Burbank, CA: Darwin Publishing, 1982.
Greenberg, Bruce C. *Greenberg's Price Guide to Lionel Trains 1901-1942*. Sykesville, MD: Greenberg Publishing, 1979.
VanCaspel, Venita. *Money Dynamics for the 1980's*. Reston, VA: Reston Publishing Co., Inc., 1980.

Periodicals

Interchange Track. P.O. Box 11851, Lexington, KY 40578.
Lion Roars. (Same as above.)
NMRA Bulletin. P.O. Box 2186, Indianapolis, IN 46206.
T.T.O.S. Bulletin. 25 West Walnut St., Pasadena, CA 91103.
Train Collectors Newsletter. P.O. Box 248, Strasburg, PA 17579.
Train Collectors Quarterly. (Same as above.)

Catalogues

Greenberg, Bruce C. *Greenberg's Price Guide to Lionel Trains: Postwar O and O-27 Trains*. Sykesville, MD: Greenberg Publications, 1982.
Hudgeons, Thomas E., ed. *Official Price Guide to Collectible Toys*. Orlando, FL: House of Collectibles, 1984.

Associations

Lionel Collector's Club, P.O. Box 11851, Lexington, KY 40578.
National Model Railroad Association, P.O. Box 2186, Indianapolis, IN 46206.
Toy Train Operating Society, Inc., 25 West Walnut St., Suite 305, Pasadena, CA 91103.
Train Collector's Association, P.O. Box 248, Strasburg, PA 17579.

MOTORCYCLES

Motorcycles and adventure seem to go together. Some very dashing individuals were quite fond of motorcycles, including

Originally created by the British to be the best touring bike ever made, the legendary Black Shadow (1948 production model here) remains a thoroughbred among aficionados, although it is extremely rare...and extremely expensive.

Lawrence of Arabia and the late film actor Steve McQueen. Marlon Brando rode into movie history on one—a wild one—and to this day the motorcyclist carries on the tradition of the knight-errant, the pony-express rider and the aristocratic equestrian out for a romp.

Part of the investment value of old motorcycles lies in their ability to transport passengers in style. Few experiences in life are as exhilarating as a brisk motorcycle ride on an empty, twisting road, and few objects can attract the eyes of passersby as effectively.

Collecting and restoring motorcycles demands a dogged persistence that exceeds that required of most other collectors. But the very challenge of the search and the intense concentration that goes into rebuilding a bike are what make motorcycle collecting so enjoyable.

History. Compared to automobiles, the hobby of collecting and restoring old motorcycles is small and specialized, much the same as the old-car hobby must have been in the 1940s and 1950s. The reason for this is not so much a lack of interest, but rather an inherent scarcity of available motorcycles regarded as "classic," and hence valuable. Even though motorcycle manufacture goes back to the earliest days of automobile development (the first "motorcycle" appeared in 1894), by the 1920s an enormous number of motorcycle builders had been wiped out, both in America and Europe, and included such names as Apache, Champion, Erie, Flanders, Greyhound, Iver-Johnson, Holley, Imperial, and Yale.

After World War II, only two American manufacturers were left: a reasonably healthy Harley Davidson and a very sick Indian. By 1953, Indian collapsed, and into this vacuum stepped the British cycle industry, which dominated world markets until the 1960s, when the Japanese, Italians and Germans took over.

Thus we find really old motorcycles, say, prior to 1965, to be very rare sights on the street, while motorcycles built after that date are relatively common. Classic motorcycles are so infrequently seen not only because of the limited numbers in which they were originally made, but also because of their basic susceptibility to weather, accidents and mechanical wear, all of which have greatly diminished potential survivors.

★ A collector in Sacramento, California, found his antique "dream bike" in a most interesting way. While visiting a motorcycle repair shop near his home, he was invited by a friendly old-timer to take a look at a cycle stored in the old man's barn. It turned out to be a 1928 Harley-Davidson with only 21,000 miles on it. When the collector asked how much the old man wanted for it, he was told that if he promised to restore it and never sell it, he could have it, free! The new owner has faithfully kept his promise, and the old Harley is running as good as new.

Values Outside the Home. Every dedicated motorcycle collector hopes to find a 1909 Pierce, 1914 Yale, or 1936 Indian Chief resting peacefully in someone's barn or warehouse, dusty but intact, waiting to be bought for a few hundred dollars. This does happen now and then, but it is not a realistic goal for newcomers to the hobby. One is more likely to see these rare cycles in museums or as carefully restored machines commanding high prices.

A more fruitful approach would be to devote one's time and energy to searching for cycles that are more modern, but not so modern that it would take thirty years for them to appreciate. Certain post-World War II motorcycles offer the advantages of reliability and parts availability—two factors that can drive the collectors of pre-war cycles crazy with frustration.

The beginning collector should consider the following three types of motorcycles before he invests:

British motorcycles: While some post-war British bikes, such as Vincent and Ariel, are rare and expensive, others, such as BSA, Norton, Royal Enfield and Triumph, are still reasonably priced and available in all stages of condition. These cycles will gain in value, especially if they are in a clean, original state. Especially sought after are racing models (better yet if they have a documented track record) and limited-production anniversary models, such as the 1977 Triumph Silver Jubilee. If one does invest in a British bike, by all means he should learn to work on it himself, since they require a good deal of maintenance.

Harley-Davidson and *Indian:* If rugged, heavy machinery is appealing, then one should consider America's two best-known makes. Harley-Davidson is the more common, the easier to get parts for, and generally the less expensive to buy and restore. While heavily customized Harley show bikes are often sold for a small fortune, the average collector is better off with unaltered bikes.

The Indian, which disappeared in 1953, is getting more and more difficult to find as a fixer-upper, and is rapidly approaching antique bikes in rarity and price.

European motorcycles: A bewildering variety of motorcycles have been manufactured in Europe but are virtually unknown in the United States. Nor is one likely to see anything but a dozen or so of the less obscure makes on American streets. These might include BMW, Benelli, CZ, DKW, Ducati, Jawa, Laverda, MV Augusta, Moto Guzzi, Puch, and Zundapp, of which only some are the big-bore type of road bike considered most valuable by the majority of collectors. Sticking with the larger-displacement BMWs, Benellis (a six cylinder!), Ducatis and Moto Guzzis would be good choices for the beginning collector. Here, as with the first two types of bikes, special racing and limited-production machines are more valuable than standard versions.

First-time investors should also be aware of several other points before choosing what to buy. These include condition and completeness (finding missing parts for cycles long out of production can be a prodigious task).

Since no price guide exists for older motorcycles, it will also be a collector's job to consult appropriate periodicals and club newsletters to get a feeling for the price range of various bikes. It is important to remember that only rare motorcycles in good condition bring high prices.

Before buying, it also makes sense to ask for full documentation on any seller's claims made for a cycle's history or rarity and to buy only what one would *enjoy* riding (some of the older cycles are a bear to handle!).

Where to Find Values. While old motorcycles do occasionally show up in the classified section of local newspapers, most of the really interesting bikes are sold through the grapevine, which may consist of popular periodicals, club newsletters, and the bulletin boards of local motorcycle repair shops. Classic car auctions will frequently feature old bikes as well, more often than not rather well restored.

★ **A California collector named Ekins bought his first old cycle about thirty years ago. It was a 1928 Henderson, for which he paid $35. After riding it many years, he sold it for $450. Five years later he bought it back for $800. The last he heard, the current owner was asking $5,000. But Mr. Ekins probably isn't tempted to buy it back, since he owns 125 other antique motorcycles.**

A Price Sampling

1947 Vincent HRD Rapide, series B, very good	$7,000
1939 Indian 4-cylinder, like new	6,000
1915 Thor twin, older restoration	5,000
1969 BMW R60 US, like new	5,000
1957 Triumph 500 cc. military bike, never run, like new	4,000
1951 Harley Davidson 74, all original, very good	3,500
1947 Indian Chief, older restoration	3,000
1956 Triumph Tiger 650, very good	2,500
1946 BSA M-20, 500 cc. single civilian model, older restoration	2,200
1956 DKW 2-cylinder, not running, incomplete	200

How to Store/Display. Motorcycles require more care and protection than automobiles. For this reason it is important to keep classic motorcycles garaged, or at least covered and out of the weather. Needless to say, it should also be kept locked when parked during even the briefest outing, preferably with a theft-proof chain looped through the frame and then secured to something permanent and immovable, such as a fence, lamppost or, better yet, a bridge.

Experienced motorcyclists will agree that one of the most important maintenance services to perform on a cycle, and especially on an old one, is to periodically tighten all of its nuts and bolts. It is also wise to invest in high-quality tires, a full face helmet and to keep the drive-chain (if applicable) lubricated and the motor well tuned. To preserve its good looks, the bike should be hosed off and then given a good coat of wax after every long ride.

Paying attention to these things will help to keep bikes both valuable and safe.

How and When to Sell. There is not yet a large market for classic motorcycles, and one has to be patient when selling one. If a bike is both beautiful and rare, it will be easy to sell. Buyers will track it down through ads run by collectors in selected periodicals and newsletters. (It is recommended not to advertise a bike in larger newspapers because it has a good chance of getting lost in the classified section where it is lumped in with modern motorcycles.)

To sell newer bikes, or those that are a bit rough, one can easily draw potential buyers by parking the faithful steed outside on a beautiful spring day with a "For Sale" sign taped to the headlight. This simple display can be pretty irresistible to bike enthusiasts looking to expand their collections.

A final word of advice. Sellers should be very careful who they let ride their motorcycles when selling. Customers should be licensed to drive a bike, and their license numbers should be recorded. Sellers can also require a cash damage deposit, as well as follow along in another vehicle.

★ A Sausalito, California, man bought a 1953 BMW Model R67 motorcycle in pieces (it had been buried in the snows of Colorado) in 1973 for $300. After getting it bolted together and running, he drove it in its disheveled state, restoring it whenever he found the time. After driving it for over 30,000 miles and spending about $1,200 on materials, he sold it in 1977 for $2,500. It was not a fantastic profit, but he got tremendous use and pleasure from the bike, driving it for four years for what he considered was free.

Little-Known Facts. The first Harley-Davidsons were sold in 1903 and were known as the "silent gray fellows" because of their quiet engines and conservative paint scheme...not exactly the image of Harley-Davidsons today!

• During World War II, the escort to the Japanese emperor often rode Rikuo motorcycles, which, judging from the name, were Japanese. But they were really Harley-Davidsons, which were manufactured in Japan before the war. The plant was seized at the outbreak of hostilities.

—Joseph L. Troise

Bibliography

Books

Kimes, Beverly Rae. *Automobile Quarterly's Complete Handbook of Automobile Hobbies.* Kutztown, PA: Automobile Quarterly.

Tax Guide for Auto Restorers and Collectors. Irvine, CA: Professional Accounting Offices, 1984.

Tragatsch, Erwin. *An Illustrated History: Motorcycles.* New York: A&W Publishers, Inc., 1981.

Periodicals

Hemmings Motor News. Box 100, Bennington, VT 05201.

Indian Motorcycle News. P.O. Box 455, Lake Elsinore, CA 92330.

Walneck's Classified Magazine. 8280 Janes, Suite 17A-1700, Woodridge, IL 60517.

NOTE: Many excellent newsletters are produced by associations devoted to one or more types of classic motorcycles. Collectors may consult *The Encyclopedia of Associations* in the reference section of their local libraries.

Catalogues

Catalogues for vintage motorcycle parts are best discovered by consulting the periodicals listed above, especially *Hemmings Motor News,* which has a section called "Cycles and Parts for Sale." Here's a sample of others offered:

Antique Cycle Supply. Cedar Springs, MI 49319.

Classic Motorbooks. P.O. Box One, Osceola, WI 54020.

Indian Motorcycle Supply. P.O. Box 1152, Aurora, IL 60507.

Sidecar Parts. 658 Lemon Hill Terrace, Fullerton, CA 92632.

Dealers

Ghost Motorcycle, 194 Main St., Port Washington, NY 11050.

M. F. Egan's, P.O. Box 738, Los Alamitos, CA 90720.

Motorcycle Classics, 628 Meridian St. NE, Huntsville, AL 35801.

Walneck's Vintage Motorcycle Sales, 8280 Janes, Suite 17A-1700, Woodridge, IL 60517.

Associations

Here is a sampling of clubs dedicated to the restoration and enjoyment of old motorcycles. Many more are listed in *The Encyclopedia of Associations* found in the reference section of local libraries.

Antique Motorcycle Club of America, c/o D. K. Wood, 14943 York Rd., Sparks, MD 21152.

Vintage Racers of Old Motorcycles (VROOM), 10200 Nevada Ave., Chatsworth, CA 91311.

MOVIE AND THEATER MEMORABILIA

In case you are of the opinion that collecting movie and theater memorabilia is just another trivial pursuit, consider the following late-1984 news items. In October, thieves in San Francisco stole a pair of ruby slippers that Judy Garland had worn in *The Wizard of Oz*. One of six pairs made for the film, the shoes sold at auction in 1972 for an average of about $2,000 per pair. The insured value of the stolen pair in 1984? $20,000!

In November, possessions from Steve McQueen's estate were auctioned off to the public in Las Vegas. Among the goods sold were a fire helmet worn by the actor in *The Towering Inferno*—it went for $1,900—and an ordinary chest of drawers that netted $800.

Two words define the world of stage and film collecting: "stars" and "hits." Especially stars. Name a great star—from this century or the last—and you will have hit on a collectors' gold mine. Name a great movie or Broadway show, on the other hand, and you *might* be mining a worthwhile vein, but not necessarily. If it is a great family movie (*Star Wars, E.T.*), something with a cult following (*Star Trek, The Rocky Horror Picture Show*) or a classic that has somehow become mythic (*Gone with the Wind, Casablanca*), there are probably a sizable number of lifelong fans who will always be eager to buy more merchandise related to their favorite show. If, on the other hand, the film is merely an Oscar winner—and particularly if it has no stars in it, like *Gandhi* or *Chariots of Fire*—interest in a show may be minimal.

History. Stage collectors' items have a history dating back at least two centuries, and many early examples are more accurately classified as antiques. *Actress glass,* with its exquisite etchings of Ellen Terry, Sarah Bernhardt and other nineteenth-century performers, commands considerable sums, as do the various medals, pendants, silverware, tea trays and ceramics commonly produced in the last century to commemorate world-famous thespians. Barbara Bel Geddes, the original Miss Ellie on *Dallas,* is an avid collector of actress glass.

But the majority of show business items—and the ones most easily found—date from this century, from 1920 on for stage and from 1930 on for film. Today's collecting can be seen as offshoots of post-World War II prosperity and pride, when those other than the wealthy could now afford to buy collectors' items, and when those other than the upper classes had some influence on popular tastes. High art in the form of classic theater would always be esteemed, but the standard show business productions that most audiences had become familiar with were no longer looked down upon. Broadway musicals and Hollywood melodramas and comedies came into their own, and their fans, many of whom had always been "secret" collectors, developed passions for acquiring artifacts from the entertainment world.

★ **Bob Latham, a high school chemistry teacher from Point Richmond, California, paid $25 for an edition of the novel *Frankenstein* published to promote the 1931 film version and illustrated with stills from it. He found the book through an ad in a collectors' newsletter. The seller believed the world was coming to an end and wanted to cash out his collection. Within three months of purchase, another collector—one with more confidence in the world's future—offered Latham over $100 for the book. Although he did not sell at that time, he was pleased to learn his special book had already quadrupled in value and confident it would continue to grow.**

Values Outside the Home. Theater fans want posters, souvenir programs (especially autographed ones), lobby photos, original cast albums, props, drawings for set designs, and sheet music from musicals. They also want personal objects that belonged to famous stars, composers, playwrights, and choreographers. Musicals are by far the most popular type of stage production for collectors.

The most famous shoes in modern movie history are Dorothy's "ruby slippers" (actually made of red sequins), coveted on her journey to Oz by the wicked witch of the West and today by film buffs and memorabilia collectors.

Movie fans want posters, lobby cards, publicity stills, sound-track albums, press kits, stars' personal belongings, and any kind of tie-in merchandise, such as toys, lunch pails, paper dolls, coloring books and cookie tins.

Show-business enthusiasts can go in one of two directions: they can get onto an already-rolling bandwagon for classic shows and stars, or they can get in on the beginning of future trends with current products and personalities. The former route is somewhat more expensive (unless one chances upon an undiscovered cache of articles), but items considered classic have consistently gone up in value over the past ten years and will continue to do so. There are some exceptions, however. Certain stars have peaked, and there is resistance to paying higher prices for their memorabilia than already exists. Humphrey Bogart is one such example. At the same time, other stars are just beginning to climb in value. The death of Richard Burton is likely to initiate a steep rise in the marketability of his memorabilia.

Choosing objects from new films is less expensive but also less dependable. Who knows what trend tomorrow will bring? Nevertheless, hobbyists can pretty much count on today's blockbuster movies to generate fans for years to come. When moviegoers return several times to see a film, its status for collectors is guaranteed.

★ **Eager to weed out the clutter in his small apartment, New Yorker David Bates decided to sell off several old sound tracks and show albums he no longer listened to. Although most brought him only $5 to $10 apiece, he was surprised to discover that two of his records were worth considerably more. An 8-inch LP of music from the film version of** *A Streetcar Named Desire,* **which he had bought new in 1951 for only a few dollars, was now commanding as much as $75 in the shops. Even more surprising was the selling price for his sound track from** *The Caine Mutiny.* **Due to a lawsuit at the time the picture was released, only a few thousand copies of the record were actually pressed, only a few hundred made their way to the shelves, and less than fifty were sold before the producer recalled the rest. The result: In 1984, collectors were offering anywhere from $500 to $2,000 for the album in top condition. In good but not excellent shape, David's copy brought him just over $1,000.**

Where to Find Values. The best sources for show business memorabilia are specialty shops, although it certainly would not hurt to check relatives' attics and even the kids' toy chest. Garage sales in non-metropolitan areas can still yield fantastic bargains, but it is often more work than it is worth to hunt them down. Most major metropolitan areas have one or two movie collectible shops, although the largest number, quite predictably, are in Los Angeles.

Theater collectors' shops are best found in New York City. Enthusiasts who live there might consider spending some time outside of stage doors, where autographs are often collected. An autograph will substantially increase an article's worth. For instance, the *Playbill* (a free guide given out at Broadway shows) is all but worthless; bearing an autograph of Mary Martin, however, will give it value of anywhere from $5 to $75.

Movie and Film Collector's World and *The Big Reel* (see "Bibliography") are excellent sources for locating memorabilia markets. Both advertise mail-order dealers and allow readers to place their own ads. In addition, they provide news on upcoming auctions, shows and conventions, several of which are held each month in various parts of the country. The columns in these publications can sometimes lead to exceptional bargains.

Another source for markets and information can be found among the thousands of celebrity fan clubs across the country. Most clubs have newsletters for their members, many of whom are anxious to buy, sell or trade merchandise pertaining to their favorite stars. Devoted fans will often pay top dollar for memorabilia since they enjoy collecting for the thrill rather than for the profit of it.

A Price Sampling

	Original price	Current price
A Star is Born, print of film, 1956 version	$100 (approx)	$695
Casablanca lobby card w/Bogart pictured	Not sold	400
Gaslight insert poster (1944)	.50	350
Mickey Mouse popcorn popper (1930s)	5.95	130
Raiders of the Lost Ark press kit (1980)	Not sold	85
Chinatown poster (1977)	6	75
Casablanca lobby card without Bogart	Not sold	50
Star Wars poster from Japan (1978)	10	45
The Terminator publicity still (1984)	12	20
Alice in Wonderland, 1951 version lobby card set	2 (approx)	15

How to Store/Display. Hobbyists can increase their chances of profit by giving great care to whatever they buy. Posters should be framed using a low acid backing; they can also be stored in airtight packaging. They should never be dry mounted, and only special tape purchased from art or surgical supply stores should be used to repair them if damaged.

Toys and other tie-in articles are best kept in their original packaging—an unassembled *Star Wars* model spaceship is worth more than an assembled one.

How and When to Sell. There is no single best time to sell most entertainment memorabilia, but there are better times than others.

Collectors should keep an eye on video releases. As soon as a new movie is sold on video cassette or shows up on cable television, it has gone out of general release and the studio that created it will no longer be producing posters and tie-ins. At that point, the supply of memorabilia is fixed. Following older films requires keeping up with the entertainment news. As mentioned earlier, a star's death will likely lead to higher prices for his or her memorabilia.

A change in status will also affect the value of an item; a minor star suddenly hits it big, or a major one makes a comeback that attracts a new generation of fans. Enthusiasts should also keep track of video sales and rentals. Some films that did poorly in general release begin to find their audience in the home market. Checking the video market will also reveal which classic films are holding on or gaining in popularity.

Collectors' periodicals and conventions can also be explored when selling. Collectors with enough merchandise should consider setting up booths of their own at conventions. Sellers should, however, stay away from flea markets; buyers there want bargains and are unlikely to give true value for an item.

The best time to sell theater memorabilia is after a successful show has had a major cast change or has closed. Items from minor successes should be sold more quickly, unless either the star or the playwright/composer/lyricist is a big name. Stage shows fade from memory more quickly than films because they cannot be seen again once they close. On the other hand, for the same reason, those that are remembered are particularly cherished.

★ **Michael Mooney, a paralegal from Kent, Ohio, and a longtime aficionado of Broadway musicals, rummaged through countless yard and garage sales gathering bits and pieces of theater memorabilia. Included in his finds were several pieces of sheet music transcribed by such greats as Irving Berlin and George Gershwin. These had apparently been given as gifts from the composers to friends or acquaintances who particularly admired their work. Presumably unaware of the sheet music's worth, the current owners sold the six song sheets for only a few dollars. Mooney immediately had the sheets appraised and discovered the lot was worth at least $500.**

Little-Known Facts. In a reversal of the usual wisdom, collecting memorabilia from certain Broadway flops can prove more lucrative than collecting from hits. The musical version of *Breakfast at Tiffany's* was a notoriously expensive flop that closed before it even got to Broadway. But because its leads, Richard Chamberlain and Mary Tyler Moore, both later became major stars, memorabilia from this show is highly sought after. The same goes for items from a more recent flop with no major stars (though it did have Eve Arden). *Moose Murders* acquired the reputation as the worst show ever to appear on Broadway, and anybody who saw it during its brief run was treated as something of a celebrity. For a short time, *Moose Murders* memorabilia enjoyed skyrocketing prices. Alas, that spurt has died out, and only time will tell if people of future decades will care enough to pay money for its detritus.

• Flop films rarely fare so well, but recently the popularity of a book called *Golden Turkeys* revived interest in some of the worst movies ever made. The camp value of *Plan 9 from Outer Space,* in which, due to the actor's untimely death, Bela Lugosi's part was played by a different actor during the last third of the movie, was quite high for a time but has since dwindled.

—John McCloud

Bibliography

Books

Chierichetti, David, and Steve Shapiro. *The Movie Poster Book.* New York: Dutton, 1979.

Dietz, James S., Jr. *Price Guide and Introduction to Movie Posters and Movie Memorabilia.* San Diego, CA: Baja Press, 1984.

Kobal, John, and V. A. Wilson. *Foyer Pleasure: The Golden Years of Cinema Lobby Cards.* London: Aurum Press, 1982.

Periodicals

American Film. American Film Institute, John F. Kennedy Center for the Performing Arts, Washington, D.C.

The Big Reel. Route 3, Madison, NC 27025.

The Film Collector/Media Sight. P.O. Box 2630, Athens, OH 45701.

Movie and Film Collector's World. 700 E. State St., Iola, WI 54990.

Movie Star News. 134 West 18th, New York, NY 10011.

Variety. 154 West 46th, New York, NY 10036.

Catalogues

Cinemonde, Poster City and Yesterdays (see "Dealers") publish annual catalogues of their merchandise; these provide good bases from which to compare prices.

Dealers

Cinema Collectors, 1507 Wilcox, Hollywood, CA 90028.
Cinemabilia, 10 W. 13th St., New York, NY 10003.
Cinemonde, 1916 Hyde St., San Francisco, CA 94109.
Collector's Showcase, 7014 Sunset Blvd., Hollywood, CA 90028.
Poster City, 3 Henry St., P.O. Box 94-F, Orangeburg, NY 10962.
Triton Gallery, 323 West 45th St., New York, NY 10036.
Woolsey's Auction Gallery, P.O. Box 651, Methuen, MA 01844.
Yesterdays, 174A Ninth Ave., New York, NY 10011.

MUSICAL INSTRUMENTS

Musical instruments and man have traveled together through the ages. Notable examples include Moses blowing the shofar as his people crossed the Red Sea, King David playing the harp as accompaniment to his Psalms, and Nero fiddling (or, in some accounts, playing his bagpipes) as Rome burned. We also associate the fife and drum with the American Revolution, and future generations will associate synthesizers and electronic instruments with our music of today.

History. The first musical instruments may have been old skulls struck with sticks or bones to produce dance beats or to communicate over distances.

Most of the early musical instruments unearthed were of simple construction, without moving parts—such as flutes, lutes, harps, and bagpipes—and were first found in Egypt. Only in the recent past (several hundred years ago) did slides, valves, keys, and other mechanical means allow a wide variety of instruments, including those that were blown, bowed, or beaten, to be developed.

★ An old Steinway grand piano, built in 1884 and used for years in the Martin Beck Theatre in New York City, was sold for $1,200 to an official with the Metropolitan Museum of Art. Several years later it was resold at auction for $390,000.

This small (11½ ") marble statuette from the year 3000 B.C. depicts a fine example of a primitive harp.

Values Outside the Home. Age is not necessarily a prime determinant of value—many old fiddles of the same vintage as Stradivarius violins are worth considerably less. Scarcity (number of instruments originally made and surviving), musical tone, artwork, and present condition all distinguish what is valuable from what is not. As John Mebane has stated, however, in his book *Treasure At Home,* "All old musical instruments are of some value."

Armies have marched to the beat of a *drum* throughout history, but the oldest existing American drums probably date from the Civil War. Snare drums, especially from military units, were tightened to improve tone by using cords on the outer shell, and the type of cord is one measure of the drum's age. Drums may also have regimental or unit names inscribed.

In the early 1700s, Antonio Stradivari, working in the Italian city of Cremona, produced about eight-hundred *violins,* which have become the world's most famous and are among the most expensive musical instruments available to collectors. Stradivarius violins had extraordinary musical tone, were well constructed, and are considered today to be works of art. The high prices and limited number of these instruments makes owning them nothing more than a dream for most collectors. And, there have been thousands of Stradivarius imitations discovered over the years.

Other nineteenth- and twentieth-century stringed instruments, such as *violas* and *cellos,* are becoming more popular and expensive as collectors' items.

Guitars and *banjos* are two instruments native to the United States that have experienced a recent resurgence in popularity. Guitars of the acoustical/non-amplified/non-electric type increased greatly in value during the 1950s and 1960s, when American folk music was the rage. Guitar brands most popular with these musicians (as well as collectors) include Martin (Martin 045), Gibson (Les Paul Sunburst, Flying V, and Explorer models), and Fender (Stratocaster and Telecaster models).

The banjo (called the *bonja* until the early 1800s) is probably the most native of all American musical instruments. Although it was used extensively in minstrel shows and popularized by black musicians, it was also used for performing classical music in the nineteenth century. Collectors especially favor five-string banjos made between 1880 and 1905 as well as Dixieland-style banjos, particularly with Manhattan, Peerless, Bruno, and Converse brand names.

The *mandolin* is a close cousin to the guitar and banjo in that strings are plucked with the finger or with a *plectrum* (pick). Mandolins were much more common in the early 1900s than they are today, and "Paddlin' Madeline Home" was probably the most popular mandolin song. Many types of mandolins were made (different sizes and numbers of strings) by manufacturers such as Washburn, Leland, and Martin.

Accordians and *concertinas* both have mechanical bellows, which, when activated by pressing combinations of keys, cause air to flow over tuned, vibrating reeds. The earliest accordians were made in

Austria, and the noted English physicist Sir Charles Wheatstone invented the concertina in 1829. The mechanical actions of these two instruments were similar, and most were made in England and Germany before 1900. Brand names include Hohner, Paragon, Clarion, and Pitzscher. Any accordians or concertinas from this era have probably already been renovated or restored, because the bellows (usually leather) did not last long with continual bending and folding.

The principle of the *harmonica*—a wind stream over a vibrating reed—is identical to accordians and concertinas, except that a harmonica player's lungs provide the wind stream directly. Harmonicas were invented in Germany, but in 1890 John F. Stratton of New York patented an improved mouth harmonica and the popularity of the instrument soared. By the end of the century the Hohner Harmonica Factory was the largest reed instrument manufacturer in the world, producing seven-million harmonicas per year with model names such as Admiral, Silver Queen, and Silver King.

Wind instruments can be divided into *reed* (woodwind) and *brass* types, and these are commonly associated with today's bands and orchestras. Single-reed (*clarinet, saxophone*) and double-reed (*oboe, bassoon, English horn*) woodwinds operate on the air-stream/vibrating-reed principle, while brass instruments use metal mouthpieces that produce tones based on the shape of the player's lips. Older wood-bodied reed instruments may not hold value over time, because the wood can become brittle, causing the instrument to lose tone. Older metal instruments are subject to metal corrosion, although they are more apt to retain their tone.

Reed instruments date back to Egypt, while the earliest brass units—bugles without moving parts—date to the time of the Roman Empire. Slides (*trombones*) and valves (*trumpets*) first appeared on European instruments in the 1500s. Because of the popularity of band and orchestral music in the United States in the nineteenth and twentieth centuries (remember *The Music Man?*), many manufacturers mass-produced wind instruments, so that a fifty-year-old trumpet or saxophone may not be worth much today. Generally, older instruments made by name companies (e.g., silver-plated instruments by G. C. Conn) are more durable and of greater value than newer, brass-plated ones.

Keyboard instruments, notably the *harpsichord* and *clavichord,* were very popular during the Baroque era in Europe, with composers such as Johann Sebastian Bach and George Frederick Handel producing many solo and concerto works. These instruments were the ancestors of today's piano, which was manufactured in the United States in large numbers over the last hundred years. Steinway and Sons have been making pianos since 1853 and have a policy of repurchasing and reselling their pianos. Any piano, whether a grand or upright, will appreciate in value if kept in good operating condition (especially the pneumatic-mechanical player pianos popular in the early 1900s).

Another keyboard instrument, the *parlor organ*—small foot-pumped organs, with several stops—is currently enjoying a renaissance as collectors are restoring them to operating condition and, in some cases, are electrifying the pumping action. Kenwood parlor organs, selling in 1905 to 1906 for $59.95, have increased in value several-fold. Collectors should contact the Reed Organ Society (Deansboro, New York 13328) for further information.

Two other musical instruments sought by collectors differ from those discussed in that they are generally not played by the musician. *Toy musical instruments* are small reproductions of the larger models and include snare drums, banjos, zithers, and fifes. The A. Schoenhut Company of Philadelphia made a miniature toy piano especially sought by collectors. *Music boxes* are limited to reproducing their own sounds but are also very desired by collectors. Music boxes were first produced in Switzerland in the early 1800s, and by the late 1800s had switched from disc to cylinder mechanisms with the capability to play up to ten tunes. Some music boxes used interchangeable cylinders and even included sets of bells. The phonograph, able to reproduce a wide spectrum of musical instrument sounds, effectively killed the music box industry, and high-quality instruments were not made after the early 1900s (see "Music Boxes").

Where to Find Values. The most valuable musical instrument collectors' items usually sell at public auction—Sotheby's in London has recently handled several Stradivarius violins. Music dealers should be consulted when searching for other rare instruments. The beginning collector could start looking in antiques shops, used-guitar stores, or pawn shops, but research into what is valuable and what is not should be done before purchasing.

A Price Sampling

Muir-Mackenzie Stradivarius	$275,000 plus
J. B. Vuillame violin	30,000-40,000
Les Paul Sunburst (Gibson) guitar	7,500-13,000
Lloyd Loar L-5 (Gibson) guitar	4,000- 5,000
Steinway medium-size grand piano (used)	2,600 plus
1865 Burdett reed pump organ	2,500 reconditioned
G. C. Conn silver-plated alto saxophone	500 plus

How to Store/Display. The best way to preserve a musical instrument is to play it and keep it in good operating condition. Parts that can deteriorate (bellows or bagpipe bags of leather, felt pads) must be kept supple and pliable. Wooden parts should not be exposed to extreme heat or dryness and should usually be lightly oiled. Metal parts should also be lubricated to prevent corrosion.

How and When to Sell. Collectors whose instruments are old but not rare will have the best chance for receiving a fair price at used-instrument dealers or pawn shops. Auctions or private placements are recommended for rarer or more valuable items.

★ **A young woman recalled that when she was a small girl, her grandfather and father had played the bagpipes they had brought with them when they immigrated to the United States from Scotland. She did not know what had happened to the two sets of pipes but thought they might still be at the family estate in Montana. Upon searching, she found them in a trunk in the attic. A friend restored both sets to playing condition—reconditioning and oiling the wood, rehemping the stocks, and tying in new leather bags and valves. For the cost of restoration, the young woman now has two very playable and very valuable sets of bagpipes (worth several thousand dollars apiece) found, literally, in the attic.**

Little-Known Facts. One of the most creative inventors of unique musical instruments is Harry Partch, who began making all of his music and instruments in the 1930s. His instruments produce music seldom heard. They are indeed unique, for, to date, no one owns a Partch instrument. They include the *kithara, zymo-xyl, boo, gourd tree,* and *chromelodeon.*

—Warren Askew

Bibliography

Books

Clemencic, Rene. *Old Musical Instruments.* New York: G. P. Putnam's Sons, 1968.

Lichtenwanger, William. *A Survey of Musical Instrument Collections in the United States and Canada.* Music Library Association, 1974.

Mebane, John. *Treasure at Home.* New York: A. S. Barnes & Co., 1964.

Ord-Hume, Arthur W. J. G. *Collecting Musical Boxes.* New York: Crown Publishers, 1967.

MUSIC BOXES

In 1897, a Swiss-born doctor added an unusual element to his treatment of a young lady suffering from a broken heart. A collector of music boxes, he charged his melancholy patient with the care and daily winding of his beautiful collection. He was gratified to see his patient recover her bright spirits even faster than he had hoped.

History. Given the cheerful nature of the Swiss, it is not surprising that the delightful mechanical music box originated in their country. In the eighteenth century, Swiss watchmakers invented and began to produce the intricate little machines that played music. These were made of either cylinders with tiny projections that lifted the tuned teeth of a music "comb," or of interchangeable steel discs with projecting studs that interacted with a "star wheel."

Providing music at the turn of a crank or the drop of a coin, music boxes eventually were the focus of entertainment in family parlors as well as in dancehalls, bars, and cafes until Edison's amazing phonograph swept them into oblivion. Some fifty years later, they emerged from cellars and attics, hotly sought after by museums and enthusiastic collectors.

★ **Sandra Holmes was puzzled when the antiques dealer she had called to appraise her late aunt's bric-a-brac showed special interest in a plain-looking little box. He showed her a concealed knob at its base. When she turned it, the box opened as if by magic, revealing a jeweled interior, and out popped a brilliant, twirling bird playing a lovely melody. He offered Sandra $800 for the exquisite antique music box.**

The Hupfeld Super Pan Orchestrion, built c. 1922, was one of the largest of its kind and capable of a virtually unlimited range of musical feats. It could produce anything from a concert pianist playing solo to a full symphony orchestra.

Values Outside the Home. Although one of their principal fascinations is the many shapes and forms they can take, music boxes may be divided into two categories: that which emphasizes the musical movement, and that which emphasizes the "box" itself. When searching for the former, the collector should look for cylinder length and sound quality, though exquisite workmanship of the casing and extra features, such as mechanical birds, also add value. On the other hand, musical toys, decorative pieces and functional objects often derive most of their value from the nature and condition of the casing in which the musical mechanism is contained rather than from the movement itself.

Some collectors focus on just one tune and try to collect all the different ways it is played. Others collect by period or by style. Musical dolls and teddy bears are popular with many collectors, while others prefer musical objects that serve a useful purpose. (Who could resist a teapot that plays "Tea for Two" while one is pouring?)

Where to Find Values. Antiques stores and specialty shops are logical places to look for music boxes, yet many collectors also passionately haunt garage sales, estate sales and flea markets. Though almost any object could turn out to be a music box, sometimes only the keenest eye will recognize that a dusty jewel case or grimy picture frame could house a music movement. Such a piece can often be bought for next to nothing.

★ **At first, Northern Californian Matt Horton planned to throw away the boxful of grimy machine parts he had found when cleaning out the storeroom of the old family-owned cafe. Then he remembered his grandfather telling him about a wonderful German music machine that had entertained patrons in the early 1900s. Matt sent off a couple of letters with photographs and descriptions to Germany, then forgot about the whole thing. Months later, he was stunned to receive an excited letter from the owner of a Popper orchestrion missing some parts—and offering Matt $1,300 for the boxful of "junk."**

A Price Sampling

Polyphone, 24″ auto changer, excellently restored	$22,500
Symphonion, in walnut case, 12″ discs	2,950
Regina #1, cherry case, coin operated	700
Jewel box, Florentine, plays "Lara's Song"	75
Ring case, enamel, ballerina twirling on lid	60
Merry-go-round, c. 1910	45
Night lamp, 7″, with revolving ballerina	30
Kitten with mouse, ceramic	20
Candy box with Christmas decoration, plays "Jingle Bells"	10
Child's musical bank, ceramic	8

How to Store/Display. If restoration of a beautiful old music box is one of the collector's greatest pleasures, it is also an undertaking he must approach with care. He should also make sure that any craftsman who repairs the intricate mechanism knows exactly what he is doing.

In caring for the outer box, one should remember that humidity is the enemy of fine woods and can also cause metal fittings to tarnish.

How and When to Sell. The owner of a rare antique music box in excellent playing condition will have no difficulty selling it to one of his fellow collectors, or to someone who collects musical instruments, or to a collector or dealer who focuses on a particular period.

Owners of boxes in which the musical movement is of secondary importance will find that the market is even wider because their boxes will also be sought by collectors of other things, such as dolls, jewel boxes, and teddy bears.

Because the kind of craftsmanship that makes music boxes so valuable is getting costlier and harder to come by, the music box collector can be confident that while his investment is giving him daily pleasure, it is also increasing in value.

★ **The old music box was grimy and it did not play, but Charles North liked what he could see of the inlaid design, and since the flea-market vendor asked for only a few dollars, he bought it. Charles took the box to a restorer, who identified it as a nineteenth-century American-made Regina. A few months later, his find restored to its old splendor and playing beautiful music, Charles advertised it for sale—and collected a cool $1,500 for it.**

Little-Known Facts. The largest music boxes ever made were the amazing *orchestrions* built in the last part of the nineteenth century, many with hundreds of flashing lights and moving parts on the outside, and seemingly an entire orchestra hidden on the inside. Some barrel-operated orchestrions measured nine feet around and more than twenty-one feet high. By contrast, some small music boxes made then could fit inside a wristwatch.

• One type of music box that struck a less than happy note was the street organ used by beggars to call attention to their misery. In nineteenth-century London young Italian boys were recruited to prey on the compassion of passersby. These unfortunate boys often slept six or seven to a bed, and they had to hand over most of their earnings to the greedy owners of the street organs they operated.

—*Vera Abriel*

Bibliography

Catalogues

Hudgeons, Thomas E. III, ed. *Official Price Guide to Music Collectibles.* Orlando, FL: House of Collectibles, 1984.

Jerry Mafden, 4624 West Woodland Rd., Edina, MA 55424 (source for pamphlets, books, and additional catalogues).

Associations
Musical Box Society International. 1300 E. Third St., St. Paul, MA 55106.

Dealers and Collectors
Eastern Musical Antiques, 10 Nowak Ln., Montville, NJ 07045.
Mechanical Music Center, Box 88, Darien, CT 06820.
Meekins Music Box Co. (restorer), P.O. Box 161, Collingswood, NJ 08108.
Richter's, 900 North Point St., San Francisco, CA 94109.

CHAPTER 15

Native American Artifacts

NATIVE AMERICAN ARTIFACTS

Lewis and Clark collected painted buffalo robes and pottery on their trip up the Missouri River; William Randolph Hearst collected Indian artwork as he scoured Europe for art treasures to store at San Simeon; Frank Lloyd Wright urged the hanging of Navajo blankets inside buildings and houses he designed; and Sir Francis Drake and his men marveled at the Pomo Indian baskets they saw in California, enough so that Drake wrote down his remarks in a diary: "Their baskets were made of rushes like a deep boat, and so well wrought as to hold water. They hung pieces of pearl shells and sometimes links of these chains on the brims to signify they were only used in the worship of their gods: they are wrought with matted-down red feathers."

Four-hundred years later, it would not be uncommon for a similar Pomo basket to sell for thousands of dollars, depending on its condition and age.

Today, the urge to collect Native American artifacts may stem partly from the romance of owning remnants of a primeval, noble culture that was nearly destroyed. Behind every object, there lies an incredible history that parallels the story of an Indian tribe.

History. There is evidence that as early as 1000 A.D. Indians in the Southwest were weaving cotton textiles. When the Spanish brought sheep to the area, Indians turned their looms to wool. The Navajos learned weaving techniques from early Pueblo neighbors and eventually began making blankets to trade with the white man.

Most prized are the Navajo blankets from the pre-1870 era, known as the Classic period. Stripe, Chief and Serape are the Classic blanket styles, made largely before the white man arrived in Navajo country. Stripe blankets are, as their name denotes, striped or banded. Chief blankets also are striped, but they incorporate diamonds and blocks as part of the pattern. Depending on the date woven and type of design, Chief blankets may be designated as first, second or third phase. Serape blankets are those with head holes that were worn like Mexican ponchos.

Kachina dolls are so popular among tourists and collectors that new versions are often as costly as antique models.

With the arrival of settlers in New Mexico and Arizona, artificial dyes and foreign yarns were introduced to native weavers. Some believe that the quality of blankets deteriorated from then on. But the blankets produced during that time—Eye Dazzlers and Germantown blankets, for example—still sell at high prices.

Around the turn of the century, traders who set up outposts in the Southwest encouraged Indians to produce heavier, larger weaves that could be used as rugs. Some traders, such as Juan Lorenzo Hubbell of Ganado, Arizona, and John B. Moore of Crystal, New Mexico, actually dictated the colors and wools they wanted and hung pictures of rug patterns in their posts for the weavers to copy.

Some have criticized such rigid setting of standards, but the traders who used them did help revitalize a dying industry and they did push the Indians to return to natural, native yarns and dyes. Rugs produced today have their roots in these efforts, and they have steadily increased in price over the past few decades. For example, a small Two Gray Hills Navajo rug, produced in the Two Gray Hills section of New Mexico, has gone from about $20 a square foot in 1964 to $70 a square foot in 1984.

American Indian basketry had a different history, particularly in Northern California, where many contend that some of the world's finest basketmakers originated. Baskets of the Pomos, Tulares, Miwoks and others took years to produce and then were used by these native Californians for decades, sometimes centuries, before they wore out. Early Russian traders, who sailed to points on the Northern California coastline, took many of these baskets back to their homeland, where they are now on display in Soviet museums. The destruction of Northern California Indians in the years to follow also meant the destruction of the basketmakers and their skills. Today only a few Indians remain who practice this centuries-old art.

Of the baskets that survived from earlier years, many are now in museum collections. Others ended up stuck in dusty corners of attics or were used by their unsuspecting owners as planters or sewing baskets.

In the past few years, a revival of interest in basketry has brought many of the remaining baskets out of their hiding places to command high prices on the market. Baskets that would have gone for $500 a few years ago are now selling for thousands. Their value appears to double every couple of years.

Interest in American Indian pottery has been rekindled recently, in part because of the existence of skilled potters who never stopped practicing their art. Historic pueblo pottery was made much like the pottery of today, with clay dug from nearby deposits that was mixed with ash, sand and shards of old pottery. No potter's wheel was used. Clay was rolled into ropes that were coiled to build the walls of pots. The pot surface was often covered with a slip of fine red or white clay and then smoothed with a stone. Various designs were put onto the clay surface using juices of plants mixed with powdered iron or manganese. Firing was done on a dung fire, which might be smothered or partly covered in order to produce various colors on the finished pot.

Historic pottery still brings in top prices. But today's artists from pueblos in New Mexico produce pottery that is also highly sought after. The Santa Clara pueblo has become famous for blackware featuring innovative carved designs. At the Acoma pueblo, potters use black-on-white designs similar to those of the early Mimbres culture. Cochiti potters are famous for their mixture of modern and historic human figures, such as Italian tenors, businessmen, two-headed people from circus shows, dancing bears and Indian storytellers.

★ **Because of the growth of interest in Indian arts in the past twenty years, few people are ignorant of the value of the artifacts they own. But there are occasional surprise finds, like the Pomo carrying basket sitting in the garage of a man whose antiques dealer told him was now worth $500, or the Christmas cards stored by a woman in a Klamath bowl, which was worth $400.**

Values Outside the Home. During the 1930s and 1940s, the collecting of Indian artwork slowed down due to the Great Depression and World War II. But since the 1940s, the demand has increased. The 1960s and 1970s were boom years for Indian jewelry. Currently most popular are Indian baskets, particularly old California Indian baskets, and Navajo blankets, with Southwestern pottery, kachina dolls and Indian beadwork following close behind.

Values of blankets are based on age and rarity of design. Classic designs from before 1875 are the most highly prized. Condition is also an important factor. Lovers of blankets who cannot afford their steepest prices should consider saddle blankets and women's blankets, which sometimes sell for less because they are smaller than standard pieces.

It is rare to find baskets made before 1900. Condition is again vital. Many baskets are damaged by collectors who have misused them or abused them. Baskets from the Klamath, Washoe, Tulare, Pomo, Pima, and Northern California tribes are highly prized.

Kachina dolls were at first painted figures that the Zuni and Hopi peoples of the Southwest gave to their children to teach them about the spirit figures that were part of annual rainmaking and growing season ceremonies.

Although they are still used for that purpose, they are now carved in great numbers for the tourist and art markets. Many of them go for very high prices; in fact, at times antique kachinas can be better bargains in terms of price. The average older kachina can sell for $250 to $1,000; newer dolls can be similar in cost.

The most prized Indian beadwork shows up on war shirts that were worn by Indian men, and on women's dresses, which are often just as beautiful in design.

Where to Find Values. Indian artifacts are available at antiques stores, special stores that deal solely in Indian objects, and auctions.

Many specialists in the field caution against buying at auctions, where prices can be inflated above market value.

Phoenix and Santa Fe are areas where Indian objects are available in great numbers, particularly during the tourist season.

Most dealers advise potential buyers to begin their collecting by reading extensively in the field that interests them before buying, and then to be sure that they are buying what they like rather than buying for investment value only.

A Price Sampling

Navajo first-phase blanket	$32,000
Hopi polychrome jar by Nampeyo	16,500
Germantown Navajo blanket, 1885-1890	5,500
Pomo basket with star design, c. 1900	5,000
Butterfly maiden kachina	4,180
Sioux beaded hide baby carrier	2,450
Two Grey Hills rug, 79″ × 60″	1,750
Woman's Navajo blanket, 1890	1,000
San Ildefonso jar, signed by famous potters Marie and Julian Martinez	850
Klamath basket bowl, small, c. 1930	400
Hoopa hat, contemporary	175

How to Store/Display. Since condition is so important to the value of Indian artifacts, correct storage is crucial.

Baskets, for example, must be kept under the right temperature and moisture conditions. Dried-out baskets can become brittle and will crack easily when handled. They should not be used to store objects that might bend or warp their shape. Baskets decorated with feathers must be protected from insect damage, and some of them should be hung like chandeliers to prevent feathers on the bottom from being crushed or worn.

Navajo blankets must be kept clean and perhaps should be dry cleaned occasionally. However, colors should be tested for fastness before the cleaning process.

Blankets are best hung on walls and should be done so in ways that prevent as much stress to the blanket as possible. Velcro strips can be carefully sewn to the blanket and fixed to strips attached to the wall. Blankets can also be hung from rods pushed through cloth sleeves sewn to the blanket back.

How and When to Sell. It is best to deal with a reputable dealer when buying or selling Indian artifacts and artwork.

Although certain objects seem to gain in popularity at various times, it is unusual for any Indian artifact to lose its value. One should not sell too soon, however, but should wait for an item's resurgence. For example, cornhusk Indian carrying bags, which a few years ago sold for $150, are now selling for $500.

★ **One collector from Marin County, California, tells of being approached by someone selling a Chumash, or California Indian, basket from the Santa Barbara area. The seller, who needed the money immediately, wanted $3,500 for the item. The collector did not buy it—someone else did and resold it a day later for almost $12,000.**

Little-Known Facts. Indian artwork has long been popular with celebrities, Robert Redford and singer/songwriter Joni Mitchell among them. Andy Williams is a longtime collector of Navajo blankets and has donated some of his to the De Young Museum in San Francisco.

• Actor James Caan wrote an article for *Architectural Digest* a few years ago that described why he collects Navajo blankets: "The world today is becoming more and more cluttered with gimmicks ... I try to live a straightforward life and I thrive on simplicity. I want the art I buy to have that quality also. Navajo blankets and rugs have that warm and comfortable essence about them, which is one of the things that initially caught my interest in Indian textiles."

—*Rebecca Larsen*

Bibliography

Books

Bedinger, Margery. *Indian Silver: Navajo and Pueblo Jewelers.* Albuquerque, NM: University of New Mexico Press, 1973.

Berlant, Anthony, and Mary Hunt Kahlenberg. *Walk in Beauty*. New York: New York Graphic Society, 1977.

Frank, Larry, and Francis Harlow. *Historic Pottery of Pueblo Indians*. New York: New York Graphic Society, Ltd., 1974.

James, H. L. *Posts and Rugs: The Story of Navajo Rugs and Their Homes*. Globe, AZ: Southwest Parks and Monuments Association, 1976.

Wright, Barton. *Hopi Kachinas: The Complete Guide to Collecting Kachina Dolls*. Flagstaff, AZ: Northland Press, 1977.

Periodicals

American Indian Art Magazine. 7314 E. Osborn Dr., Scottsdale, AZ 85251.

American Indian Basketry. P.O. Box 66124, Portland, OR 97266.

Catalogues

Indian, Eskimo and Aleut Owned and Operated Arts and Crafts Directory. Washington, DC: United States Government, Dept. of the Interior.

Dealers

American West, 2110 N. Halsted, Chicago, IL 60614.

Andrews Pueblo Pottery and Art Gallery, 400 San Felipe NW, Old Town, Albuquerque, NM 87104.

Morning Star Gallery, 513 Canyon Rd., Santa Fe, NM 87501.

Potcarrier, 347 Primrose Rd., Burlingame, CA 94010.

West of the Moon, 3464 Sacramento St., San Francisco, CA 94118.

Museums

Center of the American Indian, Oklahoma City, OK.

The Heard Museum, Phoenix, AZ.

Millicent Rogers Museum, Taos, NM.

Schoharie Museum of the Iroquois, Schoharie, NY.

Western Heritage Center, Billings, MT.

O

ODDS 'N' ENDS

We've decided that certain collectors' items simply defy classification. Some, like barbed wire and frogs, are just too darned obscure—how many of us have really given serious thought to either lately? Others, like Dionne Quintuplet memorabilia, have faded into the past and fallen victims to "out of sight, out of mind." All, however, are valuable and prove that collections do not always belong in museums. In fact, some barely qualify for the living room.

At any rate, we call this cornucopia of the sublime and the outrageous "Odds 'n' Ends."

Avon Bottles. Those of you who have ever cursed yourselves for letting the Avon Lady in—and who now have a closetful of scented bath oil beads—take heart! Her well-turned ankle might be the most important foot that ever shoved its way in your door.

Blossom Cologne bottles from 1936 are now worth over $100. White Moire Cologne bottles from the '40s have been appraised at $50. You can even sell later bottles from the '60s, but only if they are full and in their original boxes.

Keep an eye peeled for advertisements in collectors magazines. And be a little nicer to that Avon Lady! Even the recent Alpine Flask is worth about $6. Hmmm...isn't that the front door?

Barbed Wire. Most of us are not exactly moved to tears at the sight of this stuff. But to the enthusiast it is manna. Between 1868 and 1900, 757 patents were granted for barbed wire, and examples of about 700 have been found by the faithful. But since some manufacturers never bothered about patents at all, there are several hundred additional types out there somewhere. The mind boggles.

Since 1957, Jesse S. James of Maywood, California, has collected barbed wire specimens and arranged them on panels that each contain thirty pieces, eighteen inches long. But before we sneer at old Jesse, take note. Just one of his acquisitions, the Dodge Star (a type of wire patented in 1881), is worth approximately $350 per stick.

©Rick A. Kolodziej/The f-stop

It seemed that anything the Fab Four touched, however remotely, turned to gold. Early items, such as this lunch box from the mid-1960s, are the most desirable—and the most difficult to find.

Bears. A good name for this specialty might be "Bear Wars," as Ideal, the company which first came up with the concept for America's Teddy Bear, and Stieff, the manufacturer that produced bears in Germany, battle it out for first place in the collectors mart. Whatever the case, if you possess a bear made by either company before 1907, clutch it to your heart (Aw, we won't tell anybody). Both are worth up to $800.

Long feet, long noses and long curved arms are the trademarks for these antique megabears (a button on the ear signifies a Stieff bear). But it's still a bear's world. If you purchased one of the bears that Stieff made for its centennial several years ago, it has already leaped in price from $150 to $500. Makes a bear lover want to come out of hibernation....

Beatles. Money may not buy you love, but you have a chance to find out for yourself if you saved your Ringo shoes, George headscarf, or Paul beach towel.

Over a decade and a half after their breakup, the Beatles continue to retain their lofty position as the most marketable musicians in the history of popular music.

A Beatle watch was recently sold at auction for $375. A Beatle lunchbox is worth about $50. A copy of the album "Yesterday & Today" with its infamous "butcher cover" (depicting the Fab Four with chunks of meat and decapitated baby dolls) is worth about $600.

But then, some items are enough to make auctioneers gently weep. A serigraph by John Lennon of Yoko Ono was recently withdrawn at auction due to low bidding. A series of erotic lithographs of her also did not come anywhere near its appraisal price.

Sometimes, you've got to hide your love away....

Bells. Those who equate bells with grade school fire drills are obviously not acquainted with the American Bell Association. No, it's not another phone company. It's a group comprised of bell enthusiasts, such as past president Rebecca Mayer of Atlanta, Georgia, who owns over four-hundred of them (bells, not telephones).

Some of those most sought after by Rebecca and her friends include cast iron cowbells (worth $10 to $50), streetcar fare bells ($150) and, for the nostalgic, copper school bells (worth about $35), as well as decorator bells made from china or glass.

And yes, Rebecca *can* buy property and enjoy relationships with her neighbors. Bell collectors seldom ring their treasures.

Dairy Items. Dairy items are not exactly urban antiques, and most collectors would not know a contented cow from a crabby one. But all dairy paraphernalia is of some value today. Most early churns are advertised at prices well over $100.

Another popular item is the butter dish, particularly the kind made near the end of the nineteenth century. Most of these are hand carved and worth about $200. Of course, the really desirable ones are made of porcelain and created by Bennington, Royal Rudolphstadt and Wood & Sons. But prices for these are well beyond the means of the average urban collector...who, after all, continues to wonder how cows get their milk into those little cartons.

Dionne Quintuplets. The birth of the Dionne Quintuplets in 1934 resulted in an outbreak of public hysteria that has seldom been duplicated. A carnival atmosphere surrounded every move made by these five little girls. It was not coincidental that the play area next to their Canadian farmhouse was know as "Quintland."

Memorabilia from that era is extremely popular with non-hysterical collectors. Some items of interest are paper dolls ($85), spoons ($85), calendars ($40) and postcards ($350 and up).

Fay and Jimmy Rodolfos of Woburn, Massachusetts, have one of the finest collections of Dionne items in the world, including an overwhelmingly hideous lamp depicting a dour Papa Dionne with his five bundles of joy. It is not recorded whether this item is kept in their living room, or if it has had an impact on their social life.

Documents/Personal Papers. You just never know whose castoffs are going to turn up in your home.

Michael Mindlin, Jr., of New York City, was cleaning out a closet when he discovered a manuscript of the play *Anna Christie,* by Eugene O'Neill. On closer examination, he found it to be a working script, used for rehearsals, with revisions and annotations in the author's own hand. He sold it for $1,200.

Then there was that tattered copy of the Declaration of Independence found in a cellar in 1968. It turned out to be the last printed copy...and was sold for $404,000.

The point is, it pays to take a close look at the signatures on your old, moldy documents. Two rueful examples: the London man who almost ruined a document signed by Ben Franklin by using it to stiffen the cover of a book, and the tailor who merrily cut up another paper signed by Franklin for use in his paper patterns.

Feminism. Although the Equal Rights Amendment has yet to be ratified, interest in the women's movement has stimulated a growing price rise in memorabilia from its finest hours.

Political Americana consultant David Frent of Belmar, New Jersey, says that prices for sashes, buttons, felt pennants, banners and

Interest in memorabilia from the women's movement, beginning with the suffragettes, has created a whole new category of collectors' item.

ceramic and glass pieces from the Suffragist era have escalated to three or four times their original prices. For instance, buttons from the late 1800s and early 1900s may sell for $200 or more. There is also a growing interest in items representing modern feminism. Buttons that sold for $1 several years ago sell for over $5 today. A commemorative button that sold for $5 at the start of the 1977 International Women's Year Convention Weekend was worth $30 by the convention's end.

Frogs. On the other hand, for all of you women chiefly interested in the way to crooner Robert Goulet's heart, here is the answer: It's through his frogs. The handsome baritone has one of the largest collections in the world—including a gold frog-shaped ring with emeralds for eyes, and a frog-design belt buckle, both of which he wears everywhere.

"I think I've bought maybe half a dozen of the (frogs) I have," Goulet told *Collector Editions Quarterly.* "All the rest are gifts from people who know I collect them."

Some friends. But one should not underestimate the value of Goulet's frogs. He has over two-thousand of them.

Heinrich Himmler. Thomas W. Pooler of Grass Valley, California, offers top dollar for memorabilia connected with Heinrich Himmler, chief of Hitler's SS.

Pooler has been collecting flags, letters, documents, awards, medals and books for almost twenty years, and points with pride to a particularly prized acquisition...Himmler's SS membership card.

He invites fellow enthusiasts to get in touch with him about their Himmler items. Now don't all jump at once.

Kaleidoscopes. Some of us recall them as the dime store cylinders that entertained us during bouts of measles and mumps. They are even more enjoyable now. The cardboard models of the '50s and '60s are currently worth about $15, while the dignified brass and leather tubes from grandfather's study are worth over $800.

Eric Sinizer, owner of San Francisco's Light Opera Gallery, is one of the few bona fide kaleidoscope retailers in the country. His personal favorite is a sound-activated model with fiber optics that changes color based on the vibrations of stereo music. (Whatever happened to those little chunks of plastic that sort of swooshed around?)

Numisplastics. Do you destroy your old credit cards like a good citizen? Well, if you were to risk keeping them around, you could become one of the first on your block to partake of the collecting specialty known as *Numisplastics*.

Don't laugh. Walter Dinteman, author of the *Credit Card Catalogue*, believes that a thoughtfully arranged full-scale assemblage of credit cards might be sold off at a Sotheby's auction for as much as a million dollars...by the year 2000.

But until that happy day arrives, you might get a head start by hunting around for an original 1950 Diner's Club card or a 1958 Bankamericard. These two classic bits of plastic happen to be selling for well over $100 each...which is the first time we have *ever* heard of a card holder making money from these things.

Potato Mashers. "A potato masher is a beautiful object," says Byron Randall of Tomales, California. "It's the last honest kitchen tool."

Randall should know. He has 384 of them, ranging from wooden clubs to Hawaiian models to the well-worn masher used by his mother.

Although the *Guinness Book of World Records* turned him down ("I guess it's too monumental a concept," he says), most vintage potato mashers actually sell for $10 to $65 each—which makes Randall something of a pioneer. But he is not one to rest on his laurels. He's too busy looking for other potato mashers ... except the plastic kind. "They're an obscenity," he sniffs.

Pre-World War II Judaica. A specialty rich in tradition and meaning, Judaica is also filled with collectors who are not aware of their own worth. Many families have already acquired a valuable assortment of Judaica consisting simply of the ceremonial items they happen to have around the house.

You do not have to own rare, expensive, intricately wrought antiques to have a quality collection. The largest current market is for twentieth-century (pre-World War II) Judaica. In fact, a recent New York auction dealt with these contemporary art objects. Not only were most priced in the $100 to $400 range, but they sold well within their estimates.

T-Shirts. When Carter B. Smith, a San Francisco disc jockey, rebelled against endless listener contests and joked, "It is better to give than to receive," a listener took his sermon seriously enough to bless him— with a T-shirt. Ten years and almost three-thousand blessings later Smith has still not worn the same shirt twice.

He places the monetary value of his collection at approximately $15,000, although he says that as a time capsule of the past ten years, it is invaluable.

Historians apparently agree. The Smithsonian Institute recently asked Smith for a representative sampling of his shirts.

A Word to the Wise. It's all very well to begin stockpiling T-shirts, bears, credit cards and Papa Dionne lamps. But here are some words of warning.

Homer and Langley Collyer were eccentric New Yorkers who collected everything under the sun. In fact, they piled their treasures into elaborate booby traps designed to fell anyone who tried to interfere with their reclusive existence.

After Homer died in bed in 1947, the police conducted an enormous search for Langley. They had to wade through fourteen grand pianos, the chassis of a Model T Ford, old clothes, old toys, thousands of books, and scores of bicycles, sewing machines, dressmakers dummies, bolts of barbed wire, and an arsenal of modern and archaic weapons until they found his body. He had been crushed by one of his own booby traps.

Happy collecting... and hey, hey, let's be careful out there.

Bibliography

Books

Burtscher, William Jay. *The Romance Behind Walking Canes.* Philadelphia, PA: Dorrance & Co., 1948.

Hyman, Henry A. *The Where To Sell Anything Book.* New York: World Almanac Publishers, 1981.

Periodicals

American Barbed Wire Journal. P.O. Box 368, Texline, TX 79087.

"Currents in Collecting." *Collector Editions Quarterly,* 170 Fifth Ave., New York, NY 10010.

Organizations

American Bell Association, P.O. Box 286, Natrona Heights, PA 15065.

The Tobe Pasher Workshop, c/o The Jewish Museum, 1109 Fifth Ave., New York, NY 10028.

OLD WEST

It seems that more words have been written about the Old West period (1835-1910) than about any other in American history. It was a time when men were men and women were women—or was it just easier then to tell the difference? It was an era of sacrifice, bloodshed and heroes. It was also a time of determination, innovation and American ingenuity.

History. Where would we be today if all the difficulties in settling a new land had been met with "It can't be done," or "Impossible?" We would probably still be tying our horses to hitching posts. How lucky we are that a few enterprising pioneers did not accept "No" for an answer, for the results of their creativity made it possible to rein in America's new and wild frontier.

J. W. S. Perry, for example, saw the need for a bigger wagon to carry a heavier payload and one which could withstand the rigors of

Artist Frederic Remington always portrayed the American cowboy at his independent, hell-raising best. Modern fascination for all things Western has helped make all Remington canvases extremely valuable: this one, entitled "Cowboys Coming to Town for Christmas," sold for $120,000 in 1977.

the desert. So he created the Death Valley Borax Wagon, which could do both and remains today, almost one hundred years later, as a symbol of Perry's determination.

Studebaker began his automotive career making wagons, and Packard began his by making wheelbarrows. They each earned the reputation of being able to conquer the difficult in short order (the impossible just took a little longer).

Eventually those who migrated to the West were able to find lives of comfort—if measured by frontier standards. Enough tools, conveniences, gadgets, and modes of transportation had either been adapted to their new needs or else created to give settlers respite from constant labor.

But tools wore out and conveniences were replaced by better, and more, conveniences, as were gadgets and wagons. Obsolete and useless items found new homes in junk heaps, attics, cellars and sheds. And there they lay for decades, gathering dust. But they were also gaining historical and monetary value for future collectors. Little did Thomas Edison realize that when his electric light became popular, so would the lanterns that it replaced. Those lamps that blackened ceilings for so long and which were eventually stored in cellars and attics are now worth from $75 to $125 in good condition.

Other items were affected by other changes. Buttons were discarded as styles changed. Thimbles became obsolete when the foot-powered sewing machine appeared, and the toasting rack, which was an integral part of the wood stove, disappeared with the popularity of the gas stove. Today, all of these items are considered valuable to collectors of history and investments alike.

Personal items from those early pioneers have also become treasures to modern collectors. Postcards, Confederate money, letters, diaries, stamps, household items, toys and even marbles have value today. A Northern California rancher is in the process of dredging his cattle stock pond for those same marbles he threw there as a boy. He discovered that cat's eyes, spirals, swirls and sulphides are now worth $1 to $150 *each.*

★ A successful collector from Texas, who wishes to remain anonymous, never threw out anything, even when he was a child. He saved his marble collection, his empty soda bottles, even old bottle caps. As he grew older, he became interested in lost treasure and read every issue of every treasure magazine published. His goal was to make that one big find and retire.

On a weekend trip to the country, he found an abandoned house. Using his metal detector along the walls, he discovered a hiding place behind the wallpaper of an old closet. There, stacked up on the floor, were *National Geographic* magazines in almost mint condition dating back to the first issue. Each was worth $15 to $50 to collectors and even to the publishers. As news of the find became known, newspapers and magazines interviewed him and took photos. He had finally made his big find.

Values Outside the Home. While 90% of Old West collectors' items have stabilized in price, the remaining 10% have returned their investment many times over. Beginning collectors, who may not be aware of how many items are available under the heading "Old West," should consider the following as possible future buys: dishes, kitchen utensils, furniture, tools, cowboy items, barbed wire, toys, toy banks, Wells Fargo & Company items, marbles, sewing items, pens and pencils, paintings, dolls, lanterns, and railroad passes, pins and other railroad memorabilia.

These are just sixteen out of hundreds of possible categories that have value to collectors. Dolls are perhaps the hottest of these. Rare dolls are selling for $500 to $10,000 (see "Dolls"). Mechanical banks have also delighted collectors. Selling for just a few dollars in 1890 (or given away to promote saving), banks today are selling for $40 to $10,000 (see "Mechanical Banks").

A word of caution about fakes. They are everywhere, and some are good enough to fool the experts. Collectors should research their field, find out everything possible about it, and then use some common sense. If a deal sounds too good to be true, it most likely is.

Where to Find Values. Antiques and collectors shows abound. So do flea markets and garage sales. In the late 1970s and early 1980s, people began to sell their throwaways for cash. What this often meant was that they overpriced the junk and underpriced the collectors' items, unaware that they *were* collectors' items. The sharp buyer, who knew what to look for, could pick up all sorts of bargains.

It was also a time when secondhand stores suddenly became "antiques" stores. There was money to be made in trash. Anything old was labeled "antique," and its price tripled. The new collector must still be on guard for this trend, and will do well to understand a first basic rule for collecting: Not everything old *is* antique.

Antiques shops also offer something valuable to the collector. But one should not expect to buy an item there for a few cents. In fact, most likely the best bargain at an antiques shop is the friendship of its owner. Shop owners are knowledgeable people who have fully researched their subjects. This means they are also excellent sources from which to learn market prices and clues on how to spot reproductions.

★ **John Hall and his wife, Nina, of San Jose, California, have always been interested in antiques and collectors' items. Their home is filled with tools, kitchen equipment, bottles, vases, mason jars and a thousand other items. John recently picked up a wooden ice chest for $45. His immediate thought was to make a nice bookcase out of it. But he decided to check his reference books first. He was glad he did. What he had bought was an oak ice box worth $200 to $225. He did not make a bookcase out of it.**

A Price Sampling

Wells Fargo treasure box (1890s)	$750
Butter molds	25-175
Annie Oakley photo and signature	100
Handcuffs	75-100
Ice skates (1870s)	25- 50
Carbide burning lamp	25- 50
Dog tags (1800s, for dogs)	15
Dog tags (1900s, for dogs)	10

How to Store/Display. Protecting valuable objects from dust, dirt, pets, pests, kids and a harsh environment is of utmost importance if the items are to retain their value. Paper items will last a lot longer if sealed in plastic. A self-sealing freezer bag is ideal—easy to open, easy to close, and the objects can be examined without being handled.

There are many manufacturers of glass-front cases for smaller items, such as thimbles and buttons. These are almost always available at collectors' shows and well worth the price.

Restoration should be approached cautiously. Giving that toy bank a good scrubbing is not a good idea. The original paint is what adds to its value. Such items are best upgraded by dusting with a soft cloth and washing with warm soapy water. Abrasive cleansers must be avoided no matter what the item or its state of shabbiness.

It is recommended that for insurance purposes all items be photographed and accompanied by a written description. Investigators will also be able to track down a stolen item much easier if given a photo of it.

How and When to Sell. Sellers should attend antiques and collectors shows as frequently as possible. They should talk to other sellers and buyers to get ideas about the prices being asked and being paid (if one crock pot has been marked at $50, and others at $25, it is obvious which pots are going to sell and which will be returning home with their owners).

Antiques shows are by far the best places to sell wares, but they are by no means the only places. There are dozens of periodicals devoted to antiques and collectors' items, and each of them accepts advertisements. Sellers might consider taking out a small ad in a magazine that most closely matches their interests. It might be months before there is any response from an ad and months more before any deal is completed, but the ad will have reached more potential customers than would have been reached at a show.

A third alternative is club newsletters. The only problem is the difficulty in finding them. Some are so regional that unless one knows a collector who is already a subscriber, the existence of the periodical may remain forever a mystery.

★ **Valuable collectors' items can turn up in the most unexpected places and at any time. A contractor from Waco, Texas, who specializes in remodeling and dismantling old houses, won the contract for removing all the metal from several old homes being demolished in the downtown section of the community. It included the downspouts, many of which were made of lead. One of them had not drained for over fifty years. When it was taken down, a large leather bag fell out of it and split apart, spilling its contents. There on the ground lay gold coins dating back to the 1830s. Their face value came to $4,000; after they were sold at auction, the final amount paid for them was slightly over $130,000!**

Little-Known Facts. A third edition of the first cookbook by an American author published in America sold at a Sotheby's auction in October 1984 for $22,000. Out of the $874,505 spent at the auction, one buyer paid out $600,000—all of it for cookbooks.

• For every ton of trash discarded daily, one pound is kept as some type of collectors' item. More valuables are thrown out each day than are kept simply because they were not identified as such.

• If any china or pottery has the country of origin marked on its underside or surface, it entered this country as an import after 1892.

—John Shriver

Bibliography

Books

Quetermous, Steve. *Flea Market Trader.* Paducah, KY: Collector Books, 1979.

Periodicals

Americana. 29 West 38th St., New York, NY 10018.
Antique Monthly. Drawer 2, Tuscaloosa, AL 35402.
Antique Trader Weekly. P.O. Box 1050, Dubuque, IA 52001.

Antiquarian, The. P.O. Box 798, Huntington, NY 11743.

Collectibles Illustrated. Main St., Dublin, NH 03444.

Hobbies: The Magazine for Collectors. 1006 S. Michigan Ave., Chicago, IL 60605.

Treasure. 6280 Adobe Rd., Twenty-nine Palms, CA 92277.

Catalogues

Kovel, Ralph and Terry. *Kovels' Antiques & Collectibles Price List.* New York: Crown Publishers, 1984.

Hudgeon, Thomas E. III. *1985 Price Guide to Antiques and Other Collectibles.* Orlando, FL: House of Collectibles, 1984.

Clubs

Antique Outboard Motor Club, Shipyard Museum, 750 Mary St., Clayton, NY 13624.

Association for the Preservation of Political America, P.O. Box 221, Forest Hills, NY 11375.

Cola Clan, 2084 Continental Dr., Atlanta, GA 30345.

QRS Music Rolls, 1026 Niagara St., Buffalo, NY 14213.

Stein Collectors International, P.O. Box 467, Kingston, NJ 08528.

ORIENTAL ART

Oriental paintings have always produced in Western observers an awareness of mystery and an appreciation of nature and of the humor that exists there. Oriental art objects extend that appreciation through other mediums, such as jade, bronze, and lacquer, and have become some of the most precious items available to modern collectors who want to own the exquisite reminders of Oriental antiquity.

History. The art traditions of the Orient are the oldest in the world. China, whose culture dates back to 3000 B.C., originated a number of techniques for fashioning bronze vessels and ceramics, carving jade and ivory, applying enamels and lacquers, and, later, with the development of the brush and paper, rendering highly stylized images of animals, humans, and the grandeur of nature.

Bronze casting dates back to the beginning of Chinese history. Objects produced were coins, bells, spears, and vessels for cooking, serving, and ceremonials (these were invested with spirit powers). The decoration of bronze led to the development of *cloisonne*, which was a process of covering a surface with brightly colored enamels, each separated from the other by a barrier of thin metal to create "cells," and then firing the object to set the metal and the enamel. Cloisonne decorated vases, bowls, and boxes.

Jade was considered by the Chinese to possess the four virtues. It was used by the royal families as a means of identification, and it was buried with the dead. It was carved into a variety of landscapes, figures, and patterns. Carving techniques were also applied to other stones and organic material, such as ivory.

The brush appeared in China in 200 B.C., followed by paper in 100 A.D. With these new tools, artists developed painting and calligraphy as forms of creative expression.

Chinese art techniques and styles spread to neighboring Korea and Japan, where they were developed further and added to. New art forms included the Japanese woodblock print and *netsuke,* a type of intricate carving.

By the seventeenth century, members of the royal class were no longer the only patrons of art. Those of the burgeoning merchant class had also discovered a taste for the finer things and could now afford to buy them. Art production expanded to meet this need, and has been thriving ever since.

★ Collector-writer Arthur Chu tells of a young man who purchased two figurines in a thrift shop for $.35, believing they were plastic or glass. They turned out to be carved jade, worth $500.

Values Outside the Home. The field of Oriental art is so broad that opportunities for collecting are unlimited. Antique brass, jade and other stones, cloisonne, paintings and calligraphy have the most value, while modern reproductions, although beautiful and often expensive, may not appreciate.

Certain antique items produced in quantity but only during a particular era are prized by today's collectors. Examples are the netsuke, which became an essential part of the traditional Japanese garment, the kimono. Since the kimono had no pockets, the wearer had to carry personal items in purses, or carved boxes called *inro.* The inro was attached to the kimono's sash by a cord and closed by an *ojime,* or decorative bead. Dangling from the other end of the cord was the netsuke, an elaborately carved figure usually an inch and a half high. The netsuke was made of ivory but occasionally was

This eighteenth-century Japanese *No* robe exemplifies the Oriental appreciation of nature's beauty and balance, executed here on brilliant red silk and embellished by stamped gold.

fashioned from wood or other material. Those created in the eighteenth and nineteenth centuries are striking pieces, often humorously pointing out a foible peculiar to animal or man.

Netsuke, ojime, and inro are on display at major museums and avidly collected. They have also been widely counterfeited, and modern Japanese craftsmen will make reproductions of any of the historical figures on order.

Another item popular among today's collectors is *Chinese snuff bottles,* which followed quickly after the introduction of snuff into China in the mid-1600s. Although officially disapproved of, the use of snuff became a social ritual among the well-to-do classes, and the expensive containers that users carried it in became objects of conversation among their friends. Snuff boxes were carved of ivory, jade, or other organic material or stone, or made of porcelain or glass. They are now featured in Asian art museums.

The first mass-produced graphic art was the *woodblock print,* developed by Japanese artists as a process using carved blocks of wood to illustrate paper with full-color images. Because prints were readily available and affordable, since unlimited impressions of one image could be made, the emerging Japanese merchant class purchased them enthusiastically. Early artists, such as Utamaru, created pictures of actors, wrestlers and beautiful courtesans. Artists Hiroshige and Hokusai followed soon after with scenes that came to be identified as typically Oriental in their use of humor, nature and spirituality, and, occasionally, violence. "The Breaking Wave of Kanajaw" is a well-known example of the Japanese woodblock print, with its depiction of a giant wave that towers over a tiny fishing boat, threatening to carry it out to sea in what appear to be enormous claws emerging from the white foam of the wave's crest.

Where to Find Values. Oriental art can turn up anywhere, from attics to auctions. Collectors with Japanese-American backgrounds may discover that one of their grandmothers came to the United States in the early 1900s as a "picture bride." (During the turn of the century, the Japanese in America still arranged marriages for their children. Sons who had come to work in the United States learned of their future brides from photos sent to them by their brides' families in Japan.) Picture brides always brought with them their wedding kimonos, which they continued to preserve after the ceremony by carefully storing them in chests. Because there were so many wedding kimonos made during this period, collectors will not have a great deal of difficulty finding them.

Antiques dealers should be consulted in one's search for netsuke, snuff bottles and cloisonne. Collectors' organizations are good sources of information on private sales and trades. Some, such as the International Netsuke Society, hold annual conventions. The higher-priced items, such as early Chinese bronzes, Japanese woodblock prints, carved jade, and paintings, are most frequently sold at auctions or through art dealers who specialize.

A Price Sampling

Woodblock print, Hokusai artist, "Choshi in Shinosa"	$60,000
Bronze vessel, Shang dynasty, China	50,000
Bowl of carved jade, nineteenth century	11,000
Netsuke, ivory, showing monkey clutching bamboo	4,125
Glass snuff bottle with painted interior	1,000
Cloisonne vase, nineteenth century, Japanese	200
Jade duck on lotus leaf	175
Kimono, silk with embroidered cranes	150
Snuff bottle, carved amber	100
Netsuke, ivory Kabuki dancer	75

How to Store/Display. Jade is almost unbreakable but it stains easily, which means that it can also be dyed (this, of course, reduces its value). Specialists recommend that no one *but* specialists attempt to clean a piece, although they do allow that small chips in a piece can be removed by gentle sanding.

Cloisonne can be dented, which may cause pieces of the enamel to drop out. If this occurs, oftentimes the pieces can be replaced by experts trained to do restorations.

Of course, any art object can be damaged. Glass snuff bottles can break. Paper and textiles are subject to discoloration and destruction by the elements, insects and mildew. To avoid all such disasters, one should consider protecting—and displaying—pieces behind the safe glass walls of a cabinet created especially for that purpose.

If a collection is extremely valuable, items should be fully listed, photographed, and then insured.

How and When to Sell. Oriental art has been appreciating because of its limited supply and the increase in collectors. Some items are more popular than others at the moment because of the nature of the items themselves. But trends have a way of changing overnight; the clever seller will learn to foresee changes before most others recognize them, and will sell accordingly.

Selling directly to other collectors can be the most lucrative way of turning over an item, since auctions, dealers and items sold on consignment all involve commissions that are deducted from the final sale price. Collectors should consider advertising items in association journals, which are read by other collectors. *Arts of Asia* magazine is an excellent journal in which to advertise (see "Bibliography").

★ **Collector Earl Morse bought a celadon bottle from a dealer for $500 in the late '60s. It stood on a living room shelf until recently, when a dealer saw it and offered $75,000 for it. It subsequently sold at auction for $100,000. It turned out that well-to-do collectors in Hong Kong had driven up the values of this particular item.**

Little-Known Facts. An American student in Italy in the 1930s envisioned a scholarly work on the relationship of the art of Siena to its social and political environment. World War II and other events intervened. Two decades later he wrote that treatise, not about Italian art but about woodblock printmaking in the Tokagawa era, Japan. The author's name was James Michener, better known for best sellers, such as *Tales of the South Pacific, Hawaii, Chesapeake,* and *Poland.*

• It was not unusual for eighteenth-century master jade carvers to spend a lifetime working on a single item.

• A jade vessel belonging to a fourteenth-century emperor was lost for over four hundred years. It finally turned up in a monastery, where it was being used as a pickle barrel!

—*Donald Mayall*

Bibliography

Books

Bushell, Raymond. *Netsuke, Familiar and Unfamiliar.* New York: Weatherhill, 1976.

Chu, Arthur and Grace. *Oriental Antiques and Collectibles: A Guide.* New York: Crown Publishers, Inc., 1973.

———. *Oriental Cloisonne and Other Enamels: A Guide to Collecting and Repairing.* New York: Crown Publishers, Inc., 1975.

Michener, James A. *The Floating World.* New York: Random House, 1954.

Perry, Lilla S. "The Adventures and Studies of a Collector," *Chinese Snuff Bottles.* Rutland, VT: Charles E. Tuttle Co., 1960.

Warner, Langdon. *The Enduring Art of Japan.* New York: Grove Press, 1952.

Willetts, William. *Chinese Art.* Baltimore, MD: Penguin Books, 1958.

Periodicals

Arts of Asia. 1002 Metropole Bldg., 57 Peking Rd., Kowloon, Hong Kong.
Orientations. 13th Fl., 200 Lockhart Rd., Hong Kong ($44).

Catalogues

Andacht, Sandra; Nancy Garthe; and Robert Mascarelli. *Price Guide to Oriental Antiques.* Des Moines, IA: Wallace-Homestead Book Co., 1981.

Dealers

Gumps, 250 Post St., San Francisco, CA 94108.
Ronin Gallery, 605 Madison Ave., New York, NY 10022.

Associations

The International Netsuke Society, P.O. Box 16426, Honolulu, HI 96816.

ORIENTAL RUGS

Who knows when and where the first hand-knotted rug was produced? The ancient craft reaches back to the origins of the Islamic culture itself. Using portable looms that could be packed up when it was time to move the sheep to greener pastures, artists produced designs drawn from tribal culture and executed with joyous creative expression. Through the centuries, these rugs have celebrated the mysteries of the universe while they brought beauty and comfort to the stark environment of the nomadics. No less today, they can bring the highest artistic expression of the Orient to contemporary dwellings.

History. The oldest surviving example of a hand-knotted rug is the Pazyryk. It was found in 1949 when a Russian anthropologist happened onto a tomb in the frozen wastes of Siberia. It appeared that ancient grave robbers had left an opening that allowed water to seep in, preserving the solidly frozen carpet for twenty-five-hundred years. The sophisticated knotting techniques found in that rug testified to the long tradition of hand knotting that had preceded it.

The technique of knotting rugs caught on and spread along the Middle Eastern camel routes. The traditional rug-weaving world grew to include Persia (Iran), Turkey and Afghanistan, and the Caucasus, or mountainous region between the Black Sea and the Caspian. The nomadic Turkoman weavers generally ignored political boundaries when moving through Afghanistan, Persia and southern Russia. The Chinese are believed to have learned the craft from them.

Marco Polo may have been the first western connoisseur of Oriental rugs. He was so impressed with the Persian Seljuk rugs he saw on his visit in 1271 that he took some home. Venetian merchants distributed them to other parts of Europe, where they became extremely popular.

Few would deny that antique Persian carpets are the aristocrats of rugs from the East, especially those produced during what is considered the golden age of the art (from the sixteenth to the first half of the eighteenth centuries). They embody a richness of color and design that is unsurpassed. Though highly desirable (and accordingly expensive), they are seldom available today because most have permanent residence in museums and public buildings in Iran. A few belong to private collectors, and these occasionally show up at estate sales when changing tastes and lifestyles bring them to the auction block.

American decorators "discovered" Oriental rugs during the 1920s, and artisans of Persia, Turkey, and other areas of the Middle East worked tirelessly to satisfy the demand. They produced rugs in sizes that were appropriate for American rooms and in colors that were subdued by chemical washes to make them more appealing to American taste. Many were irreparably damaged by this process and were treated to an infusion of mineral oil to restore their sheen long enough to make a sale. The commercial rugs produced during this period are obviously not examples of a pure native art form and, therefore, do not interest serious collectors.

The market for Oriental rugs enjoyed a spectacular rise in the 1970s, when inflation, a weak dollar, and high prices for OPEC petroleum caused investors to become enthusiastic. Rugs that had been undervalued in the early '70s brought unheard-of prices in 1979. New Persian rugs were becoming scarcer and of uncertain quality because the shah's economic development policies pulled experienced weavers into more lucrative occupations, leaving most of the rug weaving to be done by children. Prices for the older city rugs, such as Tabriz, Kashan and others, pushed up even higher. The fall of the shah caused the important Iranian buyers to pull out of the market. Investor attention turned to the simpler tribal rugs, but the high-flying rug prices dropped in 1981, when interest rates rose and dealers were forced to sell off their inventories.

Textile Museum, Washington, D.C.

By studying rugs displayed in museums, one will discover the difference between those of investment quality and those that are merely decorative. This seventeenth-century Kashan rug from Persia's golden age is a fine example of the former, with its exquisite, intricate design.

★ **Jan David Winitz, an expert and dealer in Berkeley, California, tells of a client who so appreciated the beauty of Oriental rugs that she bought twelve of them at garage sales during the 1950s. But she wondered if the $25 to $75 apiece she had paid for them was a bit too much. It turned out she was living with a fortune: They were worth a total of $100,000.**

The price correction that tamed the fearless inflation-fueled market of the '70s remains in the '80s. New rugs are subject to the world economy, and the quality varies. India and Pakistan have brought out some very attractive rugs in recent years, but they are decorative, not of investment quality. The strength of the dollar has weakened prices of all but the most outstanding imported rugs.

Values Outside the Home. The attraction between an individual and an Oriental rug can amount to love at first sight. When this happens, a link has been established between the beholder and the artist who created it. As the collector learns more of the technical aspects of the different hand-knotted rugs, it is important to remember that they are works of art. The person who has "picked up" or inherited a rug often discovers that living with it delights both the mind and the senses with its balance and harmony.

Types of Oriental Rugs: Oriental rugs are classified many ways; a simple system is to group them under two major headings: traditional and contemporary. Traditional rugs come from one of the countries with an ancient heritage of carpet-making: Persia (Iran), the Caucasus, Central Asia, Afghanistan, Turkey, and China. These rugs may originate in cities or towns, or they may be classified as "tribal."

Tribal rugs are designed and executed by weavers who spontaneously create designs as they tie each row of knots along the weft threads. They have bold geometric designs that utilize the natural resources of the tribe, which are sheep's wool and natural vegetable and mineral dyes. Existing tribal rugs are increasing in value because production of high-quality rugs has declined in recent years. Examples of tribal rugs are Qashqai, Caucasian, Kurdish, Baluche, and Turkoman.

Traditional city rugs come from Persia and Turkey. They are produced in a workshop setting where a group of weavers may work on designs created by a professional rug designer. The designer strives for a harmonious artistic statement, and the weavers strive for perfection of execution. These rugs are elaborate, with swirls, tendrils, rosettes, and arabesques. A few of the famous rug-weaving cities include Kashan, Isfahan, Tabriz, Sarouk, and Kerman.

Town rugs are woven in larger villages near important trade routes. They are a bridge between the other two types, using floral designs that are less complex than those of city rugs and often showing some of the spontaneity of the tribal pieces. Examples include Hamadan, Heriz, Karaja, and Meymeh.

Contemporary rugs come from areas that do not have a cultural heritage of rug weaving: India, Pakistan, Bulgaria, and Roumania. The designs are often reinterpretations of traditional ones. Although the quality of these rugs is often quite high, they are seldom destined to become collector rugs. Rare exceptions are those of outstanding beauty and uniqueness.

Guidelines: It may be possible for the highly experienced investor to turn over a quick profit trading in Oriental rugs. The average collector who is interested may think of them as long-term investments that are nice to live with.

Investment-quality rugs include antiques (over one hundred years) and semi-antiques (fifty to one hundred years). The chances of an unknown Persian rug of the classical period (thirteenth to fifteenth centuries) being offered for sale are virtually nonexistent. Eighteenth- and nineteenth-century city rugs are what collectors are actively looking for, but alas, even these pieces were already scarce at the turn of the century. It is to the "younger" rugs, produced from 1850 to 1900, that seekers of choice examples must turn.

Another category that is attracting more collector interest is the semi-antique group produced between 1900 and 1960. A semi-antique rug displays traditional designs with somewhat mellowed colors.

Earnest bidding is evident for the diminishing supply of semi-antique rugs in exceptional condition. The novice would do well to look again at those rugs that are missing a few centimeters of knots near the fringe ends. Artistry, craftsmanship, design, and clarity of color can make these rugs candidates for both enjoyment and investment.

Heriz rugs are woven in villages near Tabriz, and the designs, though more rectilinear, are similar to those of their expensive city cousins. With prices ranging from $3,000 to $15,000 and higher, they are likely to increase in popularity and value.

When considering tribal rugs, remember that the most desirable rugs come from peoples with well-documented art and culture. Caucasian rugs were "discovered" after a series of major exhibitions and books put them in the spotlight during the late 1960s. Today they are among the most collectible on the market. Others with the same credentials are Anatolian rugs from the high-plains region of Turkey and Central Asian Turkoman, created by the Kurdish people of northwestern Iran, Turkey and Iraq, and those of the Baluche, located on the border between Iran and Afghanistan. The value of some of these rugs is enhanced because they are surviving examples of the artistic tradition of groups that no longer exist: the Caucasian tribespeople, the Salor, and other Turkoman tribes.

Looking at Oriental Rugs: Spontaneous admiration for a particular rug is a good indicator of personal taste. When a particular rug seems attractive, one should look at others and then come back to it. Is the attraction still there? When a rug haunts one's dreams for several days, it deserves to go home for a trial period. Most reputable dealers allow this.

Before buying, it is recommended that one look at the rug on hands and knees, checking for moth damage and areas of uneven pile caused by wear. The backside tells the story; any cracks or broken places will show up there along with evidence that the undersides of knots have been eaten away. Flat irregular areas that are brightly colored may indicate that a rug has been painted to cover worn spots. Rub a damp cloth over the area to see if any color rubs off. Many older rugs have been restored, and quality reweaving can enhance value. Check to see that the rug lies flat on the floor, since the elevated areas tend to wear more rapidly.

Differences in width between the top and bottom of a rug are not serious unless they are greater than six inches. Minor variations of one to four inches are characteristic of the hand-woven rug. A competent restoration specialist can often stretch an uneven rug into more acceptable dimensions. Frayed or missing edges can likewise be repaired. Remember, it is possible to put a deposit on a dirty rug and ask the dealer to have it washed before making the final decision.

Where to Find Values. Oriental rugs are available through established dealers, rug auctions, estate and garage sales. Established dealers with rugs on display are the most reliable source. They will usually allow you to take the rug on approval, and it can be exchanged if it proves to be a bad choice. Also, some dealers will allow the full purchase price to be applied when one chooses to trade up. A buyer should discuss these matters before making a purchase, and should have all such agreements written on the sales slip.

Few guarantees are available through rug auctions, estate and garage sales. Nomadic rug salesmen thrive on the illusion that fantastic bargains are available at their auctions. Established auction houses do have reputations to protect, and they will often offer expert advice and allow buyers to examine the rugs before the sale. Prices may get out of hand however if the rugs have attracted enthusiastic collectors. But the "all sales are final" rule prevails. Ditto for estate and garage sales, but for the knowledgeable buyer, some good investments can be found in these quarters.

A Price Sampling

Tabriz, tree of life, animals, woman, portraits, 6' × 4'	$7,500
Kirman, central medallion, floral edges, 16' × 13'8"	4,200
Sarouk, red ground, florals, Shah Abbas design, 10' × 13'	3,750
Kazak, Caucasus, 4'5" × 7'2"	3,080
Caucasian, flat woven, 1'11" × 5'	2,100
Heriz, blue field, Herati design, ivory turtle, 6' × 14"	725
Hamadan, prayer	695
Kerman, overall palmettes, rose field, 11'4" × 18'	650
Caucasian, blue ground, geometric design, ivory border, 3' × 5'	475
Hamadan, camel field, ivory, 3'2" × 7'	50

How to Store/Display. Oriental rugs are far from fragile—nomads lay them on the desert floor and camels walk on them. In the home, dirt, moths, and uneven wear are the major enemies of carpet life. And they can be warded off with a few simple precautions. Rugs should not be allowed to get dirty; they should be vacuumed weekly or whenever necessary, and turned over and vacuumed on their backsides monthly. If a rug is fragile, it should be swept with a broom going in the direction of the pile. It should be professionally washed every three to five years if it is a floor rug, five to eight for a wall hanging. Only a specialist in Oriental rugs should do this. Cleanliness will also keep moths from eating away at a rug, and moths should be tracked down in their favorite places—in carpet areas under furniture. Casters placed under furniture legs will prevent the pile from being crushed. Finally, rugs should be turned regularly, especially in homes where there are established foot patterns.

End-stopping (a process of securing the two fringe ends with a blanket stitch visible only from the back of the rug) prevents rows of knots near the fringe ends from coming loose or falling out. Edge-binding is a method of overcasting frayed edges with matching yarn. Reknotting a small worn area or reweaving a minor hole is usually not expensive, but repairing major damage can be. It is best to get estimates and look at samples of work from several recommended specialists.

How and When to Sell. One may sell privately, at an auction, or to a rug dealer. Selling privately eliminates paying a commission and it allows one to receive the total amount paid for the rug. Arranging for a private sale can be done through ads in newspapers or antiques journals and through friends or acquaintance with other rug collectors.

A well-established auction house may attract rug fanciers from distant places through advertising and catalogues. A rug will likely sell better if it is offered with other items of the same type. But selling at auction has a disadvantage: it does not guarantee that one will get the best price. A seller may be able to with a reserve (the lowest price he is willing to accept), but if the item does not sell above the reserve price, one must pay a commission for a rug he still owns. Speaking of commissions, they can run from 15% to 20%.

Selling to a dealer should be a last resort. Retail prices vary from dealer to dealer as does the price they are willing to pay. If the rug is a rare one, the seller will be in a better bargaining position, since dealers are going to be less excited about buying a rug if it is also available through wholesale outlets.

Sellers might also consider selling rugs on consignment through a dealer. Dealers are in a good position to find a buyer, and if one is willing to wait, he will get the retail price less 10% to 20% commission. If one is selling off lesser rugs in order to upgrade a collection, he may make an arrangement with the dealer to accept the present rug in partial payment for the new one. Dealer markup has already been paid on the old rug, and it is figured into the price of the new one.

★ A San Francisco Bay Area man moved into a house, where he found a rug that was old, dirty, damaged and stuffed into a rag bag. He brought the rug to a dealer to see if it was worth anything. The dealer discovered that the rug was a two-hundred-year-old Turkish Kelim. Its historical value made it worth $4,000 to $5,000.

Little-Known Facts. Sometimes there is a date recorded in Arabic numbers woven on a rug. If it was woven before 1900, chances are good that the date is correct. Skepticism is in order for those woven during the past eighty years; they were frequently antedated to give the impression of greater age.

• Collectors should not be put off by streaks of a different color in a place where the design calls for the same shade. These *abrash* are the results of variations in natural dye lots. Far from being faults, they often add charm and a luminous quality to the rug.

• Some collectors specialize in smaller Turkoman pieces, such as the *asmalyk* and *chuval*. The former is a trapping woven by a bride-to-be to decorate the flanks of her wedding camel. The latter is a Turkoman storage bag. The craftsmanship and artistry found in these smaller pieces equals that of the carpets.

—Joyce Hecht

Bibliography

Books

Eiland, Murray. *Oriental Rugs: A Comprehensive Guide.* Greenwich, CT: New York Graphic Society Limited, 1973.

Harris, Nathaniel. *Rugs and Carpets of the Orient.* London: The Hamlyn Publishing Group Limited, 1977.

Herbert, Janice Summers. *A Handbook for the American Buyer: Oriental Rugs, the Illustrated Guide.* New York: Macmillan Publishing Company, 1978.

Jacobsen, Charles. *Oriental Rugs: A Complete Guide.* Rutland, VT: Charles E. Tuttle Company, Inc., 1962.

———. *Check Points on How to Buy Oriental Rugs.* Rutland, VT: Charles E. Tuttle Company, 1968.

Winitz, Jan David, and the Breema Rug Study Society. *The Guide to Purchasing an Oriental Rug.* Oakland, CA: Breema Rug Study Society, 1984.

Periodicals

The Antiques Journal. P.O. Box 1050, Dubuque, IA 52001.

Connoisseur. National Magazine Co. Ltd., England. American edition, 250 W. 55th St., New York, NY 10019.

Catalogues

International Haji Baba Society, 7404 Valley Crest Blvd., Annandale, VA 22002.

Dealers

Breema Gallery, 6015 College Ave., Oakland, CA 94618.

Claremont Rug Co., 6087 Claremont Ave., Oakland, CA 94618.

Emmett Eiland Oriental Rugs, 1741 Solano Ave., Berkeley, CA.

International Rug Collectors' Society, 65 Rutgers, Rochester, NY 14607.

Renate Halpern Galleries, Inc., 147 West 57th St., Suite 2A, New York, NY 10019.

Associations

Breema Rug Study Society, 6015 College Ave., Oakland, CA 94618. (Lectures, workshops, research.)

P

PAINTINGS

Someone once asked Picasso, "Why do hardheaded businessmen pay hundreds of thousands of dollars for your canvases?" Picasso replied: "It's very simple—because they are hardheaded business-men."

History. The rich have always known that there is money to be made in art. Investing in art is exciting. It is also treacherous, if one puts his money in the wrong place. The art market can go down, sometimes fast and hard. Cycles of taste are short-lived. Case in point: In the golden years of the '20s, when larger-than-life portraits of English "ancestors" were popular among larger-than-life *nouveau riche* Americans, prices paid for them were in the hundreds of thousands of dollars. Today, English ancestors are not as desirable, and the portraits sell for only a fraction of the earlier prices.

Opinions about works of art are subject to change and always have been. Even the greatest classics have had their ups and downs (Rembrandt's paintings met with very little appreciation in the eighteenth century). The history of taste—which is part of the history of art—is a continuous discarding of established values, the discovering of new ones and the rediscovering of neglected ones. To survive and appreciate, a painting must be of superior quality. Even so, it is difficult to predict its future value. Nevertheless, in times of economic instability fine works of art have often been one of the safest shelters.

As masterpieces become scarcer and disappear from the market into museums and private collections, prices soar, and what is considered valuable and marketable changes dramatically. Two decades ago, for example, nineteenth- and early twentieth-century American paintings were ignored by most collectors in favor of the French Impressionists. Now that French works have been priced out of the market, paintings by American artists such as William Merritt Chase and Childe Hassam—until recently considered pale imitations of the real French thing—have been re-evaluated. They are now selling for tens of thousands of dollars.

★ A few years ago a Goodwill truck in Washington, D.C. returned with an Odilon Redon pastel. On the back of the picture were stickers from an existing New York gallery. An appraiser confirmed its authenticity, and it sold at Sotheby's for $20,000. If only the anonymous donor had known....

Values Outside the Home. Collectors should look not only at the name of the artist but also at the *painting*. A name on a canvas does not necessarily guarantee value (in fact, experts suggest that minor paintings by major artists are least likely to appreciate in the coming years). One should consider quality, condition and rarity of the painting. And a good pedigree certainly helps—if a picture once belonged to Nelson Rockefeller, one can count himself lucky—and possibly rich.

It is wise to find the best expert advice available, and to read and research the subject thoroughly. One should also seek out professionals who are active in the field. Browsing around museums and galleries can help one decide what kind of art he wants to collect.

Beginners should start in a modest manner. They can buy watercolors and drawings by lesser known but good artists for the price of a new color TV and less—a sound start for the serious collector.

Novices should also heed a few warnings before buying. Some paintings are terminally ill with too much restoration, for which there is no cure (restorations can be masked, and all but the experienced might be deceived). Signatures are occasionally tampered with, and misattributions are sometimes deliberate (just because the nameplate says a painting is by Thomas Moran, it ain't necessarily so—anyone who pleases can order a nameplate with the name of any artist he chooses).

Investing in contemporary art by living artists is clearly a speculative business. No one really knows how these works will stand the test of time. An old-master painting, on the other hand, is a more conservative placement of capital.

Tip: There has been a great deal of talk about *drawings* lately, and where there is talk there is usually a market. With more museums showing interest in them also, there is a strong probability that drawings from old masters to contemporary will increase in value.

(The masters themselves often valued their drawings as much as their finished paintings: Michelangelo gave his celebrated The Rape of Ganymede to his lover Tommaso Cavaliero, and Durer swapped a watercolor self-portrait for one of Raphael's studies for the Stanze frescoes.)

American art is gaining recognition worldwide. Although it has appreciated considerably in recent years, it is still believed to be underpriced. But prices are expected to increase dramatically in the next ten years. American subjects by American artists usually bring more money than foreign subjects by the same artists. The work of Albert Bierstadt, for example, is considered far more precious when the view is of Yosemite Valley or the Rocky Mountains rather than Swiss or Italian scenics.

Worth repeating: Buyers should look for quality, not fads, and they would do well to heed Picasso's advice: "By all means buy with your head. But do not forget to enjoy with your heart." It is well known in the art world that collectors who collect with passion are the ones who make the real profits.

Where to Find Values. New collectors should work with reputable dealers. One can call a local museum for recommendations and then find the dealer whose taste is similar and who shows interest in taking on another customer.

Buying at auction has both opportunities and pitfalls. A work should be previewed carefully before bidding begins. But bidding should not even be done if one has the slightest cause to doubt a painting's authenticity, for once a questionable piece is purchased, it will be difficult to sell.

Just because there are dealers lurking about an auction, beginners should not cut themselves out of the competition—dealers can overlook a treasure, too, and beginner's luck could lead to discovery of a sleeper.

On the other hand, an auction can be a dealer's dumping ground. The uninitiated could wind up with paintings that dealers have not been able to sell—a stigma that will probably continue to plague a work no matter who owns it.

Most dealers will return a customer's money if the customer discovers that the attribution of a work is wrong or its condition is not as good as it first seemed. Auction houses also offer some warranties, but they are usually limited to one or two years. Warranty terms and disclaimers vary sharply from house to house, so it is important to read carefully the list of sale conditions in the auction catalogue.

A Price Sampling. The following paintings were sold at top auction houses around the country. Prices are current as of 1984.

J. M. W. Turner's "Seascape: Folkestone," oil, c. 1845 (Sotheby's)	$10,250,000
Hendrik Goltzius, "Danae," oil, 1603 (Butterfield's)	675,000
Georges Rouault, "Clown," oil, c. 1940 (Phillips)	21,000
Edward Hopper, "Night in the Park," etching, 1921 (Christie's)	6,500
Reginald Marsh, "Girl on a Carousel Horse," oil, 1948 (Christie's East)	3,000
Gari Melchers, "Lee Lash Painting Outdoors," oil, 1882 (Christie's East)	2,800
Colin Campbell Cooper, "Court of the Cathedral," oil, 1878 (Christie's East)	1,800
Stanley Roy Badman, "Near Lanham, Kent," pencil and watercolor, 1930 (Christie's East)	800
Paul De Longpre, "Roses in a Bowl," watercolor, 1900 (Christie's East)	750
Hercules Brabazon, "Venice," watercolor, 1910 (Christie's East)	250

How to Store/Display. Paintings require very little maintenance. They should be protected from changes in temperature and humidity and be kept away from fireplaces, radiators, heat ducts and air conditioners. All paintings should be kept out of direct sunlight, although oil paintings are less sensitive than watercolors or prints. To keep paintings clean, nothing more sophisticated should be attempted than a light dusting with a soft feather duster.

Proper restoration is expensive and time consuming, but if a painting is valuable, it is worth every dollar and minute. Local museums are a good source for the names of professional restorers.

Contemporary art presents a whole new set of problems for restorers—and for collectors. When Picasso stuck a piece of newsprint in the middle of one of his cubist works, when Miro mixed casein with oil paint, and the German Expressionists slathered heavy paint on fragile surfaces, they were not thinking of what fifty years could do to these pieces. In many cases restorers still do not know how to prevent these non-traditional creations from deteriorating.

Collectors should keep records of their art—including photographs, slides, copies of original bills and current appraisals—off the premises in a vault or other safe place. In case of fire or theft, documented items will be protected.

How and When to Sell. Investing in art is like buying life insurance—the cash cannot be collected until the beloved subject is gone. Quality works of art will generally increase in value if one is willing to wait long enough.

Ideally, one should time his sales ahead of a recession slump, and replenish his collection at low recession prices. It is necessary to learn the current market value of a work before selling. Museum-recommended appraisers are a help here. If selling through a major auction house, one can expect to benefit from the house's publicity in newspapers, art journals and art catalogues. Auction audiences are generally overflowing. Sometimes "auction fever" overrides common sense, and the desire to bring home the prize makes for some frenzied bidding contests—in which case, the seller may reap some unexpected profits. On the other hand, a picture may not sell at all. If it does not, it is marked, and may be hard to sell the next time around.

Selling to a dealer is important if one wants a same-day sale with cash on the line. (If a painting was bought from a dealer in the first place, he may buy it back at a price close to the profit one could have made at auction.) This will save the 10% to 25% auction commission, and the net may be as good, sometimes better. A dealer may also take a painting on consignment at a 10% to 30% fee. Selling this way will sacrifice cash in hand, but the price may be better once it is sold.

Little-Known Facts. There is another "Mona Lisa" in Portland, Maine. Businessman Henry R. Reichhold purchased the fragile and damaged painting from an anonymous collector in Vienna in the early 1960s and recently donated it to the Portland Museum of Art. Scientifically dated no later than 1510, the painting has baffled scholars and intrigued the public for years. It may actually be Leonardo da Vinci's first sketch of the "Gioconda." You see, this "Mona Lisa" is not smiling, and a traditional copyist—and there were many—would never have left out that haunting identification mark.

• Some works of art are famous because of their beauty. Rembrandt's 1632 portrait of the painter Jakob de Gheyn III is famous mainly because it has been stolen so often. In the past seventeen years it has been "removed" four times from London's Dulwich Picture Gallery, the last time in May 1983. The gallery is hoping the painting will follow its usual habit and come back one day, but hopes are dimming.

—*Birgitta Hjalmarson*

★ Acquisition of Ferdinand Richardt's painting "Independence Hall, Philadelphia," 1853, may very well be the greatest bargain in American painting history. In 1961 Albert Nesle, the New York dealer in chandeliers, was in an antiques shop in Bombay, India, when he happened to see a dirty rolled-up canvas on the floor. For some reason he felt an urge to take a closer look. And behold, it was "Independence Hall, Philadelphia." He paid in piasters what amounted to $7, had it restored, and sold it to Joseph E. Levine, president of Embassy Pictures, for an undisclosed sum. Levine, in turn, donated the painting to the White House in memory of President Kennedy. Its present estimated value: half-a-million dollars.

Bibliography

Books

David, Carl. *Collecting and Care of Fine Art.* New York: Crown Publishers, Inc., 1981.

Kovel, Ralph and Terry. *Kovels' Collectors' Source Book.* New York: Crown Publishers, Inc., 1983.

Samuels, Peggy and Harold. *Everyone's Guide to Buying Art.* Englewood Cliffs, NJ: Prentice Hall, Inc., 1984.

Periodicals

Art & Antiques. 89 Fifth Ave., New York, NY 10003.

Art & Auction. 250 West 57th St., New York, NY 10019.

Art in America. 488 Madison Ave., New York, NY 10022.

ARTnews. 5 West 37th St., New York, NY 10018.

The Magazine Antiques. 551 Fifth Ave., New York, NY 10176.

The ARTnewsletter. 5 West 37th St., New York, NY 10018.

The Print Collector's Newsletter. 16 East 82nd St., New York, NY 10028.

Catalogues

Butterfield & Butterfield, 1244 Sutter St., San Francisco, CA 94109.

Christie's, 502 Park Ave., New York, NY 10022.

Christie's East, 219 East 67th St., New York, NY 10021.

Sotheby's, 1334 York Ave., New York, NY 10021.

William Doyle Galleries, 175 East 87th St., New York, NY 10028.

Dealers

Gerald Peters Gallery, 439 Camino del Monte Sol, Santa Fe, NM 87504.

Hammer Galleries, 35 West 57th St., New York, NY 10019.

International Fine Arts Association, Inc., 7422 Maple, New Orleans, LA 70118.

Keny and Johnson, 300 East Beck St., Columbus, OH 43206.

Los Angeles Fine Art Gallery, 736 North La Cienega Blvd., Los Angeles, CA 90069.

Montgomery Gallery, 824 Montgomery St., San Francisco, CA 94133.

Robert Miller, 724 Fifth Ave., New York, NY 10019.

Triangle Gallery, 95 Minna St., San Francisco, CA 94105.

Vose Galleries, 238 Newbury St., Boston, MA 02116.

Associations

International Foundation for Art Research, 46 East 70th St., New York, NY 10021.

PERSONAL POSSESSIONS

For Christmas of 1882, young Nathaniel Stevenson gave his sweetheart, Emily Primm, one of the few presents of a "personal" nature that a Victorian gentleman could give to a lady who was not his wife: a delicately engraved silver thimble. In her turn, Emily gave him a handsome cane.

Eventually Nat and Emily were married, and though they lived long and happy lives together, they could never forget the sweetness of their courting days. Today, Emily's thimble and Nat's cane are still treasured possessions; they are the focal points of a fascinating collection of personal items belonging to one of their great-great-granddaughters.

History. Personal possessions offer many of the same satisfactions that other collectors' items do: the thrill of owning something of exquisite workmanship or great scarcity, or something reflecting the history, art or social customs of a faraway place or bygone era. But more than anything else, personal effects, such as thimbles, canes, cigarette lighters, and watch fobs have a quality of intimacy not found in other collectors' items. By owning them, one feels that he is reaching back through time to touch someone else.

★ **Recovering from a skiing mishap that had resulted in a broken leg, Al Hansen bought a secondhand walking stick for $7 at a flea market. A few days later he accidentally dropped the cane and was surprised to find that its handle had come off, revealing a doctor's stethoscope concealed inside. He risked breaking his leg again as he jumped for joy when told his "cheap" cane was a rare example worth several hundred dollars.**

Values Outside the Home. Beyond recommending that he familiarize himself with his subject by reading about its history, joining clubs, and subscribing to specialized journals, one should also advise the prospective collector to take highly romanticized claims of any object with a grain of salt. Although fakes, counterfeits and misrepresentations are relatively rare, the wise collector will do a little detective work before closing any deal that offers the pen Emily Bronte used to write *Wuthering Heights,* one of Sherlock Holmes' pipes, or the key to the place where Mary stayed in Egypt.

Where to Find Values. Antiques stores specializing in the Victorian and Edwardian periods are especially good places to look for such personal items as canes, thimbles, straight or folding razors, watch fobs, inkwells or snuff boxes, particularly those of fine materials and high-quality workmanship. But flea markets and garage sales often yield unexpected treasures: among the myriads of old things laid out on those long, enticing tables may lurk a handmade razor with ivory handle, an Art Deco key, or a rare souvenir thimble.

★ During his early years in the Navy, young Ben Strout had been the typical sailor with a "girl in every port." Being a romantic at heart, he liked to hang on to some small memento of each affair. Eventually Ben married, and, years later, when cleaning the attic, his wife came upon the sentimental collection. Ben wanted to throw it out, but his clever wife had a better idea. She took the international assortment of powder cases, match covers, hand mirrors and other such items to an antiques dealer, and the money she got for them paid for their second honeymoon.

A Price Sampling

Thimbles. These little shields to protect delicate fingers date back to ancient times. Through the centuries they have been made of ivory, whales' teeth, glass, porcelain, gold and silver and often engraved or adorned with precious stones. Advertising and souvenir thimbles are also sought after by many collectors.

Gold, engraved with floral band	$75
1960 "Nixon/Lodge, Sew It Up"	10
Advertising thimble, brass, intricate design	5

Locks and Keys. Endowed with a mystical charm, locks and keys have their places in literature and history. During the Middle Ages, noblemen and women carried large collections of keys hanging

Museum of Modern Art, New York: Film Stills Archive

W. C. Fields, a master of sardonic humor, also portrayed a master at tippling and occasionally found comfort from the libations held inside his hollow walking stick.

from their girdles. When an esteemed visitor came to a walled city, he was presented its "key"—a symbolic gesture still exercised today.

Most collectors focus on a special *type* of lock or key, such as those for bicycles, prisons, even leg irons; or plain or fancy door keys, luggage keys, car keys, desk or piano keys. The wise collector will join a national organization for an exchange of information with fellow collectors.

Gold-plated key, engraved with name of
public figure $75

| Gate key, iron, bit type, 5″ | 3 |
| Car key, Ford Model T | .75 |

Razors. The value of a straight razor is determined largely by evaluating the quality of its blade and handle, and knowing who manufactured it. (With the manufacturer's name, the price rises.)

Before 1870, all razors were handmade. The handles were of natural materials, such as horn, bone, ivory, silver or pearl. Later models were machine made (mostly in Germany) and fitted with handles of synthetic materials.

Mother-of-pearl, Sample & Sons, NY;	
original box	$225
Celluloid handle, decorated with windmill	70
Plain black celluloid handle, plain blade,	
very good condition	6

Inkwells. When young, struggling Nat Stevenson wrote a love letter to his Emily, he probably dipped his pen directly into an ink bottle. But when Emily answered, she most likely dipped hers into an elaborate inkwell—one sign of a wealthy household.

Inkwells were made of glass, crystal or pottery, and from the early 1800s to the 1930s. Though it is preferred they be in good condition, glass inkwells are acceptable in spite of small chips the glass might have.

White opaque satin glass, hinged lid	$225
Dresden, porcelain, floral decoration, hinged lid	75
Glass, matching loose lid	10

How to Store/Display. One of the charms of personal possessions is that, apart from generally being quite small, by their nature they blend right into any household. Thimbles, inkwells and other small items can be displayed on shelves or in glass cases. Their care depends on the material: tortoise shell, ivory or bone may warp if subjected to heat, but they may be sponged with a soft cloth wrung out in warm, soapy water. Once the item is cleaned, many experts feel that it is best left alone: paint should not be touched up, nor should one attempt to repair chipped or broken glass or pottery.

How and Where to Sell. Advertisements in hobbyist periodicals are the best way to let other collectors know what one is offering for sale. When selecting the medium for the ad, the seller should bear in mind the possibility of "crossovers"—his turn-of-the century inkwell or early fountain pen may be of interest not only to the inkwell or pen collector, but also to the typewriter collector who wants to display his items with the enhancement of other writing implements of the period. In the same manner, the rare collector of barbershop paraphernalia may jump at a fine Sheffield razor with carved ivory handle, and the person who collects sewing machines would be happy to show off the collection with the addition of an array of thimbles.

★ During the thirty-five years that she has been teaching sewing and embroidery, Louise Masters has come into quite a collection of scissors, pincushions and thimbles left behind by her students. Going through a box of thimbles recently, she came upon an exceptionally pretty one. She was stunned to discover it was made of Meissen porcelain, worth over $2,000.

Little-Known Facts. Walking sticks concealing a variety of objects such as hunting knives, fishing rods, musical instruments, spy glasses and liberal supplies of whisky were popular in past centuries. They were so cleverly designed that a group of men could walk down a street carrying all the equipment necessary for an afternoon of hunting, fishing, music-making, "bird" watching and tippling without carrying anything other than their fashionable canes.

• Having paid the ransom for the return of her dognapped little Fido, eccentric widow Emma Wood ordered a gold-plated lock set with precious stones to secure the collar of her pampered pooch. Records show that thieves struck again undeterred—only this time they left the dog and stole the lock!

—*Vera Abriel*

Bibliography

Books

Hudgeons, Thomas E. III, ed. *Guide to Antiques and Collectibles.* Orlando, FL: House of Collectibles, Inc., 1985.

Mebane, John. *The Coming Collecting Boom.* New York: A. S. Barnes & Co., 1968.

McClinton, Katharine M. *The Complete Book of Small Antiques Collecting.* New York: Coward-McCann, Inc., 1965.

PHOTOGRAPHS

Nothing hightlights the distance between past and present like old photographs, for nothing else can capture the actual images of earlier generations. Anyone who looks carefully at those still, silent views of people and places will feel a chill of both familiarity and strangeness, because they are the legacy of our grandparents and of times long gone. Perhaps that is why there is no such thing as a valueless antique photograph; we are willing to pay good money to preserve any chance we can get to own a bit of what came before us.

History. Antique photographs divide neatly into type and period. The earliest type, known as *daguerreotypes* and produced on copper plates, were produced from 1839 to 1860. *Ambrotypes,* which were made with a wet plate on glass and were often hand touched with muted colors using a single-strand horsehair brush, were made from 1854 to 1865. What made both types so special is that they are all one of a kind; no negatives were involved in either process, and so each photo was an original split-second of history, caught forever on a gleaming, grainless surface.

Stereo views, produced from 1870 to 1905, were made for use in special viewers that produced a 3-D picture, often of a vividly photographed earthquake, fire, hurricane, or tornado-ravaged town.

Today virtually *all* photos are money in the bank. Particularly hot right now are early Native American portraits and one-half-plate outdoor mining scene daguerreotypes from California, plentiful at estate sales throughout the West, and often with a resale value of $5,000.

Library of Congress

The original of this reproduction is valuable not only because it shows President Lincoln but because it also captures him in an unstudied moment with his son Tad. (Note the heavy retouching throughout.)

★ On an obscure table in an antiques shop in Atlanta, Georgia, a dealer found a late 1840s daguerreotype of a photographer's self-portrait complete with his entire camera setup. The dealer bought the items for $20, bargained with dealers on the East and West coasts, and sold them to one of them for $6,000. He closed the sale a bit too soon, however; the next day he received another offer on the package for $12,000!

Values Outside the Home. Several basic rules apply to collecting daguerreotypes, ambrotypes, and early paper photographs. There is a direct relationship between the age of the photo and its worth—the older it is, the more valuable. This is true of size as well. The larger a photo, the bigger the price, since smaller sizes were far more plentiful. In addition, any picture in which the subject was depicted in a way other than the common unadorned portrait is automatically worth considerably more.

The best way to begin collecting is to simply scrounge through any available attic or basement, for almost all families have a rich and ready supply of old photos stacked in some dusty corner.

Where to Find Values. In general, the East Coast is a richer source of old photos than elsewhere in the country. Excellent sources for lucrative old photographs anywhere, however, are estate sales. Often the organizers of a sale simply will not take the time to sort through an old box or bag of pictures and will sell them in bulk for an astonishingly low price, occasionally under $25.

Flea markets and garage sales are other rich sources. What might be considered just an old picture of someone's great-aunt Millie could be a lucky find to collectors.

The advantage of buying photos from these three sources is avoiding dealer markup. In buying from a dealer, either at a shop, art show, or private sale, a collector can expect at least a 50% price increase. At times, of course, the increase is worth paying if it is for a rare and/or very old piece (the value of such a piece, by the way, will only increase with time).

★ A twelve-inch by fifteen-inch ambrotype, called a *mammoth plate*, portrayed an overview of Jamestown, California. On the back was a broadside by Lawrence Houseworth. A lucky collector bought it for $2,000 and sold it for $16,000.

A Price Sampling

A collector traded $400 worth of camera equipment for a French family portrait from 1845—a three-quarter-inch daguerreotype—and sold it a month later for $900.

At auction, a collector picked up an 1855 English stereo view, rare because it was not the usual portrait or disaster scene, but a still life of old cameras, a brass telescope, and a microscope, all arranged with studied carelessness on an oak table. He bought it for $300 and sold it for $900.

An 1888 ambrotype of an exquisite Asian child, along with a hand-crafted wooden case used for display, was discovered in a flea market in Kyoto, Japan. The buyer paid $100 for it and sold it for $400.

In a tattered bag of photos bought at an estate sale for $60 was a daguerreotype of a young white child seated on the lap of a black slave. Inside were engraved the girl's name and the words *"This is her private slave, Mammy Sue."* This photo alone sold for $400— each of the other photos in the bag sold for $100 up to $250.

Paper photos, which eventually took the place of daguerreotypes and ambrotypes, can often bring equally high profits to a canny collector. What was then called a *cabinet card,* entitled "Her Majesty the Queen Laughing," portrays the only known picture of Queen Victoria smiling, and indeed, she shows a toothy grin. A lucky dealer paid $25 for it and sold it for $175.

For $25 another collector bought a bag of daguerreotypes at a flea market. Most pieces went for $25 to $75, but at the bottom of the bag was an early half-plate of a dapper man, his fur-coated lady, and behind them lush trees and a lake. For that photo, the collector received $175.

An 1845 daguerreotype unearthed at a yard sale got snatched up for $10. The buyer resold it for $100.

A humorous 1880 paper photo called "Astronomy" portrays an attractive woman—Mother Nature perhaps—seated on a rock, pointing to a star-studded sky, a globe at her feet. A collector paid $7 for it and sold it for $45.

How to Store/Display. Old photos keep best in cool places. Daguerreotypes and ambrotypes were sturdy, and most have survived beautifully. They are always mounted in cases, which display attractively in a glass cabinet.

Sunlight will ruin paper photos, which should be stored in acid-free plastic sleeves and can be shown to advantage in leather-bound albums.

★ **An exquisite larger-than-usual daguerreotype (six-and-a-half inches by eight-and-a-half inches) portraying a husband and wife, was purchased for $40 and sold for $900.**

How and When to Sell. The best way to estimate the value of old photos is to attend an antique camera show and check out the prices. The advantage of selling photos to private collectors is attaining the full price of the item. Selling to a dealer will net only about 50% of the market value. However, it is best to hold on to old photographs as long as possible because prices for them can only go up as the years pass.

Little-Known Facts. Oliver Wendell Holmes called the earliest of the daguerreotypes "the mirror with a memory," and French artist Paul Delaroche echoed the fears of many when he wailed, "From today, painting is dead!"

• In Mexico, daguerreotypes and ambrotypes are tossed carelessly into the garbage, and the cases in which they came are used to store pins and buttons!

—Robin Solit

Bibliography

Books

Gilbert, George. *Photography: The Early Years.* New York: Harper and Row, 1980.
Newhall, Beaumont. *The Daguerreotype in America.* New York: Dover, 1976.
Rinhart, Floyd and Marion. *The American Daguerreotype.* Athens, GA: University of Georgia Press, 1981.

Periodicals

National Stereoscopic Association. P.O. Box 14801, Columbus, OH 43214.
Western Photographic Collectors Association. P.O. Box 4294, Whittier, CA 90607.

POLITICAL MEMORABILIA

The New Deal was yet to be a gleam in the eye of Assistant Secretary of the Navy Franklin Roosevelt when he was resoundingly defeated for the office of vice president in 1920.

The Democratic presidential ticket of James M. Cox and young Roosevelt, nominated on the 44th ballot, suffered the largest defeat of any major-party American presidential ticket up until that time. The nation clearly preferred the "return to normalcy" appeal of victorious Republicans Warren G. Harding and Calvin Coolidge. But Roosevelt supporters could later take consolation in the scandalous legacy of the Harding administration, and in the achievements of their dynamic candidate, who went on to become governor of New York and the only American president elected to four terms.

For collectors of political memorabilia, new deals can still be found daily. In 1980, a campaign button picturing both members of the unsuccessful Cox/Roosevelt ticket was bought by Chicago labor attorney Joseph Jacobs for $30,000 plus 10% commission!

History. In the early years of our country, voting was restricted to landowners, and politicking was done somewhat discreetly. Political memorabilia from those days commemorates inaugurations. Some of the most valuable items of that era are silver, copper or brass George Washington inaugural buttons, which were sewn to clothing and very difficult to find today.

A continuing American tradition has been the production of commemorative campaign medals (small medals are called *medalets*). The most scarce and valuable are made of pewter or bronze commemorating the inauguration of John Adams and Thomas Jefferson. There are few other campaign relics dating back to the eighteenth century, although the dubious art of American political songwriting made its debut then.

The American political campaign came of age in 1840 with a rematch between Martin Van Buren and William Henry Harrison. Four years prior, Van Buren had been elected president, but this time Harrison's supporters took a page from the book of "Common Man" President Andrew Jackson. Harrison conducted a "Log Cabin and Hard Cider" campaign of slogans, and this time "Tippecanoe and Tyler Too" were victorious. The 1840 election brought with it an era of flamboyant politics; rallies, parades, campaign songs, smear tactics—everything Americans have come to know and love.

Campaign collectors' items from this era include inscribed brass buttons with shanked loops on the reverse sides for attachment to clothing. Perhaps the most attractive item from the first half of the nineteenth century is a cameo brooch. Each rare and valuable brooch contains a white cameo drawing of a candidate set on an enameled background, covered with glass, and set in a brass frame. Campaign ribbons also sprang up in the early 1800s, most of them made from silk with lithographed designs.

During the nineteenth century, paper campaign materials were widely used, in part to familiarize pioneers out in the distant West with candidates from the East. Supporters could obtain portraits of their candidates, some by Kelloggs or Currier and Ives, before photographs became common. Campaign posters appeared in the late 1800s and are only lately becoming desirable to collect. Political cartoons also flourished in the mid-1800s, appearing primarily in newspapers and magazines. Popular cartoonists include Thomas Nast and Joseph Keppler. Other paper items include convention and inaugural programs, invitations, tickets, ballots, and advertising cards depicting candidates.

The use of photographs literally changed the face of campaign material in 1848. Daguerreotypes, ambrotypes and tintypes familiarized voters with candidates' faces. Ferrotypes, encased in small frames, joined the campaign trail in 1856, and by the 1860 campaign there were a few hundred different ferrotype pieces depicting presidential candidates. Scarcer buttons also show running mates.

The election of 1860 is a bonanza for collectors if only for the number of candidates who ran. The nation was split by slavery, and Republicans Abraham Lincoln and running mate Hannibal Hamlin faced two different Democratic presidential tickets, and a third ticket representing the Constitutional Party. Lincoln's emergence, however, was the historical highlight of that election. Lincoln collectors' items comprise their own vast category. Popular—and quite valuable—are photographs of Lincoln on badges, buttons and ribbons.

Shell badges became popular during Lincoln's campaign for reelection. An inscribed brass or copper-stamped shell usually framed a ferrotype, although not all shells were oval or rectangular. Later candidates distributed broom badges to "sweep out" incumbent administrations; Horace Greely looked out from a quill pen; and Winfield Hancock lost to James Abraham Garfield in 1880 despite a winning rebus-puzzle pin.

Shell badges reached their peak at the turn of the twentieth century with the development of moveable or mechanical badges. The most common mechanicals were little bug-like creatures made of silver or gold and used for the 1896 campaign, in which the Republicans stood for the gold standard and the Democrats for free silver. The wings of the silver bug opened to reveal pictures of William Jennings Bryan and running mate Arthur Sewell; the gold wings opened to reveal William McKinley and Garret Hobart. A number of mechanical badges were issued in 1896, including flags, eagles and elephants, all of which opened to show pictures of the candidates.

Campaign memorabilia has included everything from shell badges and broom blades to soap carvings and wristwatches. The "Autograph Dog" was born of Richard Nixon's 1960 presidential contest with John Kennedy.

Lanterns, torchlights, and canes were used abundantly in the grand and festive campaign parades, which flourished from the mid-1800s to the turn of the century. At their peak, in the late nineteenth century, these parades blossomed into neighborhood celebrations, featuring marching groups, fireworks and bands.

Banners were also important to American political campaigning. Some adorned campaign headquarters, other headed parades. Most banners made before 1900 are valuable because they were hand painted. Bandanas, which were popular from 1820 to the early 1900s are again popular among collectors. Most were made from inexpensive cotton, so few survive in good condition.

The invention of celluloid in the late nineteenth century made possible the familiar campaign button. By 1896, metal pin-back buttons covered with paper pictures and transparent celluloid were used by all campaigners. The celluloid process allowed the use of bold colors and imaginative designs. Buttons from 1900 to 1920 are among the most valuable, especially *jugates,* which are buttons depicting both presidential and vice-presidential candidates.

Mass-produced lithographed buttons came about with industrialization during the 1920s. An image was lithographed directly onto the metal, a process that quickly became standard campaign fare. This kind of button is easy to collect because so many of them were made and have survived (which also makes them less valuable than earlier buttons).

★ In the summer of 1958, twelve-year-old Craig Wade and his younger brother were vacationing with their uncle in Pittsfield, Massachusetts, when they came upon an old house in which they found an abandoned box. Craig opened the box and saw a lone piece of material, brown and moldy, folded in half. Like most boys would, he put the find away without much thought and eventually brought it back home to Mansfield, Massachusetts. The boy examined the material more closely at home and thought that the picture on the fabric looked like Thomas Jefferson.

The new school year came and Craig's eighth-grade class was learning about Jefferson when the boy told a teacher what he had discovered over the summer. When the teacher saw it, he knew it was a rarity. The two-by-three-inch linen banner was a celebration of Thomas Jefferson's victory over John Adams in the 1800 presidential election. It featured an oval portrait of Jefferson and an eagle to his right holding a streamer. The banner read *"Thomas Jefferson — President of the United States — John Adams is no more."*

Craig's teacher contacted a prominent attorney who connected the boy with the Smithsonian Institute, from which he promptly collected a check for $1,100 — a hefty sum for a teenager in 1959. The one-of-a-kind banner has been displayed in the Smithsonian ever since.

Values Outside the Home. Scarcity, historical interest and age are three factors that greatly determine the value of a political item. The scarcest items are the most valuable. Generally, the more historically significant an item, the more it will be worth. Age also adds to the value; McKinley items are skyrocketing now, and Teddy Roosevelt pieces are popular and command good prices.

When evaluating a political collectors' item, one should consider its construction as well. Modern alloys and mass production often lower the value of a piece.

Although an item is worth as much as the special meaning it holds for the collector, its market value is ultimately determined by what it means to the buyer. In other words, some lackluster candidates remain uninteresting forever. Even today there is not much demand for Chester A. Arthur artifacts.

The most popular candidates among collectors include the Founding Fathers (George Washington, John Adams, Thomas Jefferson, James Madison and James Monroe), Abraham Lincoln, both Roosevelts, John Kennedy, Al Smith, Andrew Jackson, and William Jennings Bryan.

The most desirable collectors' item based on historical significance is probably a George Washington inaugural button; $500 for copper or brass, up to $2,500 for silver.

Lincoln paraphernalia is more accessible. Occasionally, a Lincoln ribbon may turn up at a flea market for $20. Lincoln collectors especially should beware of reproductions and fakes. Remember that Lincoln was clean shaven when elected in 1860 and bearded by 1864. Also note that a few authentic early Lincoln items misspell his first name as "Abram."

The value of more recent lithographed buttons is based upon the candidates and the issues depicted. Generally, buttons from the late 1950s and early 1960s are now worth about $5 each; late 1960s to early 1970s buttons are worth from $2 to $3. A Kennedy/Johnson "For Experience" pictoral jugate sells for about $25, and a McKinley and Hobart jugate could fetch almost $100.

Collectors should always keep in mind the relative scarcity of buttons from a particular campaign. A McGovern/Shriver button will be worth less than a similar issue depicting the ill-fated team of McGovern/Eagleton. Landmark events also add value; Geraldine Ferraro buttons will most likely be collectors' items commemorating the first woman running on a major national presidential ticket. Buttons featuring a future president running for a local or state office also can be valuable. "Event" buttons, which are issued for or against such things as Prohibition, war, civil rights, and labor organization, also have the potential to become valuable, as do some third-party buttons, although most fetch less than concurrent presidential buttons.

Buttons are the most abundant of the political collectors' items, but articles range from posters to postcards, sheet music to coins, soap carvings to ceramics, editorial cartoons to canes. Some of the more obscure items are far more valuable than buttons, and some are mostly amusing. (A bright addition to any political collection is a British-made Liverpoolware pitcher commemorating the Watergate scandal of the early 1970s. One side of the pitcher depicts Richard Nixon's resignation of August 9, 1974; the President is surrounded by aides Haldeman, Ehrlichmann, Dean, Mitchell and Zeigler. The other side of the pitcher shows the White House flanked by an illustration of George Washington and the slogan "I Can't Tell A Lie.")

Ribbons, ties, hats, and banners have festooned candidates, supporters and campaign headquarters for more than a century. Ribbons are collected almost as fervently as buttons, so their prices are high. Old ribbons can range from $10 to more than $120 for one made of silk commemorating President Lincoln. Flags are especially sought.

Paper items, such as posters, are quickly picking up in value; collector interest is also increasing for political cartoons and postcards.

One of the most telling relics of political campaigns are the songs penned expressly for politicians. Few have heard Charles Davis' "March to the White House" written in 1924 for the losing Democrat. It can be bought today for $5. Hundreds of different songs have been published, but few are considered valuable. A picture of the politician on the cover of the sheet music generally increases its worth.

Medal and coin collection is a hobby in itself; a silver, copper or bronze commemorative is quite a find. Silver inaugural commemoratives are among the most treasured. If one was lucky enough to hide away a 1953 silver Eisenhower inaugural commemorative, he now is wealthier by more than $1,000. Official inaugural commemoratives are somewhat rare, which makes them worth more. A 1909 gold Taft piece reportedly brought $20,000 recently. Commemoratives decreased a lot both in quality and quantity when those made of aluminum were introduced at the turn of the century.

Not all medals were meant to be taken seriously; there were a number of humorous medalets minted also. Among the most popular were William Bryan dollars, which took sharp satirical aim at the Democrat who campaigned to repeal the gold standard in 1896. Silver Bryan dollars are valuable; but most Bryan tokens were made from cheap metal and were made larger than usual to suggest what Bryan's ideas would do to coinage.

Ceramic artifacts, such as plates, mugs, pitchers and bottles, have been produced since the early 1800s. A Hoover ceramic mug could bring $100, an Al Smith pitcher $60, but most fetch under $50. Like the Watergate pitcher, most older ceramics were not made in

America. Liverpoolware tankards and pitchers from the inaugurations of the first five American presidents exist and, needless to say, could bring thousands. Some Toby jugs bearing likenesses of presidents or candidates are quite beautiful. An Eisenhower Toby mug could bring $50.

Plates generally are not worth much. Exceptions include Lustreware imported from France and England in the early 1800s; an Andrew Jackson "Hero of New Orleans" pitcher is worth about $700. Tumblers are plentiful, and some, including those featuring President McKinley, average about $50. Generally, it is a good idea to carefully examine anything made before 1940 for authenticity and current market value. Modern political ceramics are probably worth more in sentimentality than in cash.

Other political souvenirs include watch fobs, which were issued in large quantities during campaigns. Many are worth up to $50 or more today. Another campaign item was the walking stick, which was first manufactured in 1840. A 1917 Woodrow Wilson inaugural stick fetches almost $100 today.

The novelty of political torches and lanterns also seems to have increased in value in today's market. Folding paper lanterns, if well preserved, can bring a few hundred dollars. Metal torchlights in all forms are also becoming valuable.

Smoking items, such as antique snuff boxes, cigar boxes and pipes, may fetch hundreds of dollars. A Truman cigar is worth $30.

Of course, no genuine political supporter would be seen during the last frantic days of a major campaign without sporting a campaign hat, which have come in many shapes and been made of all sorts of materials. Since most campaign hats are modern (post-1950), they will not command high prices.

The attic of an old political activist may include jewelry, spoons, fans, banks, and clocks, most of which have appreciated. Political toys are also increasing in value.

Where to Find Values. Garage sales and flea markets are good places to buy political items because dealer markup is low. Treasures found at a neighborhood garage sale also may be great bargains because the seller is probably not an experienced dealer. Garage sales in older neighborhoods have more to offer than those in newer developments.

Sometimes reasonably priced items can be found at antiques shops, although most antiques dealers tack on large markups. Buying at house auctions can be a good way of obtaining *boxes* of political collectors' items.

Buttons and other small political souvenirs show up at other collectors' shows, especially those exhibiting coins and stamps, and at surprisingly reasonable prices. One's older friends and relatives are also good sources of campaign pieces, especailly if they once were political activists.

A future-minded collector will make the rounds of Democratic and Republican campaign headquarters before election day and pay low prices for hats, pins, pictures, and other paraphernalia. One can also net a time capsule of valuables by helping to clean up local polling places and campaign headquarters.

A Price Sampling

William McKinley lapel button with picture, 1896	$985
Grant and Colfax cardboard jugate badge	180
Franklin Roosevelt Toby mug by Lenox, gray with white handle	175
Ramparts magazine, Nov. 1965 issue, with complete Ronald Reagan paperdoll, 4-page spread	50
Warren Harding watch fob	42
Calvin Coolidge jumbo cigar	20
Dwight Eisenhower bandana	20
John Kennedy playing cards, 1963, featuring the Kennedy family	17
McKinley/Hobart button (one inch)	15
Nixon/Agnew button (three inches)	7

How to Store/Display. It is most important that one not attempt to clean or restore an old souvenir. Cleaning will usually damage the finish by scratching it or removing the design.

Transparent display cases or frames are not recommended for most buttons. Sunlight will fade photographs and illustrations. Buttons are best stored in a soft dry environment, perhaps surrounded by felt, to avoid scratches. As interesting as they are to look at, buttons will last longer if kept in darkness, such as a lined jewelry box with many drawers in it, which is also perfect for pins and medals.

Paper items should be framed. One should use only acid-free cardboard for backing. Plexiglass or yellowed glass offers more protection than perfectly transparent materials. One should never use ordinary tapes or glues on the paper itself, which could tear it or destroy a design if it ever needed to be removed. Paper should also never be hung in direct sunlight. Air pollution is also very damaging to collectors' items. Ceramics and metals should be sealed up in cabinets or display cases and kept out of bright light.

★ John Gingerich, now of Macon, Georgia, had developed a keen eye for political memorabilia. In the late 1970s, he was visiting California to attend the national convention of the American Political Items Collectors in San Francisco. He and some friends decided to search for political collectibles, and ended up at a gun show in Los Angeles. There Gingerich spotted a jugate ribbon in a display case and negotiated its sale for $25. The ribbon turned out to be a Van Buren, the only one known so far. Gingerich estimates that he could sell it today for up to $7,000.

How and When to Sell. Demand is increasing for many campaign pieces, so that what is worth a lot today will be worth a lot more tomorrow. Collectors should hold on to those special pieces for as long as possible.

Market value of metals should be considered when eying copper, silver and other metal collectors' items. Silver pieces especially are influenced by the market.

Perhaps the easiest way to sell is to bring pieces to an antiques dealer, although this may not bring the most profit.

If one has enough to sell—and the patience to sell it—one may hold a garage sale or rent a booth at a flea market, but *only* after studying current market prices. A garage sale is inexpensive to set up, but it will only attract a limited number of people. A flea market will attract crowds, but one will have to pay to set up for business.

It may be more profitable to advertise campaign treasures in newspapers or in the advertising marts of antiques and collectors magazines. Other collectors are more able to appreciate the values of prized pieces.

There is no specific time to sell, but public excitement increases values. The anniversary of a popular president's birth or death may add to the demand for related pieces.

Little-Known Facts. William Henry Harrison's successful 1840 "Log Cabin and Hard Cider" campaign is amusing because the candidate was born into a wealthy, aristocratic Virginia family. But buttons displaying log cabins and cider jugs—and sporting the slogan "Tippecanoe and Tyler too"—convinced the public that Harrison was a man of the people and that his opponent Martin Van Buren was an effete aristocrat.

Photos of Abraham Lincoln are credited with familiarizing voters in the West with the Illinois lawman. But the newly invented photograph also could have ruined Lincoln's career; his homely appearance was sometimes the butt of editorial cartoons that referred to him as "Ape Lincoln."

—Scott Calamar

Bibliography

Books

Encyclopedia of Collectibles. Alexandria, VA: Time-Life Books, 1979.

Hake, Theodore. *The Encyclopedia of Political Buttons* (Vols 1-3). York, PA: Collectibles Press, 1974, 1977, 1978.

Hurwitz, Howard. *An Encyclopedic Dictionary of American History.* New York: Washington Square Press, 1974.

Sullivan, Edmund B. *Collecting Political Americana.* New York: Crown Publishers, Inc., 1980.

Periodicals

The Keynoter. American Political Item Collectors, 1054 Sharpsburg Dr., Huntsville, AL.

Political Americana. c/o C. W. Fishbaugh, Box 396, Shenandoah, IA 51601.

Political Bandwagon. 1632 Roberts Rd., Lancaster, PA 17601.

The Political Collector. 444 Lincoln St., York, PA 17404.

Catalogues

Flea Market Trader Revised, 3rd edition. Paducah, KY: Collector Books, 1981.

Hake's Americana and Collectibles. P.O. Box 1444, York, PA 17405.

Historicana. 1632 Roberts Rd., Lancaster, PA 17601.

Kovel, Ralph and Terry. *Kovels' Antiques and Collectibles Price List.* New York: Crown Publishers, Inc., 1984.

Dealers

Campaign Americana, P.O. Box 275, Merrick, NY 11566.

Presidential Coin and Antique Company, 6204 Little River Turnpike, Alexandria, VA 22312.

Associations

The American Political Items Collectors, c/o Joseph D. Hayes, Box 340339, San Antonio, TX 78234.

POPULAR GLASS

Glass. That magic substance formed from sand, soda, lime and fire. A fascinating substance with peculiar properties of fluidity. Pliant when hot, brittle when cold, glass can be as transparent as water or as opaque as ceramics. Fragile as a butterfly's wing or strong enough to roof a house, glass can be molded like clay, cut with a knife, spun into delicate threads, rolled into plates, pressed into sheets, and blown into goblets. The time and place of a people show themselves in the shape and color of their glassware. Those with shelves full of period glass not only own a vibrant part of history, but they participate in a lucrative hobby as well.

History. It is astonishing that in a world given to hurricanes, floods, droughts, tornadoes, monsoons, earthquakes, blizzards and hail-stones it would even occur to people to create for themselves frail containers and decorative pieces. But they do, and have, since 1600 B.C., when the ancient Egyptians began to produce glass as testaments to their love of beauty—and of the unreasonable. Bits of jewel-like glass in lapis-lazuli blue and jasper red can be seen inlaid in Tutankhamen's burial treasure and on his throne.

The first century A.D. introduced the new technology of glass-blowing, and Venice, Rome and the Rhine became the new centers of glass production. Ancient Rome even had its fanatic collectors. Pliny wrote about Petronius, Nero's master of ceremonies, who in a passionate deathbed pique, smashed to pieces a magnificent glass bowl rather than let it fall into the hands of his master after his death.

In the twelfth century, Chinese artisans produced exquisite painted glass perfume bottles. The Palestinian Jews and the people of Syria and Persia turned out thousands of hand-painted glass objects in the thirteenth and fourteenth centuries. Glassmakers in the sixteenth and seventeenth centuries experimented with form and merrily produced such items as anatomy glasses and dribble cups. In eighteenth- and nineteenth-century Germany, glass technology really expanded and gave the world cut crystal, pressed glass and all the variations familiar to us today.

★ **Goodwill Industries had sitting on their shelf a Jesse Moor backbar bottle. A wily collector snatched it up for $.25 and sold it for $75.**

Values Outside the Home. Interested collectors can begin by acquiring milk bottles (square or round, going as far back as 1866) and baby bottles (nineteenth and twentieth century, some embossed with affectionate company slogans and pictures—an especially rare nursing bottle from the '40s has a thermometer imbedded in the side). One may also find valuable medicine bottles (many embossed with unusual names and claims), snuff jars, historical and pictorial flasks, figural bottles, bitters and ink bottles, fruit jars, perfume bottles, beer bottles, wine and liquor bottles. Although prices for most bottles made after the turn of the century remain relatively low, almost any interesting glass container has the potential to appreciate in the future.

Much collectors' glassware divides into period of production. *Carnival glass,* mass produced from 1900 to 1925, was the poor man's alternative to Tiffany glass. Available by mail order, given away in huge quantities as prizes in games of chance at carnivals and circuses, Carnival glass had a face only a collector could love. Flashy, brassy, heavily patterned iridescent monstrosities appeared in average American homes as tableware, lamps, buttons, glass-leaded women's purses, commemorative items, and what were then called "Whimsys." Whimsys included such items as vases shaped like autos, bowls shaped like hats, even pieces resembling spittoons.

Original Carnival items always carry a trademark and tend to come in more mellow colors than later reproductions. Today it may fetch prices comparable to those paid for smaller Tiffany pieces.

Depression glass has been one of the hottest collectors' items in the past decade. Like Carnival glass, it was made by forcing liquid glass through pipes into molds. Made during the Great Depression, pieces were given away at weekly "dish nights" to theater patrons in the

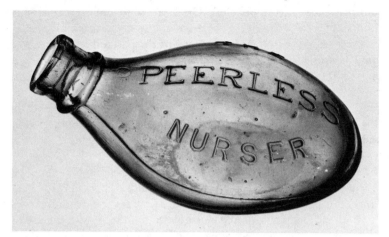

Corning Museum of Glass, Corning, NY: gift of Mrs. Frank Reynolds

The Peerless Nurser (c. 1890-1900) is a fine example of early glass production, when function was incorporated into form and manufacturers saw no need to be subtle about labeling their products.

hopes of encouraging movie attendance. It was also sold through mail-order houses and at dime stores, at times for as little as three cents apiece. Because it was made in such large quantities, it had lots of bubbles and flaws in it, which were disguised with pastel colors. The most common colors were pastel pink, green, and amber. More rare were light blue, Ritz blue, and deep ruby red; smoke and cobalt blue were extremely rare. Depression glass also came in white, creamy beige, blue, and green, which made it resemble milk glass.

Today Depression ware can still be found in attics and garages, because it was often put away as families upgraded their dish sets. Reissues were made in the 1950s using the original molds. One can distinguish original Depression ware from reissues by looking at the glass pattern: originals extend their patterns all the way to the edge of a piece; newer examples did not.

Glass specialty items should also be considered by collectors interested in the unusual. Marbles, which date back to the ancient Greeks and Romans, who used them for games and ceremonies, are excellent items to attract children to collecting. Enthusiasts should look for handmade American agates, spirals, micas, and the rare sulfides with figures inside. Also fun to collect and good moneymakers are the machine-made comic strip marbles, decorated with the faces of Bimbo, Little Orphan Annie, Sneezix, and Betty Boop.

Because of the intense interest during the past ten years in almost any glassware made before 1940, a lot of these items are becoming more difficult to find. Collectors looking toward the future can begin to pick up pieces that are only just beginning to become prized: tableware from the 1940s and 1950s (especially Fireking and Fenton), Disney and world's fair commemoratives, first-landing-on-the-moon pieces, and specialty glass containers by Avon cosmetics.

Where to Find Values. Although not the most appealing place to poke through, old dump sites can turn up a wealth of period glass, long since discarded. Energetic collectors can track down these sites through old city maps, on file in every community, or with the use of metal detectors. Many valuable pieces have already been unearthed, but there is still a lot of glass buried for those with the time and fortitude to search for it.

A fairly untapped source of glass, particularly bottles, is the ocean floor. Scuba gear and perseverance can pay off in pieces that are often undamaged and well preserved.

The more usual places, of course, such as antiques shops and shows, swap meets, flea markets, and estate sales, are also rich sources for the glass/bottle hunter.

★ **In 1976, Ann Gilmore of San Anselmo, California, inherited a number of items from an aunt who had lived for fifty-five years in the same house. As Ann was going through her aunt's household items, she discovered a small iridescent gold-colored vase. She brought it to an appraiser, who informed her that she had found a whimsy vase valued at close to $100.**

A Price Sampling

Carnival-glass punch bowl	$800
Depression-glass four-place setting, found in attic	700
Depression decanter and glass set	300
Queen Victoria commemorative plate, 1897	200
Oakland Beer bottle, 1880	80
Crackleglass bowl, c. 1920s	55
Vaseline Depression bowl	50

Bag of black onyx marbles, bought in 1902 (each)   45
Opalescent perfume bottle, c. 1930s   12
Depression glass, simple clear piece   2

How to Store/Display. Not many hidden treasures are lucrative and also beautiful and practical as well. Glassware and bottles look exquisite on backlit shelves but are also completely appropriate for domestic use. The most modest of Sunday brunches becomes elegant and unusual when served on rosy Depression plates, accompanied by wine in cut-glass goblets. *Most* old glassware is even dishwasher safe, although one should verify this with a reputable dealer before submitting a collection to the test.

Much newly acquired old glass, however, is in need of serious cleaning. Soak pieces in lukewarm water and mild soap for several days. Never subject glass to extremes in temperature, either of air or water, nor to harsh detergents or rough bristle brushes. Once clean and dry, a dull or scratched piece of glass will brighten considerably with a light rubbing of baby oil.

How and When to Sell. Glassware sets often garner a far tidier sum than single pieces. A Carnival full-place setting gives the collector a bargaining power that a sole piece does not. In addition, period glassware tends to go in and out of fashion. Interest in Depression glass peaked in 1982, so any collector now possessing various pieces would do well to hang on to them until dealers are once again hungry to purchase them.

It is important to go to shows, to see what is in demand, to contact dealers and/or one of the national glassware newsletters and associations, and to make certain that all pieces to be sold are squeaky clean.

★ Sometimes holding on to items, even when inconvenient, pays off. Mrs. Ralph Jones of Clearwater, Florida, adamantly refused to sell her set of Depression glass, even though it had to be packed and moved when she and her husband retired twelve years ago. This last year she gave her set of dishes as a wedding gift to her only granddaughter, who had always admired them. The set, which she had collected in the 1930s, is an unusual color of blue and now valued at over $250.

Little-Known Facts. The first bottled milk was delivered to neighborhoods in Oadensberg, New York, August 1886. The milkman had to make two trips, because three-quarters of the milk spilled out during the first trip. Manufacturers finally came up with a reliable cap that kept *all* of the milk inside the bottle.

• The annual marble championship in Tinsley Green, England, is that kingdom's oldest organized sporting event—ongoing since 1588.

—*Robin Solit*

Bibliography

Books

Baumann, Paul. *Collecting Antique Marbles.* Des Moines, IA: Wallace-Homestead Book Co., 1970.

Klamkin, Marian. *Collector's Guide to Carnival Glass.* New York: Hawthorn Books, 1976.

Munsey, Cecil. *Collecting Bottles.* New York: Hawthorn Books, 1970.

Rawlington, Fred. *Make Mine Milk.* Newport News, VA: Far Publications, 1970.

Periodicals

Carnival Glass News and Views. O. Joe Olson, 6063 66th St., Kansas City, MO 64131.

Depression Glass Daze. Box 57, Otisville, MI 48463.

National Depression Glass Journal. Box 268, Billings, MT 65610.

Associations

Depression Glass Daze, Box 57, Otisville, MI 48463.

International Carnival Glass Association, RR 1, Mentone, IN 46539.

Marble Collectors Society of America, P.O. Box 222, Trumball, CT 06611.

Moo (Milk Bottles Only Organization), Box 5456, Newport News, VA 23605.

PORCELAIN

The best porcelain is creamy, lustrous, and translucent. It has a sensuous touch similar to pearls or ivory. The Chinese were modeling exquisite objects from porcelain while Western man was still fashioning crude tools from rocks. Madame de Pompadour adored porcelain; she even cajoled her friend Louis XV to underwrite French factories with the national treasury.

Catherine the Great ordered 744 pieces of the stuff for the Russian court. American tycoons such as Elbert H. Gary have not minded spending a million to build a valuable collection. Prosperous Germans attempting to regain their national treasure have eagerly bid up the prices for Meissen ware. Prices fell when Portuguese collectors dropped out of the bidding following that country's revolution in 1979. The porcelain market has had its ups and downs, but it remains one of the most appealing among the decorative arts.

History. Around 850 A.D., Chinese potters of the Tang dynasty discovered that they could produce a magic substance by mixing china-clay (*kaolin*) with feldspar (*petuntse*) and quartz and firing it at temperatures around 1,350° C. The three materials fused together to form the white and partially translucent mass that came to be known as *porcelain*. With this material, exquisite objects could be created with modeled details that remain crisp and clear after firing. Enamel colors fired on the surface of the glaze tended to stay there in a bright and clear fashion. The formula for making porcelain remained an ancient Chinese secret for centuries.

The Sung dynasty produced delicately incised patterns of flowers and foliage. These included the Ting wares of Ting Chou in northeastern Hopei province and the *Lung-ch'uan* and *ch'ing-pai* wares of Chekiang and Kiangsi provinces. The latter became the center for the vast Chinese porcelain industry.

The Ming dynasty (1368-1644) saw painted decoration become more important than form. The distinctive blue underglaze achieved with a metallic oxide of cobalt was a great accomplishment of this period. The glaze was painted directly onto the body of the object prior to glazing, allowing it to be completed in a single firing. Fragile *eggshell* porcelain made during the reign of Emperor Yung Lo (1403-1424), was sometimes so delicately incised that this "secret decoration" under the glaze was visible only when the object was held to light.

Under the rule of Hsuan Te (1426-1435), the difficult-to-obtain copper-red color was produced from copper oxide in the presence of carbon monoxide in the kiln. Western imitators were unable to use this color successfully until the nineteenth century. Another innovation under Hsuan Te was the five-color Ming palette (iron-red, yellow, turquoise-blue, and green enamels) in combination with cobalt-blue underglaze.

Europeans fell in love with Chinese porcelain when Marco Polo unveiled his exotic treasures in the thirteenth century. A trickle of porcelain ware began flowing to Europe after the Portuguese established a trade route along the Cape of Good Hope. Dutch traders during the seventeenth century widened the channel for these costly imports.

During the period from the seventeenth to the late nineteenth centuries, the Chinese made and exported large quantities of porcelain pieces to the West. Earlier pieces were similar to those used in China, but later the styles were adapted to suit Western tastes. Aong the most popular of the Chinese export patterns are the *Canton* and *Rose Medallion* patterns.

Of course Europeans were eager to discover the secret and produce their own porcelain. *Soft-paste,* or *Medici,* porcelain was produced in Italy from 1575-1587. Commercial quantities of soft-paste porcelain were first made at Saint-Cloud in France during the late seventeenth century. But soft-paste porcelain is not the real thing; it lacks the hardness to hold finely detailed modeling, and the colors are soft rather than bright. Also, it scratches easily and hot liquids can cause it to crack.

French factories at Vincennes and later Sevres produced the ornate gilded porcelain coveted by Louis XV and Madame de Pompadour. In all likelihood, the factory would not have survived the profitless early days without the help of Louis' seemingly bottomless bank account.

The breakthrough for the hard-paste formula was a by-product of another of mankind's ancient preoccupations. In 1703, Augustus the Strong, Elector of Saxony, heard that an apothecary named Johann Boettger could turn base metal into gold. He promptly took the man into custody and ordered him to mix up a batch of the precious metal. Boettger teamed with a physicist named Ehrenfried Tschirnhaus, who suggested that they duplicate the process for making Chinese porcelain, which would be as good as gold. Shortly before Tschirnhaus died, Boettger discovered the Chinese *hard-paste,* or true porcelain, formula. His mixture of kaolin and petuntse yielded a beautiful, hard porcelain that was chip resistant, could be used with hot foods, and resonated a bell-like "ping" when struck with a finger. Boettger had produced "white gold."

This splendid example of a Sevres vase (1753) was created by Jean-Claude Duplessis and features two of his innovations: the lobed trumpet mouth and foliate-scroll handles.

Augustus enjoyed a European monopoly for a while as his factory at Meissen copied Chinese styles and worked the bugs out of the porcelain formula. Around 1720, the Meissen factory switched from Chinese to Japanese designs. Excellent records kept at the German factory make it possible to attribute pieces to famous modelers, such as Kirchner and Kaendler, even though they did not sign their work. During this period, many of the elaborately detailed figurines so prized by collectors were produced.

Even in those days industrial espionage was rampant, and Augustus took great precautions to guard his secret process. Workers at the Meissen factory took oaths of secrecy that were binding for life. As new technology emerged, care was taken that no one person should know everything about the process. Nevertheless, the secret leaked and rival princes learned how to make true porcelain. (Much later the discovery was independently repeated in Thuringia, England, and Russia.) During the eighteenth century, there were numerous hard-paste porcelain factories located in Switzerland and Holland, and at Vienna, Austria, Venice and Doccia in Italy, Plymouth and Bristol in England, and St. Petersburg in Russia.

Materials for making hard-paste porcelain were discovered near the French city of Limoges in 1768. However, it was not until the nineteenth century that the great expansion of Limoges porcelain production took place. The period 1770-1772 saw soft-paste porcelain gradually give way to the cheaper and more practical material of true porcelain. By 1804, the manufacture of soft paste was abandoned.

The nineteenth century saw technical improvements in porcelain making. Unfortunately, pieces produced during this period often lacked the earlier artistic qualities of originality and attention to detail. Many collectors find nineteenth-century works generally less desirable than earlier ones.

Today there is a distinct market for Chinese export porcelain and for German, French, and English wares. German porcelain is sought by Germans and people in other countries as well. Oddly, French people do not buy much French porcelain, but Americans and others do. English porcelain boomed during the 1950s, making only modest advances recently. French porcelain reached the heights during the 1960s and has not moved since. German porcelain is at the top of today's market after a period of unpopularity following World War II. The decline of the mark against the dollar has moved it down a bit from the highs of the 1970s.

★ In the 1920s, a particular British family decided to have an Oriental-type vase appraised. The family had used it for many years as an umbrella stand but now wondered if it had any value. The appraisal revealed that it was, indeed, a genuine ceramic from the Tang dynasty. It was soon sold for half a million dollars.

Values Outside the Home. The collector must first learn to distinguish between pottery and porcelain. Pottery is opaque when held to the light; porcelain is translucent. *Stoneware* (a hard non-porous type of pottery) is also slightly translucent.

The next step is to learn to differentiate between soft-paste and hard-paste porcelain. The glaze on soft paste lies on the surface instead of fusing *into* it. Therefore it is thicker and inclined to collect in hollow places. It also has a tendency to crack. Soft paste feels like soap. Where chipped, it feels coarse or granular. Sharp edges will not mark a fingernail, but almost all soft paste can be scratched by steel.

Hard-paste porcelain has a smoother, more flint-like fracture. It will mark a fingernail and it cannot be scratched by steel. One can put its unglazed underside through these tests.

An unrepaired piece should be examined carefully for hidden restorations. Ultraviolet light will reveal break lines *unless* they have been covered with lead-type paint. Holding a piece up to a bright light so that it is back lighted will reveal repaired breaks.

Repaired pieces will also feel different to the touch; material used to repair a break will feel colder than the original material surrounding it. Finally, a gentle poke at the surface with a pin will reveal whether or not a piece has been kiln fired. A glaze that is impervious to the pin scratch signifies an original, since restorations are not fired and therefore softer than originals.

The types of porcelain described in the following paragraphs provide a sampling of what's available. The best guide to collecting is an innate and informed sense of good taste. One should choose the best quality affordable and only pieces that will be enjoyable to live with.

Chinese Export Porcelain

With few exceptions, the Chinese porcelain patterns collected today are those made specifically for export during the period from the seventeenth to the late nineteenth centuries. Early pieces were the same as those used at home, but the Chinese potters soon learned to adapt the styles, shapes and colors to please their Western customers. Also, export pieces were made a little heavier so they could remain intact during rough ocean voyages.

Popular items were armorial plates sporting coats of arms, organizational insignia, or family monograms. Designers combined these foreign motifs with some Chinese design elements, which resulted in a curious but mostly harmonious melange of styles. These pieces are prized by today's collectors as are pieces with the American eagle and other patriotic embellishments.

Armorial pieces are among the easiest Chinese export items to date accurately through family records that indicate when they were ordered and paid for. Also, distinctive borders, such as the *Blue Trellis,* made only during the late 1700s and early 1800s, can also provide clues for dating. Less reliable are the potters' marks and other inscriptions occasionally found on the backs of pieces. This is because they were not standardized in the manner of silver marks.

Less expensive collectors' china are the *Canton* and *Nanking* patterns produced in abundance during the same period. Destined for families of modest means, these were dismissed as "ballast ware" by ships' captains because they were stowed deep in the damp hold to cushion the more expensive and delicate items. Motifs include stylized Chinese landscapes that would often show a bridge, a willow tree, a shrine or pagoda and perhaps a figure or two on white with blue underglaze. The *Fitzhue* pattern, named for a British trading family, is also relatively easy to find. These monochrome pieces are decorated with chrysanthemums and trellis-work borders.

Two other popular and relatively inexpensive porcelain patterns are *Rose Medallion* and *Mandarin Rose Medallion.* The former always has a center ornament or medallion and an overall floral and gold field with open spaces reserved for birds, fruits, flowers, butterflies and the like. Mandarin pieces are similar, often with distinctive borders and central designs featuring figures in a court setting.

European Porcelain

Collectors prize the bright colors of the mid-eighteenth century over the more subdued hues of the late eighteenth and nineteenth centuries. Color is important; the whiter and more translucent pieces are more desirable than those that are off-colored or gray. Generally, the fancier the shape the better. Sculptural pieces with birds, animals, or human figures fetch highest prices. Animated facial expressions and exquisitely executed details are a plus.

German artists to look for include Johann Gottlob Kirchner, who worked at Meissen on and off from 1727 to 1733. He specialized in producing lively animals, such as dogs, tropical birds, and wild boars. Another master Meissen modeler, Johann Joaquim Kaendler, who worked at the Meissen factory from 1731, is the most famous of all. Pieces attributed to him bring prices ranging from $600 to $100,000. Kaendler's life-sized birds are highly prized. He favored tropical species, but turned out a number of the more common varieties, such as jays, ducks, magpies and pheasants. Some figures are as tall as twenty inches. Because large pieces tend to crack in a kiln, few were produced. The rarities that survived bring top prices. An eagle might go for $100,000, while a small dove will fetch a mere $6,000 to $8,000.

Kaendler produced dishes for the table as well. Among his most famous is the "Swan service," commissioned by Heinrich Graf von Bruhl on the occasion of his wedding to Grafin Franziska von Kolowrat-Krakowska in 1737. Hundreds of pieces were produced, each with frolicking relief-molded swans.

Other German factories produced some quality pieces, though most experts agree that prices for Meissen are generally higher. Exceptions are the figures of flower girls, fish sellers, musicians, comedians, and romantic couples produced by Franz Anton Bustelli at Nymphenburg from 1754 to 1763. They can be worth from $10,000 to $20,000. Romantic couples made by Peter Melchior at Hochst can bring similar prices.

French porcelain made prior to 1770 is of the soft-paste variety. By 1804, the production of soft-paste was abandoned in France. While some of the early French pieces are primitive, others from St. Cloud (1678-1766), Chantilly (1725-1800), and Mennecy (1734-1806) are delightfully sophisticated. Exquisitely sculptured and decorated candlesticks can sell for $10,000.

Pieces made at the factories at Vincennes-Sevres were splashed with large areas of ground color. The most desirable colors are apple-green, turquoise-blue, and a remarkable shade of pink later named after Madame de Pompadour. To illustrate the importance of color, consider a simple mug decorated with flowers. With a natural white ground color, such a mug might be worth $500, while a similar one with turquoise could bring $1,000, and yet another with the famous *rose Pompadour* might be worth $5,000!

Exhibitions in recent years have renewed interest in French porcelain. Prices for Vincennes-Serves pieces received a boost with the Sotheby's London sale of an outstanding collection on June 12, 1984. Time will tell whether record price levels will be reached. A word of caution, however; authenticity of this type of porcelain is most difficult to establish since there are more fakes than genuine articles. Dealers are often short on expertise, causing collectors to lose their nerve.

English porcelain can be as fine as one will find anywhere, and it can be inferior. It embodies elements of everybody else's designs along with some original ideas. The botanical plates produced at the soft-paste factory in Chelsea around 1745 are sometimes thought to be the pinnacle of the English potter's art. Dishes shaped like artichokes, cabbages, lemons, sunflowers, and the like can run anywhere from $5,000 up. Collectors are less interested in the ornately gilded pieces inspired by Serves produced after 1760.

Other examples of valuable English porcelain are the interpretations of Chinese, Japanese, and Meissen designs produced at Bow and Longton Hall. These can be almost as pricey as Chelsea. The Derby factory operating in the 1760s and 1770s turned out exceptional allegorical, Oriental, and romantic figures. They go for up to $15,000.

William Billingsley was a superb painter of flowers in soft washes, roses in particular. He began creating these decorations at Derby and continued at other English factories at Pinxton, Nantgarw, Swansea, Coalport, and Worcester until his death in 1828.

The Worcester factory produced outstanding English wares. Excellent, sturdy porcelain was produced there from 1751. Early pieces were decorated with Chinese designs. The founder, Dr. John Wall, introduced a method of transfer printing that produced designs as sharp as anything on paper. Many collectors are very excited about quality transfer-printed wares, grabbing up all they can find. Designs include historical scenes, landscapes, figures, and portraits. These are often priced under $1,000.

Where to Find Values. More than a million pieces of Chinese export porcelain were shipped to the United States each year during the height of the trade. Therefore, it is entirely possible that many more first-rate specimens will find their way out of closets and attics and into the market in the near future. The most likely places to find them are the nineteenth-century port cities on the East Coast, where the pieces were first unloaded.

Dealers will often say that fine pieces of European porcelain are unavailable. This is because today's collector is the fifth generation looking for antiques, and most of the fine old pieces belong to individuals who know their value and plan to hang on to them. There is a lot of truth to this, but there are always exceptions. It will not hurt to learn to recognize quality pieces and to go browsing through garage sales, flea markets, thrift shops and antiques shops.

A reputable dealer *who has expertise in porcelain* can be one's best ally in getting started. A good one will share knowledge, answer questions, and use contacts to locate exactly the right piece(s) for a customer. Best of all, he or she will stand behind an article if it turns out to be one of the many pretenders that are all too numerous in this field. Check to find out what a particular dealer's policy is, and do not be afraid to have an expensive object appraised by an outside expert. Expect to pay a fair price for the dealer's service, because he or she will expect to make a profit.

Other possible sources include estate sales, special showings, and auctions. Prices will be high for popular items. When buying at auction, always preview any item before bidding.

★ **One day a gentleman brought a Chinese porcelain dish to Sotheby's, New York, to find out what it was worth. He had picked it up at a convent rummage sale for $3. The nuns who had been using it for sugar had acquired something they liked better for the purpose. It turned out to be rare and valuable, fetching $30,000.**

A Price Sampling

Sevres clock and vases, Louis XVI style, gilt bronze, Jewels, 3 piece	$9,500
Chinese export snuff box, swans, dog, pig, arms of Lewin of Hartford, 2″	2,200
Sevres jardiniere, turquoise, ormolu, mounted, 3 scenes 14½″	625
Rose Medallion charger, genre and floral design, 18½″	550
Chinese export basket, hilly landscape, Buddha, cricket, fruit, 10″	412
Meissen bowl, cobalt ground, raised gold, marked, 12″	379
Chelsea figurine, court jester, gold anchor, c. 1780, 9″	375

Nymphenburg figurine, lady in crinoline, 7½"	275
Worcester bud vase, hand painted, orchid panels, green, Hadley, 3½"	175
Dresden ashtray, gold trim, marked, 5½"	50

How to Store/Display. A collector's first consideration is the preservation of his precious pieces. Showing them off to best advantage can be accomplished safely with a little care. If one decides to hang valuable plates, the best plate hangers should be used. An expert can offer recommendations here. Hooks must be securely fastened into the wall and the hanging fixtures properly installed. The hangers themselves should be checked for rough edges, which would scratch gold trim.

There are advantages to keeping figurines and other porcelain pieces (including plates) on cabinet shelves behind glass. The shelves are not likely to collapse, and the glass will keep out dust. A fluorescent lighting fixture installed inside the cabinet will allow the pieces to be viewed to maximum advantage. A 25-watt bulb is adequate even for a large cabinet.

Great care must be exercised in cleaning fragile porcelain. Be particularly careful with those areas displaying gold trim, especially if it is thin or wispy. Too much rubbing could remove the gold along with the dirt. Dry cleaning to remove the surface dirt is highly recommended. Wet cleaning may be necessary for exceptionally dirty pieces or those with locked-in grime coated with oils or grease.

Pieces should first be feather dusted and then cleaned more thoroughly using a soft-bristled camel hair brush. A three-quarter-inch brush is perfect. If the item is still soiled, gentle cleaning agents can be used, and hot water (not over 160 degrees). First the piece should be soaked in plain warm or moderately hot water for a few minutes without soap to loosen grime. Then each item may be dunked a few times in a basin of hot sudsy water. If necessary, it can be rubbed gently with a rag soaked in the washing water. The final step is to rinse several times in warm water and carefully dry with a lint-free towel.

Water can become trapped inside figurines. For most articles, rinsing and thorough draining should eliminate this problem. Some items, however, have very small vent holes in inconspicuous places, which can allow water to seep in but prevent it from draining out or evaporating. The solution is to plug these holes if possible before the washing process.

How and When to Sell. The best time to sell porcelain is at the peak of an inflationary cycle. Other factors that can affect prices include publicity about a type of porcelain and sales of important collections. Revolutions and other political events that affect collectors have an impact also.

There are several options for selling pieces from a collection. Selling to an individual will net the best price because there are no commissions to pay. Arranging the sale may take some time and effort. Sellers should try advertising in publications likely to be read by potential buyers.

Selling at auction has both benefits and risks. If the sale is well publicized and offers many glamorous items to draw bidders, the price could be bid up. There are no guarantees, however, and even an innocuous event such as rain could dampen buyer enthusiasm. Also, auction houses charge 15%-20% commission on sales.

Selling to a dealer is probably the least desirable choice because he or she must buy at a price well below retail in order to stay in business. Dealers do have many customers and contacts, however, and they can likely find a buyer for a treasure faster than its owner can. Check to see if there is a dealer who will sell on consignment. The commission for a consignment sale is likely to be from 10% to 20%.

★ A dealer-collector in Palo Alto, California, picked up six beautiful translucent plates at an estate sale for $5 each. She knew they were good but was not sure what they were worth. Their Royal Dux origin made them worth more than the $250 apiece she sold them for. They later went for $600.

Little-Known Facts. The enormous demand to know the secret Meissen formula for hard-paste porcelain increased its monetary value, and seventeenth-century highways were full of wandering men knowing—or claiming to know—something about the process. All kinds of bribery, trickery and theft were employed, but alcohol proved to be the best key to unlocking the secret. Boettger of Meissen betrayed his secret when drunk, as did Joseph Jakob Ringler. The latter, who acquired his recipes by questionable means, carried them on his person in a notebook. When he was made drunk and insensible, the contents were copied. The secret spread as copies were recopied, forming the basis for further experiments.

• The French factories owed much of their success to the patronage of Madame de Pompadour. The Marquise could not get enough of the unglazed white, or "biscuit," porcelain figurines modeled after drawings by her favorite artist, Boucher. She had a similar passion for another Vincennes-Sevres specialty, soft-paste porcelain flowers. One of her detractors, the Marquis d'Argenson, noted in his memoirs that she ordered 800,000 livres worth of porcelain for her chateau and Louis XV's country houses. This scandalous extravagance, he claimed, depleted the royal coffers and ultimately led to the downfall of the monarchy.

—Joyce Hecht

Bibliography

Books

Berges, Ruth. *From Gold to Porcelain: The Art of Porcelain and Faience.* New York: Thomas Yoseloff, Publisher, 1963.

———. *The Collector's Cabinet.* London: A. S. Barnes and Co., Inc., 1980.

Berling, K. *Meissen China, An Illustrated History.* Mineola, New York: Dover, reprinted from 1910 edition.

Charles, Rollo. *Continental Porcelain of the Eighteenth Century.* London: Ernest Benn Limited, University of Toronto Press, 1964.

Cushion, John. *Porcelain.* New York: World Publishing/Times Mirror, 1973.

Gordon, Elinor. *Collecting Chinese Porcelain.* New York: Universe Books, 1977.

Godden, Geoffrey A. *Illustrated History of British Pottery and Porcelain.* London: Barrie and Jenkins, 1981.

Palmer, Arlene M. *A Winterthur Guide to Chinese Export Porcelain.* New York: Crown Publishers, Inc., 1976.

Theus, Will H. *How to Detect & Collect Antique Porcelain & Pottery.* New York: Alfred A. Knopf, 1974.

Periodicals

American Collector. P.O. Drawer C, Kermit, TX 79745.

Connoisseur. P.O. Box 10143, Des Moines, IA 50347-0143.

Dealers

Adele's Oriental and European Objects of Art, 229 Hamilton Ave., Palo Alto, CA 94301.

Almanac Antiques, 660 High St., Palo Alto, CA 94301.

C. W. Moody and J. D. Lacey Antiques, 539 Sutter, San Francisco, CA 94102.

Sharp's Antiques, 1908 Encinal Ave., Alameda, CA 94501.

Associations

National Association of Friends of Rare Porcelain, c/o Reese Palley, 1201 Boardwalk, Atlantic City, NJ 08401 (publishes newsletter).

POSTERS AND PRINTS

Abraham Lincoln in Martin Van Buren's body? Only in the world of a printmaker.

The public clamor for lithographic prints of Lincoln following his assassination was so great that unscrupulous printmakers eliminated Van Buren's head from an outdated engraver's plate and inserted the head of Lincoln. The comical result? The body of the shortest president bearing the head of the tallest.

Today, collectors value such prints for their humor as well as historical importance. And in the world of posters even more incredible oddities and beauty prevail, making a collection of posters and prints a journey into the realm of visual nostalgia.

History. The first poster may well have been the piece of Egyptian papyrus from 146 B.C. describing two escaped slaves and offering a reward for their return. Following that were the Greek *axones,* which were square columns of poster panels that listed the order of athletic contests and the names of the athletes.

Some experts claim that the "modern" poster can be traced back to 1477 in England to a public advertisement by William Caxton upon which was written at the bottom, *"Supplico Stet Cedula,"* or "Pray, do not pull down the advertisement." Safely preserved in a British library, this sheet is the earliest surviving public "poster" printed in English.

Many years after Gutenberg invented printing, the walls of Paris became the center for poster art in the 1540s. But graphics remained black and white until the late 1860s, when the invention of lithography by Alois Senefelder allowed artists to obtain grey tones, greater detail, and relief from the tedium of metal engraving. Eventually color was added to the process.

Honore Daumier was the first artist to realize the potential of lithography and used the process to print scathing satires of Paris life. Jules Cheret, after seeing some colorful American traveling-circus posters in Paris, became the first French poster artist to use color in lithographic posters. His prodigious output over fifty years made him central to the poster phenomenon. By 1890, trading and collecting his work and others, including that of Toulouse-Latrec, was a major business.

In America, magazine covers took a new twist. It meant the end of a single design printed month after month, which was practiced in England; instead poster artists were hired to do a different cover for each month and then create a poster of the cover to promote the magazine. The works of Will Bradley, Edward Penfield, Maxfield Parrish, Louis Rhead and others established a vibrant realism that was enhanced by expert production.

It was the firm of Currier and Ives that made prints as popular as posters in the United States. Aimed at a mass audience, the prints depicted townscapes, seasonal landscapes, and wildlife, all with the homey and sentimental features that Americans loved to hang on the walls of their modest homes. The prints sold in the tens of thousands. The bird prints of James Audubon were popular then too.

By the turn of the century posters were being used everywhere to announce, promote, solicit, warn, entertain and condemn. Political contests, theater, circuses, product advertising (bicycles, soap, beer, etc.), books, all kinds of events, and even underwear appeared on posters. At the same time, James McNeil Whistler was using lithographic prints to display new subject matter and new techniques. He died in 1903, but he influenced artists for decades afterward.

When World War I broke out posters became instruments of propaganda. President Wilson established a Committee of Public Information to create posters that would build morale. So effective were these wartime graphics (including the famous James Montgomery Flagg depiction of Uncle Sam pointing and saying "I want you!") that after the war, newspapers employed the idea of poster art and began creating sophisticated display ads.

From President Wilson's Committee of Information, established by him during World War II, came James Flagg's "I Want You" poster, considered one of the most famous examples of poster art from the modern era.

But the popularity of the automobile and the construction of highways began to phase out the medium-sized poster, which was gradually replaced by billboards. And although patriotic posters were used prolifically by all countries during World War II, their influence as an art form to communicate to mass audiences was quickly replaced by television after the war, never again to have the power they once had to touch many people at one time.

In the 1960s posters enjoyed a renaissance. Graphic arts became important as a mode of expression and rebellion. Andy Warhol, Roy Lichenstein and others produced posters that blurred the lines between art, fun, protest and advertising. Posters as inexpensive decorative art became immensely popular and remain so today.

★ A collector of Lincoln prints attended a country auction several years ago and found a broadside (small handbill) featuring a sharp portrait of Lincoln. The collector bid $79 and took the broadside home. He learned a few days later that the print was a rare copy of the portrait that had led an 11-year-old girl to write to Lincoln and suggest he grow a beard to improve his appearance. Today the broadside is worth several thousand dollars.

Values Outside the Home. The beginning collector must start his hobby by forgetting about the golden days of the art as it flourished in Paris at the turn of the century. Most posters from that era reside in collections or museums and are sold, if at all, for tens of thousands of dollars.

Collectors should concentrate instead on posters of social significance, such as those produced during the two world wars. Depending on their condition and subject matter, prices range from $25 to $1,000. The famous World War I poster by Howard Chandler Christy, showing a woman dressed in a man's Navy uniform and saying "Navy, Gee! I Wish I Were a Man," has been priced at $600.

Prices for these posters have held steady over the last few years, allowing a beginning collector access to the market. By specializing according to war and country—for instance, World War I European posters or those from America during World War II—a collector can make connections with the dealers who specialize in his area of interest.

Circus posters, filled with vibrant color and action scenes, are not plentiful but are sought after, particularly those printed by the Strobridge Lithograph Company. A 1914 Ringling Brothers, Barnum and Bailey poster by Strobridge was recently priced at $275.

More plentiful and sometimes just as intriguing as slices of Americana are movie posters. They are by far the most collected of all. The older ones are more valuable, depending on the movie and the stars. And movie pressbooks, issued along with the film as a publicity packet, can be found for as little as $10, such as that for the 1961 John Wayne film *The Alamo.*

Movie posters, particularly of Marilyn Monroe films, hold nearly as much appeal as the movie itself. A Monroe poster for the 1950 film *All About Eve,* could sell for as much as $200, while a 1947 Bob Hope poster for *My Favorite Brunette* might be bought for $40.

Collectors may want to focus on posters of a well-known star, or limit a collection to Academy Award winners, to posters exclusively from MGM movies.

Other subjects to consider collecting are theater, travel, magic, advertising and posters from the 1960s. Those that advertise products are fairly rare and bring prices in the $300 to $600 range, again depending on age and condition. Travel posters, usually of old steamship lines or railways, are priced slightly lower.

Collecting posters from the 1960s, which would include psychedelic and protest art, requires a concentrated search (in New York and San Francisco specifically), but will yield a valuable collection when interest in that decade is renewed.

Collecting lithographic prints gives the beginner a smorgasbord of old and new artists and categories to choose from, and many are available in just about any price range. So many Currier and Ives prints (known as "antiquarian") were lithographed in the nineteenth century that a collector can specialize in snow scenes or clipper ships or animals or birds or horses and carriages. The more sentimental antiquarian prints, such as three kittens playing, go for less than $50, while a scene of San Francisco sold for over $6,000 in 1980 and would be considerably more today.

Currier and Ives' many competitors, whose prints were of equally good quality, can also be collected, and at considerably lower prices. One name to look for is Endicott and Company among dozens of others that printed medical, legal, or stock exchange subjects and historical events. Another is McKenney and Hall, which did a series of Indian scenes and chiefs.

It must be remembered that the practice of limiting an edition of a print to enhance its value is a twentieth-century innovation. During the nineteenth century the incentive was to produce as many prints as could be sold.

The best way for a beginner to get started in acquiring a knowledge of prints is to check out pertinent books from a local library. Prints have always been popular, and art books that survey the chronology of printmaking also lend the reader a sense of history. Then one should visit an old-print shop or antiquarian-book store and browse.

The collector will learn that regional interests sometimes dominate when a value is placed upon a print. In Texas, people collect Carl Nebel's Mexican War scenes, and in San Francisco prints of Hawaii are popular. One may, therefore, find a Nebel print for sale in San Francisco priced lower than it would be in Texas.

There is also a trend in print collecting that transcends regional differences in terms of price. Because of the national popularity of President Abraham Lincoln before and after his assassinatin, hundreds of thousands of prints of him exist. From the maudlin to the downright silly, almost any Lincoln print is valuable. Prices start as low as ten dollars and go up to the thousands. A new collector might start with the clean-shaven Lincoln (prior to 1861), or focus on the bearded Lincoln (from 1861 on), or perhaps on Lincoln with his family. Currier and Ives printed thousands of copies of thirty-eight different studies of Lincoln.

New collectors of old prints of any kind should beware of fakes and reproductions, particularly of Currier and Ives. Old prints are composed of fine lines that cannot be duplicated by current photoengraving processes. Reproductions consist of rows of small dots, similiar to a newspaper photo. A beginner would not be foolish to take along a magnifying glass to an antiquarian print shop to learn to spot the differences. Old prints, sometimes stained or slightly yellowed, are also identified by a thick, high-rag content paper.

Where to Find Values. The best places to buy posters and prints are at antiquarian- and old-book stores. Dealers usually operate out of stores and include many kinds of paper memorabilia under one roof.

The second best place to buy is at advertising antiques shows, where collectors and dealers (who do not concentrate on fine arts prints) surround themselves with old magazines, files of old prints and, sometimes, posters. Items are usually marked, but there often is a little room for negotiation if one has some knowledge about the subject.

Auctions of posters and prints by well-known houses are usually held only for truly fine and rare examples, such as prints by Audubon or the coveted Currier and Ives. But at smaller country or rural auctions prints are often sold for lower prices.

A Price Sampling

"Great Race on the Mississippi" (Currier and Ives)	$11,000
"Whooping Crane" (Audubon by Havell)	10,000
"Clipper Ship Sweepstakes" (Currier and Ives)	5,000
"Eight Bells" (Winslow Homer etching)	2,500
"Babe Comes Home" (movie poster of Babe Ruth)	900
"Daybreak" (Maxfield Parrish print)	220
"Vertigo!" (movie poster)	200
"Americans All!" (World War I poster by Christy)	70
"Beauty of the Atlantic" (Currier and Ives)	50
"Latin Lovers" (movie poster with Lana Turner)	25

How to Store/Display. Paper is a fragile legacy, which means that all prints and posters require extra care. If one frames a print, it should be done with acid-free matting materials. If acid-free materials are not used, common mat boards will eventually stain the print and then cause it to deteriorate.

Rubber cement, masking or transparent tapes should never be used. A vegetable-based paste made of wheat or rice flour and water is recommended instead. The print should never touch the glass, because changes in temperature can cause condensation to form underneath it—the mat separates the print from the glass.

Unframed prints can be stored in *solanders,* which are boxes lined with all-rag paper and virtually airtight.

To store large posters, one may cut two pieces of Fom-cor (made by Monsanto and available in art supply stores) to fit the poster size and then slip the poster between the pieces and loosely tape them together. The poster should then be placed somewhere flat and out of the way, such as on the floor beneath a bed. To frame a poster, the same procedures can be followed for framing a print.

How and When to Sell. If one collects Currier and Ives prints for pleasure, it is best to hold on to them for as long as possible. The interest in Currier and Ives is similar to the public interest in diamonds; people differ on the size of a diamond they want, but not over the diamond itself. Currier and Ives prints have broad appeal and enduring qualities.

The print market remains strong because the range of prints available allows a lot of people to enjoy collecting them. If one's objective in collecting is to make money, it is best to be highly selective in buying, with an eye on resale value instead of personal taste. Consider collecting to be a business. Remember, too, that when collecting the work of Currier and Ives and others of the era, subject matter is all important, as well as condition of the piece.

Chances are if one has collected intelligently (not randomly, but with a specific focus), one will fetch the best value by selling prints through an auction house or reputable dealer. But no matter who one deals with, it is imperative to know current market prices, especially those of one's own collection.

Collectors also have the option of selling directly to buyers. The best place to do that is at the annual Great Mid-Atlantic Antique Advertising and Memorabilia Show and Sale held in Gaithersburg, Maryland. This is the most important and best attended of all such shows, and therefore gives both buyers and sellers a better chance of getting exactly what they are looking for.

★ **When Martin Dilbert of Los Angeles finally moved the old shelf in his father's garage after his father had died, he discovered a dusty railroad travel poster on the wall directly behind the shelf. It was in good condition because of the years it had spent in darkness. Dilbert learned later the poster was worth over $100.**

Little-Known Facts. Hitler was one of the originators of political pop art. As a young man he sometimes supported himself by doing commercial posters. One of his posters depicted a Vienna cathedral awash in a mountain of soap bubbles. Religion was being sold like soap, his poster asserted. Later, his deadly political doctrine made extensive use of posters.

• "Turning Out The Light," a 1905 etching done by John Sloane, portrayed a clothed woman kneeling in bed and reaching around to turn off a gas light. Stretched out next to her was a man. This and three other prints were called "vulgar" and "indecent" by the American Water Color Society.

• In the late 1800s in England, posters appeared everywhere, even on the white cliffs of Dover, a desecration that outraged the public. This led to the establishment of the Society for the Checking of Abuses in Public Advertising (SCAPA), which became a watchdog over poster-posting abuses.

—David Holmstrom

Bibliography

Books

Cogswell, Margaret, ed. *The American Poster.* New York: American Federation of Arts, 1967.

Hillier, Bevis. *Posters.* New York: Stein and Day, 1969.

Hutchison, Harold F. *The Poster: An Illustrated History from 1860.* New York: Viking Press, 1969.

Jacobowitz, Ellen S., and George H. Marcus. *American Graphics: 1860-1940.* Philadelphia, PA: Philadelphia Museum of Art, 1982.

Johnson, Una E. *American Prints and Printmakers.* New York: Doubleday & Co., 1980.

Longstreet, Stephen. *A Treasury of the World's Great Prints.* New York: Simon and Schuster, 1961.

Zeman, Zbynek. *Selling the War: Art and Propaganda in World War II.* New York: Exter Books, 1982.

Periodicals

Americana. 29 West 38th St., New York, NY 10018.

Antiquarian. Box 798, Huntington, NY 11743.

Magazine Antiques. 551 5th Ave., New York, NY 10176.

Dealers

George Theofiles, Miscellaneous Man, Box 1776, New Freedom, PA 17349 (posters, mail order).

Old Print Shop, 150 Lexington, New York, NY 10016 (posters and prints).

Rudisill's Alt Print Haus, 3 Lakewood, Medfield, MA 02052 (Currier and Ives prints).

Sergio's Old Prints, 50 Maiden Lane, San Francisco, CA 94101 (prints and posters).

Associations

American Historical Print Collectors Society, Inc., Dr. Henry A. Boorse, 338 Summit Ave., Leonia, NJ 07605.

CHAPTER 18

Quilts

QUILTS

"At your quilting, maids don't dally.
A maid who is quiltless at twenty-one
Never shall meet her bridal sun."
—embroidered on nineteenth-century quilt

In great-grandmother's day this warning was taken seriously. Every prospective bride was expected to have a dozen quilt tops before she married. (Such industry was also meant to keep young maids busy, since idle hands were believed to be the Devil's workshop.) To be quiltless invited spinsterhood. When a girl had a quilting bee in her honor, the community knew that wedding bells were not far off.

Today's rich legacy of old quilts testifies to their importance among earlier generations. Along with homemade lye soap and food "put by," they are evidence of the self-reliant nature of the times. Also, "piecing" quilts and attending quilting bees provided creative and social outlets for Early American women. Whether in the mountains or on the plains, they stitched their dreams of adventure and thirst for beauty into what would become some of the most intricate, colorful, and revealing mementos of the past.

In the 1920s, growing interest in folk art generated enthusiasm for old quilts, and early aficionados found easy pickings. Lovely old pieces turned up in trunks and barns, even in ol' Shep's bed. As the best examples began to find homes in museums and exhibitions, prices began to move up. Today it is more difficult to find valuable quilts at garage sales.

As hobbyists continue to buy up antique quilts, prices for the bold and striking Amish and other highly prized pieces get hotter. They can increase at about 10% annually. In December 1984, Sotheby's featured quilts in its Americana sale. Will this fuel even greater price increases?

History. No other type of needlework is as truly American as the patchwork quilt. Although American women did not originate either patchwork or quilting, they did combine the two ancient techniques to produce *quilts,* which became synonymous with "bedcovers." Quilts, or bedcovers, were made by "piecing," or sewing together, scraps of fabric to make a decorative top layer. This was combined

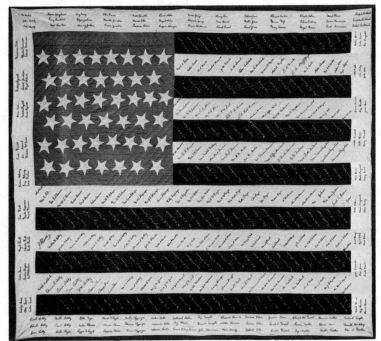

An extraordinary number of signatures (440) adds even more value to an already rare 1899 friendship flag quilt from Nebraska.

with two others—a middle for warmth and another for the bottom, or lining. The fine running stitches that "quilted" the three layers together often formed decorative patterns themselves.

Settlers from England and Holland brought the art of quilting to the Eastern Seaboard. The handsome linsey-woolsey (linen warp and wool weft) covers, first made in England, warmed many a colonial bed. From the 1600s to the 1800s, quilts took on a characteristic American style as the agile fingers of pioneer women adapted traditional designs to reflect their personal tastes and experiences. More than three-hundred patterns grew from the archetypal geometric forms. Imaginative quiltmakers took inspiration from birds lighting on a window, from log cabins, barn raisings and plowed fields. On the other hand, names such as "Kansas

Troubles," "Old Tippecanoe," "Washington's Plumes," "Union Calico," "Lincoln's Platform," and "Whig Rose," testified not only to the quiltmakers' lively interests in current events but also to opinions on them. (If the quiltmaker pieced the central design of the "Whig Rose" pattern in black, it was called "Radical Rose" and indicated that she was opposed to slavery.)

The many popular star quilt designs were spawned when seafarers' wives and daughters were inspired by the eight-point ship's wheel and the sixteen-point mariner's compass. Following their own stars as they traveled west, pioneer women made quilts with such names as "Star of St. Louis," "Star of Texas," and "Star of California" to document the journey. Though patterns were repeated many times, no two quilts were ever alike. Each was a unique artistic statement made through the individual's choice of color, fabric, and overall design.

Among the most beautiful and valuable examples of patchwork quilts are those produced in the Amish and Mennonite communities of Pennsylvania, Ohio, and Indiana. Simple geometric designs executed with a sophisticated palette of somber and bold colors make them compatible with contemporary settings. Since few of those made before 1900 have survived, most Amish and Mennonite quilts currently available were made during the 1920s and 1930s.

Bold and beautiful flowers bloomed on quilts created with appliqued patterns. Roses were very popular, along with tulips, peonies and sunflowers. Like patchwork, the technique of applique dated back to Colonial times. The quiltmaker cut small pieces of colored cloth into shapes to produce a pattern and stitched them in place on blocks of background material. These were then joined to form the quilt top. Baltimore *album quilts,* often with each block produced by a different person, are among the most beautiful and cherished of applique covers.

Victorians were attracted to the *crazies,* a type of quilt or "throw" made from scraps of leftover silk, satin, velvet, and ribbon sewed together in a hit-or-miss pattern and embellished with embroidery. Thousands were stitched up during the late eighteenth and early nineteenth centuries. But the rage died out when crazies were disdained as examples of Victorian affinities for excessive sentiment and opulence.

Quiltmaking declined after the early 1900s and was revived during the Depression. Unfortunately, the invention of the sewing machine eroded the special handcrafted artistry of earlier years. Machine-quilted pieces have little value as collectors' items nor do the many quilts that were made from kits during recent decades.

More recently, the old quilting techniques have enabled a modern art form to flower. Many contemporary quiltmakers create pieces that are not meant to be used on beds, but as hangings for walls. Works made and signed by the better artists are definitely valuable, and part of the fun of buying these items is meeting and talking to the artists who made them.

★ **Bob Montgomery and his sister were poking around in an old house Bob had bought in Bloomington, Illinois. They found some old bedcovers stored in a battered old hide-a-bed. One happened to be an unusual variation of the "Rob Peter to Pay Paul" quilt, with very fine stitching and in good condition. It was worth over $300.**

Values Outside the Home. The collector with a good sense of design and harmony can hardly go wrong in choosing a quilt that pleases the eye and shows quality craftsmanship. There are, however, certain categories of quilts that are more highly prized in the marketplace than others:

Album quilts are so called because each block, like a page in an album, has a complete design. They are usually done in applique, but sometimes combine applique with patchwork. Often these were produced by a group of women, each creating her own block. The completed blocks were pieced together to make a gift for a bride, the local minister, or a dear friend who was moving away. *Freedom quilts* were presented to young men who attained the age of twenty-one, or who completed an apprenticeship. If the individuals who created the blocks signed or personalized them, the quilt became more valuable.

A particularly fine group of album quilts were produced in the Baltimore area around 1860. Two women are given credit for these masterpieces: designer Achsah Goodwin Wilkins, and quiltmaker Mary Ford Evans. Baltimore quilts display a different design for each block, often have realistic motifs, and tend to be larger than other quilts.

Fine album quilts command higher prices than others, so enthusiasts should be prepared to pay from $4,000 up.

Amish and *Mennonite quilts* rank next in value. Quilts created by members of the Amish sect in Lancaster County, Pennsylvania, are the most expensive. Bold and abstract designs are based on simple geometric patterns that owe their impact to the dramatic use of color. Startlingly bright colors are often juxtaposed with somber ones. The religious beliefs of the Amish forbade the use of printed fabrics. Although the block patterns are plain, the wide borders of these quilts are often embellished with elaborate designs, including scallops, feathers, hearts, and wreaths.

Midwestern Amish quilts offer a greater variety of patterns and frequently are made in lighter shades of pale purple, pink, or yellow. They are also less expensive than their Pennsylvania counterparts.

Mennonite quilts are also in great demand today. They are similar to those produced by the Amish but often have more adventurous designs. Mennonite quilters sometimes used printed fabrics. The hallmarks of both Mennonite and Amish quilts are fine stitching and richness of color.

All-white quilts in very good condition follow in desirability. They were created during the late eighteenth and early nineteenth centuries, often as gifts for a bride. Only a highly accomplished seamstress would tackle one of these, which is a reasonable explanation for their scarcity. Floral and feather designs were often stuffed to stand out in relief. *Linsey-woolsey* and wool quilts made of glazed worsted also had elaborately quilted designs. Like the all-white quilts, they were made from a single piece of cloth. Surviving examples of these old bedcovers are prized for their rarity. One in good condition could bring up to $2,000.

Patriotic quilts are valued as social documents that illustrate the sentiments of an era. Popular motifs are the American eagle, shields, stars, and popular presidents, such as Washington, Lincoln, and Franklin Roosevelt. Sometimes even a real American flag could be made the focal point of a quilt. Collectors eagerly seek bedcovers with the flag motif, but even though many were produced, they are increasingly hard to find. Many date from the time of the Centennial and from the Bicentennial. Others reflect the quiltmaker's pride when her state joined the Union. Incidentally, the number of stars in the design may help to date the quilt.

Contemporary quilts are produced with both traditional and non-traditional designs. Many of the contemporary pieces are regarded as examples of visual art rather than bedcovers. Like paintings, prices vary according to the reputation of the artist. Enthusiasts may buy through a dealer or gallery. Lots of looking and comparing will help develop a sense of fair market value.

Crib quilts are enjoying a current surge of popularity. Because of their small size they can be framed or stretched and hung like paintings. Although they may lack intricate details, they are prized for their naive charm. Prices for them have risen steadily in recent years. It is important when buying to be sure that a crib quilt was *not* cut down from a larger one.

Dating Quilts

Dating quilts is a skill won by time spent studying quilts with known dates, such as those found in museums, or with dates incorporated in the design. Firm dates are, however, hard to come by without documentation of the quilt's movements from collection to collection.

Craftsmanship is a good indicator of age, and generally speaking, the finer the stitching, the older the quilt. In the 1800s, small girls were given patches of cloth to sew together as practice, since it took years to perfect the twelve to fourteen stitches to the inch required of a fine quiltmaker.

The ratio between the length and width of the quilt is another good indicator of age. More nearly square quilts are generally older than those that are greater in length than width. That is because people and the beds they sleep in have both gotten longer.

Fabric-dating is a complex skill that requires both study and observation. Also, there is a certain "slippage" factor associated with fabrics, too; as every textile lover knows, fabric is often hoarded and then passed on to succeeding generations before it is "made up."

Other Guidelines

Quilt fanciers have been looking for valuable bedcovers since the 1920s. Prices have shot up dramatically in recent years, and as prices escalate for the older and rarer examples, collector interest turns to previously undervalued examples, such as the once disdained crazies and pieces from the 1920s and 1930s.

With this in mind, beginners should look for the best quality affordable. Whatever tomorrow's vogue may be, good pieces will hold or increase in value. One should learn to recognize quality stitching and materials, and to be aware that age is more difficult to establish than condition or rarity of design.

Quilts that have been badly damaged or extensively restored should not be bought. Quilts that have faded from repeated washings or expose to sunlight also bring lower prices unless they exhibit exceptional detail. And quilts with irregular borders may have been cut and rebound, reducing value.

Whenever possible, buyers should obtain the history of a piece. Documentation adds to the value substantially, particularly if the quilt has been associated with a famous person. A quilt that is dated or signed automatically jumps in value, too. Some well-known, reputable quiltmakers are Throckmorton, Stenge, Whitehill, Kretsinger, and Evans.

Where to Find Values. Enthusiasts will meet lots of people and travel to interesting places tracking down old quilts. Families that have made quilts for years can be found and contacted if one is willing to scout country and mountain areas for them. Farm wives may have both old quilts and new ones.

Rural areas are the best places to look for bargains, and one should include in that flea markets, country auctions, antiques shops and country fairs. Quilts exist in most parts of the country, even though the Northeast is the traditional hunting ground.

In towns and cities quilts are most likely found in secondhand stores. A good dealer can offer expert advice and locate the rarer pieces, but collectors can expect to pay full retail price.

A Price Sampling. The quilt prices listed below were derived from a nationwide sampling of experts, auction houses, and specialized dealers. Remember that two quilts of the same type and age could vary greatly in price because of other variables, such as quality of workmanship and condition.

Victorian crazy quilt, with variously shaped velvet and silk colored patches embroidered with leaves, pansies, and petunias	$1,900-$2,300
Pieced calico and chintz *Friendship* quilt; red, green, brown, blue and orange, print and solid calico and chintz patches, "Square" pattern	650-850
Pieced Amish cotton basket quilt with blue and black patches, dated 1918	490-625
Pieced cotton quilt "Flower Basket" pattern, with brown and beige patches on white ground, diagonal and zig-zag quilting	475-550

Pieced Mennonite calico "Ocean Waves" quilt, with pink, blue, red, gray, and green calico and cotton patches with wide pink border	275-350
Pieced cotton and sateen Amish quilt in the "Old Maid's Puzzle" in various shades of red, rust and black	260-330
Pieced calico "Star of Bethlehem" quilt, with red, blue, orange, green, and pink calico patches on white cotton ground	225-300
Wool quilt with log cabin design, nineteenth century	190-230
Nine-patch pattern, machine quilted, c. 1890	125-175
Double wedding ring, scalloped edges, unused, 78″ × 67″	100-140

NOTE: Reprinted by permission, from The Official 1984 Price Guide to Antiques and Other Collectibles, *ed. Thomas E. Hudgeons III (Orlando, FL: The House of Collectibles, 4th edition).*

How to Store/Display. Quilts must be cleaned with extreme care, especially if they are old. Cold water, mild detergent, and a short machine cycle will bring good results. They should be sun dried if possible, but a short tumble with cool air is permissible. The best results will be had from French hand cleaning or cleaning by someone who specializes in conserving antique textiles. Quilts should not be trusted to the regular dry cleaners, since the stitches may be damaged.

No matter how a quilt is cleaned, it should *never* be ironed.

Restoring the frayed edges of a quilt may be necessary. It should be done by an expert unless its owner is also a skilled tailor. Matching fabrics and colors are important for a good appearance. Some hobbyists, however, will only buy untouched quilts.

Hanging a quilt on a wall must be done carefully in order to avoid fabric damage. The easiest way is to sew pockets of cotton fabric to the two top back corners of the quilt on the strongest part of the binding. The pockets can then be looped over the corners of a balsam-wood stretcher or a strip of wood. If a stretcher is used, the quilt must hang as freely as possible to prevent the stitches from stretching.

Quilts can be stored on hangers in an uncrowded closet, wrapped in old sheets and placed on a closet shelf, or placed in a cardboard box. Textiles must not be saved in plastic, because plastic does not allow them to breathe. If the quilt is stored folded, it should be folded a different way twice each month to prevent crease lines. When it is taken out of storage, it will do best if laid flat for a couple of hours outside to freshen in the sun.

How and When to Sell. A quality quilt will find a ready market in almost any antiques shop. Some dealers will sell a quilt on consignment for a 10% to 15% commission. Museums, including the prestigious Smithsonian, are also interested in historical quilts. Auctions are another possibility, but there is no guarantee that one will get the price he expects, and there will be a 15% to 20% commission paid to the house. A privately arranged sale will net the best value, and these can be set up through association with other quilt collectors and through ads in publications devoted to quilting and antique textiles.

Prices for quilts are currently high. Factors such as increased publicity and higher inflation will stimulate new peaks. This may be a good time to hold on to a collection unless one needs to sell.

★ When her son was born over twenty years ago, author Joyce Hecht's mother-in-law gave her an old crib quilt that had been in the family for generations. On it were pictured little boys in brightly colored overalls appliqued on a white ground with a green border. It is in beautiful condition and today worth $250.

Little-Known Facts. The number of cotton seeds that can be felt in a quilt's batting is a regional difference that may help a collector guess the age of a very old piece. In the North, quilts made before the invention of the cotton gin (1793) have more seeds in them than quilts made in the South, where slaves laboriously picked the seeds out.

• Quilting was not exclusively women's work. Two American presidents as boys helped their mothers create quilts: Dwight D. Eisenhower and Calvin Coolidge.

• Some superstitions about quilts included the following: If a young lady started to make her bridal quilt before she was actually spoken for, disaster was sure to follow; equally bad was to use the heart motif as part of a design until an engagement was final.

• Only a foolish wife would let her husband sleep under a quilt with the design known as "Wandering Foot." Any male who did so was sure to become restless, leave home to travel around the world, and never return home.

• Some old quilts display a deliberate error, or patch of color that clashes with the color scheme. These mistakes coincidentally paralleled the Near Eastern belief that it was presumptuous and unlucky for mortals to imitate God's perfection.

—Joyce Hecht

Bibliography

Books

Chase, Patti, and Mimi Dolbier. *The Contemporary Quilt: New American Quilts and Fabric Art.* New York: E. P. Dutton, Inc., 1978.

Haders, Phyllis. *The Warner Collector's Guide to American Quilts.* New York: Warner Books, 1981.

Ickis, Marguerite. *The Standard Book of Quilt Making and Collecting.* New York: Dover Publications, 1949.

Mahler, Celine Blanchard. *Once Upon a Quilt.* New York: Van Nostrand Reinhold Co., 1977.

Orlofsky, Patsy and Myron. *Quilts in America.* New York: McGraw-Hill, 1974.

Peto, Florence. *American Quilts and Coverlets: A History of Charming Native Art Together with a Manual of Instruction for Beginners.* New York: Chanticleer Press, 1949.

Secord, Robert Bishop, and Judith Reiter Weissman. *Quilts, Coverlets, Rugs, and Samplers: The Knopf Collector's Guide to American Antiques.* New York: Alfred A. Knopf, 1982.

Periodicals

Quilt World. P.O. Box 337, Seabrook, NH 03874.

Quilter's Newsletter. P.O. Box 394, Wheat Ridge, CO 80033.

Dealers

Ninepatch, 2001 Hopkins, Berkeley, CA.

Parrish and Sons Antiques, 355 Hayes St., San Francisco, CA 94102.

Herbert L. Wellerstein, Jr., Calico Antiques, P.O. Box 877, Beverly Hills, CA 90213.

Patricia Squires, The Squires Antiques, P.O. Box 1698, Lennox, MA 01240.

Associations

Santa Rosa Quilt Guild, P.O. Box 1901, Santa Rosa, CA 95402.

R

CHAPTER 19

Railroadiana

Records

RAILROADIANA

The fondness and respect accorded railroading for its creative force in history has made almost everything connected with it an object for collecting.

Railroadiana fully represents the values of a good collecting pursuit. It is romantic and historical, and its objects range from the purely mechanical to the purely aesthetic, with the potential for being worth more as time goes by. There are still enough objects out there to make collecting railroadiana rewarding. Just meeting other people with similar interests is a reward in itself. But maybe the finest payoff has little to do with who has collected what, only that it *has* been collected and preserved for the pleasure of those who follow.

History. Railroads have been with us for a little over one-hundred-fifty years. Their rapid growth led America's expansion, encouraging the settlement of land, stimulating mechanical invention, and inspiring art.

Prior to the government's involvement during the Civil War, railroad development was a disorderly affair that included freewheeling competition, investment fraud, and sabotage. Track sizes and axle widths also varied, so that often the rolling stock of one line could not be carried on the tracks of another. Multiple lines were sometimes built to serve the same towns.

After the Civil War, railroading began a golden age, characterized by the steam locomotive. Much of the sentiment of railroadiana derives from this period, which extended into the 1950s, when the last steam engines were removed from service.

From steam to diesel and electric power, from Art Nouveau to Art Deco, the practical and stylish evolution of the railroad embodies a glorious past. Through preservation and acquisition by thousands of railroad buffs, there are many objects to remember it by.

★ **Hugo Smith was walking along a stretch of railroad tracks outside Atlanta, Georgia, on a nature-study field trip, when he found a brass key among the cinders. He took it to an antiques dealer and learned that it was a railway switch box key worth $35.**

Dinner on board in the 1890s could have included blue point oysters, roast spring lamb with mint sauce, browned sweet potatoes, New York ice cream, Edam cheese, and French coffee, all for only 75¢.

Values Outside the Home. Because there are so many items available to collect, a good way to begin is by specializing in one or two categories. Very broadly, they can be designated as "paper" or "hardware." Paper items are by far the most popular, though an especially valuable possession is a "builder's plate," made of brass and affixed to a locomotive when it left the manufacturing shop.

Collecting paper memorabilia requires further specialization if one wishes to avoid feeling overwhelmed by this vast category. Timetables, posters and handbills announcing railroad schedules are the first choice among collectors, who will sometimes pay more for a bland-looking employee timetable than for a builder's plate.

Also of great interest are the annual passes that permitted free travel on a particular line. These were dispensed as benefits to employees, as courtesies to executives of other lines, and as simple bribes to those whose political goodwill it was wise to keep. Collectors of annual passes are interested in who signed them (such as a Jay

Gould or other railroad mogul) and to whom they were issued (such as a senator or president).

Other paper items include engineers' train orders, employee rule books, advertising posters and calendars, pulp novels and magazines with railroad tales, the sheet music of railroad songs, and photographs. Recently in demand have been folders publicizing the "name" trains of this century, such as the Santa Fe Railroad's California Limited and the New York Central's Wolverine. Through these colorful ads collectors relive the age of gracious travel.

As fun to collect is hardware memorabilia. Engine bells, whistles and headlights, lanterns, telegraph outfits and ticket punches are just the beginning of a nearly endless list of objects that are part of railroading. The badges, buttons and caps worn by personnel from conductors to brakemen, the locks and keys and baggage checks that helped to keep things in place or move things along, are all game for collecting.

Switch keys and "date nails" are of particular interest. The brass or bronze keys and locks signify the great responsibility of the railroad men whose job it was to unlock the switch boxes that moved the switch tracks so that one train could pass another. Loss of a key could result in a wreck. Date nails, whose broad heads were stamped with a particular year, were driven into ties as they were laid. This practice allowed railroad companies to know the longevity of their ties.

Not all hardware had to meet the elements. When the "Delmonico" was rolled onto the Chicago and Alton Railroad in 1868, it became the first railroad car devoted entirely to dining. With more than a century of refinement, a mother lode of items today come from dining cars, whose monogrammed china, silver and linens spark memories of "dinner in the diner." Obtaining a complete dinner service from a particular line is one way to approach collecting these items. Or one can seek an eclectic selection, from as many roads as possible.

Additional paper and hardware items include ashtrays, paperweights, and playing cards, and specialty items from old trolley lines or railway post offices. Items connected with railway labor unions, or materials promoting settlement of railroad land by immigrants are also valuable.

The object in railroadiana collecting is to develop the broadest representation of railroad companies, be they active today or long out of business, whether American or foreign.

Where to Find Values. A collection of railroadiana can be pursued in several ways. Many items are advertised in publications such as *Antiques Trader* and specialized railroading magazines. Dealers operate out of their homes or small shops. Some maintain warehouses and conduct a mail-order business through regularly published catalogues. A collector may write a dealer inquiring about a specific item and receive a description of a possible match and a price quote. Probably three-quarters of a dealer's business is carried out by mail.

Railroadiana is also available through membership in clubs, where it is bought, sold and traded at club meetings, shows and sales. If one wishes to go out with pick and shovel, mining for railroadiana, there are many retired railroad employees, or the executors of their estates, who may wish to part with objects from a lifetime of work. Lanterns frequently can be acquired this way.

★ **John Murphy of San Francisco, California, visited a southern Oregon town in 1977 and noticed an old timetable posted on a wall of the railroad station. He asked the station manager if he could have it, and was cordially presented with the browned sheet of paper. Mr. Murphy framed the schedule and used it as a decoration until recently, when he sold it to a local boutique for $45.**

A Price Sampling

Coffee pot, Rio Grande Western, silver c. 1900	$400
Platter, Salt Lake Route, 12″	290
Blanket, Pendleton w/UP shield	165
Cup and saucer, Atchison, Topeka & Sante Fe	165
Lantern, New York Central, bell bottom, c. 1890	85
Badge, Pullman conductor's cap	30
Tablecloth, Rock Island Zephyr, 4′ square	20
Switch key, Baltimore & Ohio, worn	16
Can, kerosene, Illinois Central, w/lid	15
Playing cards, Southern Pacific, single deck	12

How to Store/Display. Beyond its monetary value, a collection of railroadiana is a pleasure to possess, since it can be incorporated into the decor of the collector's home. A switch lamp lighting the front walk, or a hallway poster advertising the "Rocket" trains of the Chicago, Rock Island and Pacific Railroad, give a home additional distinction. Often railroadiana is collected in conjunction with a model railroading hobby.

Care of railroad collectors' items requires few special precautions for restoration, storage, and display. The common methods used to prevent rust in metal objects, to revitalize and protect wood, to avoid mildew in paper, to polish brass, and to replace or rebuild broken or missing parts will prolong the life of valued pieces.

★ **Bif Newkirk, a rancher on the eastern slope of the Colorado Rockies, had a stray railroad lantern hanging at one end of his front porch and wanted a second lantern for the other end. When he priced lanterns and could not find one for sale for less than $60, he sold his for $75.**

How and When to Sell. Collectors develop a feel for prices as they make purchases for a collection. They also develop a sense of what may be desirable to buy for trade or profitable resale. Popular today are paper objects from the turn of the century. Tomorrow may find Art Deco china at the top of a shopping list.

With this in mind, selling railroadiana is accomplished in the same ways that it is bought. A good "horse trader" can improve a collection without money changing hands at all. Also, it is good to keep in mind that items often bring a higher price in the region where they originated. Local interest in collecting is usually founded on interest in local railroads.

Any collection that represents a completed theme will be of greater value than individual items or unfinished themes. For example, a "complete" collection might consist of all the styles of lanterns used on a particular road, or all those made by a certain manufacturer, or just those few that were used for a special purpose. Themes are as various as collectors. In any case, the selling price will depend on the taste of the potential buyer.

—*Terry Parker*

Bibliography

Books

Baker, Stanley L. *Railroad Collectibles*. Paducah, KY: Collector Books, 1981.

Hughes, Stephen. *Pop Culture Mania*. New York: McGraw-Hill Book Co., 1984.

Klamkin, Charles. *Railroadiana*. New York: Funk and Wagnalls, 1976.

Periodicals

Key, Lock, and Lantern. P.O. Box 15, Spencerport, NY 14559.

Railroad Magazine. 150 East 58th St., New York, NY 10022.

Dealers

Arone, F., 377 Ashford, Dobbs Ferry, NY 10522.

Caboose Antiques, Magnolia Star Rt., Nederland, CO 80466.

Associations

Key Collectors International, P.O. Box 9397, Phoenix, AZ 85068.

Railroad Enthusiasts, P.O. Box 133, West Townsend, MA 01474.

Railroadiana Collectors Association, 405 Byron Ave., Mobile, AL 36609.

Railway and Locomotive Historical Society, P.O. Box 1194, Boston, MA 02103.

Texas Date Nail Collectors Association, Jerry Waits, 501 West Horton, Brenham, TX 77833.

RECORDS

"Play it again, Sam."
—allegedly spoken by Humphrey Bogart in the film *Casablanca*

Just as it was for Bogart in the classic film, music for most of us is a link to the past, an evoker of memories both happy and sad. The appeal—and the value—of the phonograph record is that it enables us to recall those memories in moments, simply the time it takes to press the power button of our record players to the "On" position.

History. The earliest recordings were done on metal cylinders made first from tin foil and later from wax. Today all cylinder recordings are somewhat valuable unless they have been badly damaged or warped. Prices for them are not high, however, because of the limited demand for marches, Southern plantation songs, and political speeches, which were the subjects of most cylinder impressions.

In the early twentieth century, the phonograph "disc" appeared, and companies such as Victrola and Gramophone produced hand-cranked machines to play the heavy, fragile, and easily broken shellac and wax 78s. In spite of the low quality of sound of these first discs, recordings of early opera stars, such as Enrico Caruso, Alma Gluck, and Frieda Henpel, were issued in large quantities due to the stars' popularity. Most of these discs surviving today are safe within well-protected collections.

In the 1920s, electrical recording took the 78-rpm shellac record to a slightly higher level of fidelity. But it was not until the advent of vinylite materials after World War II and two new turntable speeds (33 and 45 rpm) that "high fidelity" sound became a reality.

In the early 1950s, the "Battle of the Speeds" resulted in two new kinds of phonograph record: the seven-inch 45-rpm disc, with a large hole in the center, used to record popular music; and the twelve-inch 33-rpm long-play (LP) disc, used to record the classic repertoire (ten-inch LPs were also manufactured then). "Forty-fives" gave popular music fans a lightweight, easily storable, and inexpensive way to enjoy their favorite performers and preserve memories. "LPs" captured the entire classical music world, especially operas and symphonies, which now could be enjoyed without the interruptions and disc changing that occurred every four and a half minutes with 78 recordings (some operas had as many as thirty-nine interruptions within a twenty-record 78-rpm rendition).

The combination of improved vinyl material (which meant quieter surfaces), microgrooves, and diamond stylii stretched high-fidelity sound to the lowest and highest levels of human hearing (remember those first recordings of jet planes, trains, and bowling balls?). Since those early experiments with sound recording, there have been four more major "sound" improvements:

- *Stereophonic sound*—adding depth to the music using two channels of recorded sound to enhance realism; all records today are stereo (monaural is no longer made).
- *Quadraphonic sound*—adding more depth by increasing number of channels and speakers from two to four; this advance was rejected by the public, and little exists in quadraphonic discs.
- *Direct-to-disc recording*—capturing a performance directly on a disc, thereby bypassing tape and potential fidelity loss.
- *Digital recording*—using computers to digitally encode music; gives highest-quality fidelity on conventional LPs.

The movement towards truer sound has led to a further refinement in disc recording, the compact disc. Holograms etched on the surface of the disc are read by a laser beam. Compact discs thus differ from conventional records in that no physical contact is made between a needle and the record surface. This means that

I. F. E. Releasing Corp., courtesy Museum of Modern Art, New York

The song "As Time Goes By" captured not only lovers Rick and Ilsa in the film classic *Casablanca* but also generations of popular music lovers, who continue to discover its romantic melody and timeless lyrics.

compact discs will never wear out. They also have no surface noise and virtually no distortion. The library of compact disc music is still small but it is rapidly growing.

★ **Eddie Hoover, a resident of Castro Valley, California, bought a copy of "My Heart" (by the Mondellos) at a Goodwill store for ten cents. He sold it at a record swap to a music business executive in Los Angeles for $500.**

Values Outside the Home. Collectors divide records into "classical" and "popular" titles. Within these two classifications are many subdivisions, and even experts disagree about what is classical and what is popular. Both categories exist in recordings from all eras, and many collectors specialize within subdivisions, e.g., original issues of symphonies conducted by Leopold Stokowski on 78s.

The lists below constitute a first pass at identifying subdivisions within each title division:

Classical	*Popular*
Operas	Rock 'n' Roll
Symphonies	Rockabilly
Ballets	Jazz and blues
Instrumental solos	Rhythm and blues
and concertos	Blues
Organ music	Easy listening
Choral music	Disco
Synthesizer music	Comedy
Vocal solos	Spoken word/historical events
Religious	Pop vocal
	Pop instrumental
	Military band
	Country and Western
	Broadway shows
	Movie soundtracks

Within each subdivision are many sub-subdivisions, e.g., Italian or German operas; symphonies by Beethoven, Brahms, or Vaughan-Williams, or symphonies performed by a specific orchestra under the direction of a specific conductor; Elvis, the Beach Boys, and the Beatles in rock; "Hear It Now" by Edward R. Murrow, and the political speeches of Richard Nixon. The following categories should be considered by beginners as guides to building collections of their own:

• Many old 78-rpm orchestral sets featuring conductors such as Serge Koussevitsky, Leopold Stokowski, and Arturo Toscanini have had their sound "enhanced" and have been reissued on LPs, lowering the worth of the original 78-rpm discs. Many early LPs featured name orchestras under pseudonyms, however, making these records valuable.

- Collections of popular artists, such as Elvis Presley, the Beach Boys, Bob Dylan, and the Supremes, can bring high prices, especially if they contain recordings made early in the careers of these performers on obscure labels, e.g., early 45- and 78-rpm Sun recordings by Elvis and first-issue Beatle pressings. Reissues of early hits are virtually worthless because of the large quantities produced.
- Original 78-rpm jazz records, especially by black groups not reissued on LPs (e.g., King Oliver and his Creole Jazz Band), have brought high prices.

In addition to collecting specific composers, performances, and music types, hobbyists may want to distinguish their collections in other ways, such as:

- Record labels—especially on 78s with companies long since extinct (some labels autographed).
- Record jackets—pictures of groups, cover artwork.
- 78s versus 45s—both pressings of a given work.
- Picture discs—pictures of performers stamped into the disc.
- Original disc versus reissue—often reissue has sound electronically enhanced.

Where to Find Values. The safest way to buy used or rare phonograph records is through a reputable dealer. One of the major price determinants is condition, and merely looking at a record's surface is not enough to expose wear of the grooves, pops, pits, and scratches.

Most discs are purchased "as is" from used-record stores, with no guarantee or warranty covering condition or playability. However, record dealers will often search for specific rare records for collectors, just as they will sell them—on a commission basis.

"Mint" condition records are those that have remained unplayed or played only a few times. Occasionally, because of the rarity of a specific recording, its poor condition will not affect its worth.

How to Store/Display. Records must be stored and cared for correctly because condition is a prime determinant of price. The old shellac and wax records are fragile and breakable (and get more so with age) and must be handled with extreme care. They should be stacked vertically, not piled horizontally, because this will warp them. The newer vinyl 45s and LPs should also be stored vertically in individual jackets—the inner plastic liners are excellent for keeping dust out of the grooves. Do not store *any* records in direct sunlight, and keep them away from all sources of heat.

How and When to Sell. One of the most critical measures of value for any recording is its condition. Most collectors' guides give a five-step valuation scheme, ranging from "mint" (perfect condition) to "fair/poor." Wear, defects, cracks, digs, warps and scratches all affect the worth and saleability of a record.

Collectors who want to sell would do best to go through an established dealer, who usually sells on consignment via auction. The collector and dealer agree on a selling price (the collector will get as much as 75%) before any transaction takes place.

Other places to sell are through newspaper advertisements and at garage sales. One may also donate collections to the Archives of Recorded Sound (branches can be found at Stanford University, Yale University, and Lincoln Center) and then deduct the contribution from personal taxes.

★ **Collecting records as a hobby can lead to a career change—it happened to Ed Capizzi of Lanham, Maryland. When his personal basement collection grew to over five thousand, he had to decide to either stop collecting or start a business. His Memory Lane shop now carries over a quarter of a million records, from early Edison labels to current pop and rock stars.**

Little-Known Facts. Some of the most valuable classical LPs are little known or budget labels, such as Camden, Plymouth, and Remington. Orchestras identified as the Centennial Symphony or Festival Concert were, in fact, the Philadelphia Orchestra (Leopold Stokowski), Boston Pops (Arthur Feidler), and the London Philharmonic (Serge Koussevitzsky) performing under pseudonyms.

• The Cardboard Hit of the Week was produced from 1930 to 1932 and sold on newsstands for $.15 each (songs were actually recorded on cardboard to minimize costs, hence the name). A new "hit" was sold each week in an attempt to keep the record industry afloat during the Depression.

—Warren Askew

Bibliography

Books

Ewen, David. *All the Years of American Popular Music.* Englewood Cliffs, NJ: Prentice-Hall, 1971.

Ferrick, Barbara. *Collecting the Beatles.* Ann Arbor, MI: Pierian Press, 1982.

Leibowitz, Alan. *The Record Collector's Handbook.* New York: Everett House, 1980.

Lyons, Len. *101 Best Jazz Albums.* New York: William Morrow and Co., Inc., 1980.

Marracco, W. Thomas and Harold Gleason. *Music In America.* New York: W. W. Norton & Co., 1964.

Osborne, Jerry. *Record Collectors Price Guide.* Phoenix, AZ: O'Sullivan Woodside & Co., 1984.

S

CHAPTER 20

Scrimshaw

Sheet Music

Silver

Sports

Stamps

Stock and Bond Certificates

SCRIMSHAW

In September 1982 a single scrimshawed antique whale's tooth from the whaling ship *Susan* sold for a record $40,000 at Sotheby's in New York City. Although scrimshaw collecting is barely two decades old, many profitable opportunities await the collector now and in the future, whether one prefers the expensive, rare nautical artifacts of the American whaling period, or the more affordable contemporary pieces. With dramatic price jumps over the last few years, investment in this native American folk art will virtually guarantee substantial gains.

History. Scrimshanding most likely began around 1400 A.D., when an official Basque village seal was etched depicting a whale scene.

Discovery of the sperm whale by the American fishing fleet in the 1700s introduced not only a higher grade of whale oil but also the leisurely art of etching on ivory, practiced by nearly everyone on board, from cabin boy to ship's master.

Shortly after President John F. Kennedy settled into the White House and set up his private collection of scrimshaw, press coverage ignited immediate national interest in it. Swiss railroad heiress Barbara Johnson, who had assembled one of the world's largest collections of maritime antiques, including materials from department-store founder R. H. Macy's collection, kept the interest alive when she liquidated her collection in the early 1980s in a series of four auctions. The Americana artifacts, including some of this country's most valuable whale ivory scrimshaw, brought nearly a million dollars with the first two sales.

To help fill the demand for scrimshaw and open up new markets, groups like the Alaskan Silver and Ivory Company in Washington and the Ancient Ivory Company in Iowa (both now extinct) independently developed a pool of artists interested in working with new mediums, such as fossilized whale and animal ivory (recently discovered in ancient Eskimo hunting sites) and animal ivories from other countries. Today most of the American scrimshaw is done by professionally trained artists instead of by idle sailors, who created those stiffly drawn and etched figures more characteristic of folk art.

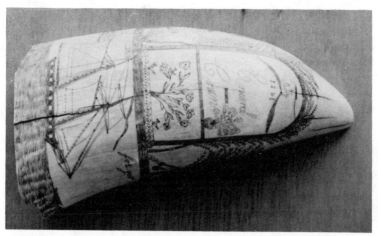

John F. Kennedy Library

It was the press coverage of President Kennedy's collection of scrimshaw that first made the public aware of this native American folk art. Shown here is a piece from the former president's collection, dated 1841.

★ **A whale's tooth was brought to a dealer in California to be cleaned and re-etched, since it was partially disfigured and covered with a dark, oily substance built up after many years of storage. As the overhaul progressed, the dealer noticed what looked like an old style of scrimshanding and immediately called the owner to get more history. He discovered that the tooth had been in the family since the early 1900s. After further examination, the dealer pronounced it to be a signed Frederick Myrick piece valued at $15,000! Of course, the original goal of re-etching the piece was quickly—and happily—abandoned.**

Values Outside the Home. Antique scrimshaw and nautical artifacts associated with the American whaling industry of the 1880s are especially prized for their historical value. A wide range of functional products portrays the average whale's practicality, with such diverse items as bird cages, cuff links, decorated walking sticks, numerous kitchen utensils and inscribed busks (flat strips of whalebone) used as corset stays.

Though a shortage of authentic pieces has sent the value of scrimshaw skyrocketing, experts believe that many pieces still wait to be discovered. (One story involving a search for lost items tells of an educated Englishman of the 1870s named James Taylor, who wanted to please his lady with a fifty-two-piece set of busks inscribed with illustrations from Shakespearean plays, the *Iliad* and other classics. He set about to give his beloved Elizabeth Royston a specially inscribed busk for every week in the year. Unfortunately, before he could deliver the remaining six, he discovered Miss Royston with another man and flashed the busks like a sword in defense of his honor. Taylor was arrested and sent to jail for assault with a deadly weapon, while his set of fifty-two scrimshawed busks were sold to an art dealer and never again seen.)

In recent years fossilized ivory and bone from ancient Arctic campsites have yielded a rich supply of scrimshanding materials, resulting in a boom for contemporary scrimshaw. These mineralized materials have taken some of the bite out of buying collectors' scrimshaw and have given the average investor an opportunity to enjoy this relatively young hobby.

Contemporary scrimshanding allows the serious collector to follow various artists as they mature and teaches them how to judge which artist and type of work will become popular and yield the greatest gains in the future. Unlike many antique pieces that lack such distinguishing marks as dates and artists' signatures, modern scrimshaw is usually signed by the artist and often authenticated through a reputable dealer who is also usually an expert and collector.

Where to Find Values. The single most important thing for collectors to remember is to purchase the best quality they can afford. It is also advised they purchase from an established dealer, who will guarantee an item. Often the dealer is himself a collector with intimate knowledge of his specialized market and able to impart insight about an individual artist. Some dealers also offer layaway plans on pieces that may run as high as thousands of dollars.

Artists' credentials are becoming hallmarks for the going price of a piece. A few years ago the Mystic International art competitions expanded its subjects to include scrimshaw. Howie Rosenfeld, a scrimshander who specializes in black/white subjects, won the Mystic competition for first place in 1982, and his winning piece sold for $10,000. The following year scrimshander Ray Peters won first place, and the average price of his work has since doubled.

A Price Sampling

Antique Scrimshaw (mint condition)

Powderhorn from 1700s	$4,700
Walking cane with brass tip, 38″ long	480
Corset stay (scrimbusk), 14″ long	250
Pie crimper with rosewood handle	200

Contemporary Scrimshaw (mint condition)

Walrus tusk with detailed whaling scene	$5,000
Detailed black "$" on fossilized ivory, 9″ long	2,000
Oval ivory animal mounted on silver belt buckle	250
Pocket knife 5″ long	75
Dime-size animal ivory pin	25

Various markets, such as Hawaii, Alaska, California, and the East Coast, show a considerable range in price for similar items.

How to Store/Display. Natural oils from the hands benefit scrimshaw. Ivory will become brittle when exposed to direct light sources, such as hot lamps and the sun. Many collectors display their pieces in special glass or plastic cases in which they have also placed a small dish of water (usually concealed). The water creates a constant humidity that will prevent the ivory from drying out.

How and When to Sell. Scrimshaw collectors, like collectors of other items, will almost always have to hold on to pieces for at least two years to realize a profit. Once a collector decides to sell, he may do so through a dealer, who will either buy the item directly or sell it through consignment.

Auctions that specialize in other art objects are good markets for scrimshaw also.

Little-Known Facts. A Japanese merchant introduced a bit of high tech to the scrimshaw market by creating a stylus that could "mass produce" etched teeth. He could carve ten teeth at a time. The teeth are now sold in the United States.

—*Billy Cache Lewis*

Bibliography

Books

Kovel, Ralph and Terry. *Kovels' Collector's Source Book.* New York: Crown Publisher, Inc., 1983.

Gilkerson, William. *The Scrimshander.* San Francisco, CA: Troubador Press, 1978.

Meyer, Charles R. *Whaling and the Art of Scrimshaw.* New York: David McKay Company, Inc., 1976.

VanCaspel, Venita. *Money Dynamics for the 1980's.* Reston, VA: Reston Publishing Company, Inc., 1980.

Catalogues

Hudgeons, Thomas E. III, ed. *Official 1985 Price Guide to Antiques and Other Collectibles.* Orlando, FL: House of Collectibles, Inc., 1984.

Ketchum, William C. *Catalog of American Collectibles.* New York: Rutledge/ Mayflower Books, 1979.

Periodicals

Nautical Brass. P.O. Box 744, Montrose, CA 91020.

Dealers

Mike Attaway, Scrimshaw Gallery Ltd., Pier 39, K-12, San Francisco, CA 94133.

FO'C'SLE, Village Fair, Sausalito, CA 94965.

Peabody Museum of Salem, East India Square, Salem, MA 01970.

Preston's, Main Street Wharf, Greenport, Long Island, NY 11944.

Associations

National Maritime Historical Society, 2 Fulton St., Brooklyn, NY 11201.

SHEET MUSIC

The encoding of music in written form is only a few hundred years old and includes the medieval religious chants of monks; the voluminous manuscripts of Johann Sebastian Bach, George Frederick Handel, Ludwig Beethoven, and other classical composers; band and orchestral music; and vocal/piano music, both classical and popular. What is being collected today, however, and also becoming more and more popular, is the *song sheet,* or printed piece of popular music for piano and/or vocal performance.

History. The first written songs were most likely the "Psalms of King David," and then only the lyrics and not the psalm tunes/chants, which had not been written down. Many of the old Hebrew and early Christian chants *were* preserved, however, and are still used in today's liturgies. History tells of Moses recounting the passage of the Israelites through the Red Sea and of Homer singing about the

Nathanial Currier (Currier & Ives) also found recognition as a sheet-music artist. His lithographs defined the romanticism of the age and often accompanied love songs.

prowess of Ulysses. Medieval composers' manuscripts were all hand produced, while minstrels performing in fairs and royal courts retained the aural tradition of music.

The first sheet music/song sheets to appear in the United States were published at the end of the eighteenth century, but the heyday for American music publishers did not occur until 1850. In the mid-1800s there were nearly as many sheet music publishers in the United States as there are record companies today. In 1840, the year's smash hit, "The Old Arm Chair," ran through twenty-three editions.

Joseph Kirby Lilly, president of the Eli Lilly Company from 1892 to 1932, was one of the first American collectors of song sheets. His particular interest was the music of Stephen Foster, and through his efforts a memorial and a collection of Stephen Foster's music was established at the University of Pittsburgh.

★ In an article entitled "Recollections of a Sheet Music Collector," by Lester S. Levy (*Notes*, XXXII/3, March 1976, pages 491-502), the successes and failures of a sheet music collector are recounted. In 1940, Levy discovered a first-edition copy of "The Star Spangled Banner" at an antique dealer's in Hagerstown, Maryland. His copy is only one of nine known first editions in existence, one of which sold in 1958 for $3,500.

Values Outside the Home. Song sheets are collected for their covers, music, and/or lyrics, although most enthusiasts are interested primarily in the covers, which reflect every facet of American life. (Inside those covers, one may find a song to suit any event in our history, including dances, games, food, clothes, social movements, prejudices, accomplishments, loves, transportation, heroes, fashions, and fads.) Covers can be further divided into medium, subject matter, or artist, such as:

- Lithography—pre-1900 black and white engravings (lithographs of Nathaniel Currier; 1835-1839)
- Painting—James M. Whistler, Gene Buck
- Early photography and color printing—photos of historical events
- Song sheets with advertising
- Art Deco—especially from 1910 to 1935
- Norman Rockwell—scenes of Americana
- Albert Varga—pinup girls
- Photographs of popular rock stars—especially the Beatles

Music sheet art is similar to poster art in that important events of the times are captured and interpreted by an artist. Much of the pre-1900 song sheets can be found stitched together into books with hard covers; thus, the individual sheet covers have been afforded extra protection over the years.

Listed below are possible categories and examples of each that can provide the basis for a song sheet collection:

- *Composers*—Irving Berlin, George M. Cohan, Victor Herbert, Ira and George Gershwin, Jerome Kern, Cole Porter, Richard Rodgers and Lorenz Hart
- *Hits without words*—Rags, marches, foxtrots, blues, cake walks
- *Alcohol and prohibition*—"Bottle's Empty, Whiskey's Gone," "Show Me the Way to Go Home," "Papa, Don't Drink Anymore"
- *Locations*—"Dixie," "Chicago," "San Francisco," "I Love Paris," "Autumn in New York"
- *Negro, minstrel, and spiritual songs*—"Jim Crow," "Oh, Dem Golden Slippers"
- *Girls' names*—"Laura," "Irene," "Ramona"
- *Transportation and communication*—"Wabash Cannonball," "Erie Canal," "Brooklyn Bridge"
- *Work*—"16 Tons," "I've Been Working on the Railroad"
- *Political songs*—"Give 'Em Hell, Harry!" "Happy Days are Here Again"
- *Patriotic songs*—"The Star Spangled Banner," "Hail Columbia"
- *Sports and games*—"Take Me Out to the Ballgame," "Batterin' Babe," "Billiards on the Brain"
- *War songs*—especially from the Civil War, "Over There" (WWI), "God Bless America" (WWII), "This is the Army"
- *Musical shows*—"Show Boat," "Pal Joey," "South Pacific"

Where to Find Values. Some of the factors that should be considered when collecting song sheets are age, popularity, scarcity, edition (first editions are especially valuable), cover artist, category (type of cover), composer(s), performer(s) and condition. In her book *Introducing the Song Sheet*, Helen Westin lists the following values for song sheets depending on their physical condition: 100% for mint or near mint items; 75% if sheet carries owner's name; 55% if the covers are separated; 50% if corners are dog-eared or frayed; 25% if sheet is torn or smeared; 10% if sheet is dirty, torn, or incomplete.

Beginners are cautioned against starting a collection blindly; that is, without having done research about composers, songs, or music. But once some kind of background has been established, new hobbyists should search salvage shops (Salvation Army, Goodwill), shops carrying old magazines and books, antiques shops, music dealers, flea markets, and other collectors (many publish catalogues that are mailed to collectors nationwide).

Information on collecting is also available from the National Sheet Music Society, Pasadena, California.

A Price Sampling. Prices are not well established for song sheets and are usually determined by negotiation between buyer and seller. Collecting sheet music is also relatively inexpensive, because new sources are continually being discovered (attics and garages), and collectors have not yet cornered the market. Serious collectors estimate, however, that prices will start to rise sharply in the 1990s as sheets become more scarce. The following are some examples of song sheet prices:

Norman Rockwell covers	$14-22
Original Beatle covers	15 plus
Art Deco covers	7 plus
Pre-World War I "mint condition" covers	3 plus

It should be mentioned that it is relatively easy to determine the publishing date of a song sheet: prior to 1917, sheets were large (13½″ × 10½″), but by 1920 they had been reduced to 12″ × 9″ to more conveniently fit piano music stands.

How to Store/Display. Because of the age of the paper in song sheets and the value stemming from the cover art itself, song sheets should be handled with care. Avoid overexposure either to hot and dry or damp, cool climate conditions. Extra protection can also be achieved by storing song sheets in individual plastic holders.

How and When to Sell. The song sheet seller will likely find himself in a bargaining/negotiating position, whether at a flea market, music dealer's, or pawn shop, due to the lack of established prices. If a collection is large enough, he can publish his own catalogue and distribute his list of sellables to other collectors, with whom he will do most of his buying, selling, and trading.

Little-Known Facts. Large public collections of sheet music/song sheets exist at the New York City Public Library, the Library of Congress, the Free Library of Philadelphia, Yale University, the University of Pittsburgh, and the University of Michigan at Ann

Arbor. Gifts of sheet music to such institutions can be treated as deductions for federal tax purposes.

• Two of the largest private sheet music collections are owned by Lester S. Levy of Baltimore, Maryland (especially pre-1900s music) and Robert Grimes of San Francisco, California (1930-1950 movie and show music).

—*Warren Askew*

Bibliography

Books

Klamkin, Mariam. *Old Sheet Music.* New York: Hawthorn Books, Inc., 1975.

Levy, Lester S. *Grace Notes in American History.* Norman, OK: University of Oklahoma Press, 1967.

———. *Flashes of Merriment.* Norman, OK: University of Oklahoma Press, 1971.

———. *Give Me Yesterday.* Norman, OK: University of Oklahoma Press, 1975.

Mebane, John. *New Horizons in Collecting: Cinderella Antiques.* New York: A. S. Barnes & Co., 1966.

Westin, Helen. *Introducing the Song Sheet.* Nashville, TN: Thomas Nelson, Inc., 1976.

SILVER

Sotheby's, New York. "$85,000 bid, do I hear $90,000? $90,000 bid, do I hear $95,000? $95,000 from the gentleman on the right. Going, going, gone!"

Actor Bill Cosby has just bought probably the finest and largest set of Tiffany's Chrysanthemum pattern flatware ever to cross the auction block. He had to pay $95,000 for it because Joan Rivers wanted it too.

History. Along with gold, silver was one of the first metals known to man. Like gold, it has been a standard by which currencies, goods, even historical betrayals have been measured (Judas Iscariot made biblical headlines for thirty pieces of it).

Silver is extremely malleable: it can be pounded, twisted and stamped with ease. It also resists oxidation. King Tut took it to his grave and it was none the worse for wear after thirty-five-hundred years.

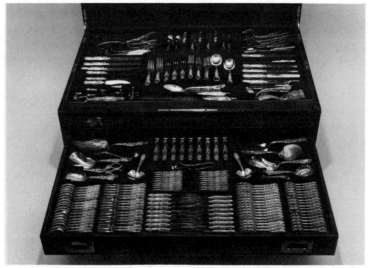

Alleged to have been recently purchased by comedian Bill
Cosby, this remarkable 684-piece Tiffany Chrysanthemum-pattern
flatware set includes such unusual items as two bonbon spoons,
a marrow spoon, asparagus tongs, and grape scissors.

Silver was really not collected as art until the late nineteenth
century. Even as late as the 1930s, a set of Regency dinner plates
might have gone into the melting pot to pay off the tax man.

Fifty years ago any respectable home had a tea and coffee service,
flatware, entree dishes, a pair of candelabrum, a wine cooler,
perhaps an epergne as well. These things were used every day. And
cleaned by servants. But who cleans silver today? Who wants to?
Those who don't, sell it. Those who do, and love their silver for what
it is, often become collectors.

★ A few years ago a small and rather strange-looking bowl turned
up at a Northern California flea market. Somebody bought it for
a couple of dollars. It spent a couple of years in a desk drawer,
until a dealer saw it, did some research, and discovered that it
was a Paul Revere ladle. Only the wood handle was missing.
Today the ladle is displayed at the De Young Museum in San
Francisco. Estimated value? At least $10,000.

Values Outside the Home. The novice collector faces a wilderness of hallmarks, styles, grades, and forms. That stunning and fanciful silver bowl one covets may well be the slowest of investments to pay off when calculating time spent talking with dealers, studying auction prices, and examining and comparing countless pieces. But bring it home and it starts paying daily dividends in the joy of owning it.

To collect successfully beginners need to know about periods, nationalities and makers. An eighteenth-century unmarked English creamer may sell for $150, whereas a similar American piece signed by Paul Revere might bring $20,000. The French take honors for the finest silver craftsmanship ever done, but their pieces are scarce because so many of them were melted down during the French Revolution.

Condition, rarity and provenance (original ownership) add significantly to the value of a piece. The less it has been tampered with, the better. All decorations should be original. A Georgian tablespoon converted into a berry spoon and embossed with fruit and leaves should not tempt the collector. The original hallmarks may be there, but it is no longer a genuine antique. And that mote-spoon by Hester Bateman *could* be a fake. The mark might be real, but it used to be a *teaspoon.* Somebody turned it into a mote-spoon and dubbed it "rare." (The mote-spoon, with its pierced bowl and pointed handle, still puzzles the experts; no one seems to know for sure what it was for.) Original coats of arms were often removed when a noble family, falling on hard times, did not want the world to know that they were selling off their silver. Or an original monogram might have been buffed off and replaced by the new owner's initials—with the best intentions maybe, but nonetheless reducing the antique value of the piece.

Best tip for novices: Buy silver that will be used and enjoyed. Do not look for bargains: Look for the best. Experienced collectors and dealers agree they never have regretted paying a fair price for a genuine article, but regretted not paying the asking price at the moment for a valuable piece that they knew would only appreciate in the future. So remember, that Victorian silver pitcher that seemed too expensive at $500 three years ago might well be worth $5,000 today.

Where to Find Values. To select a dealer, buyers will do well to follow up on recommendations from someone they trust. They can also phone local museums and ask for dealers with "sterling" reputations.

Any reputable dealer will help guide a beginning collector. Novices are also advised not to be intimidated by dealers with expensive merchandise. A dealer who routinely handles $10,000 objects is not likely to overprice items selling for $500, whereas a dealer who ordinarily handles $100 items may think that when he comes upon something for $500, it is really worth $1,000 and will mark it as such.

Collectors by all means are encouraged to buy at auction, but they must beware of the pitfalls. Everything that comes up for bid is not necessarily from an estate; sometimes it is there because a dealer has not been able to sell it. At an auction he can "dump" it. Beginners should consider having a trusted dealer do the bidding for them. He will charge a fee, but the benefit of his knowledge is worth the price.

Junk shops or flea markets are also good sources of old silver. Treasures have been known to lurk there, and no dealer has time to scout everywhere.

★ **If you want to be on the lookout for something really rare, consider the skippet, a box once designed to protect documents and treaties and such. There is a small, round eagle-crested silver skippet in the United States State Department collection. A tourist of discerning eye spotted it at a flea market in Buenos Aires, Argentina, for $300. Later it was donated to the State Department in Washington, D.C. for a hefty tax deduction. The State Department curator tells us it is worth between $15,000 and $20,000.**

A Price Sampling. The following items were sold at top auction houses across the country. Prices are current as of 1985.

Set of four George III salts by Paul Storr, London, 1813 (Sotheby's)	$198,000
Philadelphia coffee pot by Joseph Lownes, c. 1800 (Butterfield's)	5,000
Lemon strainer by Gabriel Lewin, Baltimore, 1769 (Sotheby's)	2,700
109-piece set of sterling flatware by Gorham, Versailles pattern (Butterfield's)	2,500
Creamer by Silas White Howell, Morristown, New Jersey, c. 1800 (Christie's)	1,800
George III sterling tea caddy by William Plummer, London, 1791 (Sotheby's)	1,200

Louis XVI coffee pot with maker's mark "J. G. K.," Paris,
    1788 (Butterfield's)   850
Victorian sterling shell-form bowl, Gorham, 1870
    (Butterfield's)   475
George III sterling cream jug by Charles Hougham, London,
    1773 (Butterfield's)   200
George III sterling toddy ladle by J. S., London, 1804
    (Butterfield's)   125

How to Store/Display. Silver is best washed in warm, soapy water, and dried with a soft cloth. Only cleaners recommended for silver should be used. It is that never-ending tarnishing and washing and polishing over the years that gives fine silver its beautiful patina.

Silver, easy to carry and easy to melt down, has always been very attractive to thieves. So it should be well protected wherever it is to be stored. (Back in 1660 Samuel Pepys, the famous British diarist, found this out the hard way. His July 24 entry reads: "This morning my wife in bed tells me of our being robbed of our silver tankard which vexed me all day for the negligence of my people to have the door open." The poor Pepys had *some* comfort, though, because he adds: "I hear that my man will have lost his clock with my tankard, at which I am very glad.")

★ **Some years ago a woman brought a strange looking tubular piece of silver to a show in Sausalito, California. It had been in her bottom kitchen drawer for as long as she could remember. She had no idea what it was for, but for some reason she had never thrown it out. A delighted dealer identified the "thing." It was an early American nipple feeder for nursing infants! The woman sold it to him for $440.**

When and Where to Sell. Before selling a piece, it is wise to thumb through auction catalogues for clues to its current worth. If other similar pieces actually sell for much less than their catalogue estimates (or do not sell at all), it is obviously not a good time to sell. The piece should be held on to until the market is strong again.

Once the decision has been made to sell, collectors can choose between one of two ways: by selling to a dealer for same-day, cash-on-the-line sale (one should comparative shop and offer a piece to at least a couple of dealers), or by offering it at a reputable auction house. However, the piece will do best if offered in the *right* sale. If, for example, one is selling a Victorian sauceboat, it should be handled at a Victorian sale. All the dealers and collectors with a special interest in Victorian silver would be there and prices could soar.

Little-Known Facts. In the year of 1743 Thomas Boulsover, an English cutler, was fixing a silver knife handle. As the story goes, he had the handle in a clamp and was using a copper penny to protect it. When he accidentally fused the silver and copper through careless overheating, Sheffield plate was born. With a small amount of borrowed capital, Thomas began manufacturing items made of the plate, which became tremendously successful among the great British middle class as substitutes for sterling silver. The only problem with this appealing little story is that copper pennies were not manufactured until 1797, which was fifty-four years *after* the legendary event took place. Its credibility challenged, it is still an interesting tale that has charmed silver lovers for several centuries.

—Birgitta Hjmarlson

Bibliography

Books

Fennimore, Donald L. *The Knopf Collectors' Guide to Silver & Pewter.* New York: Alfred A. Knopf, Inc., 1984.

Holland, Margaret. *Phaidon Guide to Silver.* Englewood Cliffs, NJ: Prentice Hall, Inc., 1983.

Kovel, Ralph and Terry. *Kovels' Collectors' Source Book.* New York: Crown Publishers, Inc., 1983.

Luddington, John. *Starting To Collect Silver.* Suffolk, England: Baron Publishing, 1984.

Periodicals

Art & Auction. 250 West 57th St., New York, NY 10019.

The Magazine Antiques. 551 Fifth Ave., New York, NY 10176.

The Silver Magazine. P.O. Box 1243, Whittier, CA 90609.

The Spooner. R.F.D. #1, P.O. Box 61, Shullsburg, WI 53586.

Catalogues (Issued by major auction houses)

Butterfield & Butterfield, 1244 Sutter St., San Francisco, CA 94109.

Christie's, 502 Park Ave., New York, NY 10022.

Christie's East, 219 East 67th St., New York, NY 10021.

Sotheby's, 1334 York Ave., New York, NY 10021.

William Doyle Galleries, 175 East 87th St., New York, NY 10028.

Dealers

Argentum/The Leopard's Head, 1750 Union St., San Francisco, CA 94123.

Beverly Keller Scott, P.O. Box 5628, Carmel, CA 93521.

David Orgell, 320 North Rodeo Dr., Beverly Hills, CA 90210.

Hobart House, P.O. Box 128, Haddam, CT 06438.

James Robinson, 15 East 57th St., New York, NY 10022.

Jonathan Trace, Peekskill Hollow Rd., Putnam Valley, NY 10579.

New Orleans Silversmiths, Inc., 600 Chartres St., New Orleans, LA 70130.

S. J. Shrubsole, 104 East 57th St., New York, NY 10022.

Wakefield-Scearce Galleries, Science Hill Building, Shelbyville, KY 40065.

Associations

American Spoon Collectors, P.O. Box 260, Warrensburg, MO 64093.

SPORTS MEMORABILIA

Attention sports fans! If you love your sport enough to take it home with you, you should look into collecting sports memorabilia. Every sport has its history, and stored away in attics and garages everywhere are valuable remnants of this country's early years of sports activities.

More and more people are broadening their sporting experiences by collecting mementos of their favorite sport's past. In fact, many collectors now consider the hobby more vital than following the actual sport. As its popularity has grown, the method of obtaining sports collectors' items has evolved into a sophisticated network of professional dealers who charge high prices for quality pieces. But if you have a sharp eye for a bargain and the knowledge of what is in demand, take another look at your old golf club, world series program, or fly rod—you may be surprised at its actual value.

History. America's love for sports goes back a long time, but not all the way back. The Puritans had firm convictions about a person's idle time, and local ordinances forbade colonists from playing any sort of "unlawful game in house, yard, garden or backside." Constables were ordered "to search after all manner of gaming, singing and dancing." By the nineteenth century, however, after the Olympic games were revived, sports started to take on its role as America's favorite form of recreation.

Hunting, horse racing and fishing are some of America's oldest sports, and the assortment of equipment and paraphernalia that has been made to assist the outdoorsman is phenomenal. All of it, by the way, is valuable.

Colleges have played an important role in promoting sports in America. Rowing, fencing, and track and field events were some of America's first popular participation sports, and they were usually held on campuses. Later, many college football and baseball teams started what would become long histories of homecoming traditions, which included team badges, buttons, and pennants that are now avidly sought by collectors.

Collecting professional sports memorabilia is a world of its own. Baseball cards are so popular that a separate chapter is devoted to them. But cards are not the only baseball souvenirs, and baseball is not the only sport that offers collectors' cards. There are baseball autographs, Dizzy Dean watches, game guides, yearbooks, programs, uniforms, gloves...the list is endless. And the same is true for football, basketball, golf, tennis, hockey and especially soccer.

The list of valuable sports-related items is inexhaustable, and, oddly, the hobby is rather young. Prior to the 1960s, most sports souvenirs were collected by a few die-hard fans at the stadium gates or by sending letters to the players. Today, there are so many sports collectors that dealers specializing in memorabilia operate the same way as dealers of coins, stamps or other and well-established hobbies. As the number of collectors grows, and the number of high-quality sports items diminishes, prices for popular pieces go steadily higher. Yet, there still are opportunities to find classic sports equipment, such as a Tonkin bamboo fly rod, a Gil Hodges first baseman's glove, or a MacGregor Tourney golf club for less than $200.

★ How many times have you inspected the used-club barrel at your local pro shop? One avid golfer spotted an odd-looking wooden-headed club in a New York thrift shop in 1977. It had been painted black, but the golfer noticed the name "Tommy Armour" imprinted on its head. After taking the club home—for a couple of dollars—and reading up on MacGregor's Tommy Armour series clubs and irons, he realized he had just purchased a prized "classic." After refinishing the wood, the golfer took the club to a professional tournament. It sold in fifteen minutes for $350.

College rowing was one of America's earliest popular sports. Who would have thought then (this photo was taken in 1913) that the simple equipment used would be collectors' items today?

Values Outside the Home. Any sports equipment or paraphernalia in good condition that can be authenticated as having been made before the turn of the century is valuable as a collectors' item. Sports equipment made after that date and even mass-produced items can also be valuable if they are associated with a noted personality, are the first of its kind, or have some other unique feature, such as unusual decoration or exceptionally high-quality construction.

Anglers consider George Snyder's bait-casting reels to be among the oldest reels made in America. Snyder was a Kentucky jeweler who began making reels in 1810. Other jewelers copied Snyder's design and made improvements. Some other noteworthy craftsmen who produced handmade reels were J. L. Sage, A. B. Shipley, and the Meek Brothers, also from Kentucky.

Rods and lures, including flies, are the other major types of fishing collectors' items. Bamboo fly rods and beautifully feathered flies are the most popular, and each manufacturer had its own way of identifying its product. Most handmade rods had the maker's name stamped on a metal cap at the base. Some names to look for are Sam Philippi and Hiram Leonard of Bangor, Maine. Another way of checking whether a rod was handmade is to examine its fittings. If they are silver and have a dull gray-green tarnish, characteristic of German silver, they probably were made individually. Flies are harder to identify, and there are over five-thousand patterns and sizes to differentiate. The only sure way to identify a fly's manufacturer is to find its original paper backing or envelope, which was usually marked. Red Wing Governor, the Ibis Mallard and the Black Gnat are names of several collectors' flies.

Along with fishing tackle, outdoor enthusiasts enjoy collecting guns and gunning paraphernalia (see "Firearms"). But sportsmen took more than their guns when they went into the wilderness. Other valuable items special to outdoorsmen include vintage camp stoves, tinned-iron plates and cups, dutch ovens, lanterns, wood-handled knives, and traps. Turn-of-the-century camping equipment was built to last, and today's collector often has the opportunity to put his or her collection to work. (Any hunter or camper will tell you that a pot of stew cooked in an old dutch oven over an open fire has a quality all its own.) The best authority for authenticating old camping equipment is turn-of-the-century editions of Montgomery Ward; Sears, Roebuck, and other outdoors equipment catalogues.

Golf, a more genteel outdoor sport, packs its own share of collector equipment, some of it quite valuable. Much vintage golfer's paraphernalia has been kept in good working order and is often preferred to more modern items. Clubs made in the 1920s and 1930s by MacGregor, Spalding, Hillerich & Bradsby, and McEwan are prized by collectors for their balance and handling. Prices for complete sets of "classic" clubs often go higher than $1,000. Antique-club collectors concentrate on age, and pre-1850 woods are considered the true antiques of golf. A popular style at that time was the *Phillip* club, made in Scotland and characterized by a long, five-inch head. Pre-1850 golfers used light wood clubs, or "woods," because their golf balls were covered in leather. The leather cover cut easily, so golfers *swept* the ball off the turf instead of driving it. There were few pre-1850 irons made.

Collectors look at the way the head of an old club is attached to the shaft to determine authenticity. Early clubs were usually strengthened with five or six inches of thread wound tightly around the joint and then shellacked or tarred. Less thread was used on newer clubs. Steel shafts first entered the market in the 1920s.

Baseball was actually a runner-up in the cardboard picture premium business. The tobacco firm Allen & Ginter issued the first cards using photos of pool players, boxers, oarsmen and sharp-shooters. Today, a complete set of 1952 Bowman football cards of any team is priced above $400.

Many sports collections concentrate on sports-event publications. Baseball yearbooks and world-series programs are always in demand. So are pennants, autographs and posters of old or recent sports events of renown, and uniforms, mitts, jerseys, balls and bats. But unless equipment is associated with a famous athlete (worn by a Hall of Fame player, for example), or is the first of its kind, it is not especially valuable.

Where to Find Values. The most rewarding way to obtain sports memorabilia is not to buy them but to get them directly from a sports personality or event. To a sports fan, few of life's encounters are as thrilling as getting a program autographed by a favorite sports hero. Coca-Cola's commercial featuring Mean Joe Green giving his jersey to a wide-eyed young fan captures the magic of possessing something once owned by an "immortal."

Although most sports fans will never be as lucky as the young fan in the Coke commercial, there are plenty of opportunities for them to acquire sports collectors' items secondhand. For the collector who only wants the best and is willing to pay for it, dealerships specializing in sports memorabilia are excellent sources. Counter-feits and manufactured reproductions are common, but a reputable specialist can be insurance against fraudulent merchandise. One sports price catalogue prints a warning to collectors: "As a general rule, skepticism is a worthwhile quality for the collector of sports items."

Auctions are also good sources for certain items. Decoys and firearms, for example, are often on the auction block. Other items are less frequently seen, but there are many specialized auctions and conventions that deal exclusively with sports. Most collectors' conventions and shows are advertised in hobby and collectors' magazines. A local sports collector-dealer may also be familiar with local events.

Collectors' magazines will contain classified and display advertising for sports valuables. Answering advertisements through the mail can be an effective collecting technique if one has a *specific* item in mind—there can be little confusion about Fleer football card #58, dated 1960, of George Blanda, quarterback for the Houston Oilers, for example. If an advertised item seems to only *resemble* what one is looking for, it is best avoided. One should always keep copies of sales correspondence when dealing through the mail. Guarantees should be read carefully, and one should act quickly if a decision has been made to return an item.

Short of having them given to you, the second best technique for finding sports items is to look for them among the piles of junk at flea markets, garage sales, secondhand and thrift stores. The fun comes from anticipating what one will find. Local used-merchandise sales are also great places to meet other collectors who might live just a few blocks away.

★ **One sports collector, who owns a clothing store, uses his hobby to improve business. His collection of baseball jerseys was once upgraded with his purchase of a vintage 1939 Joe DiMaggio jersey for $5,000. But rather than just store the jersey, the owner publicized his acquisition through the media. The Joe DiMaggio jersey story was picked up by the networks, and the happy store owner received over $50,000 in free national advertising.**

A Price Sampling

Football Cards

Topps, complete set, 1956	$160.00
Bowman, Y. A. Tittle, 1950	5.20
Fleer, George Blanda, 1960	5.05

Football Miscellaneous

Football, known to have been thrown for a touchdown by Norm Van Brocklin, c. 1952	390
Football, pre-1900	115

World Series Programs

1926	225
1930	180
1940	130

Baseball Miscellaneous

Baseball uniform, known to have been worn by Babe Ruth, c. 1920s	8,900
Catcher's mask, 1902	95
Fielder's glove, Larry Doby model, c. 1950	28

Golf

Set of woods and irons, MacGregor, R. Armour, 1950	1,250
Golfer's manual, H. B. Farnie, 1857	695
Set of woods and irons, Wilson, Sam Snead, 1940	500
Wedge, Walter Hagen	125

Fishing Tackle

Flies, English, set of fifty, 1880	435
Fly reel, Billinghurst, nickel plated, 1869	260
Casting rod, Heddon, 6', split bamboo, 1920	110

How to Store/Display. Collections of sports memorabilia can be as fragile as sheets of autographed paper or as tough as cast-iron camping gear. Paper items, such as picture cards, autographs, and programs, should be stored in individual acetate sheets and kept away from direct sunlight, excessive heat and moisture. Historical libraries store their older manuscripts in temperature- and humidity-regulated vaults. Collectors can create a miniature vault by using fabric-lined cabinets along with a desiccant, or drying agent.

The number of items in paper collections can add up fast so it is a good idea to organize a filing or other identification/retrieval system. In an organized collection, individual pieces tend not to be easily misplaced. Also, pieces tend to last longer in an organized collection because the collector does not have to paw through everything each time he or she wants to find something.

Other perishable sports items, such as mitts, uniforms, balls, and golf bags, have their own storage and handling guidelines. As a rule, older items made of natural materials should not be exposed to direct sunlight and excessive handling.

Most dealers think it is good business to help answer customers' questions about preserving their collections and are eager to do so. Another good source for preservation tips is consumer information on products made of materials that are used to make other consumer products. Libraries will carry consumer publications sponsored by the United States government and various trade organizations.

If one is planning to display items made from natural materials such as leather, paper, wood and cotton/wool textiles, he should keep them in a darkened room. Paper items should be mounted on acid-free paper, and, if possible, fragile pieces should be rotated from display to storage regularly.

Mechanical sports memorabilia also deserve special attention. Rust and tarnish can quickly erode the value of Dizzy Dean watches, wind-up toys and other metal souvenirs. One should use a nonabrasive cleaner, and the collection must be stored in a dry place. Any glass item placed in a display case should be regularly checked for condensation. Campers will do well to remember that if they take an antique cast-iron skillet or dutch oven along on camping trips, to keep them rust free by drying them out immediately after washing (over the fire is good) and then applying a thin coat of vegetable oil. Soaps or detergents should be avoided when washing iron cookware.

How and When to Sell. One of the best places to sell sports memorabilia is at collectors' shows and conventions. Such places are full of enthusiastic collectors, all of them eager to talk about their hobbies. Most collectors' shows require an entry fee, which can range from $10 to $50. Collectors looking to sell should always take complete sets of items to shows. Random samples are never as popular as complete groupings.

If, on the other hand, one needs to turn a collection into cash in a hurry, selling directly to a dealer is probably the quickest solution. But there will be a price to pay for the convenience—one can expect to get about half of an item's full retail value by selling to a dealer.

A big advantage to selling collectors' items on consignment is that all the work is handled by a storekeeper. One also pays for this service, of course, but if the store is in a good location, an item will be seen by more buyers than if one tried to sell it himself. Usually the seller can set his own prices.

Flea markets offer another good sales opportunity. Space rental is usually low, $10 maximum, and the larger markets draw good-sized crowds. Since most flea markets are held outdoors, it is a good idea to keep items in strong, weather-proof cases. One should also keep old leather, paper and wood items away from direct sunlight as much as possible.

If one is interested in selling at an auction house, it is important to know the commission or percentage taken by the house as its fee.

Fees generally run between 10% to 25% of an item's value. Usually the higher the sale price, the lower the percentage commission charged. Some auction houses will also provide a minimum price below which the item will not be sold. Not all houses provide minimum prices, however. In many cases, a seller will have no control over the price his item may bring. Some houses will not allow sellers to bid on their own merchandise, even to buy it back.

★ **If the timing is right, sports mementos can become collectors' items almost as soon as they become available.** On Monday, January 21, 1984, the day after Super Bowl XIX, the *San Francisco Examiner* newspaper published a souvenir edition with eight pages of Super Bowl photos and stories. On Tuesday, January 22, the edition was worth $1 to collectors.

Little-Known Facts. One of America's oldest sports, gambling, includes a great variety of collectors' devices and accessories, including instruments designed to cheat. Along with all sorts of rigged dice and card dispensers are machines that shave the edges of cards, and "hold outs," which pop the right card into the gambler's hand. Cheating devices are considered rare by collectors, probably because many are still in use....

• During its early years, golf's popularity became an issue of national defense. In 1457, the game was banned in Scotland because it interfered with archery practice. At the time, well-trained archers were considered vital to Scottish national defense; good golfers were not so important.

• During the Victorian era, fishermen casting for salmon liked to use gaudy-colored wet flies with unusual patterns and as many as twenty different kinds of feathers. Overfishing rapidly diminished the number of salmon, however, and made the survivors more selective. Today, Victorian salmon flies have all been replaced by less colorful but more realistic-looking lures.

—James W. White

Bibliography

Books

Beitz, Les. *Overlooked Treasures.* Cranbury, NY: A. S. Barnes & Co., Inc., 1976.

DiNoto, Andrea, ed. *The Encyclopedia of Collectibles.* Alexandria, VA: Time-Life Books, 1978.

Douglas, John. *Sports Memorabilia.* Des Moines, IA: Wallace-Homestead, 1976.

Keane, Martin J. *Classic Rods and Rodmakers.* Piscataway, NY: Winchester Press, 1976.

Periodicals

Antique Angler. The Antique Angler, Inc., P.O. Box 327, Stockton, NJ 08559.

Sport Fan. Bob Jasperson, 840 Conestoga Rd., Rosemont, PA 19010.

Sports Collectors News. Rt. 1, Somerset, WI 54025.

The Trader Speaks. Dan Dischley, 3 Pleasant Dr., Dept. FH, Lake Ronkonkoma, NY 11779.

Sports Collectors Digest. Krause Publications, Inc., 700 E. State St., Iola, WI 54990.

Catalogues

Hudgeons, Thomas E. III, ed. *Official 1984 Price Guide to Sports Collectibles.* Orlando, FL: House of Collectibles, 1983.

Kovel, Ralph and Terry, eds. *Kovels' on Antiques and Collectibles.* Cleveland, OH: Antiques, Inc., 1974.

Mirken, Alan, ed. *Sears, Roebuck Catalogue,* 1902 edition. New York: Crown Publishers, 1970.

Sugar, Bert R., ed. *The Sports Collectors Bible.* New York: Bobbs-Merrill Co., 1983.

Catalogue and Price Guide. Martin Friedman Specialty Co., P.O. Box 5777, Baltimore, MD 21208.

Dealers

Den's Collectors Den, P.O. Box 606, Laurel, MD 20707.

Double Play Sports Collectibles, 3653 Lawton, San Francisco, CA 94122.

Fanstand Sports Collectibles, 3418 Geary, San Francisco, CA 94118.

Martin Friedman Specialty Co., P.O. Box 5777, Baltimore, MD 21208.

Associations

Boxing Hall of Fame, 120 West 31st St., New York, NY 10001.

Golf Collectors Society, 638 Wagner Rd., Lafayette Hill, PA 19444.

Memorabilia Association, 102 Rinegold St., Peekskill, NY 10565.

National Fishing Lure Collectors Club, 652 E. Niagra Circle, Gretna, LA 70053.

STAMPS

Sylvia and Benjamin were very much in love—a circumstance made difficult by the fact that Benjamin was studying at the university two-hundred-miles away. Train fare in 1869 was beyond their means, so visits were few and far between. But they *could* afford postage, and both were avid correspondents.

Sylvia liked the little blue three-cent stamps with the picture of the locomotive, partly because she was weary of the faces of tired old men who had adorned every United States postage stamp up to that time, and partly because she enjoyed imagining that this was the locomotive that would bring Ben home to her. She bought a lot of the little blue train stamps.

What sentimentalists Sylvia and Ben were! Saving each other's letters, they would read them again and again; and when at last they were married, Sylvia tied them with ribbon and lovingly placed them in the attic trunk.

History. Postage stamps had not been around very long when Sylvia and Ben were corresponding. The first one appeared in England in 1840. One of the world's most popular stamps among collectors today, it was dubbed the "Penny Black" because of its face value and color. In a few years, postage stamps gained favor in other countries, and in 1847, the first United States general issue appeared.

The history of the postage stamp predates the history of stamp collecting by only a few months. Almost as soon as the Penny Black was issued, the hobby took off. Stamp collecting as an investment was not far behind; stamp dealers appeared before 1850.

★ Alan Woodson was a seasoned collector. Browsing through an inexpensive assortment of stamps on a dealer's counter, he found one that he believed to be rare. Although the dealer assured him that it was not, he purchased it anyway for the princely sum of ten cents. It sold a few years later for $1,800.

Smithsonian Institution

The Penny Black is prized not only because it was the first postage stamp ever made, but also because of its face value and color, which is black.

Values Outside the Home. If one of Sylvia's great-grandsons ever finds her letters in the attic, and this event is sufficient to spark an interest in collecting, he must decide how serious to get about it. The stamp collector must be sophisticated; he must be someone who knows his product. He must know about watermarks, perforations, cancelations, and how to assess a stamp's condition. He must know what makes a stamp rare.

One of the advantages of stamp collecting is that it is one of the few money-making ventures in which $20 spent each month can someday represent a valuable holding. Rare United States stamp prices have been increasing at an average compounded rate of 15%. And now and then, that truly rare find comes along that really makes it all worthwhile.

Before that $20 begins to burn a hole in his pocket, though, the fledgling collector needs to do some studying. The library is his best source of information.

The basic demand for a stamp is generated in its country of origin. Therefore, the safest choices for a resident of the United States are United States stamps. The eighteen-million Americans who collect stamps represent a huge market.

The new investor should avoid the temptation of inexpensive recent issues and modern United States plate blocks and mint sheets. These are being purchased by collectors in such large quantities that they may never be in demand. A person spending $20 each month should be buying no more than three stamps.

This does not make for much of a hobby, though, and the collector with only a few stamps is not going to learn very much. To help with his own education he should also buy an inexpensive album, collectors' tools and an assortment of stamps, so that he has an opportunity to become familiar with some of the elements of collecting. He can gradually upgrade this "auxiliary collection," learning valuable information all the while.

Age has no great bearing on the value of a stamp. Several of the world's oldest stamps can be purchased for three to five dollars each. It is rarity, and therefore demand, that creates a stamp's value, and some early issues were produced in relatively large quantities for their time. Still, older stamps are the best buy. They have had more time to become rare, and they were issued at a time when relatively fewer quantities were printed.

Whether a stamp is used or unused also makes a big difference. Sylvia's little blue locomotives can be purchased used for less than $5 today. Unused, they would be worth up to $250 each.

Even used stamps can have great value, however—especially if they contain printing errors or bear rare cancelations. One of the locomotive stamps, canceled with one of the unique imprints carved from bottle corks by early postal clerks, could be worth hundreds of dollars today.

A stamp's beauty has little to do with its value. The world's most valuable stamp, the 1856 one-cent British Guiana, looks singularly unimpressive.

How to Find Values. The wise stamp collector will visit local retailers in an effort to get acquainted. He will join a local stamp club and meet other collectors who may be willing to sell, trade or give advice. He will make a few modest purchases.

As he becomes increasingly familiar with stamps, he will begin a "want list," which he will give to his dealer. It will include the catalogue numbers of desired stamps and will indicate that he is interested only in stamps of "fine" condition or better.

Stamps are also sold at auction, and the collector who lives close enough to attend one will find it fascinating. First, though, he should go with an experienced collector just to watch.

The annual *Scott's Standard Postage Stamp Catalogue* will provide a guide to market prices for new and used stamps. Stamp periodicals are also important sources of information.

A Price Sampling. The following list reflects a range of 1984 prices secured by stamp dealers for specific issues, both unused and used, in "fine" or "very fine" condition:

	Used	*Unused*
$2.60 blue of 1930 Graf Zeppelin air mail issue*	$1,725	$3,100
$ .50 sage green of 1898 Trans-Mississippi Exploration issue*	187-275	1,080
$ .15 black Abraham Lincoln of 1861-1866 definitive issue	85-100	510-675
$ .03 ultramarine locomotive of 1869 pictorial issue	4-7	190-225
$ .06 purple of 1893 Columbian Exposition issue	40-52	92-124
$ .10 deep blue of 1922-1925 special delivery issue	.40-.50	77-83
$ .01 green of 1913 Panama Canal issue	1.60-2.00	26-31
$1.00 purple Eugene O'Neill of 1965-1979 Prominent Americans series	.05-.15	3.90-4.50
One-half cent olive-brown Nathan Hale of 1922-1925 definitive issue	.09-.12	.25-.45

* Only one sale of this item could be located

How to Store/Display. It is the sheer fun of collecting that makes it possible for the investor to smell the flowers along the way.

His essential tools will include a stamp album, tongs, hinges, watermark detector, perforation gauge and magnifying glass. To learn most quickly, he should purchase a packet of world stamps, even though he may be concentrating his investment on stamps of the United States. Purchasing too many stamps initially will lead to frustration. A packet of two thousand is sufficient to wet one's feet; otherwise, the process of sorting and classifying will be mind-boggling.

Stamps should be kept in an album or in a stock book, which is stored in a dry place at room temperature.

How and When to Sell. It is a good thing that stamp collecting is so much fun, because the average hobbyist will enjoy his collection for many years before he is able to realize a profitable return. A relatively long holding period is necessary to offset the buy-and-sell price disparity.

When it becomes advantageous to sell, dealers and auctions as well as other collectors are the best places for collectors to realize the most value for their efforts, but only if they approach the market with solid information on current market prices. Knowledge is the collector's best protection against suffering unnecessary losses.

★ **In 1918, William Robey purchased a sheet of the new $.24 "Flying Jenny" air mail issue. He saw instantly that the flying machine had been inverted, and it was only after he paid for the sheet that the error was discovered by the clerk, who then demanded the stamps back. Robey refused; it was his. He subsequently sold it to a dealer in Philadelphia for $15,000. That profit is miniscule today, for singles are now worth many thousands of dollars.**

Little-Known Facts. The first stamp collector was a young lady who placed an ad in the London *Times* in 1841 asking readers to send her Penny Blacks that they received through the mail, so that she could paper her dressing room with them. Considering that stamp's color, the resulting decor must have been less than pleasing; but her foresight, if she were around today, would have earned her millions of dollars worth of Penny Blacks for the mere cost of an ad.

• Pretty controversial, that Penny Black. Because it bore a profile of Queen Victoria, many of her subjects objected violently to the idea of licking the back of its face. Others thought the idea of *canceling* its "face"—her face?—even more objectionable.

—*Robin C. Harris*

Bibliography

Books

Blackburn, Graham. *The Postage Stamp Gazetteer.* Indianapolis, IN: Bobbs Merrill, 1976.

Blair, Arthur. *The World of Stamps and Stamp Collecting.* New York: Hamlyn, 1972.

Bruns, Franklin R. *Stamp Collecting: Your Introduction to a Fascinating Hobby.* New Jersey: Washington Press, 1974.

Cabeen, Richard M. *Standard Handbook of Stamp Collecting.* New York: Thomas Y. Crowell, 1979.

Lidman, David, and John D. Apfelbaum. *The World of Stamps and Stamp Collecting.* New York: Charles Scribner's Sons, 1981.

Mackay, James A. *The Dictionary of Stamps in Color.* New York: Macmillan, 1973.

Mackay, James A. *The World of Classic Stamps, 1840-1870.* New York: Putnam, 1972.

Thorp, Prescott H. *A Guide to Stamp Collecting.* New York: Minkus Publications, 1967.

Wagenheim, Kal. *Paper Gold.* New York: Peter H. Wyden, 1976.

Periodicals

American Philatelist. P.O. Box 800, State College, PA 16801 (monthly magazine).

The Collectors Club Philatelist. 22 E. 35th St., New York, NY 10016 (magazine of the Collectors Club of New York).

Linn's Stamp News. P.O. Box 29, Sidney, OH 45367 (weekly newspaper).

Minkus Stamp Journal. 116 W. 32nd St., New York, NY 10001 (quarterly journal).

Scott's Monthly Journal. 3 E. 57th St., New York, NY 10022.

Stamp Collector. P.O. Box 10, Albany, OR 97321 (weekly newspaper).

Stamps. 153 Waverly Place, New York, NY 10014 (weekly newspaper).

Catalogues

Harris Postage Stamp Catalog. H. E. Harris and Co., Inc., 645 Summer St., Boston, MA 02210.

Scott's Standard Postage Stamp Catalogue. (4 volumes), Scott Publishing Co., 604 Fifth Ave., New York, NY 10020.

Dealers

Earl P. L. Apfelbaum, Inc., 2006 Walnut St., Philadelphia, PA.

Bartlett and Felder, Inc., 49 Geary St., Suite 250, San Francisco, CA.

Century Stamp and Coin Co., 506 W. 7th St., Los Angeles, CA 90014.

Clark, Richard D., 1515 Cleveland Pl., Suite 461, Denver, CO.

H. E. Harris and Co., Inc., 645 Summer St., Boston, MA 02210.

Metro Coin Ltd., 4455 E. Camelback Rd., Phoenix, AZ.

Superior Stamp and Coin Co., 9301 Wilshire Blvd., Beverly Hills, CA 90210.

Associations

American Philatelic Society, P.O. Box 800, State College, PA 16801 (largest collectors association in the United States; free brochure on request).

American Stamp Dealers Association, 840 Willis Ave., Albertson, NY 11507 (dealer members have pledged to a stringent code of ethics; information is available on dealers who belong).

The Collectors Club, 22 E. 35th St., New York, NY 10016 (small society of serious collectors; non-residents welcome).

Society of Philatelic Americans, P.O. Box 904, Wilmington, DE 19809 (smaller than APS but offers similar services).

STOCK AND BOND CERTIFICATES

In fall 1928 Lucas Brown, a twenty-year-old apprentice draper invested an unexpected inheritance in the stocks and bonds of a number of "safe" companies. One year later, the catastrophic Wall Street crash turned Lucas's investment into dust. But Lucas's young bride, Molly, liked the pretty pictures on the worthless stock certificates, so she saved them and continued to add many more throughout the decades. Fifty-six years later, Lucas Brown's investment finally paid off: in September 1984, the Browns sold their collection for several thousand dollars.

History. In the past, not too many people were as perceptive as Molly Brown. *Scripophily* (the collecting of old stocks and bonds) did not catch on until the 1970s, but once its possibilities were discovered, the number of collectors rapidly grew. Here were records of history in the making, embellished and romanticized with engravings comparable to the finest prints and often bearing the signatures of famous tycoons. What other collectors' item could offer such unique blends of art, history and high finance at affordable prices? It is no wonder that soon collectors of certificates numbered in the thousands.

★ When seventy-three-year-old Betty Bauhaus tried to cash in three old stocks she had found among her late husband's papers, she was disappointed to find out that the companies had long been out of business. But the man at the Merrill Lynch office advised her to see an antiques dealer who specialized in paper items. Betty's disappointment quickly disappeared when the dealer offered her $680 for the three "worthless" certificates.

Values Outside the Home. Whether issued and canceled, issued and never canceled, or unissued, invalid stock certificates are valued most for their *vignettes,* which are the beautiful engravings of allegorical figures, portraits, or representations of a company's product or service decorating the upper halves of most—though not all—specimens. Railway trains, steamships and mining scenes are among the most popular. Famous signatures are also highly prized (the autographs of Edison, Rockefeller or of Wells and Fargo could send the value of even a plain certificate soaring). The wise collector will decide on a theme early on, building his collection topically by vignette, autograph, or industry. He should also consider the condition of the certificate, paying particular attention to the cancelation marks, since these could detract from the value of an otherwise fine specimen.

Where to Find Values. Unlike many "functional" collectors' items, such as furniture, utensils or clothing, old certificates are rarely found at church bazaars or weekend garage sales. But that is not to say that the keen collector might not come upon great finds in unexpected places. Apart from antiques shops or speciality stores, stamp shops, coin shops, flea markets, swap meets and even book stores are happy hunting grounds, while some collectors have discovered their rarest treasures in probate attorneys' offices. Nor should Aunt Sophie or Grandma be forgotten—though they themselves may not be collectors, relatives and friends are often pleased to add their "worthless" old certificates to a burgeoning collection.

★ **A young woman went to a fancy costume ball wearing a dress made entirely of old stock certificates she had found in her mother's attic. Someone at the ball advised her to show the costume to an antiques dealer. A few days later she was able to buy a whole wardrobe of dresses for the money she got for her unusual creation.**

A Price Sampling. Issued certificates are generally higher priced than unissued. Pre-1850s certificates are the rarest and most valuable. Here are some examples of recent sales or offers:

1830s New York, Providence & Boston Railroad	$295
1940s Sullivan Railroad Co.	145
1850s Sullivan Railroad Co.	95
1880s Hancock Iron Mining Co.	35
1950 Portsmouth Transit Co. (only ten issued)	25
1924 San Francisco-Sacramento Railway Co.	15
1924 National Electric Co.	10
1920 Dickson Car-Wheel Co.	9
1956 Sentinel Radio Corp.	5
1930 American Tobacco Co.	4

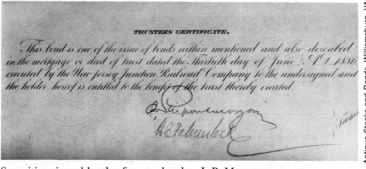

Securities signed by the famous banker J. P. Morgan are now rare because of the illegibility of his autograph (see first signature above); since it made reading his name so difficult, collectors would not recognize the name and would throw out documents bearing it.

How to Store/Display. One of the great attractions of stock and bond certificates is their portability and ease of handling. They can be slipped into clear vinyl pocket pages and stored in ordinary three-ring binders, or they may be framed and arranged in arresting wall groupings. If hung, care should be taken to avoid exposure to dampness and direct sunlight, which could cause fading and yellowing.

How and When to Sell. Other collectors of stock and bond certificates should not be the only targets for hobbyists who wish to sell. By considering their certificates' particular vignettes and signatures, those wishing to sell should also look for buyers who collect specific industry memorabilia, or autographs, or items from a particular geographic area. Really good pieces can sell well at auctions, and dealers specializing in Early Americana or paper items are always eager to see a fine or rare specimen.

★ **When a sharp operator conned Jenny Mikler into buying shares in a defunct company, she had the last laugh. She had paid $100 for the "worthless" stock certificate. As a rare collectors' item, however, it turned out to be worth $700.**

Little-Known Facts. In 1792, two-dozen merchants who used to trade various stocks beneath a cottonwood tree at the foot of Wall Street in New York City agreed to henceforth trade only with each other and to charge their customers a fixed commission. That was the beginning of the New York Stock Exchange.

• Doing up the old inn she had recently bought in Connecticut, Valerie Hopkind came upon a bundle of canceled stock certificates. Not suspecting their value as collectors' items, she used them to paper the walls of a bathroom, to great effect. She was a little chagrined to find out later that the smallest room in her house had the most expensive decor.

—Vera Abriel

Bibliography

Periodicals

Antique Securities Newsletter. P.O. Box 485, Euless, TX 76039.
Friends of Financial History Quarterly. 170 Broadway, New York, NY 10038.

Catalogues

Hudgeons, Thomas E. III, ed. *Official Price Guide to Paper Collectibles.* Orlando, FL: House of Collectibles, 1984.

Dealers

Antique Stocks & Bonds (Haley Garrison, Jr.), Drawer JH, Willamsburg, VA 23187.
George H. La Barre Galleries, P.O. Box 746, Hollis, NH 03049.
Grand Central Station, 1422 Market St., San Francisco, CA 94102.
Hollins, C., P.O. Box 11, Springfield, VA 22150.
Investors Gallery, 2524 Cedar Springs, Dallas, TX 75201.

T

TIN CANISTERS

So, you think gold is more valuable than tin, do you? Wrong. Old tin cans (dignified by the term *canisters*) may very well be the most valuable ultimate junk of all time and in some cases more valuable than gold. Made to be thrown away, old tin cans have nevertheless survived by the tens of thousands and many are highly prized by collectors. Case in point: A small tobacco can made at the turn of the century and weighing less than two ounces (empty) was bought for $1.75 fifteen years ago. Recently it sold for $450—more than the 1984 price of an ounce of gold.

History. Some credit is due Napoleon for launching the tin can industry. In the late 1700s he was losing more soldiers from their consumption of bad food than from their deaths on the battlefield. In 1795 the French government offered a prize of twelve-thousand francs to anyone who could invent a process for preserving food.

One Nicolas Appert claimed the prize a few years later with a process using large-mouthed glass bottles and boiling water. Later, two Englishmen applied somewhat the same ideas to soldered tinplate canisters.

This kind of canning was a direct hit with the British Army and Navy, which consumed huge quantities of canned vegetables and meat.

In the 1820s "canned" foods were introduced in the United States, first in glass containers, then, a few years later, in bulky, handmade tin cans (with a solder-filled hole in the top) containing finely chopped foods. When the Civil War broke out, a man named Gail Borden launched the condensed-milk industry to keep soldiers fed. When the soldiers returned home, they told their wives about canned milk.

At the beginning of the nineteenth century, can manufacturing was a cottage industry. But the Norton Brothers of Chicago invented a semi-automatic machine that soldered the side seams of cans. Production rose from a dozen cans an hour to twenty-five hundred. Later, a fully automated machine doubled can production, and Joseph Campbell started selling soup in cans for a dime each. By the

Claiming he lost more soldiers to food
contamination than from combat, Napoleon
Bonaparte influenced the French government
to offer twelve-thousand francs to anyone who
could invent a way to preserve food. Thus
began the inventive process that culminated in
the tin can.

twentieth century sixty-three different kinds of meat could be bought
in cans. The hermetically sealed vegetable won the market in the
1920s.

Tin can advertising over the years went from painted-on numbers
to paper labels to lithography applied directly to the tin. In the 1930s,
four-color lithography was introduced along with a canning
milestone: now one could buy beer in a can (see "Beer Cans").

Finally, the now-familiar aluminum cans were introduced by Coors in 1959.

★ **A married couple was out on a drive and stopped in an antiques store. There they bought an old Handmade (brand name) cigar canister for $5. Later they learned through a dealer that it was worth about $100.**

Values Outside the Home. All tins, from the oldest to the newest, are decorated to some degree, and in the world of collectors' items they fall under the heading "Advertising Antiques." The quality of lithography on the can is the key to serious collecting, along with rarity and condition.

Tins are generally divided into types: tea, tobacco, medicine, cocoa or spice, Log Cabin syrup, biscuit, cookie, peanut butter, talcum powder, beer, and tiny sample tins. These are only some of the categories.

Thousands of different tobacco tins were made during the early twentieth century, and they are the most collected today. Talcum powder tins (for men as well as for babies and women) are appealing because cute babies and smiling ladies appear on the labels. In the last six or seven years they have become increasingly popular.

Beginners can also collect cans based on the manufacturer. Ginna and Company is known for its beautiful color lithography, and Huntley and Palmer produced ingenious English biscuit tins shaped like carriages, windmills, clocks, and other familiar daily items. However, one should be prepared to pay hundreds of dollars for these unique tins.

Other ways to begin collecting are to choose cans produced during certain years, such as those made before 1900, or beer cans made prior to the 1960s. Or one can select cans that are quaint or that have delightfully zany advertising claims, such as old pharmaceutical tins (Dr. White's Cupid brand cough drops proclaimed to be good "for clearing and strengthening voices").

The point is that enthusiasts should collect what they love. If they are serious about collecting, they will do well to buy canisters only in mint condition (absolutely free of scratches, flaws or dents) or in good condition (slightly faded and scratched but not enough to mar the overall appearance of the tin).

With an eye on the future, and because just about anything is being collected these days, beginners might want to build a collection of *today's* tins—which are rapidly becoming all steel instead of tin— such as cookie tins, gourmet tins, soup and beer cans. Because technology continues to bring changes in how we live day to day, twenty years from now these ordinary items may add up to a rare collection.

But just because an antique tin is in mint condition does not guarantee it will bring a high price on the market. It has to be rare and special because of its design or shape, and somebody has to want it, perhaps to complete a set. Tins in poor condition (extremely faded, severely defective) should only be considered if they are rare.

Where to Find Values. The truly fanatical I'll-go-anywhere-to-buy-a-tin collector will arrive at an antiques show or collectors' convention two days before it opens. He knows the dealers, has specific items he is looking for, and he is willing to pay top dollar.

For this reason the beginning collector is at a disadvantage. But if one's sights are modest and his enthusiasm high, and he enjoys talking to dealers, antiques and collectors shows are plentiful and good places to learn about what is available and what one can expect to pay for it. Prices are generally lower on the East Coast, where tins are more available. Collectors shows are often announced in weekend listings of events in local newspapers.

Flea markets, antiques stores, garage sales, and out-of-the-way country stores are other good sources. Some newspapers have a classified ad heading for collectors' items and antiques. The kitchens, garages and attics of older relatives and friends can also reveal dusty valuable tins. But the beginner should stay clear of bidding on canisters at auctions and simply watch the action taking place as an educational experience.

A Price Sampling

Huntley and Palmers biscuit tins, 1880s	$550
Roly Poly figures (set of six tobacco cans shaped like plump people), 1900s	500 (each)
Gold Dust tobacco can, 1900s	300
Peter Rabbit peanut butter pail, 1920s	275
Brown's coffee can (ten pounds), 1900s	65
Colgate talcum powder, 1900s	40

Richard Hudnut talcum powder, 1930s   35
Dr. Lyon's tooth powder, 1930s   4
Prince Albert tobacco can, 1930s   1

How to Store/Display. Tin containers should never be displayed in direct sunlight or left in particularly humid places. They should be gone over lightly with a feather duster or wiped gently with a soft cloth. Older cans in mint condition should be handled as little as possible to prevent scratches. A mild liquid wax can be used to clean a can, but it should be tested on an inconspicuous place to see if it will make the colors run. Dents can be gently and carefully removed by forcing them out with the back of a wooden spoon.

How and When to Sell. One of the leading tin canister collectors in the country has never sold a single can. He collects because he loves the hunting.

But if one grows to love the hunting, as well as the buying and selling, the time to sell (assuming one's canisters are rare and in mint condition) is whenever and wherever the market is good. Dedicated buyers usually are hungry for specific items and have discretionary money. But unless one has truly valuable tins, it is usually easier to buy than sell.

★ **Colorado dealer Kathy Ralston was in a secondhand store and bought a curious old string holder that hung from a chain in the ceiling. She paid $25 for it. She soon learned that it was one of only two in existence. She eventually sold it for $2,000.**

Little-Known Facts. The first attempt to put beer in a can was done by a brewer in Montana in 1909. It failed because the end seams of the can buckled and the inside tin coating produced a foul-smelling brew.

• The plump woman on many of the Dr. Lyon's tooth powder cans is his wife.

• The term *tin can* is really a misnomer: the cans are tin-plated and made with 90% steel.

• Gail Borden's cans of condensed milk were responsible for lowering the infant mortality rate during the late 1870s.

—*John Holmstrom*

Bibliography

Books

Clark, Hyla M. *The Tin Can Book.* New York: New American Library, 1977.
Davis, Marvin and Helen. *Tobacco Tins.* Ashland, OR: Old Bottle Collecting Publications, 1970.
Liman, Ellen and Lewis. *The Collecting Book.* New York: Penguin Books, 1980.
Pettit, Ernest L. *The Book of Collecting Tin Containers with Price Guide.* Des Moines, IA: Wallace Homestead, 1977.
Wright, Larry, ed. *The Beer Can: A Complete Guide to Beer Can Collecting.* Matteson, IL: Great Lakes Living Press, 1976.

Catalogues

Hammond, Dorothy. *Pictorial Price Guide to American Antiques,* 1984-1985 edition. New York: E. P. Dutton, 1984.
Whitton, Blair. *The Knopf Collector's Guides to American Antiques.* New York: Alfred A. Knopf, Inc., 1984.

Associations

Beer Can Collectors of America (BCCA), 7500 Devonshire, St. Louis, MO 63119 (local chapters in many states).
Tin Container Collectors Association (TCCA), P.O. Box 4555, Denver, CO 80204 (also publishes newsletter, *Tintype;* write for information).

Dealers

Holt, Mary Lou, 12510 Jackson St., Grandview, MO 64030 (collector and dealer).
Nacamulli, Steve, P.O. Box 590964, San Francisco, CA 94159 (all kinds of tins).
Ralston, Dick and Kathy, 2710 Julliard, Boulder, CO 80303 (collectors and dealers).
Spiller, Dr. Burton, 300 White Spruce Blvd., Rochester, NY 14623 (peanut butter pails and others).

TOOLS

When eighty-five-year-old Samuel McLeod handed down his old pine toolbox to his grandson Andrew, he was following a family tradition that went back to the late 1700s. Nine generations of McLeods had added their favorite tools—the early ones mostly handmade—to that battered box, and though as a corporate lawyer Andy McLeod does not have much use for the carpenter's plane or the woodsman's ax, he treasures the box and its contents for capturing the essence of a vanished past.

History. Though certain basic tools have not changed much over the centuries—the carpenter who nailed the seats in Rome's colosseum two-thousand years ago probably used the same claw-hammer his counterpart would be working with in a modern stadium—the advent of the machine age in the nineteenth century meant the passing of many ancient industries and the tools that made them possible. In America, three-hundred years or more of fascinating history would be forever lost to us if not for the emergence of local and state historical societies and their interest in Early American industries. Today, "live" museums recreate the world of our ancestors with enactments of early tool use in the home, in the shop and on the farm. Following this newly awakened interest, private collectors are eager to possess antique tools, which, once cleaned and oiled, have a unique, historic beauty.

★ **Young Tim Kotts enjoyed helping out at the flea market, so he did not really mind when all he got in payment for his efforts was an old, odd-looking contraption made of wood blocks held together by a metal strap. When he showed it to an antiques dealer, any shred of disappointment turned to joy, for the strange tool turned out to be a rare nineteenth-century plane, and the dealer offered to buy it from Tim for $700!**

Values Outside the Home. Most tool collectors keep their interest to a specific period or region, or to a particular industry or craft. Some collect only primitive wooden items, such as coachmen's tools, coopers' tools and others dating from the early eighteenth to the late nineteenth centuries. Some try to limit their specialty to the simple, plain, utilitarian wrought-iron tools characteristic of the Early American period, many of them handmade by itinerant blacksmiths traveling from farm to farm.

Of the manufactured tools, folding rulers and woodworking planes, such as those produced by the Stanley Tool Company after the middle of the nineteenth century, are particularly popular. The beginner should not forget that often the toolbox itself, with its fine dovetailing and well-crafted, smoothly sliding trays, may be of considerable value.

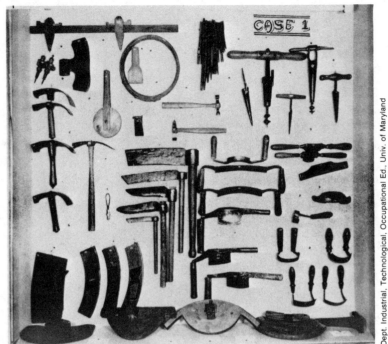

This collection of late eighteenth-century and early nineteenth-century cooper's and shipbuilder's tools shows the qualities of simplicity, functionality and fine craftsmanship that make tools valuable to collectors.

Dept. Industrial, Technological, Occupational Ed., Univ. of Maryland

---

★ **Herma Lowry was angry with her husband for cluttering up their garage with junk she was certain was older than the two of them combined. One day she had an idea. She called in an antiques dealer, who discovered that the "old junk" was in fact tools that were genuine collectors' items. He offered the Lowrys $500 for them—an offer even Stanley Lowry could not refuse.**

Where to Find Values. As in the case of the McLeods, tools are often handed down from generation to generation, until they finally find their way into a yard sale or a dealer's inventory. The market is rich in relatively inexpensive collectors' tools, but the hobbyist looking for pieces from a specific period or of a particular type would best approach specialty dealers or advertise his requirements in an appropriate periodical. It is not often that a really rare find turns up at a garage sale or church bazaar, although when it does, it is cause for celebration.

A Price Sampling. The range of factors determining the value of collectors' tools is as wide as the range of prices one can expect to pay for them. Folding rulers, as a popular example, can be worth $5 to $700 or more. Age, scarcity, materials—such as ivory or ebony—and even beauty of workmanship all play parts in setting the price for an item.

Corn sheller, wood and iron	$185
Wood tongs, scissors type	175
Handwrought iron trammel	60
Plane, Stanley Tool Co.	55
Collapsible saw in leather case	42
Soldering iron, hand-forged copper	38
Monkey wrench, wood handle, 1897	22
Tin wick-trimmer	14
Blacksmith's hand-forged tongs	3
Cast-iron plumb bob	2

How to Store/Display. Most tools may be gently cleaned with a mild steel wool and soap and water, and then rubbed with equal parts of boiled linseed oil and turpentine. This will feed and revitalize the old wood while protecting the iron parts from rust.

How to display old tools depends on the size of the individual pieces as well as on the collection as a whole. Many collectors build special stands from scrap lumber to show off their interesting objects.

★ **"This ax is so blunt, it wouldn't cut butter!"** Matt Houser said disgustedly, lugging the heavy old toolbox he had found in the attic of a house he was restoring to the local tool shop. The owner of the shop, who was an avid collector, put on his glasses to examine the rusty old things. "No wonder they're no longer in perfect shape," he said. "Some of them are more than a hundred years old. How would you like to make a deal with me?" An hour later Matt Houser walked out of the shop with a brand-new set of tools, plus $300 in cold cash.

How and Where to Sell. The wise collector will have joined an historical society or collectors' organization early on, and will have no trouble finding eager buyers among fellow members. Apart from tool collectors, buyers may be found among nostalgia buffs, collectors of Early Americana, as well as history-minded members of a particular craft or industry.

Little-Known Facts. One of the most intriguing challenges for the tool collector is identifying the original purpose of an obsolete item. Who would guess, for instance, that an odd-looking, forceps-like contraption with a curved grip was a *hog snouter*—a device used to cut the snouts of swine in such a way that would stop them from rooting.

• Contemporary tools can also make interesting collectors' items, particularly if they belonged to a celebrity. At the Steve McQueen auction in November 1984, a set of the late movie star's monkey wrenches sold for $500.

—Vera Abriel

Bibliography

Books
Bridenbaugh, Carl. *The Colonial Craftsman.* New York: University Press, 1950.

Periodicals
The Chronicle. (A quarterly publication by the Early American Industries Association.) EAIA Publications Committee, 60 Harvest Ln., Levittown, NY 11756.

Dealers
Iron Horse Antiques, Inc., R.D. 2, Poultney, VT 05764.
Ye Olde Tool Shed, P.O. Box T, Cornwall, NY 12518.

Associations
Early American Industries Association, P.O. Box 2128, Empire State Plaza Station, Albany, NY 12220.

TOYS

Of the many things that people choose to collect, toys bring back most quickly the delightful remembrances of childhood. Who among us has not felt nostalgic when confronted with a toy from our youth—a vivid reminder of those wonderful, innocent, bygone days? Toy collecting for profit, on the other hand, is not all child's play. It is serious business, albeit delightful nevertheless.

History. Children and adults have amused themselves with toys since antiquity. The word *toy* is derived from the middle English *toye,* meaning "dalliance," and referred to any object used for a plaything (as opposed to objects with a utilitarian use).

Marbles, tops, clay rattles, and carved wooden animals, including rocking horses, are just a few of the toys found in ancient Egyptian tombs. Ancient Greek and Roman children played with elaborate rattles molded in the shapes of pigs and birds.

In the second century B.C., one of the first toymakers, Hero of Alexandria, made sophisticated mechanical, hydraulic, and pneumatic "working" toys. The poet Homer wrote about humming tops spun with string, and toys were known in England as early as the fourteenth century.

Peter Breughel the Elder's 1560 painting *Kinderspielen* ("Children's Games") shows children playing with a variety of toys. In 1587, an Austrian merchant first displayed and advertised wood soldiers, sailors and tiny dancing figures as toys.

Nuremberg, Germany, was the center of mechanical toymaking from the late fourteenth to early eighteenth centuries. One of the first documented mechanical toys, "The Game of Indian Hunt," appeared in a French journal dated December 14, 1780.

In the late sixteenth century, a large cottage industry of toy woodcarvers developed in Nuremberg. Although metal toys made of lead and tinplate existed at that time, metal toys did not proliferate until the 1840s.

The first American-made toys were wooden, appearing around 1855. The period of industrialization following the Civil War was the beginning of an era of mass-produced toys in the eastern United States. By the early years of the twentieth century, the manufacture of cast-iron toys had reached its peak.

E. R. Ives & Company, founded in 1868, was perhaps the most famous American toymaker. Ives was one of those responsible for the development of the electric train (see "Model Trains").

Tinplate, first used for toys in the United States in the 1840s, began being mass produced around 1860. Sheet metal (then called sheetsteel) used for bicycles and large ridable vehicles, appeared about 1900. Plastic toys came on the market in great quantities after World War II.

Although people have always collected toys, its popularity has grown tremendously since the 1960s. The most easily collected toys

Museum of Modern Art, New York

The early Europeans' love for toys and play is beautifully illustrated in Peter Breughel the Elder's "Kinderspielen" ("Children's Games," 1560).

are those that have been mass produced since 1850. Before then, most toys were one of a kind, and therefore are quite rare today.

★ **Comic toy collector Mal Whyte paid five cents at a flea market for a five-inch-tall vinyl "Pogo" doll, one of six character dolls from the popular Walt Kelly comic strip originally packaged with Calgon soap products as premiums (c. 1968). The sets presently sell for $35 to $50, while the individual pieces bring about $6—a 1,200% increase over Whyte's five cents!**

Values Outside the Home. Due to the vast numbers of toys, their different categories and materials, there is no single set of rules for collecting. Rather, each toy sub-category has its own guidelines and price structures.

Some toy enthusiasts concentrate on a specific genre without specifying dates of manufacture, while others might specialize in toys from certain time periods or by specific manufacturers. A collector of comic toys might specialize in Disney products, while another may only collect Mickey Mouse items.

Toy collectors will profit by concentrating on areas in which they have genuine interest and knowledge. Martin Swig is a San Francisco car dealer with eight automobile franchises. Cars are his whole life. When he is not selling cars, he is racing one of his five classic Alfa Romeos. But Swig's biggest passion is collecting miniature cars. At last count, he had collected some eight hundred of them over a twenty-year period.

The main factors affecting toy prices are condition, rarity, age, size, and the manufacturer. An ideal purchase would be an old, large, rare mechanical toy from a highly valued manufacturer, still in its original box. Both toy and box would be in mint condition (retaining the original box could bump up the price from 10% to 20%). A toy in "good" condition might only bring half that of a "mint" toy.

A restored or repainted toy, on the other hand, might drop 20% to 50% or more in price. Rust on toys, even in minute particles, can drastically reduce price, as can missing or non-working parts.

A toy's age can be determined by patent numbers or manufacturers' marks (most toys manufactured after 1880 are marked). Old toy catalogues and print advertisements are valuable dating tools also.

Generally, the most valuable toys are the tin items made between the Civil War and 1900. Mechanical toys tend to command higher prices than non-mechanical if they are in good working order.

Early cast-iron toys are also popular collectors' items, especially vehicles, mechanical banks, and cap pistols. Hundreds of the small, hard plastic toys made after World War II have become prized among hobbyists. In the last few years, they have appreciated from $1 to $2 to $10 and $20 and more.

The least valuable categories generally are toys made from kits, or from wood, cloth, or paper, or handmade one-of-a-kind toys.

Unfortunately, reproductions are all too often sold as originals. Outright fakes are less common, but they do exist.

Where to Find Values. Valuable toys can be found at flea markets, garage sales, antiques shops, and general antiques shows, or through those dealers, collectors, clubs, shows, and auctions specializing in them.

Dealers are excellent sources because the novice benefits from the dealer's expertise an an added value.

Auction buying is extremely specialized and competitive. The beginner may want to attend a few toy auctions before bidding with experienced buyers. A 10% buyer's premium is usually added to bids at toy auctions.

Knowledgeable enthusiasts haunt obscure, out-of-the-way places in search of the ever elusive find. Such places include the back storage rooms of small-town toy, hardware, and five-and-dime stores.

When making a purchase, buyers should ask for a bill of sale that clearly states the condition of the toy, its age, manufacturer, origin, identifying marks and other pertinent information. If the seller has guaranteed the purchase, that should also be put in writing.

★ **A toy dealer bought an old mechanical cast-iron merry-go-round bank at a Northern California flea market. The bank has since been appraised at a whopping $7,500.**

A Price Sampling

Schonehut circus: including canvas tent, platform and ring, figures and animals, ringmaster, bisque-headed acrobats, clowns, elephants, horses, a kangaroo, an ostrich, a dromedary and others; together with a color lithographed Schoenhut catalogue	$4,180
Cast-iron and wood fire engine house: cast-iron facade with painted green doors, which spring open; wood sides with cast-iron windows and trim, sloped floor and roof; length 15″, probably by Ives	1,210
German painted metal clockwork train: locomotive tender, two passenger cars, one freight car, couplers marked "D. R. G. M."	1,045
Painted tin key-wound oceanliner: "The Island Queen," red, white and blue, with deck details, including two flagpoles fore and aft, four lifeboats, central smokestack with key on the upper deck; length 20″	990
Marx printed tin Amos 'n' Andy fresh-air taxi: key-wound car containing Amos, Andy and their dog, with horseshoe ornament on the hood; length 8″	418
Plush teddy bear: jointed limbs, felt paws, glass eyes; height 19″	286
Collection of Mickey Mouse toys: a "Movie-Jector" projector, Mouseketeer lithographed tin typewriter in original box, rubber figures of Mickey, Donald Duck, and two Mouseketeer dolls	154

Collection of cap pistols: including some made by Hubley, together with a box of caps	143
Collection of wooden toys: including early Fisher Price cow pull toy, group of painted bears, and a tool box	33
Two magic lanterns: one electrified, and with glass slide depicting winter scenes	22

SOURCE: Christie's East Auction, May 1984.

How to Store/Display. After purchase, a toy should be carefully cleaned prior to storage or display. Most experts advise against extensive restoration, however. Stripping or repainting toys decreases rather than increases value.

Metal toys should be stored in a moisture-proof environment to prevent rusting. Others should be handled as little as possible, and working toys should only be demonstrated to serious potential buyers, if at all.

Children should never be allowed to play with valuable old toys, and collectors should also follow this advice, as difficult as it may be.

How and When to Sell. Toys can be sold by the individual collector through advertisements in hobbyist publications, such as *Antique Toy World,* and through various newsletters published by special-interest clubs.

Enthusiasts can also sell directly to dealers, who then mark up their purchases for resale. Some dealers will sell toys on consignment, either for a straight commission (10% to 25%), or at a figure above the seller's asking price, the difference (which may be substantial) representing the dealer's profit.

Toys may also be sold at toy auctions. The following Butterfield & Butterfield sales commission structure is fairly typical of most auction houses. Dollar amounts represent the combined *total* a lot might bring at auction: $3,000 or more at 10%; $1,000-$3,000 at 15%; $500-$1,000 at 20%; $100-$500 at 25%; $100 or less at 35%. Some auction houses also have a minimum charge to auction an item.

Little-Known Facts. Although balls made of leather stuffed with hair, straw and papyrus have been discovered in ancient Egyptian tombs, no one knows who invented the rubber ball. Bouncing balls were not introduced to European society until late in the fifteenth century, when Columbus brought samples back with him from Haiti.

• In 1984, toy manufacturing had exploded into a $10 billion industry, with over three-thousand new items, including dolls and games, providing a bonanza for future collectors. Leading sellers were the "Trivial Pursuit" board game ($750 million in sales), "Cabbage Patch Kids," and cars and trucks that transform into fantastic robots (Tonka's "GoBots," and Hasboro Bradley's "Transformers"). The first Japanese robots and space toys were made after World War II from discarded American occupation tin cans, and sold for $4 to $5. They now sell for many times that, depending on the piece.

• A 37-inch-long model of the oceanliner *Lusitania,* manufactured by the German firm Marklin (c. 1908) holds the toy auction record of $28,600.

—*Gregory Frazier*

★ A dealer paid $7 each for seventy Japanese wind-up toys from the 1950s. He sold one of them, "Baby Robot on a Swing," to another dealer for $55. The second dealer promptly put it out on display with a $250 price tag, and sold it shortly thereafter.

Bibliography

Books
King, Constance E. *The Encyclopedia of Toys.* New York: Crown Publishers, Inc., 1978.
White, Gwen. *Antique Toys and Their Background.* New York: Arco, 1971.
Whitton, Blair. *Toys.* New York: Alfred A. Knopf, 1984.

Periodicals
Antique Toy World. 3941 Belle Plaine Ave., Chicago, IL 60618.

Dealers
S. Leonard, P.O. Box 127, Albertson, Long Island, NY 11507 (mechanical toys).

Associations
Antique Toy Collectors of America, Rt. 2, Box 5A, Parkton, MD 21120.

TOY SOLDIERS

"There were five and twenty tin soldiers, all brothers, for they had been made out of the same old tin spoon. They carried muskets and held themselves very upright, and their uniforms were red and blue, very gay indeed. The first word they heard in this world, when the lid was taken off the box was "Tin Soldiers!" It was a little boy.

—from Hans Christian Andersen's *The Constant Tin Soldier*

Little boys, and not so little boys, have for centuries delighted in their cherished toy soldier regiments. Miniature warriors arrayed in a handsome display case or on a kitchen table seem to stimulate that part of the imagination that loves to frolic in the realm of nobility and adventure.

For many, old toy soldiers recall the "campaigns" of childhood, when battles were fought on the woolly plains of a living room carpet, between a troop of Confederates rounding the corduroy sleeve of a towering winter jacket and Union soldiers waiting in the distance, guns at the ready, artillery set to fire a million rounds from the cover of a coffee table's legs. How many battles were won and lost this way? Old toy soldiers tell us, many.

History. Before their tours of duty in playrooms and on hobby benches, "toy" soldiers were employed in serious business. They guarded the tombs of the pharoahs and high-ranking princes of Egypt's Middle Kingdom. Figures of gods and goddesses, soldiers and gladiators, played their symbolic roles in Classical Greece. Through the centuries, around the world, miniature warriors and saints stood forth as votive offerings, tokens, charms and household statuettes.

The first known play soldiers were wooden knights made in twelfth-century Europe. Medieval kings and Renaissance princes afforded themselves whole armies of toy soldiers, some made of precious metals (Napoleon's son, in his short-lived job as the King of Rome, had 117 fighters made of gold). Playing with these royal troops also served as a practical way to train young rulers-to-be in the basics of field tactics.

In the eighteenth century, mass-produced tin figures brought the pleasures of toy-soldier collecting to wide-eyed boys—and their elders—worldwide, and since then has stimulated an interest that has supported commercial production of military figures for the last two-hundred years.

★ Margaret Randolph, an artist living in San Mateo, California, bought a grouping of toy soldiers in a local consignment shop to use as a subject for a small oil painting. She paid $15 for the set. Ms. Randolph had selected the soldiers for their looks only, but upon completion of her work, a viewer informed her that the pieces she had represented were worth $85.

Values Outside the Home. The rule for acquiring old toy soldiers is simple: Whenever possible, buy the best. Next comes the problem of what to buy.

Possible themes for collecting include choosing soldiers by maker, by type, by period (such as Classical or Medieval) or war, by country, or as a general representation of history.

There are four types of toy soldiers. *Flats* are essentially two-dimensional and can only be viewed from either side. *Semi-solids* are thicker than flats but not fully three-dimensional. *Solid* figures reflect lifelike dimensions from all angles. *Hollow-cast* figures are exactly that, hollow. Though today realistic soldiers are being created in plastic, collectors' toy soldiers are primarily of cast metal and "composition" substances, such as plaster, clay and papier-mache. Wooden toy soldiers and paper cutouts made over the centuries are also available but difficult to find.

Old toy soldiers were made in dimensions compatible with a child's hands, averaging around three inches high. They were meant for play, and to collectors, this purpose distinguishes "toy" soldiers from "model" soldiers. A toy soldier should be preserved to look like it did when it was made. Model soldiers are meant to be painted and otherwise altered to accurately reflect the most detailed regimental distinctions.

Metal toy soldiers were first produced as flats, made of tin. The earliest known manufacturer was Johann Gottfried Hilpert of Coburg, Germany, who miniaturized farmers, hunters, actors, and wild birds before settling down to military personnel. A 1777 flat of Frederick the Great of Prussia is considered Hilpert's best figure. Today tin flats are difficult to find. They were fragile pieces, and although they were manufactured and exported in large quantities, few survive.

Semi-solids also debuted in Germany around the middle of the nineteenth century. They were cast of metal alloys containing large

Johann Gottfried Hilpert of Coburg, Germany, was the first known metal toy soldier manufacturer. This 1777 flat of Frederick the Great of Prussia is considered his best figure.

amounts of lead. As a result, they were heftier, less brittle, and less expensive than their tin forebears, but they lacked the detail that was possible with the harder metal.

The most notable manufacturer of semi-solids was Georg Heyde of Dresden. These nearly three-dimensional figures enjoyed wide popularity for about ten years, but with the commercial production of fully three-dimensional figures in Paris around 1790, semi-solids declined, and they remained popular only in their native land.

Perhaps because of their durability, semi-solids are more obtainable than flats. Commercially made German semi-solid figures compare in quality to their solid and hollow-cast counterparts. Generally, only figures in good or excellent condition are worth collecting. Homemade figures are easy to spot for their poor workmanship and are not worth acquiring.

The French are responsible for bringing to life the first fully three-dimensional cast-metal toy soldiers. The firm Lucotte, subsequently owned by Cuperly, Blondel and Gerbeau (CBG), and then by Mignot, manufactured a wide range of castings of the French Army of the Revolution and Napoleon's *Grande Armee* of the First Empire. Captured for the ages are noble lancers and hussars, swift dragoons and stalwart line infantry.

Not to be outdone, the adaptable Heyde of Germany began producing solids of comparable quality. To battle in the marketplace he produced Persians and Greeks, Romans and Normans and great Gauls in wolfskins. Following real-world events, the field broadened to include miniatures copied from the American Civil War, the Franco-Prussian War, the British Army in India (with elephant-drawn artillery and camel-mounted outriders), the Boer War, and representations of all the combatants of World War I. Heyde's company continued to make toy soldiers during World War II, when, ironically, its factory was bombed.

CBG and Mignot produced their own exotic regiments. Soldiers included Assyrians, Egyptians, black Ethiopians with spears, the Papal Swiss Guard, Dutch Grenadiers, and Polish Lancers. Many figures were made depicting the French infantry of "the World War." There were serious young soldiers marching with slung rifles, charging with fixed bayonets, and operating automatic weapons. Motorcycle and bicycle dispatchers carried the latest news. *Chasseurs alpins* glided upon their skis, and one grouping portrayed an army band in light blue coats and scarlet trousers, the boys with cymbals, tubas and tenor horns, side drums and saxophones. Leading them was an officer carrying his sword at the salute.

These solid, cast-metal figures were usually designed with a basic body shape that was adaptable to a variety of military units. Plug-in heads and soldered-on equipment could transform the body of a Corinthian Greek into a Roman Centurian. If a soft alloy was used, a casting could be bent into different postures. Solids, along with hollow-casts, are most in demand by collectors. They are plentiful, and many are in quite good condition.

Hollow-cast toy soldiers were the creation of William Britains and Sons, Ltd. of London in 1893. Britains created his pieces by pouring metal through an entry spout into the closed halves of a mold, then pouring it out before all of it had hardened, leaving only a metal shell when the mold was opened. The resulting figures were cheaper to make than their solid-cast brethren. And they were lighter, which made them less expensive to export. Their popularity grew rapidly throughout the world.

The Britains factory had created one-hundred different pieces by 1905, and was producing five-million castings a year. Every figure was cast by hand. Movable parts were fitted and the toys hand colored in gloss paint by women working at home. By 1940, every regular regiment of the British Army had been miniaturized, as well as representatives from the armies of many other countries. Other manufacturers of hollow-casts followed the Britains mold, but none to such distinction. Britains figures are widely sought by collectors and are still available in good condition.

Lineol, a German manufacturer of composition figures, produced an unusual line of personalities; most notable were Hitler, Goebbels, Hess and Goering, with jointed arms that could be elevated into a Nazi salute. These German war leaders are very popular collectors' items. Generally, composition figures should be in good shape if they are to be added to a collection. Hobbyists should watch for cracks along the limbs.

Manufacturers of toy soldiers also reduced other worlds to catch the eye of a youngster, including farm scenes, circuses, and the American Wild West.

Identifying the manufacturer of an older figure, martial or otherwise, is often difficult, since markings were inconsistent. More recent toy soldiers, such as the Britains pieces, are identifiable by characteristic shapes and finishes. Complete sets of soldiers in their original boxes solve the identity problem, and boxed sets are much sought after by collectors.

Where to Find Values. Antiques shops, military dealers, and auction sales are the most reliable places to find toy soldiers. Christie's of New York and Lloyd Ralston Toys of Fairfield, Connecticut, are leading auctioneers. Toy soldiers also appear at swap meets and in gift boutiques. They are sometimes advertised in the classified section of the newspaper.

★ **Joe Belotti of Newark, New Jersey, bought a toy figure of an army motorcyclist and side car manufactured by William Britains. He liked the piece, paying $20 for it. But when he was offered $75 by a man to whom the dealer had referred him, he sold his toy soldier for an unexpected profit. The buyer finally completed a set long pursued.**

A Price Sampling

Mark Time, Hyderabad artillery gun team,
  limited edition of 100 sets, including 6-horse team,
  3 drivers with whips, lumber, gun and mounted
  officer with binoculars, 13 pieces in box,
  good condition $420
Britains, 21st Empress of India's Lancers (box #100),
  mounted at the trot in review order, trumpter, pre-WWI
  set dated 1903, original box, 5 pieces, very good
  condition   300
Mignot, French ambulance, drawn by 4-horse team, horse
  handler, driver with whip, original box, excellent
  condition   220
Johillco, Band of the Coldstream Guards, full instrumen-
  tation and drum major, 20 pieces tied in original
  box, mint condition   170
Heyde, German infantry, WWI, attacking with fixed
  bayonets, officer with extended sword, no box,
  11 pieces, very good condition   90
Britains, Scots guards (box #75), 7 pieces tied in
  original box, excellent condition   77
Authenticast, Russian infantry advancing with rifles at the
  ready, 14 pieces, no box, excellent condition   45
Britains, Boy Scout signallers (box #163), 6 pieces tied
  in original box, excellent condition   35

How to Store/Display. In addition to careful handling, old toy soldiers will require some special care. Do not expose paper soldiers to direct sunlight or spot lamps, and keep them dry in a ventilated atmosphere with no more than 60% humidity. Composition soldiers will shrink and crack in very dry conditions, but the wire armatures supporting their outer substance are liable to corrode if the humidity is high. So they are best kept in an atmosphere with 50% relative humidity. Woodworm is the chief enemy of wooden soldiers, leaving little holes and a powder residue. Infected pieces with still-active insects should be treated with woodworm fluid.

Metal soldiers are mostly alloys of tin and lead. Depending on their manufacturing process, they may corrode at points due to electro-chemical reactions. Lead carbonate will appear as a white/grey powder on the surface, which in its early stages can be treated with an ion-exchange resin, then coated with a protective layer of clear lacquer to prevent a recurrence.

Touching up the paint or repairing some other deteriorated aspect of a toy soldier is acceptable from the collector's viewpoint, though points of restoration should remain detectable to avoid the work being labeled as an attempted forgery.

Any old object such as a toy soldier will not react well to abrupt changes in its environment. Care should be taken to make a shift in temperature or humidity a gradual experience for the material.

★ **Irene Smith was traveling in Paris when she purchased a set of Mignot toy soldiers for about $100. Returning to her La Jolla, California, home, a friend informed her that the purchase was worth twice that in the United States.**

How and When to Sell. Since interest in old toy soldiers is growing, it is probable that their value will be rising in years to come. Interest also has been growing for American dime-store soldiers, such as the metal figures manufactured by Barclay and Manoil between 1935 and 1942. Veterans of this era may still be found in the old toy box in the attic.

Soldiers sold at auction will be more attractive if offered in boxed sets. If one wants to sell individual pieces, he will be best off by selling to a dealer, who will usually want the piece to complete a set of his own or to sell to another collector.

Since most collectors are active buyers and sellers throughout the year, a beginner will have no trouble building a collection and eventually upgrading it or selling it off.

— *Terry Parker*

Bibliography

Books

Garratt, John G. *Collecting Model Soldiers.* New York: Arco Publishing Company, Inc., 1975.

Harris, Henry. *Collecting Model Soldiers.* London: Abelard-Schuman Ltd., 1969.

McKenzie, Ian. *Collecting Old Toy Soldiers.* London: B. T. Batsford Ltd., 1975.

Dealers

Old Model and Toy Soldiers Hospital, 590 Monroe St., Santa Clara, CA 95050.

War and Peace Miniatures, 31 West Main St., Webster, NY.

Associations

American Model Soldier Society, 1524 El Camino Real, San Carlos, CA 94070.

TVS, RADIOS AND PHONOGRAPHS

Phonographs and radios were once the centers of attention in American homes. Families clustered around the radio or hovered over the "talking machine." As years passed, those items became infused with sentimental value. Sell that set? Heck no! We listened to Charlie McCarthy on it!

Today, a combination of sentimental value and the scarcity of replacement parts has made old working radios, phonographs and, only recently, televisions once again valuable.

History. Who invented the phonograph? If you guessed Thomas Edison, you were half right. It was 1877 when Edison first recorded and, to his astonishment, heard his own voice reciting back to him the nursery rhyme "Mary Had a Little Lamb." The Edison talking machine was patented and sold in 1878, and it brought him immediate national acclaim. But the great inventor could not perfect the device and only envisioned it as a business transcription machine. So he dropped it and went on to invent the carbon filament lightbulb and a system to distribute electricity.

At the same time, Alexander Graham Bell astonished his assistant by transmitting the words "Watson, come here, I want you." Bell's invention of the telephone brought him the French Volta Prize and the equivalent of $10,000, which he used to set up a sound laboratory.

Edison's phonograph used tinfoil-covered cylinders to record and reproduce sound, but Bell and associates found that a wax-coated cardboard cylinder was superior and lasted longer. They approached Edison to market a joint improved product but he refused. Bell's *graphophone* (the generic name Bell used for his new machine) was patented and became very popular, spurring Edison to return to perfecting his phonograph. Edison emerged from his workshop with a new phonograph that incorporated some of Bell's ideas.

Concurrent with this, German immigrant Emile Berliner developed the flat record, which could be mass produced. From this grew the double-sided flat record, which became standard after 1905 (see "Records").

The most popular manufacturers of early phonographs were Edison, Columbia and Victor, and there was fierce competition between the three. Columbia and Edison sold cylinder-playing phonographs, but Victor was oriented towards the future and incorporated Berliner's flat-disk record design.

During Abraham Lincoln's era the thought of transmitting and receiving sound waves through thin air was judged to be sheer fantasy. But by the turn of the century, the idea of the radio would become a reality. By 1895 James Maxwell and Heinrich Hertz isolated the theories of electromagnetic waves, and Guglielmo Marconi had demonstrated a wireless telegraph.

The first transatlantic broadcast was orchestrated by Marconi in 1901. It was not the most interesting radio program—he broadcast the letter S—but it was a successful one.

It took Lee De Forest's 1906 invention of the vacuum electron tube before voice and music could be transmitted. Yet it was not until 1920 that the first commercial radio station, KDKA, was created by Westinghouse in Pittsburgh, Pennsylvania. Westinghouse, RCA, Atwater-Kent, Zenith, and Crosley became some of the first manufacturers of radios.

Introduction of the transistor by Bell Laboratories in 1948 ended the era of the classic plug-in radio while inadvertently making obsolete radios valuable as collectors' items. The most notable came from the 1930s and were novelty items, such as Dionne Quintuplet and Charlie McCarthy sets. Art Deco pieces were also produced then, some of which were made of chrome and tinted glass, or were brightly colored, or shaped like microphones, telephones, and books.

Television eclipsed both the miracles of the wireless and of the "talking machine." The father of television technology was Vladimir Zworykin, a Russian-born American physicist. Television testing began in the mid-1920s, and by 1927 a TV program had been carried by wire from Washington, D.C. to New York.

NBC TV first went on the air April 30, 1939, but television technology was slowed by FCC standardization and the approach of World War II. In 1945 the FCC allocated thirteen VHF frequencies (they later took one back). By that time there were 16,500 TV sets in America. UHF was introduced in 1952, a year after the first commercial color broadcast.

★ As the owner of a radio and television repair and sales shop in San Rafael, California, Zeke Lakeman now has plenty of opportunity to spot old treasure.

About six years ago he was visiting an elderly customer on a service call when he noticed an old phonograph. It had not been cleaned or oiled in about forty-five years, but Lakeman suspected that it could be restored.

The phonograph contained memories, the customer told him. It had been purchased new shortly after the turn of the century. It was broken, missing a belt and the needle, and the finish was deteriorated. But the customer agreed to take $100 for it.

Lakeman restored the 1902 Edison Home machine to working order—it plays two-minute tin cylinders—and it is worth almost $1,000 today.

Values Outside the Home. This is a good field for the beginning but persistent collector with plenty of space in his home. Old radios and phonographs are not only available, but they will likely increase in price. An attic or basement and those of relatives and friends are good places to begin a search.

The most valuable items are phonographs, radios or first-generation televisions with all the parts intact and working; buying on appearance only is like buying a used car without looking at the engine: one may pay a high price for a fine-looking piece only to find that it does not work and that parts are not made anymore or else cost as much as the initial purchase.

At the turn of the century, one could have bought a phonograph for as little as $7.50 or as much as $300. An oak Edison "Opera" sold for less than $100 during 1912 (an expensive set then). Today it could fetch $3,200. Early phonographs, especially those of the three largest manufacturers, are relatively plentiful. More valuable are the less familiar makes, such as Zonophone or Reginaphone.

One can still find cylinders for the early phonographs, and old radio signs and shop displays with manufacturers' logos make interesting collectors' items. Stereo was not introduced until the 1950s; however, the advent of digital compact-disc players may mean that the vinyl disc and its player will go the way of the metal cylinder, making stereos valuable as collectors' items.

Collecting radios is a limited hobby. One is not going to unearth a two-hundred-year-old set for the simple reason that home sets have only been around for the last sixty-five years. And only the first twenty-eight of those years produced valuable sets (there is little demand for radios manufactured after the introduction of the transistor). Early radios are sought after as well as later models made with Bakelite. Art Deco sets are also popular and command good prices, especially those made of mirrored and colored glass. In general, most pre-transistor radios appreciate in value.

Crystal sets sold cheaply when new, and they can be picked up for a reasonable price today. Wooden "cathedral" radios, from the '20s and '30s, are slowly disappearing. They were common buys a few years ago but are becoming harder to find.

Television collection is a more elusive hobby. The field is just opening up, since televisions are such a relatively new invention. The small first-generation models of unusual design are attracting the most attention. A 1949 three-inch Pilot with a microscopic screen coupled with a chassis to rival the size of a modern console has become a collectors' item.

Elusiveness in this field has also given rise to rumors. There is an unconfirmed tale about an early Philco, its screen supported by a small frame above the cabinet, that sold for $3,000.

Where to Find Values. Collectors will not find many of these items at flea markets. There are few flea markets with plug outlets to test the electrical models, and vendors will most likely not have spare parts. One may pay premium prices for a useless shell at a flea market.

Estate sales and garage sales, especially those held in older neighborhoods, yield the best finds. Some of the sets may even work. Antiques dealers are not usually experts in this area. They value these pieces more for age and appearance than workability, and often set very high prices. Collectors will do better to look in the classified section of the more widely read newspapers for possible private sales.

It is also an advantage to patronize longtime local radio and TV stores. Occasionally, reconditioned pieces sell for very reasonable prices.

★ **Shortly after World War II, Karl Frick of Santa Barbara, California, stepped into a junk shop and noticed a curious phonograph. The old record player was broken and seemed to be one of the cheaper early models. Frick paid $5 for it, and because he was mechanically inclined, he got the original Edison Home phonograph to play. It would sell for at least $250 today.**

A Price Sampling

Columbia phonograph with wood horn	$1,500
RCA Victor "Schoolhouse" phonograph with wood horn	1,250
Edison cylinder standard phonograph with wood horn	325
Majestic Charlie McCarthy radio	310
Pepsi-Cola bottle-shaped radio, c. 1940s	200
Atwater-Kent Model 20 radio with horn and tubes	150
Philco Bakelite radio (battery)	65
Emerson Mickey Mouse radio, 1935	35
Emerson wood table radio, c. 1937	18
Dick Tracy radio, c. 1961	10

How to Store/Display. One of the biggest challenges of collecting these mechanical marvels is restoring them to working condition, which greatly increases their value.

It is rare to find an authentic old radio or phonograph in working order. It is rarer still that it will remain in working order, and tracking down spare parts is difficult.

The do-it-yourselfer can refer to classified ads in antique and collectors' magazines to find copies of original repair manuals. Older libraries may carry back copies of radio magazines, some with printed wiring diagrams. Occasionally, schematics are pasted on the inside of a radio, but they are often illegible, browned by hot tubes. If by chance the manufacturer still exists, it may be able to provide needed information, but hardly ever can it provide a replacement part. Pre-tube era devices are easier to restore than the later models that used tubes because tubes are so difficult to find. Local antique-radio clubs in many cities can help locate parts and information. Also, some collectors will buy pieces just for spare parts. The cabinet of a phonograph or radio is usually easier to restore than its mechanical innards. Some refinishers can do astounding jobs with warped, cracked and broken wood. Common sense dictates care of the cabinet; too much heat or direct sunlight will dry or warp the finish. Lemon oil is the best polish for those old cabinets.

How and When to Sell. Generally, the workmanship of a phonograph or radio will withstand the wear and tear of time, and an old top-of-the-line model will increase in value proportionately to its original price. A working artifact in good condition will only increase in value, not decrease, so it should be held on to. Restoring an old radio could cost $75 to $100, but the investment is usually worth it whether one sells or not.

If one must sell, it is advised to place an ad in antiques and collectors magazines—other collectors will appreciate what these items are worth. But they may also try to take advantage of ignorance, so beginners should have a piece appraised before selling it.

★ **It pays to shop around.** Fifteen years ago Paul Giganti of San Carlos, California, found a treasure in an unlikely place. While in nearby Santa Cruz, Giganti met a collector of Nazi memorabilia who had a radio for sale. Giganti figured the Atwater-Kent Standard "breadboard" set was worth about $35, and he was glad to pay $15 for it, especially since it required no restoration. It is now worth about $400.

Little-Known Facts. When one buys a GE radio, he is buying one of Thomas Edison's direct descendants. "General Electric Company" is the modern name for the organization founded by the inventor (original name of the firm was the Edison General Electric Company). RCA is a descendant of companies founded by Emile

Berliner, inventor of disc records; and the original Columbia phonograph used the designs of Alexander Graham Bell.

• If you think Lassie's been around for a long time, consider RCA's logo, "Nipper," the white dog fascinated by his master's voice, which presumably is sounding forth from a horn speaker. Nipper belonged to the brother of British painter Francis Barraud and has been gracing American RCA Victor products and British phonographs for one hundred years. Barraud built a career upon painting Nipper for RCA and its British sister company.

• The first commercial radio broadcast was a news report announcing Warren G. Harding's election to the presidency. The news was broadcast November 2, 1920, on KDKA in Pittsburgh.

—*Scott Calamar*

Bibliography

Books

Bruce, Robert V. *Bell: Alexander Graham Bell and the Conquest of Solitude.* Boston, MA: Little, Brown and Co., 1973.

Clark, Ronald W. *Edison: The Man Who Made the Future.* New York: G. P. Putnam's Sons, 1977.

Encyclopedia of Collectibles (Phonographs to Quilts). Alexandria, VA: Time-Life Books, 1979.

Encyclopedia of Collectibles (Radios to Signs). Alexandria, VA: Time-Life Books, 1980.

History of Music Machines. Prepared by the Smithsonian Institution. New York: Drake Publishers Inc., 1975.

Ketchum, William C., Jr. *The Catalog of American Collectibles.* New York: Rutledge Mayflower, 1979.

Shanks, Bob. *The Cool Fire.* New York: W. W. Norton and Sons, 1976.

Periodicals

The Horn Speaker and Radio Age. P.O. Box 53012, Dallas, TX 75253.

Catalogues

Kovel, Ralph and Terry. *Kovels' Antiques & Collectibles Price List.* New York: Crown Publishers, 1984.

Frick, Karl, ed. *Phonograph Parts.* 940 Canon Rd., Santa Barbara, CA 93110, 1984 edition.

Murphy, Catherine. *The Antique Trader Price Guide to Antiques.* Dubuque, IA: Babka Publishing, 1984.

Quetermous, Steve, ed. *Flea Market Trader.* Paducah, KY: Collector Books, 1981.

Dealers

Everything Audio, 16756 NE 4 Ct., N. Miami Beach, FL 33162.

Musical Americana, 1684 Lafayette, Santa Clara, CA 95050.

Westland Radio & TV, 1541 Fourth St., San Rafael, CA 94901.

Associations

Antique Wireless Association, Main St., Holcomb, NJ 14469.

Phonograph and Gramophone Society, 148 W. Finchley, London N3 1PG, England.

U

CHAPTER 22

Utensils

UTENSILS

Not all antiques need to be kept under glass or locked in a safe deposit box. And who says that antiques should not be used but only admired, preferably from a safe distance? Certainly not the collectors of kitchen gadgets. An easily identifiable group, they are the ones whose kitchens are half buried under interesting objects of copper, brass, pewter, wood, and tin, all of it displayed on racks and shelves and hooks, or spilling out of kitcen drawers. If a visitor should ask about their treasures, they will pull them out one by one, and tell stories of delectable corn muffins and homemade maple syrup.

History. Social change was responsible for turning kitchen utensils into collectors' items. Breadmaking tools, for instance, ended up in junk shops when busy homemakers started buying their bread from stores. Canners and preserve jars were discarded when the Jolly Green Giant became a frequent visitor. And sadirons (what Grandma used to heat on her wood-burning stove and then press our clothes with) were gleefully thrown away as soon as electricity was brought into American homes.

Yesterday's obsolete tools have become today's antiques for other reasons also: historical interest, nostalgic yearnings, and interior decorating fashion.

The official United States Customs definition of *antique* is any item over one-hundred years old, but many kitchen gadgets of the 1920s and 1930s are already considered articles worth collecting. Kitchenware does not have to be old to be valuable, just out of date and in demand.

Before the nineteenth century, kitchen tools were handmade, often quickly and crudely. But the finer objects had a beauty of form that mass production could never duplicate.

During the nineteenth century, mass production brought uniformity of design and execution. Popular kitchen utensils were made of tinware (sheet iron coated with tin), then painted and often

The simple beauty and usefulness of early kitchen utensils is what makes them so appealing to modern collectors, who are used to high-tech plastic gadgets and pages of operating instructions.

varnished. Wire work improved during this period, and wire baskets replaced wicker.

In the twentieth century, aluminum, plastic, and Pyrex appeared, and both hand and electric gadgets helped make kitchen work easier. Among the utensils patented during the 1920s were a grapefruit corer, an aluminum cookie and doughnut cutter, a pastry blender with a Bakelite handle, and a tinned eggbeater with a glass bowl and tin cover.

★ An East Coast farmer bought a box of junk at a sale for $.50. In the box was a piece of pewter, which another buyer at the sale recognized as valuable. The second buyer paid the farmer $400 for the piece, then sold it again at a good profit. The third buyer sold it to a museum for $5,000. (The storyteller did not specify what the pewter object was, but it does not matter.)

Values Outside the Home. The hobbyist interested in kitchenware may want to build a collection around a particular material, such as wood, tin or iron. Any kitchen utensils now made of metal or plastic, such as potato mashers, scoops, mortars and pestles, even sieves and knives, were probably once made of wood, and of course many still are. Tin was used for trays, graters, molds, pudding steamers, cookie cutters, match holders, milk or syrup containers, coffeepots, canisters, and even cabinets (those pie safes with punched-tin backs designed to keep baked good fresh).

The collector specializing in iron will want, say, an iron utensil rack from which to hang pots and pans, and a selection of hand-forged tools, such as ladles, skimmers, and long forks. He may want to display an iron tea kettle on top of a hot wood stove—it will also add moisture to the air—and he can decorate his fireplace with Early American sawtooth trammels, chains, and "S" hooks. He can store matches in a wrought-iron wall match holder, and his garlic, onions, and potatoes in hanging wire baskets. He might want to decorate his kitchen walls with cast-iron baking pans, which he can also use to turn out delicious muffins, waffles, and cornbread.

Another alternative for the new hobbyist is to base a collection on one type of item, such as butter prints. Prices for butter prints begin at $25 and go up to $650 for an eighteenth-century piece with a thick-cut tulip design.

Cabbage or slaw cutters come in many sizes and prices. There is even a giant version, which had been designed to grate three or four cabbages at once directly into a sauerkraut barrel.

Storage containers are another good category to focus on, if the collector has a roomy kitchen. Complete sets of tin canisters are hard to find and therefore valuable. Toleware (tinplate that was usually painted or elaborately decorated) biscuit tins have been known to sell for $1,000. Salt-glazed stoneware crocks, hanging baskets, blown-glass cruets, or wood buckets can be not only decorative but lucrative—and useful as well.

A particular historical period will also make a good focal point for a kitchen collection, although collectors will need to learn how to date utensils. Older painted tin trays, for example, had lapped edges, while those on newer versions were welded. Wirework techniques improved in the early 1800s, so that skimming ladles made before that period appeared more crude. And scrapple pans made of sheet rather than cast iron were made after 1900.

Cost, too, may determine what kind of collectors' utensils to buy. The beginner will find kitchenware in a wide range of prices. In general, the more unique an item, the more expensive it will be. Decoration, too, adds to the cost. The new collector might want to start with something inexpensive, such as wooden potato mashers (also called "stompers"). These sell for $5 to $15. Cookie cutters are also good low-cost purchases; most are still available for $3 to $10. A maple rolling pin can be bought for $5, although a milk-glass version with a holder for water may go as high as $90, and a stoneware version can cost over $150.

The items mentioned here are currently popular, but they are examples only. The new collector should allow necessity, imagination, and taste to govern the theme of a collection beyond the current fad, especially if items are going to be displayed on the kitchen walls.

Where to Find Values. The northeastern part of the United States, especially New England and the Pennsylvania Dutch region, is rich in collectors' utensils. A weekend spent in the country could be the start of a happy collecting career.

Collectors also enjoy buying at shows. *Antique Trader Weekly,* a trade publication, advertises shows. And ordering by mail from reputable firms is an ideal way to shop, especially among buyers living in remote locations.

Flea markets, junk shops, and garage sales are also excellent places to find undervalued kitchenware, if a wily dealer has not gotten there first.

Newsletters put out by collectors' associations often carry tips on buying and publish classified ads from members. They are also an avenue through which one can meet other collectors.

A Price Sampling

Crock, 1800s; Crolius, NY	$1,900
Skillet, cast iron, deep pan, long handles, 11″ × 20″	210
Stove-top toaster, tin, Hobluck Pyramid	125
Crock, 3-gallon, stoneware; Geddes, NY; 10½″	75
Kitchen Aid Mixmaster, working	55
Egg basket, wire, chicken shaped	40
Eggbeater, Holt's, patented 1899	25
Chocolate mold shaped like turkey	15
Pyrex refrigerator set, 3 pieces	12
Wearever ricer; aluminum cone, legs; No. 8, 9″	6

How to Store/Display. Kitchen gadgets are easier to keep than some antiques. After all, if a kitchen tool has survived over a hundred years of use, chances are it will not damage easily.

Collectors have devised imaginative ways to display kitchen objects, such as using tin milk containers as umbrella stands, or tin graters as lamp reflectors.

There is some dispute over whether to refinish or restore old kitchenware. As it applies to all antiques, an unbroken original is best, and a bad restoration is worse than none.

However, everything needs cleaning, and anything old will eventually need some restoration. The local library is the best place to find specific directions for the care of antiques.

The wise collector also keeps a catalogue of all items, noting each piece's descripton, date and place of acquisition, price paid, current value if known, current location if lent out, and any other pertinent comments. Each item in a large collection should be given a catalogue number, and an accompanying photo is always recommended, in case of theft, for insurance and recovery purposes.

How and When to Sell. According to experienced collectors, the prices of kitchen collectors' items rises to a maximum and then levels off for a few years, but they rarely fall.

A collector wanting to sell all or part of a collection should pay attention to shows, classified ads, and local shops to see what the market is offering before he actually offers items of his own for sale.

There is not a tremendous turnover in kitchenware. Collectors often keep their utensils for a generation. This makes them harder to find, and thus more valuable. Placing classified ads in collectors' periodicals will ferret out buyers searching for particular items.

Members of collecting organizations can sell their wares through personal contacts or classified ads placed in club newsletters. However, club members have a mutual interest in keeping prices down.

Little-Known Facts. "Spiders" are cast-iron pans with legs. The legs were used to regulate heat when cooking in an open fireplace. For more heat, the legs were sunk deep into the ashes; for low heat, the pan stood higher in the hearth.

• Until modern times, salt was expensive and precious. A salt box was hung in an honored place in the kitchen. Table salt was served in a *master salt*, usually made of pressed glass. Later, salt was served in tiny individual dishes with tiny spoons. Salt shakers appeared when salt became more available, and less expensive.

• New England tinware was painted in delicate shades of light-blue, green, and lavender. Pennsylvania Dutch tinware was painted in bright colors—red, yellow, and green—with simple designs. The normal background color on tinware was black or brown. Light-cream backgrounds were rare—and expensive.

• Pewter utensils were used in Early American taverns and inns because they could not break. Then during the Revolutionary War, all pewter items not absolutely essential to civilians were donated for bullets. Earthenware replaced pewter for everyday use, because it was less expensive. At the other end of the social scale, pewter was replaced by silver.

—Elinor Lindheimer

Bibliography

Books

Campbell-Franklin, Linda. *Three Hundred Years of Kitchen Collectibles.* Des Moines, IA: Wallace-Homestead, 1983.

Cole, Ann Kilborn. *How to Collect the "New" Antiques.* New York: David McKay Co., Inc., 1966.

McClinton, Katherine M. *The Complete Book of American Country Antiques.* New York: Coward-McCann, Inc., 1967.

Rockmore, Cynthia and Julian. *The Room-by-Room Book of American Antiques.* New York: Hawthorn Books, 1970.

Weiss, Jeffrey. *Kitchen Antiques.* New York: Harper & Row, 1980.

Periodicals

The Antique Trader Weekly. P.O. Box 1050, Dubuque, IA 52001.

Maine Antique Digest. P.O. Box 354, Waldobora, ME 04572.

Catalogues

Wurtsboro Wholesale Antiques, P.O. Box 386, Wurtsboro, NY 12790 ($3).

Dealers

Jack's Emporium, P.O. Box 950, Fredericksburg, TX 78624.

John A. Wilson, 812 Bellecrest Rd., Lancaster, PA 17601.

Kookin', 85 Carl St., San Francisco, CA 94117.

Les Zakarin, P.O. Box 616, Midtown Station, NY 10018.

Wine Country Antiques, 13471 Main, Hopland, CA 95449.

Associations

American Graniteware Association, P.O. Box 605, Downer's Grove, IL 60515.

Club of the Friends of Ancient Smoothing Irons, P.O. Box 215, Carlsbad, CA 92008.

Cookie Cutter Collectors Club, 5426 27th St., N.W., Washington, DC 20015.

Figural Bottle Openers Collectors Club, c/o Barbara Rosen, Six Shoshone Trail, Wayne, NJ 07470.

International Correspondence of Corkscrew Addicts, 275 Windsor St., Hartford, CT 06120.

Pewter Collectors Club of America, 2363 Henbird Ln., Lancaster, PA 17601.

CHAPTER 23

Vintage Clothing

VINTAGE CLOTHING

What is vintage clothing? It is a little older than new, a little younger than antique, and full of lively history. Fast gaining fame with the fashionable and the avid collector, French, English and American clothing from the 1880s through the 1960s can be profitable as well as a versatile addition to any wardrobe.

History. Since the moment Adam and Eve first donned fig leaves in Eden, body coverings have been a very important part of life. Much more than a simple need, clothing is a reflection of history, and styles have been influenced by economic needs, social structures, technology, and the mass media. But as fashion critics love to point out, there is nothing new under the sun, and anything that is "in" today was probably popular at least once or twice in years past.

Even the sumptuous French clothing of the eighteenth century was much like that of the Renaissance period. But Queen Victoria's accession to the British throne in 1837 coincided with a new era of respectability and fashion in Britain as well as the United States and France. Technology created new fabrics and the sewing machine, and suddenly the ready-made trade let even the less fortunate be *"a la mode."*

In the twentieth century, women rebelled against their position in society as feminine objects and concocted the "boyish look." But throughout the changing fashions of the roaring '20s and the fluctuating '30s and '40s, Victorian touches such as leg-o-mutton sleeves, fitted bodices, boned corsets and floor-length gowns came and went once again. The '50s saw closets full of classics, as well as the return of the 1890s shirtwaist and the 1920s chemise, or straight shift. And then came the '60s: Miniskirts, plastic, and flower children were in vogue, and so were vintage clothing stores. Thrift shops became havens for the fashion conscious.

Throughout the '70s and '80s, people have moved toward the mixture of old and new, an appreciation of hand-sewn pieces, and an "individualist" appearance. Currently, everything from Victorian and Edwardian whites to paisleys and beaded sweaters from the '50s can be found in stylish wardrobes. So what's new? Not much. What's

The 1940s zoot suit looks almost conservative by today's "anything goes" fashion standards, although in its time it was considered outlandish.

in? Just about everything. No matter how silly an old outfit may look now, the odds are that it will be the cat's meow in ten or twenty years, and therefore worth a pretty penny to some eager shopper.

★ One San Francisco vintage clothing dealer said she could go on and on about finds she has made, but perhaps her favorite one was a gold velvet and lame opera coat from the 1940s that she found in Ohio in 1981 for under $100. She is now about ready to sell the piece and is certain it is worth more than $400 in today's market.

Values Outside the Home. As the current trends seem to be toward individuality and a well-dressed, eye-catching appearance, good condition and mix-and-match potential are musts for vintage clothes. Buyers should check pieces carefully and look for new/old stock; that is, clothes that were never worn. Victorian and Edwardian hand-embroidered whites are very popular and absolutely exquisite when in good condition, as are beaded sweaters from the '50s. In fact, most hand-sewn and hand-beaded items are good investments, as are rare pieces and designer clothes by such as Coco Chanel, Claire McCardell, Dior, and Adrian.

Collectors should keep an eye out for anything that is truly a good example of its period and should try to look ahead: It is an advantage to keep abreast of new and upcoming revivals (such as '50s clothes for the new-wave look), and to snatch things up before their prices reflect sudden popularity. For the clothes lover who is neither dealer nor collector, the best attack is to forget labels and look for wearable sizes and styles from the 1920s through the 1950s. One should also be prepared to do a bit of repair work here and there and to look for creative possibilities in seemingly ruined clothes.

Where to Find Values. The starting line for a vintage-clothes shopping spree should be one's own nooks, crannies—and grannies. Once the home territory is thoroughly picked over, collectors should browse around nearby thrift, used clothing, costume, and vintage clothing stores, where clothes are nicely displayed and easy to try on. A word of warning, however: bargains are far less common in these shops than they once were. Overheads are high, and owners know what sells well.

Bargains do exist, however, at flea markets, auctions and estate sales, all of which are advertised in local newspapers. Two large flea markets in the United States are the weekly swap meet at the Rose Bowl in Pasadena, California, and the Brimfield, Massachusetts, flea market, which is held about three times a year. Before rolling off to a far away sale though, buyers should check its reputation from a friend who has been there. It is best to arrive early for best selection and to never be afraid to bargain tactfully, especially for a group of items. Merchandise should be examined carefully before buying, especially at auctions, where pieces can soil and suffer from manhandling. Finally, collectors should go to a few auctions just to observe. Many require registration, a small entrance fee, a 10% premium over the winning bid price, and sales tax.

A Price Sampling

c. 1960 Diagonally pleated cream chiffon evening dress, belonged to Marilyn Monroe	$1,835
c. 1895 Chinese (Mandarin) robe, heavily embroidered silk, knee length, mint condition	450
c. 1925 French gold lame/lace flapper gown, excellent condition	225
c. 1970 white empire-waist wedding gown with train, good condition	125
c. 1900 French white bobbin-lace camisole, mint condition	75
c. 1920 pink drop-waist flapper dress, silk, some beading, good condition	50
c. 1880 small black purse covered with jet beads, excellent condition	35
c. 1930 white seed-pearled cloth gloves, excellent condition	25
c. 1950 hand-sequined gold lambswool sweater, very good condition	20
c. 1940 man's dress grey-black striped pants, good condition	12

How to Store/Display. With the exception of items such as leather jackets and fur coats, most vintage clothing does not require specialized or unusual cleaning agents. Items in good condition can be dry cleaned, but only establishments recommended by dealers should be patronized, because some use chemicals that will turn a silk dress into confetti. White cottons can be hand washed with a mild soap, or brightened slowly with a mild bleach. Beaded items should be dry cleaned rarely or simply aired and lightly vacuumed.

Once clean, garmets should be laid flat or rolled in drawers lined with acid-free tissue or paper, or unbleached muslin. Some collectors like to adorn their homes with well-dressed forms or mannequins, but generally one should not hang up old clothes, especially beaded garments. If hanging is absolutely necessary, one should use a padded hanger covered with muslin. Vintage clothes should never be stored in a basement or attic, and plastic bags, paper, cardboard, and unsealed drawers should also be avoided. The storage area should be kept dark, dry (under 50% humidity), at room temperature (65°-75°F), sealed, and bug free. In addition, vintage clothes should be guarded against food stains, drink and smoke, which are some of its worst enemies.

How and When to Sell. The old adage, "One person's junk is another person's treasure" is most appropriate in the vintage-clothing trade. Heirs to an atticful of finery will find that newspaper ads and publicity in the nearest college town can spark a very successful estate sale. A local dealer or collector can help with pricing. On the other hand, the owner of one or a few pieces can call dealers, describe the clothes, and request a price. Though they often buy clothes from wholesalers, retailers will sometimes pay 30% to 50% of the appraised or retail value of a piece, so sellers should be polite and try not to reach for the moon.

Other options for the seller are flea markets, where spaces are available for a small fee, and auctions, which sometimes charge a consignor's fee of 5% to 25%. If clothing is not in tip-top shape, a charitable donation and the opportunity for a tax write-off might be in order.

Every dealer finds that some items sell especially well in his or her area. Victorian and Edwardian cotton whites, anything that is hand embroidered or beaded, sweaters and ensembles from the '50s, flapper dresses, designer suits and dresses, corday and beaded evening purses, hats (some locations), and Victorian costume clothing are in demand lately. Wedding dresses and accessories move well in winter and spring; evening wear is popular, and bustles and corsets are rare enough that some dealers will pay a premium for them.

★ When a couple from Montana found they had inherited closetsful of clothing from a great aunt, they were uncertain about what to do with it all. After deciding to keep a few items and then hold an estate sale, they were thrilled to find that the university in their town was full of eager buyers. The couple was left with a comfortable sum and the knowledge that the clothing was in appreciative hands.

Little-Known Facts. When Napoleon Bonaparte divorced Josephine in 1809, she retired to Malmaison with only her clothes to console her. And what a consolation they must have been! An inventory of her wardrobe listed no less than 676 dresses, 49 court costumes, 252 hats and headdresses, 60 cashmere shawls, 785 pairs of slippers, 413 pairs of stockings, and 498 embroidered chemises.

• Tweed, originally known as "twill cloth," was first made on hand looms in Scotland, near the Tweed River. It is said that a draper there was trying to read a wet invoice once and mistook the word "twill" for "tweed." He continued to refer to the cloth as tweed, and since then the name has stuck.

• On another note, the tuxedo was simply known as a "formal evening coat" until it was brought to New York from England in the 1880s and paraded around Tuxedo Park.

• The permanent wave was invented by Charles Nestle in 1906, and that year only eighteen women dared risk the process. Why? Because the operation took twelve hours and cost $1,000.

—Cynthia White Tolles

Bibliography

Books

Dolan, Maryanne. *Vintage Clothing 1880-1960.* Florence, AL: Books Americana, Inc., 1984.

Irick-Nauer, Tina. *The First Guide to Antique and Vintage Clothes—Fashions for Women, 1840-1940.* New York: E. P. Dutton, Inc., 1983.

Kennett, Frances. *The Collectors Book of Fashion.* New York: Crown Publishers, Inc., 1983.

Love, Harriet. *Harriet Love's Guide to Vintage Chic.* New York: Holt, Rinehart and Winston, 1982.

Mailand, Harold F. *Considerations for the Care of Textiles and Costumes.* Available through Indianapolis Museum of Art, 1200 West 38th St., Indianapolis, IN 46208.

Malouff, Sheila. *Collectible Clothing With Prices.* Des Moines, IA: Wallace-Homestead Co., 1983.

Maurois, Andre. *The Edwardian Era.* New York: D. Appleton-Century Company, 1933.

Periodicals

American Collector. P.O. Drawer C, Kermit, TX 79745.

Antiques and the Arts Weekly. Newtown Bee, Newtown, CT 06470 (good source for locating auctions, especially on the East Coast).

Vintage Ventures, Around and About. P.O. Box 1678, New Milford, CT 06776.

Dealers

Garbo's, 641 Main Strasse, Covington, KY 41011.

Golden Oldies, 2027 Broadway, Boulder, CO 80302.

Harriet Love, 412 W. Broadway, New York, NY 10012.

Painted Lady, 1838 Divisadero St., San Francisco, CA 94115.

Sotheby's, 1334 York Ave., New York, NY 10021 (other branches located all over the United States).

The Way We Wore, 1839 Divisadero St., San Francisco, CA 94115.

Associations

Art and Antique Dealers League of America, 353 E. 53rd St., #2G, New York, NY 10022.

The Costume Society of America, 330 W. 42nd St., Suite 1702, New York, NY 10036.

Museum of Costume and Fashion Research Centre, 4 Circus, Bath, Avon, BA1 2EW, England (the museum will help to identify clothing and send requested information).

W

CHAPTER 24

Weavings

Wine

WEAVINGS

No one knows how long ago man learned to weave, but it is clearly an ancient art. The poet Homer in 700 B.C. used a loom as a focal point for his epic "The Odyssey," in which he tells how Odysseus' wife, Penelope, spent her days weaving a shroud for her father-in-law, Laertes, while waiting for her husband to come home from the Trojan War.

The world of weavings now open to the collector touches every continent of the world: Flemish tapestries from the Medieval era, colorful clothing from the Indians of South America, batiks from Indonesia, bed coverings from Early American times, linens of Scandinavia, and many more.

History. Reaching their peak in the Medieval and Renaissance periods were *tapestries,* fabrics woven with designs or pictures that oftentimes told stories and were used for wall hangings or curtains.

Although fragments of tapestries created in early Egyptian and Greek times still exist today, most for sale to contemporary buyers date from the sixteenth century onwards.

In Western Europe, tapestry weaving began in the eleventh or twelfth century, and by the fourteenth century, there were three great weaving centers: Arras (in Flanders), Paris, and London. Later, significant workshops for tapestries were set up in other parts of Europe, which included cities in Italy, Spain, Holland and Denmark. Even in the United States, what became a famed tapestry works was created in New York City in 1893 by William Baumgarten, who operated it until 1912.

Among the tapestries most popular with visitors to European museums are the *mille-fleur* (thousand flower), which often show beautiful Medieval ladies in settings of thousands of tiny flowers, sometimes with a unicorn nearby. Many were woven in the French Loire Valley during the 1500s.

From America's early years came a variety of bed coverings, most of them little known to the average collector, who assumes that our ancestors covered themselves only with quilts.

An 1830 coverlet originating from either New York or New Jersey displays the elaborate effects of the Jacquard attachment, including eagles, doves, and flowers. Note the initials and date in each corner.

In almost every Colonial home stood a spinning wheel and loom. Most all cloth required by a family was made by the housewife with the help of her children. In Massachusetts, for example, in the 1640s, an ordinance made it compulsory for each family to spin a certain amount of yarn each year or face heavy fines. Later, much of the labors of weaving were taken over by traveling journeymen.

Among the textiles from this period of our history were *bed rugs,* which were fabrics made of heavy wool knotted or hooked to form a kind of pile on top of wool that was woven. Among early references to bed rugs was a letter that Governor John Winthrop wrote from Massachusetts in 1630 to his son in England, urging him to bring a store of "rugges both to use and to sell." A bed rug such as the governor referred to scored one of the biggest sales for an antique textile in the past few years. It sold in Massachusetts in 1983 for $55,000.

Bed rugs often feature large floral representations with winding stems, creating effects similar to crewel patterns.

Linsey-woolsey coverlets from the eighteenth and nineteenth centuries were more sedate. They were often woven on looms on which homespun linen was used for the warp, and wool in indigo or red was used for the weft (see "Quilts"). The fabric that came off the loom was then basted to a piece of homespun linen used as a bottom. A thin pad of unwashed wool was fitted in between the layers. Then the whole was stretched on a quilt frame for the final, artful stiching together.

From early America also came *coverlets* made of linen and wool. Some were woven in patterns of diamonds and squares. Some were done in a geometric double-weave style, so that the reverse side of the coverlet was a mirror image of the front. Early weavers would share their patterns and developed hundreds of variations, each with a special title: "Cluster of Vines," "Dogwood Blossom," "Orange Peeling," "Rattlesnake Snow Trail," "Blazing Star," and others.

In 1820, there arrived in America a sophisticated new loom that used an attachment developed by a French weaver, Joseph Jacquard. The Jacquard attachment consisted of a series of cards with large and small punched holes that activated the harnesses of the loom and allowed the weaver to make a pattern. Elaborate patterns and complicated borders were suddenly possible: stars, shields, eagles, ribbons, mottos and figures of George Washington, Mount Vernon and the Capitol.

From the Scandinavian countries, such as Sweden, came linen weavings with patterns preserved by families for centuries. Among the most unusual woven goods were *wall and ceiling hangings* done in white linen with colored designs. The hangings were fastened to the rafters of homes and would extend down as far as the top of the wall, where they were finished off with braided fringe. Others were tacked on walls. The hangings made a room resemble the inside of a tent. In some parts of Sweden, the custom persisted through the nineteenth century.

From out of Central and Southern America came the colorful pieces of clothing handwoven in Guatemala, Bolivia, and Peru and which in themselves have become works of art to be displayed on walls. Guatemalans produced *huipils* (women's blouses), *cortes* (skirts of standard length) and *refajos* (wraparound skirts). Ponchos, shawls, sashes and *chullos*, or knitted caps, are the products of Peru most commonly seen on today's market. From Bolivia came *llicllas* (mantles), *ajsus* (skirts), and *chuspas* (coca bags).

Across the world, from Indonesia, came the dyed cloth known as *batik*, which began to soar in popularity in this country in the 1960s and is now used by such designers as Issey Miyake of Tokyo and Hector Herrera of Mexico.

True batik is white cotton waxed with a pattern and then dyed and boiled to remove the wax.

In the modern era, artists such as Dorothy Liebes, Loja and Eliel Saarinen of Finland, Lenore Tawney, and others have created woven masterpieces that have turned weaving into a modern art form.

★ A New York collector tells of going into an antiques store many years ago and finding a neatly folded watermelon-pink linsey-woolsey spread for sale for $10. It had been discovered in a local attic wrapped in mothproof paper and marked with the year "1835." The dealer obviously had no idea of the market value of the spread, or she would have priced it many times higher than $10.

Values Outside the Home

• *Tapestries.* Many people are apprehensive about buying tapestries as collectors' items or artwork because they believe that most are too large and are seen only in museums and castles. But small tapestries are abundant. Many later tapestries depict scenes of home life and nature, which modern collectors sometimes prefer to religious subjects. Their value has increased steadily, and some of them, such as the *mille fleur* examples mentioned earlier, have increased in price many times in the past thirty years.

• *Coverlets.* Most coverlets and similar Early American bedcoverings usually range from $400 to $1,500, depending on their quality of design and how well preserved they are. In that respect, their cost is not as great as quilts from the same period, which some believe are currently selling at prices inflated far above their true value.

Most popular coverlet patterns are eagles and similar Early American motifs. Coverlets from the 1800s are often dated and marked with their place of origin—a real advantage for a collector in a resale.

• *South American textiles.* Currently, among the most highly valued textiles from South America are antique Bolivian blankets, often resembling old Navajo blankets in striped styles. Some from the eighteenth century have been known to sell for $10,000. Also highly prized are antique wool bags, in which Bolivians carried coca leaves to chew, and old belts.

Contemporary blankets from Peru, Bolivia, and other South American countries sell for much less, some as low as $50 or $60.

• *Batiks.* Authentic batik is becoming more and more expensive as labor costs rise, but it is also a good place to put one's money because it is becoming rare. Antique (which for batik means pre-World War II) sarongs of two yards in length can be purchased at prices ranging from $200 to $2,000. New batik sells for $150 to $200.

Where to Find Values. The collector interested in antique textiles should purchase them from a reputable dealer. Antiques stores that specialize in a specific type of textile, such as Early American bedcovers or French tapestries, will provide a wider variety of choices for the buyer. Often, the best values in fabrics from foreign countries will be found in the countries themselves.

A Price Sampling

Flemish tapestry, 8′ × 14′, 1600s	$3,000
French *verdure*, or nature-study, tapestry, 7′ × 6′	1,500
French Aubusson tapestry, 5′ × 7′, 1847	1,300
Peruvian Indian tapestries, 4′ × 5′, featuring scenes of wildlife, villages, or copies of Impressionist paintings	200-700
American coverlet, early-1800s, New York, red, white and blue	700
Nineteenth-century woolen coverlet with eagles	600
Woolen coverlet for full-size bed, 1841	575
Jacquard coverlet, double woven, mid-1800s	475
Contemporary Egyptian tapestries, scenes of life on Nile, 2′ × 3′	450
Art Deco tapestry from Belgium, 3′ × 4′	55

How to Store/Display. Even tapestries from the sixteenth century have survived with little care and attention, although heat can dry them out and make them brittle. A monthly vacuuming and occasional cleaning can keep them in shape. Batiks, precious wall hangings, coverlets, and similar fabrics should not be cleaned in any way before consulting an expert familiar with such items.

How and When to Sell. Some of the items mentioned in this chapter are less known to collectors and therefore may be selling at lower prices than the more familiar items. That means that they are still relatively good as buys, will appreciate steadily over the next few years, and might soar in price if they should become either more rare or more popular. Many collectors, for example, are now hanging on to coverlets, believing that they will catch on eventually in the same way that quilts have.

Little-Known Facts. It is true that many of the famous tapestries hang in castles and museums. For example, "Jason and the Golden Fleece," from the 1740s, hangs in the ballroom of Buckingham Palace, sometimes home of Queen Elizabeth II.

• They are also, however, the focal point of many a celebrity's decorating scheme. The Russian-born prima ballerina Natalia Makarova has used a Flemish tapestry as the main piece of artwork in her Park Avenue apartment dining room in New York.

• Among the most famous of earlier tapestries is the "Bayeux," supposedly ordered by a French bishop who was half-brother of William the Conqueror. The tapestry, made between 1066 and 1068 in an English monastery and composed of colored woolen stitches on a long linen cloth, depicts a series of episodes surrounding the Norman invasion of England in 1066.

• Original weavers of bed coverlets used a bizarre method for dyeing yarn. They placed earthenware dye pots next to their fireplaces and added urine saved up from bedroom chamber pots. In this they dissolved indigo and then added the yarn, which sat there until it turned just the right color.

—*Rebecca Larsen*

Bibliography

Books

Atwater, Mary Meigs. *The Shuttle-Craft Book of American Hand-Weaving*. New York: MacMillan Co., 1966.

Constantine, Mildred, and Jack Lenor Larsen. *Beyond Craft: The Art Fabric.* New York: Van Nostrand Reinhold Co., 1972.

Lord, Priscilla Sawyer, and Daniel J. Foley. *The Folk Arts and Crafts of New England.* Philadelphia, PA: Chilton Book Co., 1970.

Panyella, August. *Folk Art of the Americas.* New York: Harry N. Abrams, 1981.

Plath, Iona. *The Decorative Arts of Sweden.* New York: Dover Publications Inc., 1966.

Safford, Carleton L., and Robert Bishop. *America's Quilts and Coverlets.* New York: Weathervane Books, 1974.

Dealers

America Hurrah, 766 Madison Ave., New York, NY 10021 (American folk art).

Berger/Yorke, 904 Irving St., San Francisco, CA 94122 (Bolivian weavings).

The Blue Candlestick, 14320 S. Saratoga-Sunnyvale Rd., Saratoga, CA 95070 (American country antiques).

Nancy Borden, P.O. Box 4381, Portsmouth, NH 03801 (Early American textile reproductions).

Joseph Kilejian, 135 N. La Brea, Los Angeles, CA 90036 (Tapestries and textiles).

Parrish & Sons, 355 Hayes St., San Francisco, CA 94102 (American antiques).

Vojtech Blau Inc., 800 B Fifth Ave., New York, NY 10021 (Tapestries).

WINE

"Good wine is a good familiar creature if it be well used."—Othello

By the mid-1980s America will have consumed more than 410 million gallons of wine—more than twice the amount it consumed ten years ago. Why? Partly because Europeans are convincing Americans that wine can be part of their daily diet. Foreign wines are flowing into this country at top speed, and the shelves they reach are already crowded with prize-winning American selections.

But how does anyone decide which wines to take home? Or what will taste good now? Or ten years from now? And are Grandad's old wines worth anything beyond sentimentality? Experts agree that the answers to these questions lie with an understanding of the wine industry, which includes a love for its history and an appreciation of its romance.

History. Unlike many things people consider valuable enough to collect, most of the wine we value and have access to today is not

Library of Congress

Among Noah's achievements, though lesser known, was that of vintner.

antique. But its origins date back to at least 3000 B.C. in the area of Asia now known as northern Iran. According to Genesis, even Noah was a grape grower and wine drinker, though he probably failed at any marketing attempts, considering the beastly nature of his clientele. As civilization moved westward through Egypt, the Mediterranean islands, Greece, Rome and central Europe, so did the grapevine.

Just as "Chippendale" is a great name in furniture, so is France a benchmark of quality in the world of wine. Its Bordeaux, Burgundy, Graves and Champagne regions have ideal climates for grape growing, and winemakers there have been perfecting their craft and maintaining high standards for centuries.

The most valuable and delicious wines in the world are made from a small number of specific grape varieties. The important red grapes are Cabernet Sauvignon, Merlot, Pinot Noir, Zinfandel and Petite Sirah. The white varieties are Johannisberg (or White) Riesling, Chardonnay, Chenin Blanc, Sauvignon Blanc and Gewurztraminer. More and more domestic wine made from these grapes is receiving international attention, and the abundance of quality products available today gives the wine buyer ample opportunity to sip the finest.

★ One young wine enthusiast purchased a case of Chateau Margaux 1973 for only $16 a bottle in 1977. Two years later the price had more than doubled, and just knowing that was enough for the man. He held on to his precious investment and enjoyed his "success" on special occasions in the following years.

Values Outside the Home. A selective buyer might start with an array of dry white wines and add a few rose, red, sparkling and fortified wines for a superb collection. White wines and roses are generally not long-term cellar candidates, but they are preferred by many to the heavier red wines. Well-balanced reds are very rewarding, since many are drinkable now, while others will mature over time into rich blends of complex flavors and aromas. Vintage Champagne will also age well, though most sparkling and dessert wines are best when drunk soon after their release.

In order to make satisfying purchases, one can learn a little about classification systems used in wine-producing regions and spend time sampling those wines. A fine French wine carries a label bearing its specific chateau or commune *appellation,* or origin; e.g. "Chateau Montrachet." The best California wine is named for the grape variety from which it is made (e.g. Robert Mondavi Cabernet Sauvignon) with the exception of some dessert and sparkling wines.

There are other key phrases to search for on wine labels, and since wine books are as numerous as wine bottles these days, learning the basics is easy. But one should not just read about wine! It is more fun to take advantage of the many delightful, inexpensive selections begging for attention—and tasting. Though there are risks in trial and error, the rewards are countless.

Where to Find Values. Many critics advise private wine investors to buy exclusively from merchants who sell only wine and are therefore well versed in the mechanics of handling and storing it. Small and large stores alike usually sell a case (twelve bottles) of wine for 10% or 20% less than the regular retail price. Wine merchants also offer advice by the magnum, and many shops post critics' columns and wine awards to help indecisive shoppers.

Auctions are another haven for very fine wine, and London boasts the crown princes of auction firms, Sotheby's and Christie's, both of which have full-time wine departments. Buyers look through catalogues of the merchandise to be sold and inevitably see a few gems, such as the 1806 Lafite, which sold for $9,800 in 1981. Most states are not licensed to hold public auctions, but organizations such as California's Napa Valley Hospital hold wine auctions annually as fund raisers. Wineries and collectors donate wine to the various causes, and buyers can tiptoe away with some lovely selections—and very empty pockets.

One can also buy wine directly from its maker: Wineries not only allow the public to sample their products but also sell their wares on the spot. In addition, some wineries offer wine futures, or the pre-sale of a certain wine for the next two or three vintages before it ever reaches the bottle. This is risky for the buyer, of course. But if one has grown fond of a certain wine that is consistently good but only produced in small quantities, the chance may be worth taking.

A Price Sampling

1956 Beaulieu Vineyards Private Reserve Cabernet Sauvignon/CA	$540.00
1961 Chateau Palmer/Bordeaux, France	299.00
1970 Robert Mondavi Cabernet Sauvignon/CA	100.00
1976 Chateau Haut-Brion/Graves, France	62.50
1976 Dom Perignon/Champagne, France	36.00
1979 Beaulieu Vineyards Private Reserve Cabernet Sauvignon/CA	23.75
1982 Chateau Montelena Alexander Valley Chardonnay/ CA	13.00
1983 Chateau Ste. Michelle Johannisberg Riesling/ WA	7.49
1981 Edmeades Vineyards Pinot Noir/CA	6.00
1983 Milbara Coonawarra Fume Blanc/Australia	5.50

How to Store/Display. The rules of storing and aging wine are important but relatively simple to follow. A wine "cellar" can be anything from a small cupboard to a corner of the garage, or a full-fledged artificially cooled room below the house devoted solely to storing cases of wine. Collectors who lack space can check with local merchants, many of whom will store bottles for a small fee.

The area chosen should be dark, clean, well ventilated and kept at a constant temperature of about 10° C, or 50° F. Temperatures much above or below that are unfavorable for maturation of the wine. Bottles are properly stored on their sides (except in the cases of some fortified wines) so that the wine keeps the cork moist and tightly wedged in place. This, in turn, helps prevent air from entering the bottle and oxidizing the wine, which would ruin its delicate flavors. Most wine merchants and variety stores now carry plain wine racks, and magazines such as *Sunset* and *Popular Mechanics* can offer simple alternatives. Cardboard wine cases hold up for a short time but may collapse quickly in a damp cellar. Additionally, a log or cellar book is a handy tool that allows one to note purchases, inventory, and specific characteristics of wines as they are sampled.

How and When to Sell. Buying wine for investment and resale purposes is a popular practice in some circles and can be a fruitful one. Many British connoisseurs lay down two cases of a special wine, sell one case when its value has doubled, and keep the other in the cellar for sipping. Such sellers can find a market at wine auctions, and can also find merchants and private collectors who are willing to trade wines or buy from a private cache. Auctions are also resources for people who have received a sudden "wine windfall" and would rather be enjoying a sudden cash windfall.

The "when" of selling depends on a wine's vintage, quality, and rarity. Generally, when a great vintage is followed by a few lean years, its wines will be especially valuable. But guessing which wines will bring the highest price may appear to require a blindfold and a lot of luck at times. The wine enthusiast who feels that way should just sit back and enjoy his favorite ten-year-old Bordeaux. He has invested in his own happiness, and that may be his finest decision ever.

★ **When Beaulieu Vineyards in California released its 1979 Private Reserve Cabernet Sauvignon, a lucky collector snatched up a case for about $16 per bottle. The 1984 price of this wine is $23.75 per bottle, and its price promises to rise even more. With a return of 50% on her investment already, the collector is sitting pretty but will hold on to her case a little longer before considering a sale.**

Little-Known Facts. In the *Devil's Dictionary*, Ambrose Bierce's sharp wit leaves no stone unturned, including one subject dear to his heart:

Wine, n: Fermented grape-juice known to the Women's Christian Temperance Union as "liquor," sometimes as "rum."
Wine, madam, is God's next best gift to man.

• In the past, Italy's wine industry has been raked over the coals and accused of making wine from such non-grape substances as beet sugar and ox blood. Even film star Tony Curtis documented similar atrocities in a letter to columnist Joyce Haber:

> Some of the big [Italian] manufacturers were discovered making wine out of old water, banana peels, parts of rubber tires and other everyday little things that you might find anywhere.

• J. W. E. Blandy, Esq., a wine collector in London, inherited the Dr. Michael Grabham collection of legendary Madeira wine and decided to sell selected bottles at Sotheby's. Each bottle brought about $100 to $200, and all had lived famous lives. About one bottle Winston Churchill was reputed to have remarked, "Do you realize, gentlemen, when this wine was made, Marie Antoinette was still living?"

—Cynthia White Tolles

Bibliography

Books

Amerine, Maynard A., and Vernon L. Singleton. *Wine: An Introduction.* Berkeley, CA: University of California Press, 1977.

Blumberg, Robert S., and Hurst Hannum. *Fine Wines of California.* New York: Doubleday, 1984.

Fadiman, Clifton, and Sam Aaron. *Wine Buyer's Guide.* New York: Abrams, 1977.

Johnson, Hugh. *The World Atlas of Wine.* New York: Simon and Schuster, 1978.

Lichine, Alexis. *Alexis Lichine's New Encyclopedia of Wines and Spirits.* New York: Alfred A. Knopf, 1984.

Paterson, John. *The International Book of Wines.* London: The Hamlyn Publishing Group Limited, 1975.

Periodicals

Wine Country, Napa Valley Magazine, Inc., 1701 Park Rd., Suite 4, Benicia, CA 94510.

Wine Spectator, M. Shanken Communications, Inc., 400 E. 51st St., New York, NY 10022.

Wine and Spirit, Haymarket Publishing Ltd., 38-42 Hampton Rd., Teddington, Middlesex, TW11 0JE, England.

Wines and Vines, Hiaring Co., 1800 Lincoln Ave., San Rafael, CA 94901.

Catalogues

Generally available at auctions sponsored by dealers and auction houses.

Dealers

California Wine Merchant, 3237 Pierce St., San Francisco, CA 94123.

Draper and Esquin, 655 Sutter St., San Francisco, CA 94102.

Heublein, Farmington, CT (best reached by phone at 800/243-4348).

Sotheby's, 34-35 New Bond St., London, W1A 2AA, England.

Associations

American Wine Society, 3006 Latta Rd., Rochester, NY 14612 (offers excellent quarterly journal to subscribers).

Brotherhood of the Knights of the Vine, P.O. Box 13285, Sacramento, CA 95813.

International Society of Wine Tasters, 60 Sheridan Ave., Williston Park, NY 11596.

Les Amis du Vin, 2302 Perkins Pl., Silver Spring, MD 20910.

Wine Appreciation Guild, 155 Connecticut St., San Francisco, CA 94107 (valuable publications offered).

Chapter 25

XYZs of Collecting

Many acquisitions bring continuous satisfaction, others perpetual self-chastisement. Before you invest, it will pay good dividends to investigate and consider certain pro and con factors with respect to each purchase. Ask the following questions:

1. Is it beautiful? Do most people find it attractive? Does it have artistic merit?
2. Does it possess charm or quaintness? Do you feel drawn to it, a deep sense of attachment?
3. Are there features that emphasize your heritage, background, or family ties?
4. Are you interested only because certain others have acquired similar pieces?
5. Does it stand out distinctly from other similar items? Is it likely to be confused with less desirable examples?
6. Can you be sure it is authentic, original, and as represented? Is it signed or documented in some way?
7. Is the workmanship of high quality? Did it require great skill to produce?
8. Are you buying this because if you wait it will no longer be available? Should you take more time to decide?
9. Does it have intrinsic value? Is the asking price in line with actual cost of production?
10. Will many others appreciate it as a gift or legacy?
11. How important is it historically? In its own right? Or for what it represents?
12. Could a much less expensive version easily be produced that would appear to be identical?

13. Is it associated with very important people or events?

14. Will its present acceptance be likely to be maintained or, better yet, increase in the future?

15. Is this something that can be easily carried, displayed, and enjoyed without excessive installation, care, or protection?

16. Does this item have additional attraction and value because it is one link in a continuing chain? Is it one of a definite set or combination?

17. Will it be easy to dispose of at a fair value? And in what manner?

18. Are there so many examples readily available that the supply is quite likely to be greater than the demand?

19. Are all the people involved with this item people that are well known and trusted?

20. For what reasons *other than financial gain* are you interested in acquiring this example?

After considering all these things, if you like it, buy it, with the idea of keeping it for its present merit and not its future worth.

From *Limited Edition Collectibles: A Handbook with Prices,* copyright © 1974 by John Hotchkiss. A Hawthorn Book. Reprinted by permission of E. P. Dutton, Inc.

Index

Celebrity Index